MILLER'S COLLECTORS CARS

Yearbook & Price Guide 2000

≢BROOKS

SPECIALIST AUCTIONEERS & VALUERS

World Leaders in the Sale of Collectors' Motor Cars and Automobilia

The Brooks team are the world's leading specialists in the sale of Collectors' Motor Cars at auction from veteran to modern day classics, from the sedate to Formula 1. Brooks' extensive sale calendar includes general and specialist sales at famous venues throughout the world: Goodwood, Beaulieu, The London Motor Show, Monte Carlo, Stuttgart (at the Mercedes-Benz Museum), Paris, Geneva, the Nürburgring, Gstaad and California.

Brooks offers you the services of a formidable but wholly approachable team of enthusiasts' whether buying or selling historic collectors' cars, motorcycles or automobilia. We can find or place any important car in the world. We also offer a valuation service for insurance, probate and family division.

To discuss any of Brooks' services please call Malcom Barber, James Knight or Nick Lumby in London on 0171 228 8000 or Stewart Skilbeck on 01757 638894 (North of England and Scotland) Simon Kidston or Max Girardo at Brooks Europe in Geneva on +41 (0) 22 300 3160 Paul Clark at Brooks USA on +1 (415) 391 40000

Catalogue subscriptions are available. Please call catalogue sales on 0171 228 8000 or Fax 0171 585 0830.

≢BROOKS

SPECIALIST AUCTIONEERS & VALUERS

MILLER'S COLLECTORS CARS
Yearbook & Price Guide 2000

General Editor
Dave Selby

Foreword by
Louis Klemantaski

MILLER'S COLLECTORS CARS YEARBOOK AND PRICE GUIDE 2000

Created and designed by
Miller's Publications
The Cellars, High Street
Tenterden, Kent TN30 6BN
Telephone: 01580 766411
Fax: 01580 766100

General Editor: Dave Selby
Editorial and Production Co-ordinator: Ian Penberthy
Editorial Assistants: Carol Gillings, Shirley Reeves, Jo Wood
Designers: Kari Reeves, Shirley Reeves, Alex Warder
Advertisement Designer: Simon Cook
Advertising Executives: Jill Jackson, Melinda Williams
Production Assistants: Gillian Charles, Léonie Sidgwick
Additional Photography: Ian Booth, Brooklands Museum, Neill Bruce,
Classic & Sportscar Magazine, John Colley, Bob Dunsmore,
Bruno Grégoire, LAT Photographic, Charles Leith, Bob Masters,
David Merewether, David Phipps, Robin Saker,
Marc Souvrain, William Taylor, Hal Thoms, Eoin Young
Indexer: Hilary Bird

First published in Great Britain in 1999
by Miller's, a division of Mitchell Beazley,
imprints of Octopus Publishing Group Ltd,
2–4 Heron Quays, London E14 4JP

© 1999 Octopus Publishing Group Ltd

A CIP catalogue record for this book is
available from the British Library

ISBN 1 84000 174 7

Colour and black and white Illustrations and film output by CK Litho, Whitstable, Kent
Printed and bound by Toppan Printing Co, (HK) Ltd, China

Front cover illustration:

1965 Ferrari Le Mans Berlinetta. **£1,000,000+ BKS**

Contents

Acknowledgements

The publishers would like to acknowledge the great assistance given by our consultants:

Chris Alford	Newland Cottage, Hassocks, West Sussex BN6 8NU
Malcolm Barber	81 Westside, London SW4 9AY Tel: 0171 228 8000
Rex Cadman	The Old Rectory, 45 Sandwich Road, Ash, Nr Canterbury, Kent CT3 2AF
Peter Card	81 Westside, London SW4 9AY Tel: 0171 228 8000
Tom Falconer	Claremont Corvette, Snodland, Kent ME6 5NA
Paul Foulkes-Halbard	Foulkes-Halbard of Filching, Filching Manor, Jevington Road, Wannock, Polegate, E Sussex BN26 5QA
Tony Gosnell	Tel: 01428 722933
David Hayhoe	Grand Prix Contact Club, 28 Pine Avenue, West Wickham, Kent BR4 0LW
Simon Johnson	Military Vehicle Trust, 7 Carter Fold, Mellor, Lancs BB2 7ER
Bill King	Cheffins, Grain & Comins, 2 Clifton Road, Cambs CB2 4BW
Brian Page	Classic Assessments, Stonechat House, Moorymead Close, Watton-at-Stone, Herts SG14 3HF
Tim Schofield	Coys, 2–4 Queen's Gate Mews, London SW7 5QJ
Mike Smith	Chiltern House, Ashendon, Aylesbury, Bucks HP18 0HB
Neil Tuckett	Marstonfields, North Marston, Bucks MK18 3PG
Toby Wilson	Sotheby's, 34–35 New Bond Street, London W1A 2AA Tel: 0171 293 5000

We would like to extend our thanks to all auction houses, their press offices, and dealers who have assisted us in the production of this book, along with the organisers and press offices of the following events:

Beaulieu September Autojumble & Automart

Louis Vuitton Classic

London Classic Car Show

Goodwood Festival of Speed

RAC British Grand Prix

Coys International Historic Festival

Beltring '99 – The War and Peace Show

Rétromobile, Paris

Technics, Essen

Classic & Prestige Vehicle Auctions

Serving London, the south west, central and south east of England

Barons offer regular sales throughout the year at the prestigious Sandown Park venue. With extensive free car parking, on site hotel, full restaurant and bar facilities and the 10,000 square foot Esher Hall, this venue offers unrivalled facilities and easy access.

Entering your car into a Barons auction is simplicity itself.

We can send you our information pack and entry form.

You may enter a car by Fax or Telephone.

You can enter a car via our Web Site.

Whichever method you choose, you can be assured of the highest levels of service and promotion, with a data base running into many thousands, our interactive web site and targeted advertising, your car will be seen by the largest possible audience.

Barons not only offer unrivalled levels of service, we also offer some of the most competitive rates in the business, with an entry fee of only £75.00 + VAT and commissions of 5% + VAT.

Visit Barons Web Site at www.barons-auctions.com

Fax-U-Back information line: 09067 110060
EMail: info@barons-auctions.com
Call Laurence Sayers Gillan or Ian Murray on
(023 80) 840081 or 741314   Fax: (023 80) 840767

Barons (Specialist Vehicle Auctioneers) Ltd – Brooklands House – 33 New Road
Hythe – Southampton SO45 6BN

How to use this book

It is our aim to make the guide easy to use. Marques are listed alphabetically and then chronologically. Commercial Vehicles, Children's Cars, Replica Vehicles, Restoration Projects, Racing & Rallying and Military Vehicles are located after the marques, towards the end of the book. In the Automobilia section objects are grouped alphabetically by type. If you cannot find what you are looking for please consult the index which starts on page 348.

Miller's Starter Marque

Starter Minis: *All models.*
- Whether yours is a 1959 car with sliding windows, cord door-pulls and external hinges, or a 1995 model, all Minis are classics. Even though modern Minis are still closely related to the 1959 original, the early cars have an extra, subtle charm. Parts are rarely a problem, but the Mini's major enemy is rust.
- Before looking underneath, inspect the roof panel, guttering and pillars supporting the roof. If they are rusted or show that filler has been used, the rest of the structure may be in similar, or worse, shape.
- Examine floorpans from above and below, joints with the inner sills, front and rear bulkheads, crossmember and jacking points. If the subframe has welded plates, check that they've been properly attached. Look inside the parcel compartment on each side of the rear seat, beneath the rear seat, and in all corners of the boot, spare-wheel well and battery container. These are all common rust spots.
- Clicking from beneath the front of the car indicates wear in the driveshaft constant-velocity joints – not easy or cheap to rectify.
- Rear radius-arm support bearings deteriorate rapidly unless regularly lubricated; check the grease points ahead of each rear wheel for signs of recent attention.
- The A-series engine is generally reliable and long-lived. However, expect timing-chain rattle on older units; burnt exhaust valves may be evident on high-mileage examples, as may exhaust smoke under hard acceleration, indicating cylinder/piston wear.
- Mini Coopers can be worth more than double the ordinary classic Minis. Consequently, fakes abound. It's not just a question of checking the uprated specification – twin carbs, disc brakes, badges and the like – but also of unravelling engine and chassis numbers, and subtle tell-tale signs that you'll only learn about from club experts and professionals. First join the club (see Directory of Clubs), then go shopping.
- Pick of the bunch: Of the original generation of Coopers, the best all-round performer is the 1275S, 60mph coming up in 10.9 seconds, and puff running out just shy of the ton. As usual, the aficionados prefer the first-of-breed purity of earlier cars with sliding windows, etc.

1964 Austin Mini Cooper S, 1275cc, completely restored, 1,000 miles covered since, engine rebuilt stainless steel exhaust, twin fuel tanks, reclining seats, finished in ivory with black roof, excellent condition.
£11,000–12,000 COYS

1965 Austin Mini Cooper S, 1385cc high-performance engine, restored 1997 at a cost of £22,000, finished in ivory with dark green interior, sunroof, concours condition.
£7,000–8,000 BKS

Racing car manufacturer John Cooper already knew quite a bit about tuning BMC's A-series engine before a test drive in a prototype Mini convinced him of the car's competition potential. The result, launched in 1961, was the Mini Cooper. With a tuned 997cc engine, it soon established its credentials as a rally and race winner. The 1071cc Mini Cooper S of 1963 took engine development a stage further and provided the basis for the 970 S and 1275 S of 1964. The latter pumped out 76bhp and was good for a genuine 100mph.

Did You Know?
Mini designer Alec Issigonis didn't approve when John Cooper approached him with plans for a hot Mini. The creator of the miniature marvel stuck to his vision of a car that would provide 'everyman transport', but Cooper went over his head, got the go-ahead to breathe magic on the Mini and created an unlikely sporting legend.

◀ **1970 Morris Mini Cooper S,** Wood & Pickett conversion, 1275cc, knock-off Minilite wheels, Webasto sunroof, finished in Sable with beige leather upholstery, leather dashboard, electric tinted windows, 17,286 miles from new.
£13,000–15,000 BKS

The Mini was never more luxurious than when upgraded by Wood & Pickett. This car belonged to film star Lawrence Harvey until his death in 1973.

MINI Model	ENGINE cc/cyl	DATES	CONDITION 1	2	3
Mini	848/4	1959–67	£3,500	£1,800	–
Mini Countryman	848/4	1961–67	£2,500	£1,200	–
Cooper Mk I	997/4	1961–67	£8,000	£5,000	£2,500
Cooper Mk II	998/4	1967–69	£6,000	£4,000	£1,500
Cooper S Mk I	var/4	1963–67	£7,000	£5,000	£2,000
Cooper S Mk II	1275/4	1967–71	£6,000	£5,000	£2,000
Innocenti Mini Cooper	998/4	1966–75	£4,500	£2,000	£1,000

210 **MINI**

Caption
provides a brief description of the vehicle or item, and could include comments on its history, mileage, any restoration work carried out and current condition.

Source Code
refers to the 'Key to Illustrations' on page 330 which lists the details of where the item was photographed, and whether a dealer or auction house. Advertisers are also indicated on this page.

Miller's Starter Marque
refers to selected marques that offer affordable, reliable and interesting classic motoring.

Information Box
covers relevant information on marques, designers, racing drivers and special events.

Price Guide
these are worked out by a team of trade and auction house experts, and are based on actual prices realised. Remember that Miller's is a PRICE GUIDE not a PRICE LIST and prices are affected by many variables such as location, condition, desirability and so on. Don't forget that if you are selling, it is quite likely you will be offered less than the price range. Price ranges for items sold at auction include the buyer's premium.

Price Boxes
give the value of a particular model, dependent on condition and are compiled by our team of experts, car clubs and private collectors.
Condition 1 refers to a vehicle in top class condition, but not concours d'élégance standard, either fully restored or in very good original condition.
Condition 2 refers to a good, clean roadworthy vehicle, both mechanically and bodily sound.
Condition 3 refers to a runner, but in need of attention, probably to both bodywork and mechanics. It must have a current MOT.
Restoration projects are vehicles that fail to make the Condition 3 grading.

10

11

Foreword

Browsing through the thousands of photographic images that have been carefully selected for this ninth edition of *Miller's Collectors Cars Yearbook and Price Guide* recalls a lifetime full of the richest motoring memories. Although much of my working life has been spent behind the lens trying to capture the drama, excitement and fluid movement of cars in motion, the rhythmic beat of the internal combustion engine has also run like a pulse throughout my entire life.

I was born in 1912 in what was then Manchuria, where my father was one of the first motor car importers. Before the age of eight, I can remember 'helping' in the workshops and still vividly recall the thrill of awaiting the arrival of any new model at all. Back then, we applied no critical judgements or comparisons, as any car at all was an object of desire.

At school in England, as motoring gathered momentum, I recall the emergence and proliferation of the splendid little Austin 7 as it became commonplace on our roads. Indeed, on finishing school, I became the proud owner of an Austin sports model. In the 1950s, through my work as a photographer, I was privileged to navigate on no less than five Mille Miglias in Aston Martins and Ferraris, partnering great drivers like Reg Parnell, Paul Frere and Peter Collins.

I am lucky indeed, for not only do I have the memories, but also I have the photographs. Even so, for me, Miller's impressive compendium rekindles magical memories of cars I remember well, and some I had nearly forgotten. In addition, it has introduced me to some I never knew existed at all. I hope it brings the reader similar pleasure, and with its wealth of practical information encourages a few more enthusiasts to make their own living memories out of motoring nostalgia.

Louis Klemantaski.

State of the Market

Despite the predictions of recession that have hung over the British economy for most of the last 12 months, there has been precious little sign of it in the collectors' vehicle market, which has probably enjoyed its most buoyant year since the end of the 1980s. Indeed, the British economy appears to be well on the mend in other sectors as well, so there is no reason to suppose that the present healthy state of the market will not continue.

To a degree, the continued strength of sterling has curtailed the participation in British sales of overseas bidders, although not at the top end of the market. At Brooks' annual Goodwood sale, in June, which concentrates on sports and racing cars, a 1930 Bentley 4½ Litre Supercharged Vanden Plas tourer achieved virtually the same price made at the same venue in June the year before, at £375,500, but this was totally eclipsed by the £683,500 paid for a 1962 Aston Martin DB4GT Zagato Coupé, the highest auction price in the UK during the last year. A 1955 DB3S sports racer sold for £293,000, while several other cars exceeded £100,000. At a more down-to-earth level, a concours-condition 1970 Jaguar E-Type Series II roadster made £34,500, and a 1954 3.4 litre Jaguar XK120M drophead sold for £29,900.

Sotheby's, alone among the major houses, appears to have reduced its activities in the collectors' car market, holding only four sales since last June. However, at Hendon in July 1998, it achieved £58,700 for a 1973 Ferrari Dino 246 GTS, and £46,600 for the 1929 Alvis Silver Eagle Special 'The Green Car', while a collection of 'barn-discovery' Rolls-Royces, which did well in an otherwise lacklustre December sale, confirmed that single-owner collections and 'King Tut's Tomb' can always be relied upon to generate interest.

Brooks first American sale took place at Quail Lodge, Carmel, California, in August 1998, during the Pebble Beach concours weekend. In all, 80 per cent of lots entered were sold, totalling £3.18 million. Top price of the day was the £426,144 paid for a 1908 12.7 litre Grand Prix Mors racer, and a more modern racer – a 1967 Ford GT Mk IV (one of only 12 built) made £246,113. A return to Paris by Brooks in September firmly established this venue, two cars exceeding £350,000, a 1928 Hispano-Suiza selling for £58,267, and a 1932 Alfa Romeo 6C 1750 supercharged GT going to a Spanish collector for £89,641.

December saw Brooks at Gstaad, Switzerland for the first time. In a sale totalling £3.3 million, the highest price for a car in a European auction in 1998 was achieved, a 1965 Ferrari 250 LM Berlinetta making £1,075,000. A 1953 Ferrari 250 Mille Miglia Berlinetta made £422,000 in the same sale, and a 1936 Alfa Romeo V12 racing engine, thought to be worthless by the widow of Enrico Nardi, realised an astonishing £114,000.

The same month saw Brooks' annual Olympia sale, which included motorcycles and Formula 1 memorabilia. There, a 1935 2 litre ERA D-Type realised £406,300 to make top price of the day. A quarter of a million was raised by the Formula 1 memorabilia. In 1998, Coy's annual auction at Silverstone fielded a marathon 148 lots. Top price of the day was the £370,538 paid for a 1959 Ferrari 250 Spyder California with full history (most important), while a 1987 ex-Le Mans Kremer Porsche made £117,938. Coy's has held fewer sales in the past 12 months, concentrating on quality rather than quantity and producing some excellent prices.

Of the provincial houses, H&H in Buxton has continued its run of successful regional sales, with a high percentage of vehicles sold each time. H&H also sells the occasional high-priced vehicle, while BCA recently sold a 1932 Delage D8 8S drophead for £71,000. Christie's has been concentrating its efforts in the USA, the Pebble Beach sale continuing as one of the highlights of the US calendar. It has also managed to secure a number of prestigious single-owner collections. The sale held at Tarrytown, New York, in April 1999, was typical, totalling £3.5 million, with an almost completely original 1913 Mercer Type 35 J Raceabout making £579,000. Its sale in Geneva included cars from the Hans Dursteler Collection, top price being the £281,000 paid for the ex-Reg Parnell 1948 Maserati 4 CLT/48 supercharged Grand Prix monoposto racer. At Nine Elms in London, Christie's also did well, however, with £196,750 paid for a 1934 MG K3 supercharged Magnette.

Brooks' April 1999 sale at Olympia established a record for a spring sale anywhere with a £2 million result. Top price was the £579,000 paid for a 1932 Alfa Romeo 8C 2300 (the chimney sweep's car), while a 1904 Mercedes Simplex rocketed to £265,500.

Low- to medium-range classics have also done well, although the more mundane family cars of the 1930s, 1940s, 1950s and 1960s remain reasonably priced. Non-exotic American cars from all eras are also cheap in Britain and excellent value for money, but the top prices, as always, have been paid for luxury cars by prestigious manufacturers, and sports and racing cars with good provenance.

If anything, the market is showing a distinct, but modest, upturn as this is being written. We have seen a truly excellent year, and I have every confidence for the future.

Malcolm Barber

Investing in Pleasure

Investment isn't a word that's bandied about so freely these days in connection with classic and collectable cars – and it's a good thing, too. Thankfully, the climate in the classic car world has long since moved on from the late 1980s, when Gordon Gecko greed inspired a crazy inflationary spiral.

For a brief period, the simple nostalgic pleasures of a tremendously enjoyable recreational pursuit were subverted and distorted. Instead of a happy glow of pride and a growing memory bank of summer days spent behind the wheel, some owners spoke of their cars in the language of the stock market. Where once an E-Type Jaguar was described as a 3.4, 4.2, roadster or fixed-head coupé, now it was tagged an 'appreciating asset', a 'commodity' and an 'investment'. Instead of someone coming up to you in the supermarket car park and saying, 'What'll she do, mister?', they were just as likely to ask, 'What's she worth?'

Well, in the early 1990s, this false market collapsed in a big way as, for example, Jaguar E-Type roadsters that were worth £100,000 and more at the height of the boom fell back to a quarter of that over-inflated value.

All that's a long time ago now, but it's taken a while for all the shock waves to dissipate. There were those who, for many years after, held a dogged sentimental attachment to those peak market values, deluding themselves that their particular car was the only one in the world to buck the downward trend. Well, they've finally come to accept the reality of the market place. There's one anecdote – maybe apocryphal, but oft repeated – that sums up the atmosphere of those times: when an owner of a Ferrari Daytona 365 GTB/4 phoned an auction house for a valuation, he was asked, 'Does sir want this morning's price or this afternoon's price?'

Similarly, in those days when the hobby was treated by some as an investment arena, the commodities they traded in were sometimes of dubious quality. In some cases, cars were being traded onwards before they'd even been driven, and the eventual owners who actually wanted to drive them were often sadly disappointed when they discovered the compromised integrity beneath the shiny paintwork. These were cars for buying and selling, not driving, and I recall an old market traders' tale of the case of sardines that was sold from one trader to another for ever increasing profit. That was until someone tasted one and complained to the last vendor, who replied, 'They're not for eating, they're for buying and selling.'

Most of the 'sardine' cars have long since been flushed out, and today the market is stable, bustling and thankfully free of the wild fluctuations that once tempted speculators. In short, it has found its own level, with reassuringly steady prices. However, there is a batch of cars that seem undervalued, and it's no surprise that these were the cars whose values spiralled into orbit during the boom. Mk II Jaguars and E-Types are particularly enticing at the moment, along with the so-called Big Healeys, the 100/4, 100/6 and 3000 models. Triumph Stags are less than half of their over-inflated peak value and these days look like a lot of car for the money. Likewise, most DB-series Aston Martins and several Ferrari models, from the 246 GT Dino to the 365 GTB/4 Daytona, rate as bargains compared to their stratospheric values of old.

These apart, the general stability in the market is tremendously beneficial and healthy for the hobby. Today, it's far easier for enthusiasts to gauge the real market value of the cars they own and the next they may buy. The result is generally increased traffic, with more cars to choose from as enthusiasts trade up, down and sideways between themselves in search of new enjoyable driving and owning experiences, rather than trying to sell high and buy low and become 'players' in an unpredictable market.

That's the healthy reality of today's classic car market, yet – and it never ceases to amaze me – I am still approached regularly by newspapers, TV and enthusiasts for advice about 'investing' in classic cars. I simply tell them what a wise auctioneer told me a while ago: 'A keen angler wouldn't sit on a riverbank and tell fisherman's tales about what a fantastic investment his fishing rod was. He'd use it to catch fish. But it's something some classic car enthusiasts still persist in doing and it's a great way to spoil the pleasure of a tremendously enjoyable recreational pursuit. The investment is in the driving pleasure and joy of ownership. If you've bought sensibly, you'll also have something that won't lose capital value in real terms, and compared with rampant new-car depreciation that's something to smile about.'

Those are wise words. To avoid 'buyer's remorse', don't invest; buy a car that will give you more smiles per mile as you enjoy driving it and cherish the cosy glow of nostalgia. Why not dream a little, and with the help of this latest edition of *Miller's Collectors Cars Yearbook and Price Guide* it's my hope that some of you will turn your dreams into driving reality.

Dave Selby

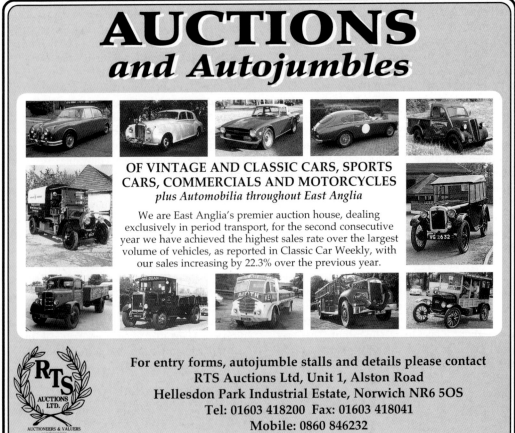

18

Abarth

1964 Abarth 2400 Coupé, coachwork by Allemano, 2323cc, overhead-valve, 6 cylinder in-line engine, aluminium head, iron block, 140bhp at 5,600rpm, 4-speed manual gearbox, left-hand drive, independent front suspension with torsion bar, wishbones and anti-roll bar, live rear axle with semi-elliptic leaf springs, disc brakes all-round, alloy wheels, red with tan interior, fitted black leather luggage.
£25,000–28,000 C

This particular car is believed to be the last production machine and was made especially for the 1964 Geneva show. It has remained in the Abarth family until recently.

AC

From its early days producing three-wheeled tradesmen's vehicles, AC graduated to building four-wheeled cars before WWI, and in the 1920s and 1930s offered a range of high-quality sporting cars. Immediate post-war products were idiosyncratic, if not inelegant, until the launch of the lovely Ace in 1954. Later, endowed with a mighty American Ford V8, this dainty sports car was transformed into the potent and legendary AC Cobra. Cobra mechanics and underpinnings also spawned the AC 427 and 428, a luxury GT that combined US power and British engineering with an elegant Italian body courtesy of Frua. Only 80 of these well-bred, but macho, GTs were built before the fuel crisis of October 1973 stifled demand. In 1979, AC resumed production with the 3 litre V6 mid-engined 3000ME. It was never beautiful, but it looked extremely purposeful. Sadly, its 120mph top speed didn't match its aggressive posture. Only 82 were built, and they remain affordable oddballs with a certain 'What is it?' appeal.

◀ **1955 AC Ace,** 2 litres, 6 cylinders, overhead camshaft, 90bhp at 4,500rpm, twin-tube ladder-frame chassis, all-independent suspension, original right-hand drive, 103mph top speed, 0–60mph in 11.4 seconds, restored in late 1970s, metallic pale green, beige leather upholstery, wood-rimmed steering wheel.
£21,500–24,500 BKS

Production of the Ace ceased in 1964, but its spirit lived on in the Shelby American AC Cobra.

AC Model	ENGINE cc/cyl	DATES	CONDITION 1	2	3
Sociable	636/1	1907–12	£10,500	£9,000	£4,500
12/24 (Anzani)	1498/4	1919–27	£14,000	£11,500	£7,500
16/40	1991/6	1920–28	£18,000	£15,000	£11,000
16/60 Drophead/Saloon	1991/6	1937–40	£24,000	£21,000	£15,500
16/70 Sports Tourer	1991/6	1937–40	£35,000	£26,000	£18,000
16/80 Competition 2-Seater	1991/6	1937–40	£55,000	£45,000	£35,000

AC Model	ENGINE cc/cyl	DATES	CONDITION 1	2	3
2 litre	1991/6	1947–55	£7,000	£4,000	£1,500
Buckland	1991/6	1949–54	£8,500	£5,500	£2,500
Ace	1991/6	1953–63	£30,000	£25,000	£18,000
Ace Bristol	1971/6	1954–63	£42,000	£30,000	£25,000
Ace 2.6	1553/6	1961–62	£38,000	£32,000	£29,000
Aceca	1991/6	1954–63	£22,000	£16,000	£11,000
Aceca Bristol	1971/6	1956–63	£28,000	£20,000	£12,000
Greyhound Bristol	1971/6	1961–63	£16,000	£12,000	£8,000
Cobra Mk II 289	4735/8	1963–64	£90,000	£80,000	£60,000
Cobra Mk III 427	6998/8	1965–67	£125,000	£100,000	£80,000
Cobra Mk IV	5340/8	1987–	£55,000	£40,000	£28,000
428 Frua	7014/8	1967–73	£19,000	£15,000	£10,000
428 Frua Convertible	7014/8	1967–73	£28,000	£20,000	£16,000
3000 ME	2994/6	1976–84	£15,000	£10,000	£8,000

Racing history for Cobra will put the price to over £100,000–120,000.

▶ **1988 AC Cobra Mk IV,** V8 engine, rack-and-pinion steering, finished in Cobalt blue with magnolia leather interior, 5,000 miles from new, always dry-stored, summer use only.
£30,000–32,000 BKS

Production of the Cobra ended in 1968 after 1,029 cars had been built. It resumed in 1980 under the auspices of Brooklands-based Autokraft, which had acquired the AC name.

◀ **1997 AC Cobra Mk IV,** 4948cc, V8, left-hand drive, finished in red with white stripes, full weather equipment, owned by AC Cars from new, 3,246 miles recorded, excellent condition.
£32,000–37,000 BRIT

The Mk IV Cobra, powered by a 4948cc Ford engine, was offered for sale from 1984. During 1987, Ford finally granted Autokraft the right to use the Cobra name. Although lacking the macho brutality of the earliest models, the Mk IV is far more satisfactory as a road machine.

AJS

◀ **1931 AJS Richmond 9hp Saloon,** Coventry-Climax engine, 4-speed manual gearbox, blue with matching interior upholstery and trim, history file, original instruction booklet, good condition throughout.
£4,000–5,000 H&H

The A. J. Stevens company was best known for motorcycles, but it built cars from 1930 until 1931, when it went into liquidation. Production was taken over by Willys-Overland-Crossley until it ceased completely in 1933. AJS produced about 3,300 examples of this rather expensive, quality light saloon car, of which relatively few remain. This particular example was owned by the Stevens family, the manufacturers, for most of its life. It was one of the last 300 produced.

Alfa Romeo

Keen drivers have good reason to be grateful to Alfa Romeo, for almost from the company's foundation, in Milan in 1910, Alfa models have carried sporting genes. There are simply too many lithe, lean and nimble Alfas to mention, and for periods in its history, the company's eager road cars have basked in the reflected glory of race-track victories, most notably during the 1920s, when Alfa Romeo began to dominate Grand Prix racing.

Although Alfa Romeo gradually moved towards the automotive mainstream, higher volume production and more affordable models after 1945, the cars' sporting genes have persisted to this day. Virtually every Alfa of the 1960s and 1970s was a rewarding driver's car. Although sometimes marred by fragile electrics and a readiness to rust, many flaws were easily forgiven once you got behind the wheel.

1929 Alfa Romeo Supercharged 6C 1500 Super Sport, coachwork by Zagato, 1.5 litre, double-overhead-camshaft engine, Roots supercharger, approximately 78bhp, restored, very good condition.
£200,000–250,000 BKS

This extremely important Alfa Romeo began life as a 3rd Series 1500 Super Sport and was one of the three works cars entered by Stiles for the Brooklands Double Twelve. Works driver/mechanic Giulio Ramponi was to co-drive with Count Giovanni 'Johnny' Lurani, but as Lurani recalled in his autobiography *Racing Around the World*, 'I remained in the pits complete with helmet, goggles and gloves, ready to relieve Ramponi, but Giulio kept on and never left the driving seat. I hoped...to have a chance during the second day...but in vain!' Ramponi went on to gain a memorable victory.

A handmade, sterling silver, 1:14 scale model of the 1932 Scuderia Ferrari Alfa Romeo Monza, mounted on a slate stand with a silver plaque.
£7,200–7,800 BKS

1954 Alfa Romeo 1900SS Coupé America, coachwork by Ghia, finished in red with beige interior trim, restored 1995.
£27,000–30,000 BKS

Designed by Giovanni Savonuzzi, who had joined Ghia from Cisitalia, this car reflected his keen interest in vehicle aerodynamics.

ALFA ROMEO Model	ENGINE cc/cyl	DATES	CONDITION 1	2	3
24HP	4084/4	1910–11	£25,000	£16,000	£12,000
12HP	2413/4	1910–11	£18,000	£11,000	£8,000
40–60	6028/4	1913–15	£32,000	£24,000	£14,000
RL	2916/6	1921–22	£30,000	£24,000	£14,000
RM	1944/4	1924–25	£28,000	£17,000	£13,000
6C 1500	1487/6	1927–28	£50,000*	£20,000+	£10,000+
6C 1750	1752/6	1923–33	£100,000+	£80,000+	-
6C 1900	1917/6	1933	£18,000	£15,000	£12,000
6C 2300	2309/6	1934	£22,000	£18,000	£15,000
6C 2500 SS Cabriolet/Spider	2443/6	1939–45	£100,000	£50,000	£40,000
6C 2500 SS Coupé	2443/6	1939–45	£60,000	£40,000	£30,000
8C 2300 Monza/Short Chassis	2300/8	1931–34	£1,000,000+	£400,000+	£200,000
8C 2900	2900/8	1935–39	£1,000,000+	£500,000+	£300,000

Value is very dependent on sporting history, body style and engine type.
*The high price on this model is dependent on whether it is 1500 supercharged/double overhead cam.

Miller's Starter Marque

Alfa Romeos: *1750 and 2000 GTV; 1300 Junior Spider, 1600 Duetto Spider, 1750 and 2000 Spider Veloce; 1300 and 1600 GT Junior; Alfasud ti and Sprint.*

- Responsive, eager and sweet twin-cam engines, finely balanced chassis, nimble handling and delightful looks are some of the characteristic traits of classic Alfas from the mid-1960s onwards. They are also eminently affordable. For the kind of money that would buy you an MGB or Triumph TR, you could be a little more adventurous and acquire an engaging Alfa Romeo sporting saloon or convertible.
- The bad news is that the unfortunate reputation Alfas of the 1960s and 1970s earned for rusting was deserved. Even that has an advantage, however, because the suspicion still lingers and helps keep prices comparatively low. In fact, most Alfas from that period will have had major surgery at least once, so you should be able to find one with plenty of metal. Even so, take a magnet along. Classic Alfa owners – or *Alfisti* as they prefer to call themselves – have a saying: 'You pay for the engineering and the engine, but the body comes free.'
- Bear in mind, too, that maintenance costs are likely to be higher than they would be for an MG or Triumph TR.

1955 Alfa Romeo 1900 Super Sprint, coachwork by Touring, 1975cc, 4 cylinder engine, double overhead camshafts, 5-speed all-syncromesh gearbox, double A-arm front suspension with anti-roll bar, live rear axle located by radius arms, Alfin 4-wheel hydraulic drum brakes, left-hand drive, 120mph top speed, good condition.
£20,000–23,000 C

The Super Sprint Coupé was intended as a family-size, sporting two-door coupé. Its heart-shaped, vertical front grille and similarly-sized horizontal air intakes would become the trademark of future models.

1959 Alfa Romeo Giulietta Sprint Special Coupé, 1290cc, alloy cylinder block, 100bhp, 5-speed gearbox, left-hand drive, 125mph top speed, refurbished in 1991, major overhaul in 1994, approximately 81,400km from new, very original condition.
£7,500–10,000 BKS

Alfa Romeo's successful Giulietta range debuted in 1954 with the arrival of the Bertone-styled Sprint coupé; the Berlina saloon did not appear until the following year. Introduced in 1959, the Sprint Special is recognised as the ultimate Giulietta.

1961 Alfa Romeo Giulietta SS, 1290cc, 4 cylinders, double overhead camshafts, 100bhp at 6,500rpm, 5-speed gearbox, left-hand drive, 120mph top speed, finished in silver with red leather interior, good condition.
£9,000–12,000 BRIT

In all, 1,366 examples of the Giulietta SS were produced between 1959 and 1962.

> A known continuous history can add value to and enhance the enjoyment of a car.

1959 Alfa Romeo Giulietta Spider, coachwork by Pininfarina, 1290cc, 4 cylinder, double-overhead-camshaft, engine, ground-up restoration 1996/7, rebuilt engine, new stainless steel exhaust system, new 5-speed gearbox, repainted in Rosso Alfa, retrimmed in black leather with red piping, new hood.
£12,000–15,000 COYS

For many *Alfisti*, the Giulietta Spider is the archetypal post-war Alfa Romeo, and for the purists, the first series (code-numbered 750) is the most desirable. Although similar in appearance to the later 101 series, the shorter-wheelbase 750 is more attractive. This example, being a late 750-series car, incorporates several improvements that were built in to the 101 range, most notably revisions to the front suspension.

ALFA ROMEO Model	ENGINE cc/cyl	DATES	CONDITION 1	2	3
2000 Spider	1974/4	1958–61	£14,000	£9,000	£4,000
2600 Sprint	2584/6	1962–66	£11,000	£7,500	£4,000
2600 Spider	2584/6	1962–65	£13,000	£8,000	£5,000
Giulietta Sprint	1290/4	1955–62	£10,000	£7,000	£4,000
Giulietta Spider	1290/4	1956–62	£11,000	£6,000	£4,500
Giulia Saloon	1570/4	1962–72	£5,000	£3,000	£1,500
Giulia Sprint (rhd)	1570/4	1962–68	£10,500	£6,000	£2,000
Giulia Spider (rhd)	1570/4	1962–65	£11,000	£8,000	£4,000
Giulia SS	1570/4	1962–66	£16,000	£11,000	£5,000
GT 1300 Junior	1290/4	1966–77	£7,000	£5,500	£2,000
Giulia Sprint GT	1570/4	1962–68	£7,500	£5,000	£2,000
1600GT Junior	1570/4	1972–75	£7,000	£4,000	£2,000
1750/2000 Berlina	1779/4 1962/4	1967–77	£4,000	£2,000	£1,000
1750GTV	1779/4	1967–72	£7,000	£6,000	£2,000
2000GTV	1962/4	1971–77	£6,500	£4,000	£2,000
1600/1750 (Duetto)	1570/4 1779/4	1966–67	£10,000	£7,500	£5,000
1750/2000 Spider (Kamm)	1779/4 1962/4	1967–78	£9,000	£6,000	£3,000
Montreal	2593/8	1970–77	£10,000	£8,000	£5,000
Junior Zagato 1300	1290/4	1968–74	£7,000	£5,000	£3,000
Junior Zagato 1600	1570/4	1968–74	£8,000	£6,000	£4,000
Alfetta GT/GTV (chrome)	1962/4	1972–86	£4,000	£2,500	£1,000
Alfasud	1186/4 1490/4	1972–83	£2,000	£1,000	£500
Alfasud ti	1186/4 1490/4	1974–81	£2,500	£1,200	£900
Alfasud Sprint	1284/4 1490/4	1976–85	£3,000	£2,000	£1,000
GTV6	2492/6	1981–	£4,000	£2,500	£1,000

◄ **1968 Alfa Romeo Spider Duetto,** 1779cc, 4 cylinders, double overhead camshafts,132bhp at 5,500rpm, 5-speed manual gearbox, disc brakes all-round, left-hand drive, finished in red with black interior, black hood.
£8,000–10,000 Pou

Alfa Romeo Spider

When the new Spider was first seen at the Geneva Motor Show in 1966, Alfa launched a competition to name the car. After ploughing through 140,000 entries with suggestions like Lollobrigida, Bardot and Nuvolari, they chose Duetto, which neatly summed up the two's-company-three's-a-crowd image.

1961 Alfa Romeo Giulietta Spider Veloce, coachwork by Pininfarina, 1290cc, double overhead camshafts, 5-speed gearbox, restored in 1996, genuine Veloce specification, red with black interior, good condition.
£11,000–14,000 BKS

1972 Alfa Romeo 2000 Spider Veloce, 1962cc,
4 cylinders, 5-speed manual gearbox, new rear wings
and full respray in 1991, silver with black interior.
£3,750–5,000 H&H

1973 Alfa Romeo 2000 Spider Veloce, 1962cc,
4 cylinder, double-overhead-camshaft engine,
5-speed manual gearbox, left-hand drive, recently
restored, resprayed in silver, black interior.
£3,500–4,500 H&H

1974 Alfa Romeo 2000 Spider Veloce, 1962cc,
refurbished, new brake discs, master cylinder, petrol
tank, exhaust system and water pump, finished in red,
original black upholstery, canvas hood in good condition.
£5,000–6,000 BRIT

1988 Alfa Romeo Spider Mk III Cloverleaf, coachwork
by Pininfarina, 2 litres, good condition.
£8,500–9,500 LOM

1990 Alfa Romeo Spider S4, 2 litres, fuel injection, 5-speed manual gearbox, power steering, Rosso red with
oatmeal interior and black hood, good condition throughout.
£11,000–13,000 BLE

1992 Alfa Romeo Spider Veloce, coachwork by Pininfarina, 2 litres, burgundy metallic with tan leather interior,
electric windows, door mirrors and aerial, good condition.
£10,500–12,500 CARS

1964 Alfa Romeo Giulia Spider 1600, coachwork by Pininfarina, 1.6 litre, 4 cylinder, double-overhead-camshaft engine, 92bhp, 5-speed gearbox, right-hand drive, 109mph top speed, finished in red with black interior, dry stored since 1983, in need of restoration.
£4,000–5,500 BKS

1967 Alfa Romeo Giulia Sprint GTC Cabriolet, coachwork by Bertone, 1.6 litre, 4 cylinder, double-overhead-camshaft engine, 106bhp, 5-speed manual gearbox, disc brakes all-round, 112mph top speed, restored 1991, factory-fitted chassis reinforcement, finished in Rosso red with grey upholstery, good condition.
£7,000–10,000 BKS

The GTA competition version enjoyed considerable success, winning the European Touring Car Championship three years running, from 1966 to 1968. Almost as rare as the GTA was the cabriolet-bodied GTC, 999 examples of which were produced between 1965 and 1966.

Restored Values

The cost of a professional restoration will have an influence on, but no direct relation to, a car's market value. A restored car can have a market value lower than the cost of its restoration.

1968 Alfa Romeo Giulia 1750GTV Series I, 1788cc, 4 cylinder, double-overhead-camshaft engine, 118bhp, 5-speed manual gearbox, independent front suspension, coil-sprung live rear axle, disc brakes all-round, right-hand drive, restored in 1991, yellow with black interior, good condition.
£1,750–2,500 BKS

▶ **1972 Alfa Romeo 1600GT Junior,** 1.6 litre, bodywork refurbished and resprayed in 1990, block and cylinder head replaced, 36,000 miles from new, good condition.
£3,750–4,500 BKS

Unquestionably one of the world's finest sports saloons from the moment of its introduction in 1963, the Bertone-styled Giulia enjoyed a lengthy production life, finally disappearing from the Alfa range 14 years later. The 1600GT Junior was built between 1972 and 1977, initially in two-headlamp form, and later with the four-headlamp front end shared by the contemporary 2000GTV.

1972 Alfa Romeo 2000GTV, coachwork by Bertone, 2 litres, good condition.
£12,000–14,000 LOM

◄ 1975 Alfa Romeo
Montreal, 2593cc, double-overhead-camshaft V8, fuel injection, 200bhp at 6,500rpm, 5-speed manual gearbox, independent front suspension, coil-sprung live rear axle, disc brakes all-round, 14in alloy wheels, left-hand drive, 220km/h top speed.
£9,500–11,000 Pou

1980 Alfa Romeo Alfetta GTV SE, 2 litre, extensively restored, engine uprated, 11:1 compression ratio, reconditioned cylinder head, sports camshafts, K & N air-induction system, 4–2–1 exhaust manifold, tuned exhaust with twin tailpipes, lowered and uprated suspension, brakes overhauled, reconditioned alloy wheels, louvred GTV6 bonnet, resprayed Gioalo Fly yellow, interior in excellent condition, Recarro-style black GTV6 seats, new carpet, original wooden steering wheel, aluminium racing pedals, 64,000 miles from new.
£8,000–9,000 LOM

The SE was a special-edition model that benefited from a full Webasto sunroof, special alloy wheels, air conditioning, and a wooden steering wheel and gear lever.

1975 Alfa Romeo Alfetta 1.8GT, right-hand drive, finished in silver, good condition.
£9,000–10,000 LOM

This particular car is one of only three right-hand drive examples known to exist.

Miller's is a price GUIDE not a price LIST

◄ **1980 Alfa Romeo Alfetta GTV,** 1962cc, 4 cylinders, 5-speed gearbox, full alloy roll cage, front and rear sump guards, alloy wheels, Cibié spot lights, fire extinguisher, red with grey and black interior trim.
£2,500–3,500 H&H

1984 Alfa Romeo Alfetta 2000GTV, 1962cc, 5-speed manual gearbox, reconditioned cylinder head, bare-metal respray in silver, newly treated with underseal, fully rustproofed, dark green and black interior trim.
£1,500–2,000 H&H

1990 Alfa Romeo 75 Sport, white with black trim, alloy wheels, red interior.
£9,000–10,000 LOM

1993 Alfa Romeo SZ, coachwork by Zagato, 3 litre, double-overhead-camshaft V6, 206bhp, 5-speed transaxle, cockpit-adjustable suspension, 253km/h top speed, 0–100km/h in 7 seconds, finished in Rosso Alfa with light tan leather interior, 5,000km from new.
£20,000–24,000 BKS

◄ **1993 Alfa Romeo SZ,** coachwork by Zagato, 2959cc, 6 cylinders, 5-speed manual gearbox, finished in Alfa red with black leather interior trim, 37,000km from new, one of only 250 left-hand drive models made, excellent condition.
£21,000–25,000 H&H

Alvis

Founded in 1919, Alvis soon gained a reputation for building fine sporting cars. The company was also an early pioneer of front-wheel drive, which featured on the 12/75 model of 1928. In the 1930s, as Alvis models became increasingly luxurious, the company's best cars began to rival those from Bentley. After 1945, the cars were a little more mundane and sometimes outright quirky, as with the unsuccessful, whale-like TB14 and TB21. Elegance returned in 1956, however, with the Graber-styled TD21, which evolved into the TD, TE and TF models. Then Rover took control in 1966 and Alvis production ceased.

1934 Alvis Speed 20SB Saloon, 2511cc, 6 cylinders, 4-speed manual gearbox, restored c1990, 543 miles covered since, finished in two-tone blue, blue and grey upholstery and trim, dry-stored since 1991.
£23,000–26,000 H&H

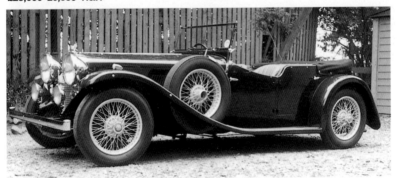

◀ **1934 Alvis Speed 20 Tourer,** coachwork by Cross & Ellis, fully restored 1997, all mechanics overhauled, wheels rebuilt, new wiring loom, new chrome, new duck hood, tonneau and sidescreens, finished in British Racing green, new beige hide interior, new carpets, matching numbers, excellent condition throughout.
£39,000–42,000 Mot

ALVIS Model	ENGINE cc/cyl	DATES	CONDITION 1	2	3
12/50	1496/4	1923–32	£20,000	£13,000	£7,000
Silver Eagle	2148	1929–37	£16,000	£12,000	£8,000
Silver Eagle DHC	2148	1929–37	£18,000	£13,000	£9,000
12/60	1645/4	1931–32	£15,000	£10,000	£7,000
Speed 20 (tourer)	2511/6	1932–36	£35,000	£28,000	£18,000
Speed 20 (closed)	2511/6	1932–36	£22,000	£15,000	£11,000
Crested Eagle	3571/6	1933–39	£10,000	£7,000	£4,000
Firefly (tourer)	1496/4	1932–34	£12,000	£10,000	£6,000
Firefly (closed)	1496/6	1932–34	£7,000	£5,000	£4,000
Firebird (tourer)	1842/4	1934–39	£13,000	£10,000	£6,000
Firebird (closed)	1842/4	1934–39	£7,000	£5,000	£4,000
Speed 25 (tourer)	3571/6	1936–40	£38,500	£30,000	£20,000
Speed 25 (closed)	3571/6	1936–40	£23,000	£17,000	£12,000
3.5 litre	3571/6	1935–36	£35,000	£25,000	£18,000
4.3 litre	4387/6	1936–40	£44,000	£30,000	£22,000
Silver Crest	2362/6	1936–40	£14,000	£10,000	£7,000
TA	3571/6	1936–39	£18,000	£12,000	£8,000
12/70	1842/4	1937–40	£10,000	£8,000	£6,000

◄ **1935 Alvis Speed 20SC Tourer,** coachwork by Vanden Plas, 2762cc, 90mph top speed, all mechanical components in sound condition, engine rebuilt, 11,000 miles covered since, high-ratio rear axle fitted, steering rebuilt, brakes relined, new clutch, instruments fully functional, finished in British Racing green, grey double duck hood, burgundy leather interior, correct tools including wheel hammer and grease gun, complete service record.
£27,500–32,500 BRIT

Introduced in 1932, the Speed 20 was powered by a 20hp engine similar to that used in the previous Silver Eagle series. It was endowed with excellent performance and represented outstanding value at under £700. The low-slung chassis proved ideal for the various styles of sporting coachwork offered at the time.

▶ **1961 Alvis TD21 Saloon,** 2993cc, 6 cylinders, automatic transmission, restored, finished in British Racing green, cream leather interior, burr walnut trim, good condition.
£8,500–10,000 BRIT

Introduced as the TA21, the 3 litre series progressed through the TB and TC21, and by 1958 the Park Ward-bodied TD21 was in production – an elegant and distinctive motor car offered in Saloon and Drophead Coupé form.

1961 Alvis TD21 Saloon, coachwork by Park Ward, restored 1986/89, gearbox modified to accommodate overdrive, resprayed in British Racing green, chrome trim replated, wheels rebuilt, tan upholstery, good condition.
£5,000–7,000 S

Herman Graber, of Berne, built bodies to special order on Alvis chassis, culminating in the TC108G show car, displayed in Paris in 1955. Park Ward was responsible for the production versions from 1958, and they are regarded by many as among the most beautiful in existence.

ALVIS Model	ENGINE cc/cyl	DATES	CONDITION 1	2	3
TA14	1892/4	1946–50	£9,500	£8,000	£4,500
TA14 DHC	1892/4	1946–50	£14,000	£11,000	£5,000
TB14 Roadster	1892/4	1949–50	£15,000	£10,000	£8,000
TB21 Roadster	2993/6	1951	£16,000	£10,000	£7,000
TA21/TC21	2993/6	1950–55	£12,000	£9,000	£5,000
TA21/TC21 DHC	2993/6	1950–55	£17,000	£13,000	£10,000
TC21/100 Grey Lady	2993/6	1953–56	£13,000	£11,000	£5,000
TC21/100 DHC	2993/6	1954–56	£19,000	£15,000	£9,000
TD21	2993/6	1956–62	£11,000	£8,000	£4,000
TD21 DHC	2993/6	1956–62	£22,000	£16,000	£10,000
TE21	2993/6	1963–67	£15,000	£10,000	£7,000
TE21 DHC	2993/6	1963–67	£22,000	£16,000	£8,000
TF21	2993/6	1966–67	£16,000	£12,000	£8,000
TF21 DHC	2993/6	1966–67	£28,000	£17,000	£13,000

Armstrong-Siddeley

◀ **1952 Armstrong-Siddeley Whitley Saloon,** 2309cc, 6 cylinders, 4-speed manual gearbox, resprayed in white, period valve radio, original owner's manual, good condition throughout.
£2,400–3,300 H&H

Miller's is a price GUIDE not a price LIST

ARMSTRONG–SIDDELEY Model	ENGINE cc/cyl	DATES	CONDITION 1	2	3
Hurricane	1991/6	1945–53	£10,000	£7,000	£4,000
Typhoon	1991/6	1946–50	£7,000	£3,000	£2,000
Lancaster/Whitley	1991/6				
	2306/6	1945–53	£8,000	£5,500	£2,500
Sapphire 234/236	2290/4				
	2309/6	1955–58	£7,500	£5,000	£3,000
Sapphire 346	3440/6	1953–58	£9,000	£5,000	£2,000
Star Sapphire	3990/6	1958–60	£10,000	£7,000	£4,000

Arrol-Johnston

◀ **1913 Arrol-Johnston 15.9hp Four-Seater Tourer,** 4 cylinder engine, shaft drive, rear-wheel brakes, electric lighting, finished in grey with green upholstery, 5,604 miles from new, requires recommissioning.
£15,000–17,000 BKS

Sir William Arrol and George Johnston formed the Mo-Car Syndicate in Glasgow in 1897. Their early Dogcarts were sturdily constructed in the Scottish Highlands and were powered by a flat-twin engine. Coachwork had a varnished wood finish, and dos-à-dos seating arrangements were favoured. By 1913, the Pullinger-designed Arrol-Johnston was much more conventional. It featured a 'coal-scuttle' bonnet, with the radiator behind the engine. The company offered two 4 cylinder models in 1913, an 11.9hp and a 15.9hp, together with a limited-production 6 cylinder car.

ASA

1965 ASA 411, 1092cc, 4 cylinder in-line engine, twin Weber 40DCOE carburettors, 104bhp at 7,500rpm, front disc brakes, rear drum brakes, centre-lock alloy wheels.
£14,000–17,000 Pou

Aston Martin

Bamford and Martin Ltd was set up in 1913 by engineers Robert Bamford and Lionel Martin from a base in London's South Kensington, initially tuning and developing Singer 10s. In 1919, the first prototype Aston Martins were produced – the name was formed from the Aston Clinton Hillclimb and Lionel Martin's surname – although the cars were not available for sale for another two years or more.

Although the company achieved considerable sporting success, its financial basis was always flimsy with frequent changes of ownership.

In 1947, the company was taken over by tractor manufacturer David Brown, whose initials gave name to the memorable DB series. With losses of £1 million a year, Brown relinquished ownership in 1972, and since 1987 Ford has been the custodian of one of the most charismatic British sporting marques. But one mark of the enduring appeal of these classic motor cars is the high number of survivors. Of the 12,000 or so Astons built up to the launch of the DB7, it's reckoned that around two-thirds have survived in one form or another.

◀ **1937 Aston Martin 15/98 Four-Door Saloon,** 2 litre, overhead-camshaft 4 cylinder engine, 98bhp, Moss synchromesh gearbox, Girling rod-operated brakes, 85mph top speed, restored 1988/97, finished in British Racing green with beige interior.
£12,500–14,000 BKS

The Aston Martin 15/98 resulted from the company's policy of developing and refining its products, the car's predecessor being the Mk II. Short- and long-chassis models were built. Aston Martin's troubles of this period kept production low – only 176 2 litre cars of all types were completed between 1936 and 1939.

1950 Aston Martin DB2 Coupé, 2.6 litres, 6 cylinders, overhead camshaft, finished in British Racing green, restored.
£85,000–100,000 BKS

This particular DB2 was one of three Coupés prepared by Aston Martin for the second post-war Le Mans 24-hour race in 1950. It was to be driven by Eric Thompson and Jack Fairman; Reg Parnell was paired with Charles Brackenbury, and George Abecassis with Lance Macklin to drive the other two. Unfortunately, en route to the Sarthe circuit, Fairman missed a corner and overturned the car. It proved impossible to repair the damage in time for the race, so the DB2 was returned to the Feltham works and rebuilt in time for Thompson to drive it in the *Daily Express* One-Hour Production Car Race, at Silverstone, on August 26. Thereafter, it enjoyed a varied career on road and track, being driven by such notables as Moss, Collins, Salvadori, Rolt, Macklin, Abecassis and Rob Walker, not forgetting Eric Thompson himself.

ASTON MARTIN Model	ENGINE cc/cyl	DATES	CONDITION 1	2	3
Lionel Martin Cars	1486/4	1921–25	£26,000+	£18,000	£16,000
International	1486/4	1927–32	£36,000	£20,000	£16,000
Le Mans	1486/4	1932–33	£52,000	£38,000	£32,000
Mk II	1486/4	1934–36	£40,000	£30,000	£25,000
Ulster	1486/4	1934–36	£80,000+	£50,000	-
2 Litre	1950/4	1936–40	£30,000	£20,000	£12,000

Value is dependent upon racing history, originality and completeness.
Add 40 per cent if a competition winner or works team car.

Aston Martin DB2/4 Mk I & II (1953–57)

Body styles: Four-seater saloon, fixed-head coupé, drophead coupé.
Engine: Double-overhead-camshaft, six-cylinder, 2580cc, 2922cc from 1954.
Power output: 125bhp at 5,000rpm (2580cc); 140bhp at 5,000rpm (2992cc).
Transmission: Four-speed manual.
Brakes: Drums all round.
Maximum speed: 115–120+mph.
0–60mph: 12.6 seconds (2580cc); 10 seconds (2992cc).
Production: 763.
Evolved from the two-seater DB2, the 2/4 added two more occasional rear seats for practicality; as for the styling, the DB2/4 merely states what it is,

suggesting honest durability rather than the Gucci-loafer glitz that came later when Astons clothed themselves in Italian designer wear. And indeed, the whole thing is something of a durable brogue. With its solid chassis and confident gait to match its 115mph plus pace, it's also pretty rugged, at least compared with the delicate nerves of later, far more complex and highly-strung Astons. In fact, the DB2/4 is the nearest thing to a viable DIY Aston, with an engine that's not as marginally tuned as later models and Triumph Herald-like access under that one-piece bonnet. Cheaper to own and run than a Bond-era Aston, understated and, quite possibly, under-valued too, that's the DB2/4.

1955 Aston Martin DB2/4, engine recently rebuilt with new pistons, liners, valves and guides, converted to unleaded fuel, new water pump and carburettors, brakes and suspension overhauled, resprayed.
£17,000–20,000 CGC

◀ **1957 Aston Martin DB Mk III Coupé,** rebuilt DBA 6 cylinder engine, twin SU carburettors, 162bhp, left-hand drive, finished in metallic silver, original tobacco leather upholstery.
£21,500–24,000 BKS

The DB Mk III was built between 1956 and 1959, and was the first road-going Aston Martin with the handsome new radiator aperture designed by Bert Thickpenny (and previously seen on the competition DB3S), which would become an Aston Martin hallmark. Production totalled 529 cars.

▶ **1963 Aston Martin DB4 Series V Vantage,** 3670cc, 6 cylinders, double overhead camshafts, triple Weber DCOE carburettors, 285bhp at 5,750rpm, 4-speed plus overdrive gearbox, independent front suspension, coil-sprung live rear axle, disc brakes all-round, Borrani wheels, 240km/h top speed.
£50,000–55,000 Pou

1961 Aston Martin DB4 Series IV Vantage Convertible, coachwork by Touring, 3670cc, 6 cylinders, 9:1 compression ratio, triple SU HD8 carburettors, 266bhp at 5,700rpm, 4-speed David Brown gearbox, twin-plate Borg & Beck clutch, oil cooler, independent coil-spring/wishbone front suspension, coil-sprung live rear axle located by Watts linkage and parallel trailing arms, disc brakes all-round, finished in Chariot red, chromed wire wheels, black leather interior and hood.
£65,000–70,000 COYS

The DB4, made its debut at the 1958 London Motor Show. Successor to the DB Mk III, it was the first production Aston Martin to employ Tadek Marek's new twin-cam, all aluminium straight-six engine and a lightweight aluminium body designed by Touring, using its *Superleggera* method of construction. Performance of 140mph, 0–60mph in around 9 seconds, and 0–100mph in 20 seconds put it among the fastest grand tourers available. Introduced in 1961, the Series IV benefited from myriad detail changes.

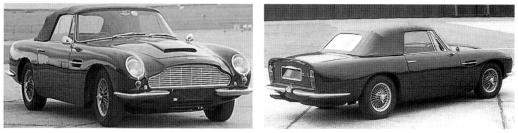

1967 Aston Martin DB6 Vantage Volante Convertible, 3995cc, 6 cylinders, triple SU carburettors, 325bhp, converted to ZF manual gearbox, restored 1990, finished in British Racing green, good condition.
£60,000–70,000 BKS

The culmination of Aston Martin's long-running DB line, the DB6 was introduced in 1965. However, it abandoned the *Superleggera* body structure of its predecessors in favour of a conventional steel fabrication. The wheelbase was 4in longer than before, resulting in an extensive restyle, with an increased windscreen rake, raised roofline and reshaped rear quarter-windows. Opening front quarter-lights made a reappearance, but the major change was at the rear, where a Kamm-style tail with spoiler improved the aerodynamics, greatly enhancing stability at high speed. After 37 Volante convertibles had been completed on the DB5 short-wheelbase chassis, a switch was made to the DB6 chassis in October 1966. Distinguishable by its flared wheel arches and DBS wheels, the Mk II DB6, introduced in 1969, could be had with AE Brico electronic fuel injection. In total, 1,575 DB6s were made between 1965 and 1970, plus 140 long-wheelbase Volantes.

Aston Martin DB4 (1958–63)

Body styles: Fixed-head coupé or convertible.
Construction: Pressed-steel and tubular inner chassis frame, aluminium-alloy outer panels.
Engine: Double-overhead-camshaft, six-cylinder, 3670cc; or, for some GTs, 3749cc.
Power output: 240bhp at 5,500rpm.
Transmission: Four-speed manual with optional overdrive.
Suspension: Independent front with wishbones, coil springs and telescopic dampers; live rear axle located by trailing arms and Watts linkage, with coil springs and lever-arm dampers.
Brakes: Servo-assisted Dunlop discs front and rear.
Maximum speed: 140+mph.
0–60mph: 8 seconds (less for GT/GT Zagato).
0–100mph: 20.1 seconds (less for GT/GT Zagato).
Average fuel consumption: 14.22mpg.
Production: 1,040 (fixed-head); 70 (convertible): 95 fixed-head DB4 GT (including 19 Zagato).
The debut of the DB4 in 1958 heralded the beginning of the Aston Martin glory

years, ushering in the breed of classic six-cylinder DB models that propelled Aston Martin on to the world stage. Earlier post-war Astons were fine sporting enthusiasts' road cars, but with the DB4, Aston Martins acquired a new grace, sophistication and refinement that was, for many, the ultimate expression of the grand tourer theme. Clothed in an Italian designer suit by Carrozzeria Touring of Milan, it possessed a graceful yet powerful elegance. Under the aluminium body was Tadek Marek's fabulous double-overhead-camshaft, straight-six engine, which had been developed from Aston Martin's energetic racing programme. In short, the DB4 looked superb and went like stink. The DB5, which followed, will forever be remembered as the James Bond Aston, and the final expression of the theme came with the bigger, heavier DB6.

1968 Aston Martin DB6 Mk I, 3995cc, completely restored.
£25,000–30,000 SCS

1974 Aston Martin V8, 5340cc, engine overhauled, mechanically sound, new inner sills, finished in red, tan upholstery, well maintained, history file.
£15,000–18,000 BRIT

Following the take-over of Aston Martin by Company Developments early in 1972, the DBS V8 was replaced by a new model, designated simply 'V8'. Although retaining much of the William Towns design, the V8 was instantly recognisable by its restyled front with single headlamps.

1971 Aston Martin DBS V8, double overhead camshafts, Lucas fuel injection, 350bhp, 3-speed automatic transmission, 4-wheel disc brakes, extensive mechanical overhaul in 1989, resprayed in metallic blue, 70,000 miles from new, original specification throughout.
£15,000–18,000 C

A new V8 engine, with light-alloy block and heads, was developed from the Aston Martin DBS of 1967, but production delays held it back until 1969. It was worth waiting for, however: in its initial fuel-injected form, it gave 350bhp and abundant torque. Installed in a superb chassis, clad with splendid four-seater bodywork, it propelled the V8 Aston Martin from 0 to 50mph in 5.4 seconds.

1976 Aston Martin V8.
£16,000–19,000 BLE

◄ **1979 Aston Martin V8 Oscar India,** automatic, 58,000 miles from new, full service history.
£23,000–26,000 VIC

ASTON MARTIN Model	ENGINE cc/cyl	DATES	CONDITION 1	2	3
DB1	1970/4	1948–50	£30,000+	£20,000	£16,000
DB2	2580/6	1950–53	£30,000+	£18,000	£14,000
DB2 Conv	2580/6	1951–53	£35,000+	£28,000+	£17,000
DB2/4 Mk I/II	2580/6 2922/6	1953–57	£30,000	£18,000	£14,000
DB2/4 Mk II Conv	2580/6 2922/6	1953–57	£40,000	£25,000	£15,000
DB2/4 Mk III	2580/6 2922/6	1957–59	£35,000	£22,000	£15,000
DB2/4 Mk III Conv	2580/6 2922/6	1957–59	£38,000+	£26,000	£20,000
DB Mk III Conv	2922/6	1957–59	£46,000	£28,000	£18,000
DB Mk III	2922/6	1957–59	£35,000	£22,000	£15,000
DB4	3670/6	1959–63	£35,000	£22,000	£16,000
DB4 Conv	3670/6	1961–63	£60,000	£35,000	-
DB4 GT	3670/6	1961–63	£100,000+	£80,000	-
DB5	3995/6	1964–65	£35,000	£26,000	£20,000
DB5 Conv	3995/6	1964–65	£50,000+	£38,000	-
DB6	3995/6	1965–69	£30,000	£20,000	£16,000
DB6 Mk I auto	3995/6	1965–69	£28,000	£18,000	£14,000
DB6 Mk I Volante	3995/6	1965–71	£50,000+	£32,000	£28,000
DB6 Mk II Volante	3995/6	1969–70	£52,000+	£40,000	£30,000
DBS	3995/6	1967–72	£15,000+	£15,000	£9,000
AM Vantage	5340/8	1977–78	£20,000	£15,000	£10,000
V8 Vantage Oscar India	5340/8	1978–82	£40,000+	£25,000	£20,000
V8 Volante	5340/8	1978–82	£40,000+	£30,000	£25,000

Works/competition history is an important factor.

1987 Aston Martin V8 Vantage, 400bhp, manual gearbox, left-hand drive, British Racing green with beige Connolly hide interior, one of only 350 examples made, 16,120km from new, excellent condition throughout.
£40,000–45,000 BKS

1987 Aston Martin V8 Volante, 5340cc, double overhead camshafts, fuel injection, 300bhp at 5,000rpm, 3-speed automatic transmission, independent suspension all-round, 4-wheel Girling disc brakes, alloy wheels, 240km/h top speed.
£42,000–46,000 Pou

◄ **1989 Aston Martin 'PoW' Vantage Volante,** 12,000 miles from new, full service history, outstanding condition.
£120,000–130,000 MEE

This particular car is one of 22 built to the same specification as that of HRH Prince of Wales' Vantage Volante.

► **1990 Aston Martin Virage,** manual gearbox, 45,000 miles from new, excellent condition.
£50,000–55,000 MEE

1995 Aston Martin DB7, 4-speed electronically-controlled automatic transmission, left-hand drive, finished in British Racing green with magnolia leather interior, electrically heated seats.
£48,000–54,000 BKS

Ford's acquisition of Aston Martin in 1987 ensured the company's future, and the former's take-over of Jaguar two years later made possible a revival of the DB line, dormant since the end of DB6 production in 1970. Jaguar's axed XJS replacement – the XJ41 – was deemed more suitable as an 'entry-level' Aston Martin, and work on the project began toward the end of 1991, responsibility for the final design being given to Tom Walkinshaw's JaguarSport company. A shortened and modified XJ6 saloon platform formed the basis for the DB7. Brilliantly styled in a manner reminiscent of the traditional Aston Martin, the body employed composite-material panels in its construction. The engine was a 3.2 litre version of the twin-camshaft, four-valves-per-cylinder AJ-6 unit. Equipped with a water-cooled Eaton supercharger, it developed 335bhp, sufficient to propel the DB7 to 160mph.

Atalanta

1939 Atalanta 4.3 Litre Cabriolet, coachwork by Abbott, side-valve V12, 3-speed synchromesh gearbox, 100+mph top speed, restored, finished in navy blue with black hood.
£45,000–50,000 BKS

A short-lived marque, Atalanta Motors was the brainchild of Aston Martin's A.C. Bertelli and Alfred Gough, designer of the overhead-camshaft Frazer-Nash engine. Founded in 1937, the firm specialised in hand-built sports cars of advanced design, the exclusive and expensive Atalantas being unique among British cars of the day in featuring all-independent suspension. The chassis was a substantial X-braced affair, fitted with hydraulic brakes, while the use of Hiduminium alloy for the suspension links and Elektron magnesium alloy for the huge 16in diameter brake drums helped keep unsprung weight to a minimum. Gough 4 cylinder engines powered the majority of Atalantas (not that there were many – approximately 20 cars of all types are thought to have been built), but in 1938 the company launched the Lincoln Zephyr-powered 4.3 litre model. The V12 Atalanta was rated highly, but the marque did not reappear after WWII.

Auburn

1935 Auburn 851 Speedster, fitted with mid-1950s Packard V8 engine, non-original gearbox, rear axle and brakes, restored, finished in red, running order, good condition throughout.
£39,000–44,000 BKS

Of all the cars launched during the mid-1930s, the Auburn Speedster, unveiled at the 1935 New York Auto Show, was intended to stimulate showroom traffic. Its dramatic styling by Gordon Miller Buehrig was inspired by his earlier design for a Weymann-bodied Duesenberg speedster, yet it was created largely from existing parts. The new limited-production Speedster was based on the centre section of the 1933 Auburn Speedster, but the addition of teardrop wings and external exhaust pipes created a stunning new look that certainly boosted Auburn sales.

Austin

The Austin name finally disappeared in 1987, yet throughout the company's life, from its formation in 1905, the marque ran through the mainstream of the British motor industry. Rarely were Austins glamorous, but generally they possessed the stout virtues of solid dependability based on sensible engineering, rather than fanciful technical wizardry. At various times in its history, Austin was the largest British car maker. As for the cars, Austin's greatest legacy must surely be the two modest machines that transformed British motoring on each side of WWII.

The Austin 7 of 1922 brought motoring *en masse* to the middle classes, and in 1959, the new Austin Se7en, as it was originally badged, brought motoring to millions in a pocket-sized world-beater better known as the Mini. Today, only a few early Austins are beyond the pocket of the ordinary enthusiast, and virtually every post-war model can be maintained with relative ease by a competent home mechanic. From the 1950s into the 1970s, many Austins were offered with only slight variations in trim, decoration and specification as Morris, MG, Wolseley, Riley and Vanden Plas models.

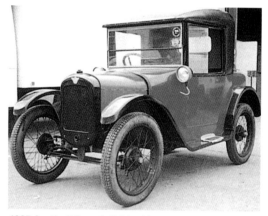

1925 Austin 7 Coupé, finished in red and black, new headlining and door and interior trim, seats, radiator cap, door handles and magneto missing.
£8,000–9,000 BKS

Austin's Coupé of 1925, built on the well-proven Austin 7 chassis, was aimed at the independent woman driver and was a very snug fixed-head two-seater. The top was panelled in aluminium and clad in black Rexine, access to the boot being provided by tilting the seats forward. A useful external luggage grid sat on top of the boot. The headlamps were scuttle-mounted, and there was a two-piece opening windscreen and a three-piece bonnet. Mechanically, the car was as the standard Austin 7.

1929 Austin 7 Top Hat Saloon, 750cc, 4 cylinders, 3-speed manual gearbox, original black fabric bodywork, red bonnet, red interior trim, good condition throughout.
£4,500–5,500 H&H

Between 1928 and 1931, over 18,000 Austin 7s were made in various guises. This particular car is believed to be one of 80 of this model to survive.

Austin Aside

The Austin 7 will fit on a full-size billiard table – that's because the original plans for the car were drawn up on a billiard table at Herbert Austin's home, Lickey Grange.

AUSTIN Model	ENGINE cc/cyl	DATES	CONDITION 1	2	3
25/30	4900/4	1906	£35,000	£25,000	£20,000
20/4	3600/4	1919–29	£20,000	£12,000	£6,000
12	1661/4	1922–26	£8,000	£5,000	£2,000
7/Chummy	747/4	1924–39	£7,000	£5,000	£2,500
7 Coachbuilt/Nippy/Opal etc	747/4	1924–39	£10,000	£9,000	£7,000
12/4	1861/4	1927–35	£5,500	£5,000	£2,000
16	2249/6	1928–36	£9,000	£7,000	£4,000
20/6	3400/6	1928–38	£12,500	£10,000	£8,000
12/6	1496/6	1932–37	£6,000	£4,000	£1,500
12/4	1535/4	1933–39	£5,000	£3,500	£1,500
10 and 10/4	1125/4	1932–47	£4,000	£3,000	£1,000
10 and 10/4 Conv	1125/4	1933–47	£5,000	£3,500	£1,000
18	2510/6	1934–39	£8,000	£5,000	£3,000
14	1711/6	1937–39	£6,000	£4,000	£2,000
Big Seven	900/4	1938–39	£4,000	£2,500	£1,500
8	900/4	1939–47	£3,000	£2,000	£1,000
28	4016/6	1939	£6,000	£4,000	£2,000

Prices for early Austin models are dependent on body style, landaulet, tourer, etc.

Miller's Starter Marque

Starter Austins: *Austin 7; A55/60 Cambridge; A90/95/99/105/110 Westminster; Metropolitan; A30/35/40; 1100 and 1300.*

- Although, in general, post-war Austin models were pretty popular, not all of them are in plentiful supply. Those listed above are blessed with a good survival rate, spares and club support, and normally possess the Austin virtue of durability.
- From the pre-war period, the Austin 7 is eminently viable as a run-while-you-restore car, with little to baffle the home mechanic.
- One of the most engaging Austins of the post-war era is the cute Austin/Nash Metropolitan, which came in a choice of dazzling ice-cream colours: red, yellow and turquoise over white. The hardtop versions had white roofs and lower bodies, making them resemble sandwiches with a variety of sickly fillings. Initially, the Metropolitan was built by Austin for the American Nash company as a 'sub-compact', or two-thirds scale 'Yank tank'. It was available in the UK from 1957.

1930 Austin 7 Saloon, 747cc, later 4 cylinder engine and 4-speed gearbox, engine rebuilt, all mechanical components in good condition.
£3,250–4,000 BRIT

1931 Austin 7 Swallow Sports Saloon, restored in 1996, finished in black and cream, black interior, excellent condition throughout.
£7,000–8,000 BKS

The 7's success led to a host of special-bodied variants from independent coachbuilders, none more famous than those produced by the Swallow Sidecar Company of Blackpool. The pretty two-tone Sports Saloon brought the Swallow name to the attention of the car-buying public and paved the way for the stylish SS sporting models of the 1930s which, in turn, led to the famous Jaguar marque.

1931 Austin 7 Roadster, finished in brown with white bonnet and hood.
£3,500–4,500 FHF

1931 Austin 7 Tourer, finished in blue with black wings, full weather equipment, correct and original specification.
£5,000–5,500 AS

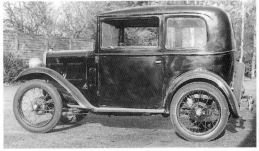

1932 Austin 7 Saloon, 747cc, 4 cylinders, unrestored, good original condition.
£2,000–2,500 DB

Austin 7 (1922–39)

Engine: Four-cylinder, 747.5cc.
Power output: 13–23bhp.
Transmission: Three-speed manual; four-speed from 1933.
Maximum speed: 45+mph.
Price in 1923: £165.
The diminutive Austin 7 introduced real motoring in miniature to first-time car owners all over the world. From its launch in 1922, it was acclaimed as a 'scaled-down motor car, rather than scaled-up motorcycling' and eventually sold more than 375,000. Today, its cheeky charm will still raise a chuckle, even if you're stuck behind one teetering along a country lane with the crazy meandering gait of a drunk pushing a supermarket trolley. The Austin 7 offers an affordable introduction to vintage-style motoring and the friendly competition of The Vintage Sportscar Club.

1934 Austin 7 Box Saloon, finished in blue with black wings, blue interior trim, excellent condition throughout.
£4,500–5,000 **AS**

1934 Austin 7 Two-Seater Special, engine rebored and fitted with close-tolerance main bearings, double-valve springs and special head gasket, lowered suspension, 1925 radiator surround, one-off body built with ash frame and marine-grade plywood floor, finished in French blue with light blue interior.
£2,500–3,000 **S**

1936 Austin 7 Opal Tourer, 747cc, 4 cylinders, 4-speed manual gearbox, dark green with matching green interior trim and upholstery, older restoration.
£4,250–4,750 **H&H**

1935 Austin 7 Ruby Saloon, black, original condition.
£2,750–3,250 **AS**

1937 Austin 7 Ruby, 747cc, 4 cylinders, good mechanical condition, engine rebuilt 1996/97 gearbox and steering overhauled, new sunshine roof, resprayed in Dove grey, original blue leather seats, original specification.
£3,500–4,000 **BRIT**

In August 1934, along with the rest of the Austin range, the 7 received a comprehensive facelift, giving it altogether more modern lines and ensuring its continued success as a best-seller. The 7 range comprised the Opal two-seat tourer, Open Road four-seat tourer, Pearl cabriolet and Ruby saloon. The spare wheel was carried undercover on all models, while the revised front end incorporated a painted radiator surround that matched the rest of the coachwork. In keeping with established Austin tradition, the wings and wheels were black, irrespective of body colour.

Austin Aside

The Austin 7 was made under licence in several countries: by Nissan in Japan, as the Rosengart in France, the Bantam in the USA, and the Dixi in Germany. The last was the first car built by BMW.

1937 Austin 7 Ruby Deluxe, fully restored to original specification, finished in dark blue with black wings, original leather seats.
£3,500–4,000 AS

1934 Austin 10/4 Deluxe Saloon, 1125cc, side-valve engine, 4-speed gearbox, 12 volt electrics, chromed radiator surround, restored in 1991, finished in Westminster green over black, green leather interior, original tools.
£3,000–3,500 LF

1938 Austin 10 Cambridge, 1125cc, 4 cylinder side-valve engine, Easiclene wheels, restored, black coachwork in good condition, all mechanical components good, new wiring loom, interior partially renovated.
£2,500–3,000 BRIT

1928 Austin 16/6 Burnham Saloon, body-off restoration, very good mechanical condition, finished in blue and black with blue interior.
£9,000–10,000 CGC

1939 Austin 8, finished in dark blue with black wings, original, 2 owners from new.
£1,000–1,500 LF

1936 Austin 10 Deluxe Cabriolet, 948cc, fully restored, good condition.
£6,500–7,500 CVPG

1935 Austin Light 12/4 Ascot Saloon, 1535cc, 4 cylinder side-valve engine, 4-speed gearbox, engine reconditioned in 1988, good mechanical condition, black with tan leather seats, original.
£3,250–3,750 BKS

One of a complex series of 12hp cars marketed by Austin in the 1930s, the Light 12/4 was conventional in all respects. The new Ascot body style was introduced for the 1933 saloons and was coachbuilt in vintage tradition. The Deluxe version came with a Pytchley sunroof and a choice of leather or Bedford cord upholstery. It retailed at £218. The Light 12/4 was produced from 1933 to 1936 and offered in Open Road tourer, Elton two-seater and light van forms alongside the Ascot.

1928 Austin 16/6 Burnham Saloon, 2249cc, 36bhp, maroon and black, good condition.
£18,000–20,000 CVPS

◀ **1948 Austin 16 Saloon,** 2199cc, 4 cylinders, finished in black with brown leather trim, original interior in need of tidying, brightwork in need of replating, correct throughout, non-runner. **£2,750–3,250 BRIT**

Produced between 1945 and 1949, the Austin 16 was a robust and powerful motor car. It was well appointed and appealed to a clientele whose resources could not quite stretch to a Wolseley or a Rover.

1935 Austin 18/6 Saloon, 2366cc, 6 cylinders, engine restored in 1989, finished in grey and black, interior upholstered in blue leather with wood trim, 2 occasional seats and map pockets fitted. **£6,800–7,400 S**

▶ **1950 Austin A90 Atlantic Convertible,** 2660cc, overhead-valve 4 cylinder engine, 88bhp, restored 1990/97, finished in red with cream leather interior, hydraulic hood and windows, very good condition. **£9,000–11,000 BKS**

Aimed at the US market and styled accordingly, the A90 Atlantic met with a cool reception from American buyers, despite setting a speed record at Indianapolis in 1949 by averaging over 70mph for seven days and nights. Based on A70 Hampshire running gear, the A90 was built between 1948 and 1950; the convertible was joined by a sports saloon in 1949.

Austin A30/A35 (1951–59)

Body styles: Two- and four-door saloons, Countryman estate, van and pick-up.
Engine: Overhead-valve, four-cylinder, 803cc (A30); 948cc (A35).
Power output: 28bhp at 4,500rpm (A30); 34bhp at 5,100rpm (A35).
Transmission: Four-speed manual.
Brakes: Hydro-mechanical drums.
Top speed: 65mph (A30); 75mph (A35).
0–60mph: 38 seconds (A30); 29 seconds (A35).
Fuel consumption: 35–45mpg.
Production: 576,672.
Price in 1951: £529.

When the baby Austin A30 appeared in 1951, the peanut-shaped four-seater was intended to rival the Morris Minor launched in 1948. But shortly after the Austin appeared, the two rivals merged under the BMC banner. Even though it was a moderate success,

the Austin was overshadowed by the million-selling Minor. Nevertheless, the A30 was a pert and capable economy package. It was the first Austin to feature unitary construction, and initially was powered by a peppy little 803cc, overhead-valve engine, the first of the famous A-series engines that went on to power the Mini and Metro.

In 1956, the A30 was updated to become the A35. Externally, it featured a larger rear window and other detail changes, but underneath it had a 948cc engine that considerably improved performance. Production of the saloon model came to an end in 1959 with the arrival of the Mini, but the A35 van continued to be manufactured until 1968.

Pick of the bunch: The bigger-engined A35. If the conditions were right, with a following gale, you might even contemplate overtaking.

1951–56 Austin A30 Four-Door Saloon, 803cc, 4 cylinders, 4-speed manual gearbox, good condition.
£800–1,100 AUS

1953 Austin A30, 803cc, overhead-valve engine, 4-speed gearbox, resprayed in black, new carpets, early 4-door example with sliding windows and 'lift-out' boot, fair condition.
£750–1,000 LF

1966 Austin A35 Van Conversion, 948cc, 4 cylinders, 4-speed manual gearbox, fitted with side windows, good condition.
£750–1,000 AUS

◀ **1958 Austin A35 Saloon,** 948cc, 4 cylinders, 4-speed manual gearbox, finished in light blue with black interior trim, 39,000 miles from new, good condition, history file.
£450–600 H&H

AUSTIN Model	ENGINE cc/cyl	DATES	CONDITION 1	2	3
16	2199/4	1945–49	£3,000	£2,000	£1,000
A40 Devon	1200/4	1947–52	£2,000	£1,200	£750
A40 Sports	1200/4	1950–53	£6,000	£4,000	£2,000
A40 Somerset	1200/4	1952–54	£2,000	£1,500	£750
A40 Somerset DHC	1200/4	1954	£5,000	£4,000	£2,500
A40 Dorset 2 door	1200/4	1947–48	£2,000	£1,500	£1,000
A70 Hampshire	2199/4	1948–50	£3,000	£1,500	£1,000
A70 Hereford	2199/4	1950–54	£3,000	£1,500	£1,000
A90 Atlantic DHC	2660/4	1949–52	£10,000	£6,000	£4,000
A90 Atlantic	2660/4	1949–52	£6,000	£4,000	£3,000
A40/A50 Cambridge	1200/4	1954–57	£1,200	£750	£500
A55 Mk I Cambridge	1489/4	1957–59	£1,000	£750	£500
A55 Mk II	1489/4	1959–61	£1,000	£750	£500
A60 Cambridge	1622/4	1961–69	£1,000	£750	£500
A90/95 Westminster	2639/6	1954–59	£2,000	£1,500	£750
A99 Westminster	2912/6	1959–61	£1,500	£1,000	£500
A105 Westminster	2639/6	1956–59	£3,000	£1,500	£750
A110 Mk I/II	2912/6	1961–68	£2,000	£1,500	£750
Nash Metropolitan	1489/4	1957–61	£3,500	£2,000	£750
Nash Metropolitan DHC	1489/4	1957–61	£6,000	£3,000	£1,500
A30	803/4	1952–56	£1,500	£800	-
A30 Countryman	803/4	1954–56	£1,500	£1,000	-
A35	948/4	1956–59	£1,000	£500	-
A35 Countryman	948/4	1956–62	£1,500	£1,000	-
A40 Farina Mk I	948/4	1958–62	£1,250	£750	£200
A40 Mk I Countryman	948/4	1959–62	£1,500	£1,000	£400
A40 Farina Mk II	1098/4	1962–67	£1,000	£750	-
A40 Mk II Countryman	1098/4	1962–67	£1,200	£750	£300
1100	1098/4	1963–73	£1,000	£750	-
1300 Mk I/II	1275/4	1967–74	£750	£500	-
1300GT	1275/4	1969–74	£1,800	£1,000	£750
1800/2200	1800/2200/4	1964–75	£1,500	£900	£600
3 Litre	2912/6	1968–71	£3,000	£1,500	£500

◄ **1952 Austin A40 Devon Saloon,** 1200cc, 4 cylinder engine, coil-spring independent front suspension, resprayed in black, mechanical components in good condition.
£1,300–1,500 BRIT

Introduced in 1947 to replace the Austin 10, the A40 was available in both two- and four-door versions, designated Dorset and Devon respectively. The styling of the new model was by Dick Burzi and clearly was influenced by the Chevrolet Master Series of 1940 and 1941.

1953 Austin A40 Somerset, Gold Seal engine, Zenith carburettor, 42bhp, column gearchange, body in fair condition, brightwork in need of attention, interior in good condition.
£1,000–1,500 LF

1967 Austin A40 Farina Mk II, 1098cc, 4 cylinders, 4-speed manual gearbox, finished in light green and cream, light tan interior, one owner from new, winter stored, 7,279 miles from new, excellent condition throughout.
£2,600–3,200 H&H

1969 Austin Vanden Plas 1300, 40,000 miles recorded, two owners from new.
£2,500–3,000 WILM

1973 Austin Princess Vanden Plas 1300, automatic transmission, one owner, 15,000 miles from new, full service history.
£3,000–3,250 UMC

Austin-Healey

The marriage that created an enduring piece of sports car magic was consummated at the 1952 London Motor Show. Donald Mitchell Healey, rally driver and engineer, had already sewn up a deal with Austin boss Leonard Lord, in 1951, for the rugged four-cylinder engines and transmissions of the Austin A90 Atlantic. Healey's dream was of a cheap, true 100mph sports car, the Healey Hundred. Overnight, it became the Austin-Healey 100 when Leonard

Lord decided that he wanted to build the car everyone was talking about. The Big Healey, as it became known, slotted in perfectly, and about 80 per cent of all production went Stateside. Over the years, this rugged bruiser became increasingly civilised. In 1956, it received a six-cylinder engine in place of the four, but in 1959, the 3000 was born. This became increasingly refined – with front disc brakes, then wind-up windows – and ever faster.

1953 Austin-Healey 100/4 BN1, 2660cc, overhead-valve, 4 cylinder engine, restored, finished in light blue metallic, black interior, excellent condition throughout.
£17,000–20,000 BC

1956 Austin-Healey 100/6, 2.6 litres, manual gearbox with overdrive, completely restored, 120 miles covered since, finished in Healey blue over cream, blue leather interior, excellent condition throughout.
£13,500–17,000 BKS

The need to boost the Austin-Healey 100's flagging sales led to a major revamp of the sports car for 1956. In place of the original Austin A90 4 cylinder engine was a BMC C-series 2.6 litre six. The chassis was also lengthened to allow the inclusion of two occasional seats. Power was increased from 90 to 102bhp, but the inevitable weight gain meant that there was little improvement in performance. Similar in appearance to its predecessor, the 100/6 was easily distinguishable by its 'crinkle' radiator grille and bonnet-top air intake.

▶ **1957 Austin-Healey 100/6,** restored 1992/96, finished in red with off-white vinyl upholstery.
£11,000–13,000 BKS

1957 Austin-Healey 100/6, 2639cc, 6 cylinders, original UK specification, finished in black, original red interior trim piped in white, mechanically and structurally in very good condition, cream vinyl hood, good condition throughout.
£10,000–12,000 BRIT

1958 Austin-Healey 100/6, 2639cc, 6 cylinders, left-hand drive, extensively restored, engine rebuilt 1997, converted to unleaded fuel, new fuel lines, carburettors and gearbox rebuilt, new 72-spoke chromed wire wheels, finished in Healey blue with dark blue interior and hood, tonneau cover and sidescreens, excellent condition throughout.
£15,000–17,000 COYS

It was with an Austin-Healey 100/6 in basic production trim that Tommy Wisdom and Cecil Winby won their class in the 1957 Mille Miglia, while in 1958 three works 100/6s took the Manufacturers' Team Prize at Sebring. That year saw the first factory rally team of 100/6s demonstrate their potential; among their drivers was Pat Moss, sister of Stirling. The 100/6's final works victory was on the 1969 Tulip Rally – by which time the engine was producing 160bhp – when Jack Sears and Peter Garnier won the GT category, beating Aston Martin, Ferrari and Mercedes Benz.

◄ **1962 Austin-Healey 3000 Mk II,** 2912cc, 6 cylinders, restored, finished in Healey blue over ivory, dark blue interior, excellent condition.
£15,000–17,000 COYS

A development of the Austin-Healey 100/6, the 3000 was launched in March 1959, in two-seat BN7 and 2+2 BT7 guise. It had a strong ladder chassis with independent coil-spring and wishbone front suspension, and a leaf-sprung rear axle located by a Panhard rod. Front disc brakes were fitted for the first time. The original 6 cylinder engine was enlarged to 2912cc and produced 124bhp at 4,600rpm. It was mated to a 4-speed gearbox, and could propel the car to 110mph (116mph overdrive).

1962 Austin-Healey 3000 Mk II, 2912cc, 6 cylinders, triple SU carburettors, 132bhp at 4,750rpm, 4-speed gearbox with overdrive, Girling hydraulic front disc brakes, chromed wire wheels, finished in British Racing green, black interior and hood, left-hand drive.
£17,000–19,000 Pou

AUSTIN-HEALEY	ENGINE	DATES	CONDITION		
Model	cc/cyl		1	2	3
100 BN 1/2	2660/4	1953–56	£20,000	£14,000	£8,000
100/6, BN4/BN6	2639/6	1956–59	£18,000	£13,500	£8,000
3000 Mk I	2912/6	1959–61	£20,000	£13,000	£8,500
3000 Mk II	2912/6	1961–62	£22,000	£15,000	£9,000
3000 Mk IIA	2912/6	1962–64	£23,000	£15,000	£11,000
3000 Mk III	2912/6	1964–68	£24,000	£17,000	£11,000
Sprite Mk I	948/4	1958–61	£10,000	£6,000	£3,000
Sprite Mk II	948/4	1961–64	£5,000	£3,000	£2,000
Sprite Mk III	1098/4	1964–66	£4,500	£3,000	£1,500
Sprite Mk IV	1275/4	1966–71	£5,000	£3,000	£1,500

◀ **1965 Austin-Healey 3000 Mk III,** 2912cc, 148bhp, manual gearbox with overdrive, 121mph top speed, 0–60mph in under 10 seconds, total rebuild 1989, 4,000 miles covered since, further restoration in 1997, converted to unleaded petrol, modified exhaust system, chromed 72-spoke wire wheels, Waxoyled bodyshell, finished in white with black leather interior, walnut-veneered dashboard, Motolita steering wheel, alarm, original radio, excellent condition.
£20,000–23,000 BKS

▶ **1966 Austin-Healey 3000 Mk III BJ8,** 2912cc, 6 cylinders, 4-speed manual gearbox with overdrive, original right-hand drive model, unused for 20 years, chassis-up restoration, full engine rebuild, new stainless steel exhaust system, new radiator, water pump, fuel tank, brake pipes and discs, extra cooling fan, new wings, sills and door skins, resprayed in Colorado red over white, new wiring loom and dashboard, new black leather upholstery piped in red, new carpets and hood, excellent condition throughout.
£15,000–17,000 H&H

◀ **1967 Austin-Healey 3000 Mk III,** 148bhp, manual gearbox with overdrive, finished in blue with matching leather interior, little use since 1973, 41,000 miles from new.
£13,500–16,000 BKS

The Austin-Healey 3000 Mk III, with its more powerful engine, appeared in the spring of 1964, being followed later in the year by the Phase II version. The latter featured revised rear suspension intended to eliminate axle tramp. By the time production ended in 1967, over 16,000 Phase II 3000s – the car's most popular variant – had been built.

1959 Austin-Healey Sprite Mk I, 948cc, overhead-valve, 4 cylinder engine, original right-hand drive model, complete mechanical and body restoration, new hood and tonneau cover.
£5,000–6,500 BRIT

The 'Frog-eye' Sprite got its nickname from the headlamp pods on the bonnet, but originally Donald Healey wanted to use retractable lamps, like the later Lotus Elan. Cost ruled these out, however, and helped to create a car of great character. This particular car was owned by the British hillclimb champion Martyn Griffiths for over 17 years.

1960 Austin-Healey Sprite Mk I, 948cc, 4 cylinders, 4-speed manual gearbox, imported from USA, restored early 1990s, converted to right-hand drive, original steel bonnet, finished in red with black interior trim, heater, 64,000 miles from new, good condition.
£5,000–6,000 H&H

1960 Austin-Healey Sprite Mk I, 948cc, 4 cylinders, restored, finished in red, good condition throughout. £6,000–7,000 **BRIT**

The immortal 'Frog-eye' Sprite was produced between March 1958 and July 1961. Based on proven BMC mechanical components, it provided economical sports car motoring with an affordable price tag, gaining a strong and loyal following.

Bartholomew

◄ **1902 Bartholomew 3hp Spindle-Back Two-Seater,** chassis no. 1, engine no. 19, single-cylinder, 3hp two-stroke engine, 2-speed gearbox with Champion clutch, chain drive to rear axle, restored, finished in black and red. £8,000–10,000 **BKS**

While Henry Ford and Ransom E. Olds were making huge strides in developing the US motor industry, there were many engineers who dreamed of creating a car that would beat the world. Among them was George Edison Bartholomew, who built this, his one and only motor car. Like many early American cars, it was based on the lines of a horse-drawn buggy.

Bayliss Thomas

◄ **1925 Bayliss Thomas Four-Door Tourer,** believed to be a 12hp model, four-seater coachwork, finished in black with matching interior, last run 1990, unrestored. £5,000–6,000 **BKS**

Better known for its bicycles and motorcycles, the Excelsior Motor Company, of Tyseley Green, Birmingham, launched the short-lived Bayliss Thomas car in 1921, the marque taking its name from the company's founders. Models ranging from 9 to 13hp were produced, using Coventry-Simplex and Meadows engines mated to Bayliss Thomas' own 3-speed gearbox. Production is thought to have ended around 1929, after over 1,000 cars had been produced.

Bentley

Walter Owen Bentley founded Bentley Motors in 1919, and over the next 12 years produced just 3,024 cars. The first production Bentley, the four-cylinder 3 Litre, appeared in 1922; two years later, a 3 Litre won the Le Mans 24-hour race, and Bentleys won again in 1927, 1928, 1929 and 1930. Yet despite race-track glory, the company's finances were always precarious, and Bentley launched its luxury 8 Litre model in 1931, on the eve of a depression. That move resulted in the company falling into the hands of Rolls-Royce.

The next generation of Bentleys, produced at Rolls-Royce's Derby plant, are now known as the 'Derby Bentleys'. The first new car under Rolls-Royce ownership was the 3½ Litre, which essentially employed a tuned version of the Rolls-Royce 20/25 six-cylinder, 3669cc engine that gave a lusty 105bhp and powered Bentleys to 90mph – sometimes more. Later, the engine was boosted to 4257cc to become the 4¼ Litre, with lighter-bodied cars nudging 100mph. It was in this era that Bentleys were dubbed 'The Silent Sports Car', and British coachbuilders graced the sporting models with some enduringly stylish bodies. Today, the quality, elegance and originality of coachwork has a significant bearing on the overall value of a car.

After 1945, Bentley and Rolls-Royce models began to converge, initially with the R-Type Bentley. The standard factory-bodied R-Type was really only a slightly more sporting Rolls-Royce Silver Dawn with a Bentley badge. However, while the standard-bodied Rolls-Royce and Bentley were close kin, one Bentley of this period stood alone, with no Rolls-Royce counterpart. That was the beautiful Bentley R-Type Continental, which had an exquisite fastback body developed in the wind-tunnel and crafted in aluminium by H.J. Mulliner. With the advent of monocoque construction, the era of the great coachbuilt Bentleys came to an end, the S- and T-series models being little more than alternatively badged versions of the Rolls-Royce Silver Cloud and Silver Shadow. Today, many consider the Bentley models to be a touch more discreet than their Rolls-Royce counterparts, and they can often be bought for slightly less.

1924 Bentley 3 Litre TT Replica, one of the last TT models to be built, originally fitted with three-seater Park Ward coachwork, later rebodied with Vanden Plas-style four-seat tourer coachwork, Alfin brake drums, finished in green with matching interior, more recent complete body overhaul, very sound condition.
£65,000–70,000 BKS

W.O. Bentley debuted his new 3 Litre car at the 1919 Olympia Motor Exhibition. In only mildly developed form, this was the model that became a legend in motor racing history and has become the archetypal vintage sports car. Early success in the 1922 Isle of Man Tourist Trophy, led to the introduction of the TT Replica (later known as the Speed Model) on the existing 9ft 9½in-wheelbase standard chassis. An increase in compression ratio raised maximum power from 70 to 80bhp, providing a top speed of 90mph.

1923 Bentley 3 Litre Blue Label, coachwork by Vanden Plas, recently restored, excellent condition throughout.
£70,000–80,000 SVV

1927 Bentley 3 Litre Speed Model Doctor's Coupé, coachwork by Freestone & Webb, matching engine numbers, twin SU Sloper carburettors, C-type gearbox, short-wheelbase chassis, dickey seat, wind-up windows, recent mechanical overhaul, new Allen counter-balanced crankshaft and connecting rods, running gear to correct factory specification, coachwork and interior restored late 1980s, finished in dark green with tan interior.
£67,500–72,500 BKS

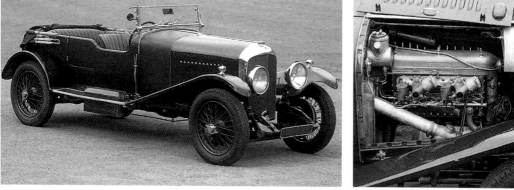

1928 Bentley 4½ Litre Four-Seat Tourer, Vanden Plas-style fabric-covered coachwork, fold-flat windscreen, aero screens, side wind deflectors, rear-mounted spare wheel, running board-mounted toolbox, leather spring gaiters, finished in green with black leather interior, appropriate instrumentation, history file.
£90,000–100,000 BKS

Bentley's original experimental 4.5 litre engine was used in the 1927 Le Mans practice car, and probably went on to be fitted in the first production 4½ Litre chassis, campaigned at Le Mans that year by Callingham and Clement and affectionately known as 'Old Mother Gun'. The 4½ Litre enjoyed a four-year production run, being fitted with closed and open sporting bodywork. Originally, this particular example had lightweight Gurney Nutting Weymann-type saloon coachwork. Like so many Weymann-bodied cars, however, the coachwork did not stand the test of time, and it has been rebodied in Vanden Plas tourer style.

1931 Bentley 8 Litre Convertible Victoria, all-metal coachwork by Walter Murphy, restored 1992, finished in silver with matching interior, black hood, excellent condition throughout.
£600,000+ BLK

Of the hundred 8 Litre Bentley chassis produced, this is the only example to have been fitted with an American body from new.

1931 Bentley 8 Litre Sports Saloon, coachwork by Mulliner, overhead-camshaft, 6 cylinder engine, unused for over 15 years, recent complete restoration, finished in green with black wings and hood.
£400,000+ BLK

Bentley's last successful model to leave the old Cricklewood factory was the magnificent 8 Litre. With closed bodywork, it could attain 100mph. This car was delivered new to William K. Vanderbilt Jr.

1935 Bentley 3½ Litre Two-Seater Sports Special, originally fitted with Thrupp & Maberley saloon coachwork, converted to a sports special in the 1970s, chassis shortened by approximately 14in, bonnet line lowered, finished in black with matching upholstery, chassis, bodywork and engine in good condition, offered with Derby hub pullers, wheel spanner and starting handle.
£34,000–38,000 BKS

1937 Bentley 4¼ Litre Four-Door Saloon, coachwork by Mulliner, 4257cc, extensively restored 1986/87, including new plywood floor, new radiator, overhauled cylinder head, crankshaft damper and water pump, stainless steel exhaust system, bodywork sound, finished in black, original part-worn beige interior, some micro-blistering of paintwork, little recent use, history file.
£12,000–14,000 BKS

1937 Bentley 4¼ Litre Special Saloon, coachwork by Park Ward, believed to be one of only three built to this design, finished in black over blue, brown hide interior, good condition throughout.
£18,000–21,000 RCC

BENTLEY Model	ENGINE cc/cyl	DATES	CONDITION 1	2	3
3 Litre	2996/4	1920–27	£100,000	£75,000	£40,000
Speed Six	6597/6	1926–32	£300,000	£250,000	£160,000
4½ Litre	4398/4	1927–31	£175,000	£125,000	£80,000
4½ Litre Supercharged	4398/4	1929–32	£600,000+	£300,000	£200,000
8 Litre	7983/6	1930–32	£350,000	£250,000	£100,000
3½ Litre Saloon & DHC	3699/6	1934–37	£70,000	£30,000	£15,000
4¼ Litre Saloon & DHC	4257/6	1937–39	£70,000	£35,000	£20,000
Mk V	4257/6	1939–41	£45,000	£25,000	£20,000

Prices are very dependent on engine type, chassis length, matching chassis and engine numbers, body style and original extras, like supercharger, gearbox ratio, racing history and originality.

1937 Bentley 4¼ Litre Sportsman Tourer, four-door, boat-tail coachwork by Diskon & Molyneux, 4257cc, 6 cylinder, pushrod overhead-valve engine, twin SU carburettors, 125bhp at 4,500rpm, 4-speed manual gearbox, semi-elliptic springs all-round, hydraulic shock absorbers with 'ride control', mechanical 4-wheel brakes, Rolls-Royce mechanical servo, finished in Mustard yellow with black double-duck hood, aero screens fitted for rear passengers, Notek driving light, Lucas headlights, Butlers Atlantic sidelights, period-style dashboard, recently recommissioned.
£36,000–40,000 C

This car was originally supplied with Park Ward saloon coachwork, but it was rebodied as a four-door tourer in Australia during the mid-1970s.

1951 Bentley R-Type Saloon, 4566cc,
6 cylinders, finished in Burnt green and Buttermilk with magnolia interior, restored good condition.
£12,000–14,000 BLE

1952 Bentley R-Type Saloon, 4566cc, 6 cylinders, finished in two-tone grey, good condition throughout.
£12,000–14,000 BLE

1954 Bentley R-Type Standard Steel Saloon,
automatic transmission, rebuilt 1991/96, finished in dark blue with beige leather upholstery, original specification in all major respects.
£11,000–13,000 BKS

Launched in 1952, the R-Type was powered by a 4566cc version of the renowned F-head, 6 cylinder engine, first seen in the Mk VI of 1946, albeit in 4250cc form. The new engine developed an estimated 150bhp. The R-Type was offered with a choice of manual or automatic transmissions.

1954 Bentley R-Type Standard Steel Saloon, 4566cc,
6 cylinder inlet-over-exhaust engine, automatic transmission, independent front suspension, partially restored 1984/85, transmission overhauled 1994, finished in Midnight blue over Shell grey, blue leather interior, original Radiomobile radio, full toolkit, comprehensive history file, excellent condition throughout.
£12,500–14,000 BKS

▶ **1954 Bentley R-Type Saloon,** 4566cc, 6 cylinder F-head engine, automatic transmission, independent front suspension, restored 1984/87, engine rebuilt, 4,000 miles covered since, gearbox overhauled, finished in Midnight blue with grey leather interior, 61,000 miles from new, original specification, good condition.
£15,000–17,000 BKS

BENTLEY Model	ENGINE cc/cyl	DATES	CONDITION 1	2	3
Abbreviations: HJM = H.J. Mulliner; PW = Park Ward; M/PW = Mulliner/Park Ward					
Mk VI Standard Steel	4257/6				
	4566/6	1946–52	£16,000	£10,000	£5,000
Mk VI Coachbuilt	4257/6				
	4566/6	1946–52	£25,000	£20,000	£12,000
Mk VI Coachbuilt DHC	4566/6	1946–52	£40,000+	£30,000	£20,000
R-Type Standard Steel	4566/6	1952–55	£12,000	£10,000	£7,000
R-Type Coachbuilt	4566/6	1952–55	£25,000	£20,000	£15,000
R-Type Coachbuilt DHC	4566/6				
	4887/6	1952–55	£50,000	£35,000	£25,000
R-Type Cont (HJM)	4887/6	1952–55	£80,000+	£40,000	£29,000
S1 Standard Steel	4887/6	1955–59	£15,000	£10,000	£7,000
S1 Cont 2-door (PW)	4877/6	1955–59	£30,000	£25,000	£20,000
S1 Cont Drophead	4877/6	1955–59	£80,000+	£75,000	£50,000
S1 Cont F'back (HJM)	4877/6	1955–58	£50,000	£35,000	£25,000
S2 Standard Steel	6230/8	1959–62	£15,000	£9,000	£6,000
S2 Cont 2-door (HJM)	6230/8	1959–62	£60,000	£40,000	£30,000
S2 Flying Spur (HJM)	6230/8	1959–62	£45,000	£33,000	£22,000
S2 Conv (PW)	6230/8	1959–62	£60,000+	£50,000	£35,000
S3 Standard Steel	6230/8	1962–65	£16,000	£11,000	£9,000
S3 Cont/Flying Spur	6230/8	1962–65	£45,000	£30,000	£25,000
S3 2-door (M/PW)	6230/8	1962–65	£30,000	£25,000	£10,000
S3 Conv (modern conversion - only made one original)	6230/8	1962–65	£40,000	£28,000	£20,000
T1	6230/6				
	6750/8	1965–77	£10,000	£8,000	£4,000
T1 2-door (M/PW)	6230/6				
	6750/8	1965–70	£15,000	£12,000	£9,000
T1 Drophead (M/PW)	6230/6				
	6750/8	1965–70	£30,000	£20,000	£12,000

1954 Bentley R-Type Saloon, coachwork by James Young, 4566cc, 6 cylinders, automatic transmission, finished in green with matching interior trim and upholstery.
£9,500–11,500 H&H

1955 Bentley R-Type Saloon, automatic transmission, very original, good condition.
£11,000–13,000 BLE

1955 Bentley R-Type Continental, coachwork by Mulliner, 4887cc, 6 cylinders, high-compression cylinder head with larger inlet valves, twin SU carburettors, 178bhp, 4-speed gearbox, alternator, resprayed in Astrakhan, original beige leather upholstery, seat belts, factory-fitted 3-spoke steering wheel, period HMV radio, altimeter and compass, original chrome and veneers in very good condition, factory tools.
£100,000–110,000 BKS

1955 Bentley S1 Saloon, 4887cc, 6 cylinders, 4-speed automatic transmission, blue over silver, blue and grey leather interior trim.
£8,500–11,000 H&H

1957 Bentley S1 Continental Two-Door Coupé, coachwork by Park Ward, 4887cc, 6 cylinders, left-hand drive, finished in Dawn blue, good mechanical condition, sound coachwork, 66,300 miles from new.
£27,500–32,500 BRIT

Following on from the R-Type Continental, the S-series met with much acclaim from the motoring Press. *The Autocar* stated, '...the latest Bentley model offers a degree of safety, comfort and performance that is beyond the experience and perhaps even the imagination of the majority of the world's motorists – a modern magic carpet capable of annihilating great distances.' When fitted to the Continental, the 4.9 litre engine was uprated slightly, while the transmission benefited from higher gearing, making for relaxed cruising.

Auction Prices

Miller's only includes cars declared sold. Our guide prices take into account the buyer's premium, VAT on the premium, and the extent of any published catalogue information relating to condition and provenance. To identify cars sold at auction cross-refer the source codes at the ends of photo captions with the Key to Illustrations on page 330.

1956 Bentley S1 Continental, automatic transmission, finished in maroon, new leather upholstery, beige carpets, excellent veneers and brightwork, overhauled 1992, including attention to suspension, steering, brakes, engine and exhaust system, little use since.
£40,000–50,000 BKS

Mulliner fastback styling had first appeared on the R-Type as early as 1952, but it had a timeless elegance, and similar sensational styling was offered on the S-series cars. The aerodynamic shape, formed from lightweight aluminium panels, was developed in a wind tunnel.

▶ 1956 Bentley S1 Saloon, 4887cc, 6 cylinders, overhauled 1980, 5,000 miles covered since, finished in black over silver, grey hide upholstery with navy piping, transmission in need of attention, bodywork sound.
£5,000–7,000 BRIT

Various styles of coachwork were available on the S-series, although the standard steel saloon was the most common. The S1 remained in production until 1959, when it was superseded by the S2, powered by a 6.2 litre V8 engine.

1958 Bentley S1 Flying Spur Four-Door Saloon, coachwork by Mulliner, 4887cc, 6 cylinders, finished in dark blue with blue leather interior, well maintained, service history, excellent condition throughout.
£22,000–25,000 BRIT

This particular car was featured in the TV series *The New Statesman,* driven by the character Alan B'stard, played by Rik Mayall.

◄ **1960 Bentley S2 Four-Door Saloon,** finished in Smoke green over Sage green, cream leather interior, good condition throughout.
£8,000–10,000 BKS

Introduced in 1959, the Rolls-Royce Silver Cloud II and Bentley S2 were unchanged in appearance from their Silver Cloud and S-Type predecessors, but their performance was considerably enhanced by a new 6230cc, aluminium V8 engine. Power-assisted steering had become standard, while a manual gearbox was no longer available. The Silver Cloud II and S2 remained in production until superseded by the restyled Cloud III and S3 in 1962.

1961 Bentley S2 Flying Spur Four-Door Saloon, coachwork by Mulliner Park Ward, 6230cc V8, 4-speed automatic transmission, power steering, electric windows, cruise control, hand-wound aerial, refurbished 1994/95, new laminated windscreen, rear screen and rubbers, resprayed in Shell grey, grey leather upholstery, new rear cushion, squab and armrest, new centre console armrest, new door trims, all interior woodwork renovated and relacquered, good condition throughout.
£33,000–38,000 BKS

1962 Bentley S2 Continental, coachwork by Mulliner, 6230cc V8, finished in Claret metallic with matching carpets and magnolia hide upholstery, restored 1992/96, good condition throughout.
£37,000–45,000 BKS

1964 Bentley S3 Four-Door Saloon, finished in silver over Midnight blue, grey leather upholstery piped in dark blue, good condition.
£11,000–13,000 BKS

Replacing the S2 in 1962, the S3 continued to use the 6.2 litre V8 engine. However, it had larger carburettors, a new distributor, raised compression and a four-speed automatic transmission as standard. Among the changes to its appearance were four-headlamp lighting, the removal of the side lights from the tops of the wings, and a slightly lower radiator shell. Inside, the front bench seat was replaced by separate seats.

◄ **1964 Bentley S3 Continental Drophead Coupé,** restored, finished in black with tan hood, excellent condition.
£65,000–75,000 COHN

1967 Bentley T1 Saloon, 6750cc V8, finished in Sage green with beige hide upholstery, 45,000 miles from new, original condition, extensive history.
£11,000–13,000 COYS

In 1965, Rolls-Royce unveiled a completely new Bentley. Sharing the same specification as the Silver Shadow, the T-Type featured unitary construction, self-levelling independent suspension, servo-assisted disc brakes all-round and a 4-speed automatic transmission. The well-tried V8 was basically the same as it had been in the S3.

1972 Bentley Corniche Two-Door Convertible, coachwork by Mulliner Park Ward, restored 1997, finished in blue with grey leather interior, one of only 45 built, good condition throughout.
£25,000–30,000 BKS

Introduced in March 1971, the Corniche was a revised version of the Mulliner Park Ward-bodied two-door variants of the Rolls-Royce Silver Shadow and Bentley T-series saloons. The engine was the familiar 6750cc aluminium V8 which, in Corniche form, produced around ten per cent more power than standard and was capable of propelling the car to a top speed in excess of 120mph, with sports car-beating acceleration to match.

1978 Bentley T2 Saloon, 6750cc V8, 3-speed automatic transmission, finished in Le Mans blue, Parchment leather interior trim and upholstery, excellent condition throughout, history file.
£7,500–9,000 H&H

Miller's is a price GUIDE not a price LIST

Berliet

1920s Berliet Automobiles double-sided enamel sign, shield-shaped, locomotive logo, 43½in (110.5cm) high.
£480–500 LF

In 1905, Berliet signed an agreement with the American Locomotive Company whereby certain Berliets would be built in the USA under the name Alco. To celebrate this alliance, the Berliet radiator badge was redesigned to incorporate the front view of an American locomotive.

1930 Berliet V 1L 8CV Saloon, right-hand drive, reburbished 1990/91, finished in blue and black, cloth-trimmed interior, in need of recommissioning.
£4,600–5,400 BRIT

Latterly better known for its commercial vehicles, Berliet was a producer of motor cars between 1895 and 1939. By the 1920s, the company offered a comprehensive range of cars, and sales were buoyant. As the 1930s dawned, one of the most popular models was the V 1L 8CV, a 1.5 litre car that was well proportioned and rugged.

Bizzarrini

Giotto Bizzarrini has carved himself a reputation as an engineering genius, understandably when one considers his achievements. He was responsible for designing the legendary Ferrari 250 GTO, and after leaving Ferrari, he created Lamborghini's magnificent quad-camshaft V12 engine. His next project was a collaboration with Renzo Rivolta, for whom he designed a luxury, high-performance gran turismo, which entered production as the Iso Rivolta. Bizzarrini was keen to continue race development and persuaded Rivolta to allow him to build a two-seat coupé, with which the company could go racing. Logically, he reasoned that beating Ferrari on the race-tracks, would lead to improved sales of the road cars. The Iso Grifo A3L ensued. This was a two-seat coupé, bodied by Bertone and incorporating a tuned Chevrolet Corvette engine.

While the A3L was being built for road use, a competition version, the A3C, was designed. The prototype was displayed at the 1963 Turin show. Its original shape had been sketched by Bizzarrini himself, then refined after experiments in the University of Pisa's wind-tunnel. Finally, Giorgetto Giugiaro added his touches while employed at Bertone's design studio. Eventually, Bizzarrini went into production on his own, and the car was sold as the Bizzarrini 5300GT.

1965 Bizzarrini 5300GT Strada, coachwork by Bertone, 5300cc Chevrolet V8, 365bhp, 305km/h top speed, restored little use since, excellent condition throughout.
£80,000–85,000 COYS

This particular car was owned by Giotto Bizzarrini from new, being used by him as a development 'mule' to test new competition and production modifications.

BMW

Via aero engines, then motorcycles, Bayerische Motoren Werke moved into car manufacture in 1928 with the Dixi, an Austin 7 built under licence. From these humble beginnings, BMW went on to produce some fine pre-war touring cars. In 1940, a streamlined BMW 328 won Italy's Mille Miglia. After the end of WWII, the company came close to oblivion on a number of occasions. In the mid-1950s, for example, the beautiful and excruciatingly expensive 507 nearly brought BMW to its knees, but salvation came from the other end of the market in the shape of the Isetta microcar (see Microcars section). The latter was built from 1955 to 1965, and although in its early years it generated considerable profit, by the early 1960s, sales had fallen off sharply, as 'real cars' in miniature – such as the Mini – had begun to claim the market. In the 1960s, the company got back on course with the stylish, pert and capable '02 series two-door saloons, and began to build its modern reputation as a producer of fine executive, luxury and sporting machines.

1959 BMW 507 Series II Roadster, 3168cc V8, twin carburettors, 173bhp at 5,000rpm, front disc brakes, Rudge wheels, hardtop, 124mph top speed, completely restored, engine overhauled, finished in white, original black leather interior piped in white, maintained regardless of cost, 14,000 miles from new, excellent condition.
£125,000–140,000 COYS

BMW's V8 had first appeared in 2.6 litre form in the 502 saloon of 1954, which offered impressive performance and fine roadholding courtesy of all-independent, torsion-bar suspension. In 1955, BMW introduced the 507, a beautiful two-seater roadster, which was based on the 502, but with a shortened chassis. It was propelled by a higher-compression-ratio version of the 3168cc V8, while the body panels were crafted in aluminium over a steel frame. The 507's combination of looks and performance, plus the glamour of a V8 engine, had few rivals, only Ferrari and Pegaso offering similarly exotic packages.

1969 BMW 1600 Two-Door Saloon, 1573cc, overhead-camshaft 4 cylinder engine, 85bhp, all-independent suspension, front disc brakes, resprayed in green, tan vinyl upholstery, regularly serviced, 47,756 miles from new, sound condition.
£1,750–2,000 BKS

The foundation of BMW's post-war resurgence was the 1500 saloon and its derivatives. Endowed with attractive styling, more than adequate performance, reasonable economy and excellent controllability, the 1600 family proved very successful, nearly 400,000 of all types being produced between 1968 and 1976.

1973 BMW 2002 Tii Two-Door Saloon, 1990cc, overhead-camshaft 4 cylinder engine, Kugelfischer fuel injection, 130bhp, all-independent suspension, front disc brakes, near 120mph top speed, finished in blue with black upholstery, 40,000 miles recorded, good condition.
£1,300–1,700 BKS

BMW Model	ENGINE cc/cyl	DATES	CONDITION 1	2	3
Dixi	747/4	1927–32	£7,000	£3,000	£2,000
303	1175/6	1934–36	£11,000	£8,000	£5,000
309	843/4	1933–34	£6,000	£4,000	£2,000
315	1490/6	1935–36	£9,000	£7,000	£5,000
319	1911/6	1935–37	£10,000	£9,000	£6,000
326	1971/6	1936–37	£12,000	£10,000	£8,000
320 series	1971/6	1937–38	£12,000	£10,000	£8,000
327/328	1971/6	1937–40	£30,000+	£18,000	£10,000
328	1971/6	1937–40	£60,000+	-	-

◄ **1975 BMW 2002 Tii Two-Door Saloon,** fuel injection, 130bhp, near 120mph top speed, good bodywork, finished in Aqua blue with black interior, 35,000 miles from new, completely original, excellent condition, toolkit.
£3,400–3,800 BKS

Endowed with attractive styling, reasonable economy and excellent controllability, the 2002 Tii proved outstandingly successful, almost 39,000 being produced between 1971 and 1975.

► **1975 BMW 2002 Tii Lux Two-Door Saloon,** styling by Michelotti, 1990cc, overhead-camshaft, 4 cylinder engine, Kugelfischer fuel injection, 130bhp, 4-speed gearbox, semi-trailing-arm independent rear suspension, Lux Turbo wheels, restored with all correct BMW parts including factory engine, less than 2,000 miles covered since, finished in bronze with fawn interior trim and upholstery, bodywork and interior in excellent condition.
£4,750–5,250 BKS

1975 BMW 2002 Turbo, finished in silver, black seats, 78,000km recorded, unrestored, good condition throughout.
£4,000–5,000 BKS

The BMW 2002 Turbo was Europe's first turbocharged car; in fact, when it was launched in 1973, it was the world's only turbocharged production model. Unfortunately, its arrival coincided with the OPEC oil crisis, which restricted sales and its production life. The 2002 had a deep front spoiler, one of the earliest instances of modern motor racing aerodynamics being applied to a road car. It could top 130mph and outperform almost every other vehicle on the road.

1973 BMW 3.0 CSi, 3 litres, restored, original, excellent condition.
£8,000–10,000 MUN

1973 BMW 3.0 CSi Coupé, 2986cc, 6 cylinders, 4-speed manual gearbox, alloy wheels, finished in white, original black leather interior, good condition throughout.
£4,000–5,000 H&H

1974 BMW 3.0 CSi Two-Door Coupé, new cylinder head, fitted with later 5-speed overdrive gearbox, 4-wheel ventilated disc brakes, power steering, Alpina alloy wheels, Ziebarted from new, recent brake overhaul, bodywork in good condition, but with isolated blemishes, resprayed in original Ruben red, black cloth interior, 2002 sports steering wheel, full service history, complete toolkit.
£6,000–7,000 BKS

BMW returned to 6 cylinder power for its top-of-the-range models in 1968 with the launch of the 2500 and 2800 saloons. Also new was the 2800CS coupé, although the latter's running gear had more in common with the existing 4 cylinder 2000C/CS. The introduction of the similarly-styled 3.0 litre CS in 1971 brought many improvements: with 180bhp on tap, it was good for around 130mph. The 200bhp Bosch fuel-injected CSi – introduced in 1972 – was even quicker.

1981 BMW Mk I 535i, 3.5 litres, finished in silver grey, good condition throughout.
£3,500–4,500 MUN

1971 BMW 3.0 S Saloon, 2985cc, resprayed in original Malaga red, original black vinyl interior in excellent condition, fully Waxoyled.
£2,750–3,250 H&H

1974 BMW 3.0 CSi Coupé, 2986cc, 6 cylinders, 5-speed gearbox, restored, suspension rebuilt, new interior, new stainless steel and chrome fittings, finished in red with black interior trim, 66,980 miles recorded, excellent condition.
£4,250–5,250 H&H

1981 BMW M1 Coupé, 3500cc, 6 cylinders, 277bhp, 160+mph top speed, 0–60mph in 5.5 seconds, engine rebuilt at a cost of £8,000, £6,000 respray, unused since, 13,000km from new, excellent condition.
£40,000–45,000 COYS

BMW's glorious M1 supercar is a rare mix of stunning performance and practicality. The original concept was for a car that could compete in the Ferrari-type marketplace, but which provided BMW-style reliability. The bodywork was styled by Giugiaro's Ital Design, the stunning coupé accommodating two people and a mid-mounted, 6 cylinder, twin-cam, 24 valve BMW Motorsport engine with fuel injection. Handling was viceless and reliability excellent. Furthermore, levels of comfort were of a degree unheard of in a mid-engined supercar at that time. Today, the M1 is seen as a great car, but something of a missed opportunity for BMW, who never exploited its sales potential.

1981 BMW M1 Coupé, 3.5 litres, 6 cylinders, double overhead camshafts, 4 valves per cylinder, 277bhp, 5-speed ZF transaxle, 260km/h top speed, finished in Alpine white with black leather and cloth chequered seats, 33,000km recorded, excellent condition throughout.
£37,000–42,000 BKS

1979 BMW 635 CSi Coupé, 3453cc, 6 cylinders, 5-speed gearbox, finished in red with black interior trim and upholstery, 68,500 miles from new.
£2,300–2,800 H&H

BMW Model	ENGINE cc/cyl	DATES	CONDITION 1	2	3
501	2077/6	1952–56	£9,000	£7,000	£3,500
501 V8/502	2580,8				
	3168/8	1955–63	£10,000+	£5,000	£3,000
503 FHC/DHC	3168/8	1956–59	£25,000+	£20,000	£15,000
507	3168/8	1956–59	£100,000	£70,000	£50,000
Isetta (4 wheels)	247/1	1955–62	£7,000	£3,000	£1,200
Isetta (3 wheels)	298/1	1958–64	£8,000	£2,500	£1,500
Isetta 600	585/2	1958–59	£3,000	£1,800	£500
1500/1800/2000	var/4	1962–68	£1,800	£800	£500
2000CS	1990/4	1966–69	£5,500	£4,000	£1,500
1500/1600/1602	1499/4				
	1573/4	1966–75	£3,000+	£1,500	£800
1600 Cabriolet	1573/4	1967–71	£6,000	£4,500	£2,000
2800CS	2788/6	1968–71	£5,000	£4,000	£1,500
1602	1990/4	1968–74	£3,000	£1,500	£1,000
2002	1990/4	1968–74	£3,000	£2,000	£1,000
2002 Tii	1990/4	1971–75	£4,500	£2,500	£1,200
2002 Touring	1990/4	1971–74	£3,500	£2,000	£1,000
2002 Cabriolet	1990/4	1971–75	£5,000+	£3,000	£2,500
2002 Turbo	1990/4	1973–74	£10,000	£6,000	£4,000
3.0 CSa/CSi	2986/6	1972–75	£8,000	£6,000	£4,000
3.0 CSL	3003/6				
	3153/6	1972–75	£16,000	£10,000	£7,500
MI	3500/6	1978–85	£60,000	£40,000	£30,000
633/635 CS/CSI	3210/3453/6	1976–85	£7,000	£3,000	£2,000
M535i	3453/6	1979–81	£4,500	£3,000	£2,500

1982 BMW 635 CSi Coupé, 3500cc, 6 cylinders, 4-speed automatic gearbox, ABS, power-assisted steering, electric windows, electric tilt and slide sunroof, finished in Henna red with black leather interior, central locking, trip computer, stereo, 86,900 miles from new, excellent condition throughout. £3,000–3,500 H&H

1984 BMW 635 CSi Coupé, 3430cc, 6 cylinders, ABS, power steering, finished in silver with grey interior, electric sunroof, windows and seat adjustment, trip computer, air conditioning, good condition throughout. £4,500–5,000 BRIT

Cross Reference
See Colour Review

Miller's Starter Marque

Starter BMWs: *1502, 1602, 2002, 2002 Touring.*

- The '02 series two-door saloons were launched in Germany in 1968. When they arrived in the UK in 1971, they were not particularly cheap: the 2002 model was £120 more than a Rover P6 2000, and only £170 less than a Mk II 3.4 Jaguar – yet on the BMW there was not a piece of polished wood or hide trim in sight. Instead, the '02 models rewarded sporting drivers with spirited performance and pert handling. They are easy to live with and generally robust, with good availability of reasonably priced spares.
- **Performance:** All, except the 1502, are good for 100mph, and the fuel-injected 2002 Tii offers a sizzling 0–60mph time of 8.2 seconds with a 118mph top speed. This and the twin-carb 2002 Tii are the best buys in performance terms, but many will have been mistreated by a succession of boy racers. The 1602, plain 2002 and 1502 make sensible down-market alternatives.
- **Rust:** Particular points to watch include the jacking points, which can fall out and allow the sills to rot from the inside. Look in the boot, too. Generally though, rust problems are no worse than on any other steel monocoque saloon.
- **Engines:** BMW engines are famed for their smooth and reliable performance: if looked after, they are good for more than 80,000 miles. On starting from cold, listen for rattling from the top end, which indicates camshaft/follower wear. These engines need an oil change every 5,000 miles, so look for documentation that confirms regular maintenance.
- All in all, this Beemer's pretty straightforward, but there are a couple of more exotic options. Cabriolets are undoubtedly desirable, but have some nasty rust-traps, particularly behind the rear seat where the hood is stowed. If you are not careful, Cabriolet restoration costs could spiral beyond reach.
- Likewise, the rare 2002 Turbo is an enthusiast's car rather than a daily driver. For a start, only 51 were sold in the UK. If you can find one, you'll get performance – and shattering bills to match.

1985 BMW M635 CSi, 3.5 litres, 6 cylinders, excellent condition.
£10,000–13,000 MUN

1985 BMW M635 CSi, 3.5 litres, finished in white with black trim, good condition.
£10,000–13,000 MUN

1988 BMW 635CSi Coupé, 53,000 miles from new, service history, good condition.
£9,000–11,000 VIC

1986 BMW M6 Coupé, 3453cc, tuned 24 valve, 6 cylinder engine, 286bhp, 5-speed gearbox, finished in Royal blue with blue leather interior trim, Recaro seats, service history.
£6,750–8,000 H&H

▶ **1986 BMW E30 M3,** 2.3 litre engine, finished in white, alloy wheels, spoilers, sunroof, good condition throughout.
£10,000–12,000 MUN

Bristol

In 1947, as wartime aviation contracts came to an end, the Bristol Aeroplane Company branched out into car manufacture with an anglicised version of the pre-war BMW 327. The company's first model, the 400, clearly owed plenty to aircraft construction and design techniques, having a light-alloy outer skin and a streamlined shape developed in the wind-tunnel. The six-cylinder engine was derived from a pre-war BMW unit. Only 700 examples of the 400 had been produced by the time production came to an end in 1950, and ever since Bristols have continued to be made in small numbers, providing handcrafted luxury for those who could afford them.

In 1962, the company switched from six-cylinder engines, adopting Chrysler V8s in a quest for refined power. Bristol enthusiasts tend to fall into two camps, some favouring the leaner six-cylinder models, while others prefer the easy power of the V8-engined cars.

◄ **1949 Bristol 400,** fitted with more powerful 85C engine, independent front suspension, rack-and-pinion steering, restored, finished in maroon with tan leather interior, excellent condition throughout.
£15,000–17,000 BRIT

The Bristol Aeroplane Company's diversification into motor car manufacture began with the 400 model, in 1947. It utilised a box-section chassis based on the BMW 326 design, as a result of Bristol's association with AFN Ltd, the BMW importers. The new car boasted an up-to-date technical specification, and with its handsome, aerodynamic coachwork, it was capable of 95mph.

1953 Bristol 403 Saloon, 2 litres, 6 cylinders, restored, good condition.
£12,000–14,000 BKS

1959 Bristol 406 Two-Door Saloon, 2216cc, 6 cylinders, finished in red with original grey upholstery, walnut dashboard, in need of recommissioning.
£5,000–6,000 S

Dealer Prices

Miller's guide prices for dealer cars take into account the value of any guarantees or warranties that may be included in the purchase. Dealers must also observe additional statutory consumer regulations that do not apply to private sellers. This is factored into our dealer guide prices. To identify dealer cars cross-refer the source codes at the ends of photo captions with the Key to Illustrations on page 330.

BRISTOL Model	ENGINE cc/cyl	DATES	CONDITION 1	2	3
400	1971/6	1947–50	£18,000	£14,000	£8,000
401 FHC/DHC	1971/6	1949–53	£28,000	£14,000	£8,000
402	1971/6	1949–50	£22,000	£19,000	£12,000
403	1971/6	1953–55	£20,000	£14,000	£10,000
404 Coupé	1971/6	1953–57	£22,000	£15,000	£12,000
405	1971/6	1954–58	£17,000	£13,000	£10,000
405 Drophead	1971/6	1954–56	£25,000	£22,000	£18,000
406	2216/6	1958–61	£15,000	£11,000	£7,000
407	5130/8	1962–63	£15,000	£8,000	£6,000
408	5130/8	1964–65	£14,000	£10,000	£8,000
409	5211/8	1966–67	£14,000	£11,000	£7,000
410	5211/8	1969	£14,000	£10,000	£6,000
411 Mk 1–3	6277/8	1970–73	£16,000	£11,000	£8,000
411 Mk 4–5	6556/8	1974–76	£12,500	£9,500	£7,000
412	5900/8				
	6556/8	1975–82	£15,000	£9,000	£6,000
603	5211/8				
	5900/8	1976–82	£12,000	£8,000	£5,000

1965 Bristol 408 Saloon, 5130cc Chrysler V8, good condition throughout.
£4,000–5,000 PALM

BSA

1936 BSA Scout 55 10hp Coupé, 4 cylinders, 3-speed manual gearbox, wire wheels, two-door, two-seater coachwork with fabric top, rear-mounted spare wheel, finished in black with red leather upholstery, internal access to luggage space behind seats, original leather trim in fair condition, all electrical equipment working, good running order, in need of tidying.
£3,000–4,000 H&H

Although production of the BSA Scout averaged over 2,000 units a year between 1935 until the outbreak of WWII, relatively few of these elegant sports models have survived. It was Britain's only volume-produced, front-wheel-drive model during the 1930s and featured independently-sprung front wheels with inboard brakes.

◄ 1930 Alfa Romeo 6C 1750 Gran Sport Spyder, coachwork by Zagato, double overhead camshafts, Roots-type supercharger, restored, engine rebuilt, original body frame (possibly repanelled), hood frame and floorpan.
£150,000–170,000 BKS

The 6C 1750 of 1929 set new benchmarks in sports car design, reflecting the brilliance of Vittorio Jano, and for almost the next decade, the annals of motor sport would be littered with the successes of its derivatives. The model was linked inextricably with events such as the Mille Miglia and the TT races. The supercharged Gran Sport offered 100mph performance and superb handling.

► 1931/33 Alfa Romeo 8C 1750 Le Mans, 2.6 litre, 8 cylinder in-line engine, double overhead camshafts, 165bhp at 5,000rpm, 4-speed manual gearbox, semi-elliptic leaf springs, mechanically-operated 4-wheel drum brakes, well maintained, full racing history.
£450,000+ C

This particular Alfa Romeo Special began life as a long-chassis, late-series Gran Turismo with drophead coupé coachwork. It was purchased in 1950 by Viscount Ridley, who fitted an 8C engine and gearbox to the chassis, adding larger brakes and heavier springing. Subsequently, it was rebodied in the style of the Leslie Hawthorn Le Mans-winning car.

1931 Alfa Romeo 6C 1750 GT 'Fugientem Incurro Diem' Berlinetta, coachwork by Touring, 6 cylinders, double overhead camshafts, supercharged, Memini twin-choke carburettor, 3.16m wheelbase, flexible wooden bumpers, restored 1993/94, only 500km since, finished in light blue with black wings, blue cloth upholstery and grey headlining, black marbled dashboard.
£140,000–160,000 BKS
The first name in the log book of this particular sporting *berlinetta* is that of Cavaliere Benito Mussolini. The car is fitted with one of the celebrated Touring *'Fugientem Incurro Diem'* Coupé-Royal aerodynamic *berlinetta* bodies.

◄ 1932 Alfa Romeo 6C 1750 'Gran Turismo Compressore' Saloon, coachwork by Touring, 6 cylinders, double overhead camshafts, supercharged, finished in pale green, light grey cloth upholstery, excellent original condition.
£90,000–100,000 BKS

Only 159 GTC chassis were built between 1931 and 1932. This car was delivered new to an owner in Rome, then sold to a convent in Southern Italy, where it remained for 20 years.

1939 Alfa Romeo 6C 2500 SS Tipo 256 'Ala Spessa' Spider, coachwork by Touring, channel-section chassis, coil-spring and trailing-arm front suspension, swing rear axles on torsion bars, aluminium body panels on steel tubing frame, bought as a chassis with all correct mechanical parts, restored to 'Ala Spessa' specifications, correct in all details, concours condition, FIVA passport.
£85,000–95,000 BKS

The Alfa Romeo 6C 2500 SS *Tipo 256* replaced the 8C 2900 as the company's main sports racing car during 1938. It was available in various states of tune, the type number being Alfa Romeo's new method of designating a competition car (*256* – 2.5 litres/six cylinders). Scuderia Ferrari was responsible for building the *Tipo 256* during 1939, shortening the 6C 2500 chassis and uprating the engine with higher compression and three carburettors. Most of the 15–25 *Tipo 256s* built (estimates vary) were fitted with Spider Corsa bodies with cycle wings. From about 1939, however, Italian coachbuilders, notably Touring, began experimenting with aerodynamic shapes, such as the '*Ala Spessa*' (wide-wing) body. Only two of the latter were built as development cars early in 1939, but neither has survived.

◀ 1955 Alfa Romeo 1900 Sprint Series II Coupé, *Superleggera* coachwork by Touring, double-overhead-camshaft, 4 cylinder engine, 5-speed gearbox, wishbone and coil-spring independent front suspension, approximately £44,000 spent on restoration, fitted with later 2 litre engine, Alfin brake drums, new wiring harness, bare-metal respray, Connolly leather upholstery, excellent condition.
£39,000–45,000 BKS

Launched in 1951, the 1900 Sprint featured cabriolet bodywork by Pininfarina and coupé bodywork by Touring, both utilising the 100bhp engine of the 1900Ti sports saloon. The model was upgraded for 1954, gaining a 1975cc engine and 5-speed gearbox.

▶ 1960 Alfa Romeo Giulietta Spider, 1290cc, 4 cylinders, double overhead camshafts, Solex carburettors, 80bhp at 5,800rpm, 4-speed manual synchromesh gearbox, wishbone and coil-spring independent front suspension, coil-spring rear suspension, 4-wheel drum brakes, red with black and red interior, black hood, left-hand drive, partial restoration, paintwork and interior in good condition, electrics in need of minor attention, original toolkit, good condition.
£12,500–14,000 C

◀ 1929 Alvis Special Silver Eagle 'The Green Car', 2511cc, 6 cylinder engine, triple SU carburettors, dry-sump oil system, close-ratio gearbox, modified Alvis 12/50 chassis, streamlined boat-tail, streamlined undertray and front dumb-iron fairing, 46 trophies included.
£47,000–52,000 S

This well-known race-bred Alvis enjoyed a long and illustrious racing career, being the only Alvis to win an International Grand Prix at Phoenix Park, Dublin, in 1938. The original 2 litre power unit was later replaced by a Speed 20 2511cc, 6 cylinder, overhead-valve engine, producing 130bhp.

▶ **1930 Aston Martin 1½ Litre International Tourer,** one of 14 long-chassis cars built, older restoration, engine completely rebuilt, oil supply modified with in-line filter, water pump, dynamo, clutch, starter motor and fuel pump overhauled, new silencer and exhaust system, finished in green with green leather interior, good condition throughout. **£33,000–36,000 BKS**

◀ **1954 Aston Martin DB2/4,** 2589cc Vantage engine, double overhead camshafts, 125bhp, 111mph top speed, 0–60mph in 12.6 seconds, rebuilt to original specification, mechanical components and bodywork replaced or repaired as necessary, new bonnet, resprayed in maroon, reupholstered in grey leather. **£28,000–32,000 BKS**

The launch of the DB2/4, in October 1953, heralded a new generation of four-seat sports cars from the Newport Pagnell factory. Its hatchback rear window was copied by many manufacturers from the 1960s onwards.

▶ **1955 Aston Martin DB2/4 Mk I Drophead Coupé,** 3 litres, 6 cylinders, double overhead camshafts, 140bhp, rectangular-tubing chassis, trailing-arm independent front suspension, 118mph top speed, left-hand drive, restored 1993/96, engine top-end rebuilt, bare-metal respray in Royal blue, all rubber seals replaced, brightwork replated, new Connolly leather upholstery and Wilton carpeting, good condition throughout. **£40,000–45,000 BKS**

A total of 565 DB2/4 Mk I models were produced before being superseded by the Mk II in October 1955.

1959 Aston Martin DB4GT, coachwork by Touring, 3.7 litres, 6 cylinders, double overhead camshafts, 302bhp at 6,000rpm, early-style bonnet scoop and grille, cathedral rear lights, original Perspex rear quarter-windows and screen, Borrani wire wheels, chassis structure in good order, finished in original Dubonnet Rosso with Slate grey hide, paintwork dulled and micro-blistered in places, original carpets, headlining replaced, seat belt mountings, non-standard door mirror, competition-type cut-out switch in driver's-side rear quarter-window, 27,000 miles from new, recently recommissioned, possibly in need of new back axle. **£130,000–140,000 BKS**

In 1959, Aston Martin won the Le Mans 24-hour race and the Sports Car World Championship. Later that year, the company introduced its race-bred DB4GT. This featured an aluminium-skinned body by Touring in their *Superleggera* (super lightweight) style.

◄ 1957 Aston Martin DB2/4 Mk I Arnolt Coupé, coachwork by Bertone, completely restored mid-1980s, good condition throughout. £80,000–90,000 BKS

American industrialist Stanley Harold 'Wacky' Arnolt was able to indulge his love of cars when, in 1952, he bought a stake in Bertone and arranged for the manufacture of Bertone-bodied Arnolt MGs. By far the least well-known of Arnolt's creations, however, is the Aston Martin. The British manufacturer is believed to have supplied seven DB2/4 chassis in the mid-1950s, six of which were bodied as roadsters, the seventh being a coupé.

▶ 1962 Aston Martin DB4GT Zagato Coupé, 3670cc, 6-cylinders, double overhead camshafts, 314bhp at 6,000rpm, 4-speed manual gearbox, tube-framed, aluminium-panelled body, left-hand drive, restored. £680,000+ BKS

No more than 19 of these, competition-bred coupés were built, and only eight of them had left-hand drive. This particular car exhibits unique features. Its tail treatment is sleeker than the standard model, while the nose intake grille is reminiscent of the style seen on the early-1950s DB3. This car achieved the UK record auction price in 1998.

1964 Aston Martin DB5, 3995cc, 6 cylinder, double-overhead-camshaft engine, 282bhp, 5-speed gearbox, independent front suspension by double wishbones and coil springs, live rear axle with parallel radius arms and Watts linkage, 4-wheel disc brakes, restored, new timing chains, overhauled water pump, reconditioned dampers, new clutch and wheel centre-lock spinners, all rusted sills, box-sections, outriggers, bumper mountings, rear radius arm locating points and jacking points replaced with new metal, corroded aluminium panels replaced, bare-metal respray, new windscreen, external chrome fittings replated, leather upholstery refurbished, excellent condition. £45,000–50,000 C

This car was used by renowned French special-effects man Remy Julienne to practise the high-speed car chases and stunts that featured in the James Bond film *Goldeneye*. The suspension, brakes and tyres were all modified to make this possible. The Aston Martin served as a test-bed for modifications that were made to identical vehicles used during the filming.

◄ 1978 Aston Martin V8 Vantage, 5340cc, Weber IDA carburettors, 380bhp at 6,000rpm, stiffened suspension, Koni dampers, deep front air dam, bolt-on boot spoiler, blanked off radiator grille and bonnet air scoop, 170mph top speed, 0–60mph in 5.3 seconds, restored 1990, painted red with magnolia upholstery, matching red carpets, recent attention to sills and jacking points, well maintained. £20,000–23,000 COYS

◀ **1928 Austin 7 Chummy,** 747cc, 4 cylinders, restored, mechanical components and bodywork in good condition, finished in maroon with black wings, trimmed in black leatherette, hood and sidescreens of correct material and serviceable, little recent use. **£5,500–7,000 BRIT**

The introduction in 1922 of the diminutive Austin 7 changed British motorists' opinion of economy cars. Today, enthusiasm for the Austin 7 is as great as ever. One of the most popular models was the four-seater Tourer or Chummy, as it was known. Designed to carry two adults and two children, this car really was the progenitor of popular family motoring and, effectively, Britain's answer to the Ford Model T.

▶ **1930 Austin 7 Ulster Sports,** 747cc, 4 cylinder, unsupercharged full-pressure engine, original body tub, restored, finished in red with black leather seating and hood, completely original and genuine, little recent use, excellent condition throughout. **£8,000–9,000 H&H**

◀ **1965 Austin-Healey 3000 Mk III Phase 2,** 2912cc, 6 cylinders, left-hand drive, recently restored, all mechanical components overhauled, new wiring loom, new floors, sills, outriggers and wings, bare-metal respray, new glass, chrome, road wheels and stainless steel exhaust, new leather upholstery, carpets, hood and tonneau, excellent condition throughout, Heritage Trust certificate. **£18,000–21,000 COYS**

The ultimate Healey model arrived in early 1964 with the introduction of the 3000 Mk III. It sported myriad changes, most notably more power, twin 2in SU carburettors and a revised exhaust system. The interior was far more refined, the old steel dash panel being replaced by wood veneer, the seats covered in leather and a console placed between the front seats.

1927 Bentley 3/4½ Litre Tourer, replica fabric-covered coachwork in the style of 'Mother Gun', engine uprated to 4½ litre specification, Le Mans-specification 3 Litre chassis, windscreen and separate aero screens, centre-mounted Marchal driving light, radiator and offside-headlamp stoneguards, external oil tank filler, quick-release radiator filler cap, Le Mans-style quick-fill rear fuel tank, cockpit brake adjusters, bucket seats, appropriate instruments. **£85,000–95,000 BKS**

This car was built as a replica of the celebrated Bentley works car, the original 'Mother Gun' having been steadily modified far beyond its 1927 specification.

► **1930 Bentley Speed Six Corsica Coupé,** 6.5 litres, 12ft 8½in-wheelbase chassis, completely restored in 1998, finished in black with grey interior, excellent condition. **£1,200,000+ BLK**

1930 Bentley 4½ Litre Supercharged Four-Seater Tourer, coachwork by Vanden Plas, 'D' type gearbox, very original. **£375,000+ BKS**

First shown at the 1929 London Motor Show, the 'Blower Bentley' was developed as a private venture by Sir Henry Birkin to extract more performance from the 4½ Litre model, which was becoming outclassed on the circuits of Europe. Only 50 production supercharged 4½ Litre Bentleys were built. Among the few cars of their day capable of 100mph on the open road, they have always been regarded as the supercars of their era.

► **1934 Bentley 3½ Litre Saloon,** coachwork by Park Ward, recently restored, interior retrimmed, excellent condition. **£25,000–30,000 COYS**

The coachwork fitted to this particular car was draughted by the gifted designer and engineer Sir Roy Fedden, and built for him by Park Ward in June 1934. Park Ward was sufficiently impressed to use the design as the basis for a run of production bodies, which differed only in the mounting of the spare wheel and the line of the front wings, this being the only example to have helmet wings that turn with the front wheels.

◄ **1935 Bentley 3½ Litre Drophead Foursome Coupé,** three-position coachwork by Carlton Carriage Company, 6 cylinder engine to original specification, two-tone paintwork, folding hood in good order, twin side-mounted spares, silver wire-spoked wheels, trafficators, biscuit leather upholstery, good original condition. **£23,000–27,000 S**

◄ 1935 Bentley 3½ Litre Coupé, coachwork by Kellner, 6 cylinder engine, 105bhp, 5-speed gearbox, centralised lubrication system, leaf-spring suspension, hydraulic shock absorbers, power-assisted brakes, Marchal lamps, Perspex sunroof, dickey seat, recent total cosmetic restoration, engine top-end rebuilt, new clutch, high-ratio final drive, suspension and fuel system overhauled, excellent condition throughout, large history file.
£60,000–70,000 COYS

The first of the Derby Bentleys, and also the first to be marketed as 'The Silent Sports Car', the 3½ Litre soon gained a reputation for pace and fine handling. This 3½ is one of only three bodied by Kellner.

1939 Bentley 4¼ Litre Saloon, coachwork by Vanden Plas, overdrive, new exhaust system, original leather upholstery, correct specification and complete, good selection of tools, stored for some time, in need of some refurbishment, running well.
£21,000–22,500 RCC

► 1953 Bentley R-Type Standard Steel Saloon, automatic transmission, left-hand drive, finished in black over silver, original blue/grey leather upholstery, body and chassis sound, in need of minor attention.
£15,000–16,500 RCC

This particular Bentley R-Type was delivered new to Belgium.

◄ 1955 Bentley R-Type Continental, coachwork by H.J. Mulliner, 4887cc, F-head 6 cylinder engine, 4-speed manual gearbox with synchromesh on upper 3 ratios and right-hand change, close-ratio gearset and 3.7:1 final-drive ratio, 120mph top speed, fitted with high-level, full-flow oil filter, sunroof, finished in silver, original burgundy leather interior trim showing slight creasing, toolkit virtually complete, well maintained.
£70,000–80,000 BKS

◄ **1957 BMW 507,** all-aluminium, 3.2 litre, pushrod V8 engine, 150bhp, hand-formed aluminium bodywork. **£140,000–160,000 BLK**

The 507 made its debut at the 1955 Paris show. Although it was well received, it did not enter production until 1957. Only 254 BMW 507s were built, production being stopped in 1959.

► **1953 Bristol 401,** 2 litre, 6 cylinder engine, 85bhp, dry-stored 15 years, refurbished, reconditioned cylinder head with new valves and guides, new stainless steel exhaust, brakes overhauled, bare-metal respray, brightwork rechromed, interior refurbished. **£10,500–13,000 BKS**

Launched in 1949, the Bristol 401 was a more aerodynamic derivative of the mechanically similar 400, its bodywork having been developed in the wind tunnel of the parent Bristol Aeroplane Company. With aluminium panelling over a tubular steel frame, the Bristol weighed a mere 2,700lb.

1928 Bugatti Type 35B Grand Prix, chassis no. 4938, engine no. 192T, restored mid-1980s, excellent condition, award winner. **£400,000+ BLK**

Raced in 1928 by the great Louis Chiron, this Type 35B won two or three Grands Prix of the period. It was presented to Chiron as a gift by Ettore Bugatti in recognition of his racing successes.

► **1934 Bugatti Type 57 'Ventoux',** 3257cc, 8 cylinder in-line engine, 4-speed manual gearbox, cable-operated brakes, restored, good condition. **£60,000–70,000 Pou**

◄ **1937 Bugatti Type 57C Cabriolet,** three-position coachwork by Gangloff, 3257cc, 8 cylinder in-line engine, Roots supercharger, 162bhp at 5,000rpm, 4-speed gearbox, hydraulic brakes, right-hand drive, 170km/h top speed, restored, excellent condition. **£170,000–190,000 Pou**

▶ **1903 Cadillac Model A 6½hp Rear-Entrance Tonneau,** wooden wheels, brass fittings, including oil and acetylene lamps, deep-buttoned red leather upholstery, older restoration showing signs of deterioration, engine valve gear dismantled.
£20,000–23,000 BKS

The Cadillac Automobile Company was established in 1902. Its first production car, the Model A, was powered by a single-cylinder horizontal engine of about 1.5 litres, mounted under the floor and driving through a 2-speed epicyclic gearbox with chain drive to the rear axle. It was a basic, but successful, design that Cadillac retained for about five years.

◀ **1938 Cadillac Series 38–90 Fleetwood Limousine,** 16 cylinder engine, left-hand drive, completely restored, excellent condition.
£65,000–75,000 BLK

Cadillac introduced new body styles for 1938, together with a new V16 engine. This particular car once belonged to the renowned comedian W.C. Fields.

▶ **1932 Chrysler Imperial CL Convertible Roadster,** coachwork by LeBaron, 8 cylinder in-line engine, 6.3 litres, 125bhp at 3,200rpm, 4-speed gearbox, hydraulic brakes, hydraulic shock absorbers, 95+mph top speed, complete body-off restoration, concours winner.
£140,000–160,000 BKS

Apart from a handful of chassis, LeBaron was responsible for the coachwork on all of Chrysler's 1932 CL Custom Imperials. Arguably the ultimate of the Customs was the Convertible Roadster.

1911 Daimler 20hp Open Drive Landaulette, coachwork by Maythorn, electric starter, brass acetylene headlamps, oil/electric side and opera lamps, opening windscreen, fold-down landaulette rear, speaking tube to chauffeur, restored, rear compartment upholstered in Bedford cord with silk trimming, leather trimmed chauffeur's compartment, original condition.
£50,000–60,000 BKS

Daimler offered a range of touring cars in 1911: the 4 cylinder 15hp model; the 38hp car, as supplied to Queen Alexandra; and the mighty 57hp, six-cylinder types, built in landaulette, limousine and shooting-brake form for King George V, all such cars being bodied by Hooper. Unusually, this car carries open-drive landaulette coachwork by Maythorn, built to the order of Prince Louis Alexander Battenberg of Hesse, grandson of Queen Victoria and First Sea Lord from 1912 to 1914.

◄ **1950 Delahaye 235M Ghia Pillarless Saloon,** restored 1990, concours condition.
£100,000–120,000 BLK

This Ghia-bodied Delahaye was designed by Felice Mario Boano. Incorporated in the design are wide oval grille openings and streamlined fairings that conceal the wheels, but can be swung up out of the way. It was one of the last Delahayes to be built.

1929 Duesenberg J Murphy Convertible Coupé, restored, excellent condition.
£600,000+ BLK

Of the 470 Duesenbergs produced, the Murphy Convertible Coupé was the most popular, a total of 55 being built.

► **1953 Ferrari 250 Mille Miglia Berlinetta,** two-seater coachwork by Pinin Farina, 3 litre V12 engine, right-hand drive, interior and bucket seats upholstered in leather, older restoration.
£425,000+ BKS

The prototype 250MM was unveiled as an unbodied chassis at the 1952 Paris Salon. It reappeared with its refined, yet aggressive-looking, Pinin Farina body at the Geneva Salon in 1953. Thirty-one 250MMs were subsequently constructed at Ferrari's Maranello factory, 17 of them being completed as Berlinettas.

◄ **1957 Ferrari 250GT Spyder Series 1,** coachwork by Pininfarina, fitted with later outside-plug engine, 15in wheels, disc brakes and high-ratio differential (original included), converted to right-hand drive, finished in red with black leather interior, pristine condition.
£215,000–230,000 BKS

► **1961 Ferrari 250GT SWB California Spyder Replica,** based on Ferrari 250GTE, chassis no. 2437GT, competition-specification 3 litre V12, 4-speed gearbox with overdrive, left-hand drive, excellent condition.
£90,000–100,000 BKS

The sleek styling of the classic California Spyder, was the zenith of 250GT production. Only 49 long-wheelbase and 55 short-wheelbase examples left the factory between 1957 and 1963. To create this replica, a 250GTE chassis was shortened and fitted with new aluminium coachwork.

◄ **1961 Ferrari 250GT Cabriolet Series II,** coachwork by Pininfarina, 3 litre V12, 240bhp, 4-speed gearbox with overdrive, engine rebuilt, 6,300km covered since, suspension overhauled, brakes overhauled, Borrani wire wheels, original detachable hardtop, tonneau cover, resprayed in red, light tan leather interior, toolkit, excellent condition.
£95,000–110,000 BKS

► **1961 Ferrari 250GTE Coupé,** coachwork by Pininfarina, chassis no. 2513GT, engine no. 2513GT, 3 litre V12, restored 1995/97, 1,219km covered since, original leather interior, period radio, excellent condition.
£42,000–48,000 BKS

With four seats, Pininfarina coachwork, 240bhp and refinements such as disc brakes all-round, the GTE was the first Ferrari to make a significant impact on the customer profile. Previous Ferraris had been made for single men; the 250GTE was aimed at the man on the move who also had a family.

◄ **1969 Ferrari 365 GT 2+2 Coupé,** coachwork by Pininfarina, 4.4 litre, overhead-camshaft V12, 320bhp at 6,600rpm, hydro-pneumatic, self-levelling independent suspension all-round, power steering, 152mph top speed, 0–60mph in 7.2 seconds, leather upholstery, air conditioning, recent cosmetic improvements.
£15,000–18,000 COYS

► **1973 Ferrari 365 GTB/4 Daytona Berlinetta,** coachwork by Pininfarina, chassis no. 15837, engine no. 15837, 4390cc V12, 4 overhead camshafts, 352bhp at 7,500rpm, 5-speed transaxle, oval-tubing chassis, all-independent wishbone and coil-spring suspension, servo-assisted ventilated disc brakes all-round, 170+mph top speed, right-hand drive, complete body restoration 1989, leather interior, mechanical overhaul 1990, 31,000 miles recorded, very good condition.
£55,000–65,000 BKS

1965 Ferrari 500 Superfast Coupé, coachwork by Pininfarina, chassis no. 6679SF, engine no. 6679SF, 4963cc V12 engine, 400bhp at 6,500rpm, 175mph top speed.
£115,000–130,000 COYS

The culmination of a series of aerodynamic and high-performance grand tourers by Pininfarina, the Ferrari 500 Superfast was produced in very limited numbers following its debut at the 1964 Geneva show. It was an evolution of the 410 and 400 Superamerica and was considered the ultimate grand tourer of its day. This particular 500 Superfast was purchased new by the renowned comic actor Peter Sellers.

1967 Ford GT40, 4727cc V8 engine, Weber carburettors, rigid steel monocoque chassis, Borrani wire wheels, older restoration, finished in yellow, little use in recent years, excellent condition throughout.
£165,000–180,000 COYS

When Henry Ford II committed his company to the World Sportscar Championship, he gave his engineers an unlimited budget to gain the greatest prize: victory at Le Mans. The project was contracted out to Ford Advanced Vehicles, headed by John Wyer, and the car they created was the GT40. Of simple construction, it boasted great strength, a useful attribute in endurance racing. Proof of that is the car's extraordinary competition record. As well as a very successful racing car, the GT40 was turned into a road-going GT, offering the ultimate looks and performance of the day.

◄ **1953 Healey Silverstone Replica,** 2.4 litre Riley engine, rebuilt to competition level, with flowed head and tuned stainless steel exhausts, headlamps tucked away behind radiator grille, cycle-type wings, black leather bucket seats and carpets.
£10,000–13,000 S

A Tickford drophead coupé body was originally fitted to this chassis and the car was first registered in January 1953. The drophead was acquired 25 years later by a Healey enthusiast who painstakingly rebuilt the car to Silverstone specification, using a former TT Silverstone as reference for the restoration.

1924 Hispano-Suiza H6B 37.2hp Tulip-wood Sports Torpedo, 6.6 litres, 6 cylinders, aluminium block, overhead camshaft, 4-wheel brakes with iron liners in alloy drums, servo-mechanism, restored mechanically, engine noisy and in need of overhaul.
£125,000–140,000 BKS

For the 1924 racing season, André Dubonnet, ordered an H6 with a 'type sport' chassis and commissioned Nieuport-Astra, aircraft manufacturers, to build a racing body using contemporary aircraft practice to combine light weight with high strength. This was the sensational 'tulip-wood' car that Dubonnet drove so spiritedly in the 1924 Targa Florio. British engineer Roy Middleton had long coveted Dubonnet's 'tulip-wood' H6, and the discovery of an H6B chassis during the 1980s gave him the opportunity of building his dream car. Although Dubonnet's car had been constructed from laminated mahogany and not tulip-wood at all, Middleton elected to use real tulip-wood, entrusting the work to Carl Douglas Racing Shells.

1948 Jaguar 1½ Litre Four-Door Saloon, 1775cc, 4 cylinder overhead-valve engine, Girling mechanical brakes, hypoid-bevel back axle, pressed-steel body, rebuilt in 1980, well maintained, concours winner.
£15,000–17,000 BKS

▶ **1948 Jaguar Mk IV 3½ Litre Drophead Coupé,** 6 cylinder, 7-bearing, overhead-valve engine, 4-speed manual gearbox, hypoid-bevel rear axle, 120in wheelbase, beam front/live rear axles on semi-elliptic springs, Girling mechanical brakes, all-steel coachwork, finished in Old English white with red leather upholstery, well maintained, concours winner.
£30,000–35,000 BKS

1955 Jaguar Mk VIIM Four-Door Saloon, 3.4 litre, 6 cylinder engine, 190bhp, manual gearbox, torsion-bar independent front suspension, cruiciform-braced chassis, restored, fewer than 66,000 miles from new, concours winner, excellent condition.
£17,250–19,000 BKS

1954 Jaguar XK120 Drophead Coupé, matching chassis and engine numbers, 3.4 litre, 6 cylinder engine, left-hand drive, complete body-off restoration 1991/94, original body panels retained with exception of doors, finished in black with cream interior, burr-walnut dashboard, complete toolkit, concours winner, excellent condition throughout.
£50,000–55,000 BKS

◀ **1966 Jaguar Mk II 3.8 Saloon,** 3442cc, double-overhead-camshaft, 6 cylinder engine, manual gearbox with overdrive, restored, finished in red, uprated engine, gearbox, brakes and suspension, wire wheels, good condition throughout, history file.
£14,000–17,000 UMC

▶ **1967 Jaguar Mk II 2.4 Litre Saloon,** 6 cylinder engine, 120bhp, manual gearbox with overdrive, finished in Old English white with navy blue leather interior and wood cappings, chromed wire wheels, unrestored, very original, well maintained.
£5,000–7,000 COYS

Introduced in 1959, the Mk II cars would rank among the best-loved Jaguars ever made. Today, they are regarded as classics.

◀ **1969 Jaguar E-Type Series II Roadster,** 4235cc, double-overhead-camshaft, 6 cylinder in-line engine, manual gearbox, original right-hand drive model, finished in Carmine red with black leather interior, engine overhauled, good condition throughout.
£17,000–20,000 BRIT

▶ **1970 Jaguar E-Type Coupé,** 4-speed manual gearbox, rebuilt to original factory specification, new exhaust system, chromed wire wheels, resprayed in Gunmetal grey, black leather upholstery and black carpets.
£10,000–12,000 S

The 150mph E-Type had a distinctive body line, showing the influence of Malcolm Sayers' E1A 1958 prototype, in turn recalling Alfa Romeo's *Disco Volante* bodystyle.

1974 Jaguar E-Type Series III Roadster, 5343cc V12, 272bhp, manual gearbox, 140+mph top speed, resprayed in red, new hood and tonneau cover, 53,000 miles from new, original, good condition.
£18,000–21,000 COYS

Bugatti

After Roy Nockolds, silkscreen print depicting Constantini driving works Bugatti Type 35 in the 1926 Targa Florio, hand-coloured by Nicky Hales, 24½x17¼in (62x44cm).
£115–130 BKS

1925 Bugatti Type 35 Grand Prix Two-Seater, chassis no. 4610, engine no. 57, restored to original specification.
£180,000–220,000 BKS

The Type 35 Bugatti was destined to become probably the most successful racing car of all time. This particular car is a very early example. Invoiced for delivery to racing driver Malcolm Campbell, it was only the fourth Type 35 supplied to Britain.

1928 Bugatti Type 44 Sports Two-Seater, coachwork by Corsica, chassis no. 44415, engine no. 44415, 3 litre, 8 cylinder in-line engine, aluminium-panelled two-seater body.
£75,000–85,000 BKS

Believed to be the oldest surviving Bugatti with coachwork by the London coachbuilder Corsica, this 1928 Type 44 Bugatti was originally fitted with a Harrington fabric saloon body.

1934 Bugatti Type 49 Cabriolet Convertible, coachwork by Gangloff, 3247cc, overhead camshaft, two spark plugs per cylinder, dual Scintilla magneto, engine-driven fan, restored 1985 to original condition, engine completely rebuilt, dual spare wheels.
£100,000–120,000 BKS

Around 470 examples were produced during 1930–34. Derived from the 3 litre T44, the T49 had superior torque and performance.

BUGATTI Model	ENGINE cc/cyl	DATES	CONDITION 1	2	3
13/22/23	1496/4	1919–26	£40,000	£32,000	£25,000
30	1991/8	1922–36	£45,000	£35,000	£30,000
32	1992/8	1923	£45,000	£35,000	£30,000
35A	1991/8	1924–30	£110,000+	£90,000	£80,500
38 (30 update)	1991/8	1926–28	£44,500	£34,000	£28,000
39	1493/8	1926–29	£120,000	£90,000	£80,000
39A Supercharged	1496/8	1926–29	£140,000+	-	-
35T	2262/8	1926–30	£140,000+	-	-
37 GP Car	1496/4	1926–30	£110,000+	£90,000	£75,000
40	1496/4	1926–30	£50,000	£42,000	£35,000
38A	1991/8	1927–28	£48,000	£40,000	£35,000
35B Supercharged	2262/8	1927–30	£300,000+	£170,000+	-
35C	1991/8	1927–30	£170,000+	-	-
37A	1496/4	1927–30	£125,000+	-	-
44	2991/8	1927–30	£50,000+	£40,000	£35,000
45	3801/16	1927–30	£150,000+	-	-
43/43A Tourer	2262/8	1927–31	£180,000+	-	-
35A	1991/8	1928–30	£140,000	£110,000	£90,000
46	5359/8	1929–36	£140,000	£110,000	£90,000
40A	1627/4	1930	£55,000	£45,000	£35,500
49	3257/8	1930–34	£60,000+	£45,000	£35,500
57 Closed	3257/8	1934–40	£40,000+	£35,000	£30,000
57 Open	3257/8	1936–38	£80,000+	£60,000	£55,000
57S	3257/8	1936–38	£250,000+	-	-
57SC Supercharged	3257/8	1936–39	£250,000+	-	-
57G	3257/8	1937–40	£250,000+	-	-
57C	3257/8	1939–40	£140,000+	-	-

Racing history is an important factor with the GP cars.

Buick

BUICK Model	ENGINE cc/cyl	DATES	CONDITION 1	2	3
Veteran	various	1903–09	£18,500	£12,000	£8,000
18/20	3881/6	1918–22	£12,000	£5,000	£2,000
Series 22	2587/4	1922–24	£9,000	£5,000	£3,000
Series 24/6	3393/6	1923–30	£9,000	£5,000	£3,000
Light 8	3616/8	1931	£18,000	£14,500	£11,000
Straight 8	4467/8	1931	£22,000	£18,000	£10,000
50 Series	3857/8	1931–39	£18,500	£15,000	£8,000
60 Series	5247/8	1936–39	£19,000	£15,000	£8,000
90 Series	5648/8	1934–35	£20,000	£15,500	£9,000
40 Series	4064/8	1936–39	£19,000	£14,000	£10,000
80/90	5247/8	1936–39	£25,000	£20,000	£15,000
McLaughlin	5247/8	1937–40	£22,000	£15,000	£10,000

Various chassis lengths and bodies will affect value. Buick chassis fitted with British bodies prior to 1916 were called Bedford-Buicks. Right-hand drive can add a premium of 25 per cent.

1936 Buick 8 Limited Limousine, coachwork by McLaughlin, 5247cc, 8 cylinders, hydraulic jacks all round, finished in black with beige West of England cloth trim, cabinets in partition housing canteen equipment, silver cocktail shaker and cups, silver sandwich box and vacuum ice jar, silver smoker's set, jewel box and hot water bottle, radio, 2 clocks, very good condition, formerly owned by HM King Edward VIII, original log book detailing the first owner as, 'HM The King, St James Palace, SW1'.
£48,000–54,000 COYS

Visually, this Royal Buick was similar to a standard Limited, but for the deletion of the rear quarter-windows and fitting of a smaller rear screen to increase privacy. Inside, quarter companions replaced the quarter-lights, built up individually in wood, each housing a mirror and lamp plus a heavily-chromed reading lamp with universal movement. Privacy was further enhanced by a silk blind for the rear window that could be operated electrically from either the passenger or driver's compartment. Within nine months of delivery of the Buick, King Edward VIII was in the midst of the abdication crisis.

BUICK Model	ENGINE cu in/cyl	DATES	CONDITION 1	2	3
Special/Super 4 Door	248/8				
	364/8	1950–59	£6,000	£4,000	£2,000
Special/Super Riviera	263/8				
	332/8	1050–56	£8,000	£6,000	£3,000
Special/Super Convertible	263/8				
	332/8	1950–56	£8,500	£5,500	£3,000
Roadmaster 4-door	320/8				
	365/8	1950–58	£11,000	£8,000	£6,000
Roadmaster Riviera	320/8				
	364/8	1950–58	£9,000	£7,000	£5,000
Roadmaster Convertible	320/8				
	364/8	1950–58	£14,500	£11,000	£7,000
Special/Super Riviera	364/8	1957–59	£10,750	£7,500	£5,000
Special/Super Convertible	364/8	1957–58	£13,500	£11,000	£6,000

Cadillac

The very first Cadillac, known retrospectively as the Model A, was completed on October 17, 1902. That first product of the company, founded by Henry Martin Leland, was distinguished by its considerable refinement compared with other offerings of the time, and ever since, the Cadillac name has been a by-word for prestige motoring. In 1909, the young company was acquired by General Motors, where it has remained pre-eminent as the flagship marque. But Cadillacs were not merely luxurious; at many stages throughout its history, the company has been at the forefront in the practical application of innovation and technology. In 1912, Cadillac became 'the car that has no crank', with the introduction of the electric self-starter; electric lights also appeared that year. In 1914, it introduced its first V8

engine. In 1929, Cadillac offered safety glass and a synchromesh gearbox, and in 1930, the extravagant V16 arrived, followed closely by the V12 models.

Not surprisingly, sales plummeted during the depression following the Wall Street Crash, and the extravagant excess was reined in to match the slimmer wallets of the day. Even so, Cadillac suffered less than many other luxury-car manufacturers, and in the years after 1935, nearly half of all cars sold in the USA costing more than $1,500 (£950) were Cadillacs.

A name that can't be omitted is that of stylist Harley Earl. He drafted his first Cadillacs in 1928 and went on to create the ultimate automotive expression of the American dream: fins, chrome and bullet-shaped bumpers. Of his creations, none is more iconic than the 1959 Cadillac.

1930 Cadillac 452 Madam X Coupé, V16, restored, finished in red, excellent condition.
£130,000–140,000 BLK

This coupé is referred to as a 'Madam X' because of the slant of its windscreen.

1938 Cadillac V16 Convertible Coupé, side-valve engine, restored, first example built with this body style, concours condition.
£60,000–65,000 RM

1949 Cadillac Series 62 Convertible Coupé, 5424cc V8, 4-speed automatic transmission, hydraulically-operated hood, seats and windows, manually adjustable door-mounted spotlamps, light tan canvas hood, finished in red with tang leather upholstery, excellent condition.
£23,000–28,000 BKS

Cadillac's all-new V8 engine, introduced in 1949, had a smoothness never experienced before in a V8. Although smaller in capacity than its predecessor (5.4 litres), the high-compression, lightweight engine provided a top speed of 100mph and 0–60mph in 12 seconds.

CADILLAC (pre-war) Model	ENGINE cc/cyl	DATES	CONDITION 1	2	3
Type 57–61	5153/8	1915–23	£20,000+	£14,000	£6,000
Series 314	5153/8	1926–27	£22,000	£15,000	£6,000
Type V63	5153/8	1924–27	£20,000	£13,000	£5,000
Series 341	5578/8	1928–29	£22,000	£15,000	£6,000
Series 353–5	5289/8	1930–31	£32,500+	£22,000	£12,000
V16	7406/16	1931–32	£50,000+	£32,000+	£18,000
V12	6030/12	1932–37	£42,000+	£25,000	£15,000
V8	5790/8	1935–36	£30,000+	£15,000	£6,000
V16	7034/16	1937–40	£50,000+	£30,000	£18,000

1953 Cadillac Ghia Coupé, completely restored late 1980s, finished in black with beige interior, 34,320 miles from new.
£200,000+ BLK

In 1953, Cadillac commissioned Ghia to design and build a European-styled coupé. Three chassis were reportedly shipped to Ghia, but only two examples are known to have been built. This car is believed to have been owned by actress Rita Hayworth.

1957 Cadillac Eldorado Biarritz Convertible, restored, finished in black with white interior, once owned by The Who rock band, good condition throughout.
£22,000–25,000 PALM

1962 Cadillac Sedan de Ville, 6384cc V8, 325bhp at 4,800rpm, 3-speed automatic transmission, converted to right-hand drive, restored 1980s, concours condition.
£6,000–9,000 C

In the early 1960s, GM's chief stylist Harley Earl retired, his place being taken by William Mitchell. A little more restrained than Earl, Mitchell eased back on the chrome, trimmed the Cadillac's tailfins and emphasised scupltured body lines. But the Cadillac was still the ideal celebrity's car. This Sedan de Ville has long been recognised as a car that was originally supplied to Marilyn Monroe in 1962.

CADILLAC Model	ENGINE cu in/cyl	DATES	CONDITION 1	2	3
4-door sedan	331/8	1949	£8,000	£4,500	£3,000
2-door fastback	331/8	1949	£10,000	£8,000	£5,000
Convertible	331/8	1949	£22,000	£12,000	£10,000
Series 62 4-door	331/8				
	365/8	1950–55	£7,000	£5,500	£3,000
Sedan de Ville	365/8	1956–58	£8,000	£6,000	£4,000
Coupe de Ville	331/8				
	365/8	1950–58	£12,500	£9,500	£3,500
Convertible	331/8				
	365/8	1950–58	£25,000	£20,000	£10,000
Eldorado	331/8	1953–55	£35,000	£30,000	£18,000
Eldorado Seville	365/8	1956–58	£11,500	£9,000	£5,500
Eldorado Biarritz	365/8	1956–58	£30,000	£20,000	£15,000
Sedan de Ville	390/8	1959	£12,000	£9,500	£5,000
Coupe de Ville	390/8	1959	£15,000	£9,000	£5,500
Convertible	390/8	1959	£28,000	£20,000	£10,000
Eldorado Seville	390/8	1959	£13,000	£10,000	£6,000
Eldorado Biarritz	390/8	1959	£30,000	£20,000	£14,000
Sedan de Ville	390/8	1960	£10,000	£8,000	£4,500
Convertible	390/8	1960	£27,000+	£14,000	£7,500
Eldorado Biarritz	390/8	1960	£25,000+	£17,000	£10,000
Sedan de Ville	390/8				
	429/8	1961–64	£7,000	£5,000	£3,000
Coupe de Ville	390/8				
	429/8	1961–64	£8,000	£6,000	£4,000
Convertible	390/8				
	429/8	1961–64	£20,000	£9,000	£7,000
Eldorado Biarritz	390/8				
	429/8	1961–64	£19,500	£14,000	£9,000

Caterham

◄ **1988 Caterham Super 7,** 1599cc Ford crossflow engine, 4-speed Ford manual gearbox, Morris Marina 1.8 rear axle, long-cockpit format, tonneau cover, 747 miles from new, excellent condition throughout. **£9,500–11,000 BRIT**

Caterham Cars acquired the rights to the Lotus Super 7 following Lotus' change of direction towards more upmarket sports cars. Steady development has ensured that the car has remained a firm favourite.

Chevrolet

In 1910, when William C. Durant lost control of General Motors, the firm he had founded in 1908, he immediately set about making his comeback. In 1911, he set up his new company, naming it after Swiss-born racing driver Louis Chevrolet, who helped design their first car. By 1916, Durant's fortunes had soared so dramatically that his company actually bought General Motors. However, by 1920, as the post-war depression took hold, Durant lost both companies. His legacy, however, is a marque that ever since has steered a steady course through the mainstream of American motoring, running head to head with Ford in the competition for the affections and wallets of working Americans.

◄ **1926 Chevrolet Superior B1 Four-Seater Tourer,** 2500cc, 4 cylinder engine, 3-speed manual gearbox, right-hand drive, restored, resprayed in yellow with black wings, new red interior, new hood and weather equipment. **£6,750–7,750 H&H**

1957 Chevrolet Bel Air Convertible, body-off restoration, excellent condition throughout. **£23,000–27,000 PALM**

Chevrolet 150, 210, Bel Air, 1955–57

Body styles: Two- and four-door saloon, two- and four-door pillarless coupé, convertible, two- and four-door estate, Nomad sports estate.
Engine: straight-six, 3862cc; V8, 4350cc and 4674cc (1957 only).
Power output: 123–136bhp (six-cylinder models); 162–225bhp (4350cc V8); 185–283bhp (4674cc V8).
Transmission: Three-speed manual, optional overdrive; two- and three-speed automatic.
Top speed: 108mph (1956 Turbo-Fire V8).
0–60mph: 10.7 seconds (1956 Turbo-Fire V8).
'Go all the way, then back off,' was what General Motors' styling chief, Harley Earl, told his design team to do for the 1955 Chevrolet range. At a stroke, Chevrolet shed its image as a maker of dull, reliable granny-mobiles and assaulted an affluent younger generation with a three-year model range so mythic that enthusiasts have coined their own name for the 1955–57 models – Tri-Chevys. Gone was the paunchy rotundity; in its place crisp, clean lines that inclined forward and made the car look ever so eager. And it was. For the first time in its history, Chevrolet offered a V8 engine option. The injection of potent V8 power was as rejuvenating as Viagra, allowing Chevrolet to advertise the car as 'the hot one'. The line kicked off with the plain-Jane 150; the mid-range 210 added a little more equipment and extra chrome garnish; while at the top was the luxury Bel Air, a model that earned the nickname 'baby Cadillac'.
Of the three model years, 1957 is considered the ultimate classic, no model more so than the awesome V8 Ramjet with fuel-injected 4.7 litre engine. In American, that's 283cu in, and with a power output of 283bhp to match, Chevrolet claimed it was the first production engine to offer the magic one horsepower per cubic inch.

CHEVROLET Model	ENGINE cc/cyl	DATES	CONDITION 1	2	3
H4/H490 K Series	2801/4	1914–29	£9,000	£5,000	£2,000
FA5	2699/4	1918	£8,000	£5,000	£2,000
D5	5792/8	1918–19	£10,000	£6,000	£3,000
FB50	3660/4	1919–21	£7,000	£4,000	£2,000
AA	2801/4	1928–32	£5,000	£3,000	£1,000
AB/C	3180/6	1929–36	£6,000	£4,000	£2,000
Master	3358/6	1934–37	£9,000	£5,000	£2,000
Master De Luxe	3548/6	1938–41	£9,000	£6,000	£4,000

1956 Chevrolet Corvette, 4342cc V8, finished in Venetian red with white side panels, red and cream interior, 71,500 miles from new, very good condition.
£17,000–19,000 BRIT

▶ **1960 Chevrolet Corvette,** V8, 4-speed manual gearbox, hard and soft tops, restored, excellent condition throughout.
£23,000–27,000 COR

1965 Chevrolet Corvette Sting Ray Roadster, 5.7 litres, manual gearbox, finished in Glen green with beige leather interior, knock-off wheels, hard and soft tops.
£16,000–18,000 COR

1970 Chevrolet Corvette Stingray Roadster, manual gearbox, hard and soft tops.
£14,000–16,500 COR

CHEVROLET Model	ENGINE cu in/cyl	DATES	CONDITION 1	2	3
Stylemaster	216/6	1942–48	£8,000	£4,000	£1,000
Fleetmaster	216/6	1942–48	£8,000	£4,000	£1,000
Fleetline	216/6	1942–51	£8,000	£5,000	£2,000
Styleline	216/6	1949–52	£8,000	£6,000	£2,000
Bel Air 4-door	235/6	1953–54	£6,000	£4,000	£3,000
Bel Air Sport Coupe	235/6	1953–54	£7,000	£4,500	£3,500
Bel Air Convertible	235/6	1953–54	£12,500	£9,500	£6,000
Bel Air 4-door	283/8	1955–57	£8,000	£4,000	£3,000
Bel Air Sport Coupe	283/8	1955–56	£11,000	£7,000	£4,000
Bel Air Convertible	283/8	1955–56	£16,000	£11,000	£7,000
Bel Air Sport Coupe	283/8	1957	£11,000	£7,500	£4,500
Bel Air Convertible	283/8	1957	£14,500+	£10,500+	£8,000
Impala Sport Sedan	235/6, 348/8	1958	£12,500	£9,000	£5,500
Impala Convertible	235/6, 348/8	1958	£14,500	£11,000	£7,500
Impala Sport Sedan	235/6, 348/8	1959	£8,000	£5,000	£4,000
Impala Convertible	235/6, 348/8	1959	£14,000	£10,000	£5,000
Corvette roadster	235/6	1953	£18,000+	£14,000	£10,000
Corvette roadster	235/6, 283/8	1954–57	£20,000+	£13,000	£9,000
Corvette roadster	283, 327/8	1958–62	£20,000+	£12,000	£9,000
Corvette Sting Ray	327, 427/8	1963–67	£15,500+	£12,000	£10,000
Corvette Stingray DHC	327, 427/8	1963–66	£22,000+	£15,000	£8,000
Corvette DHC	427/8	1967	£16,000+	£13,000	£10,000

Value will be affected by build options, rare coachbuilt options, high-performance engine specifications, etc.

1976 Chevrolet Corvette Stingray, 5.7 litre V8, automatic transmission, good condition.
£7,000–8,500 **COR**

1979 Chevrolet Corvette, 5.7 litre V8, automatic transmission, resprayed and retrimmed, lift-out glass roof panels, good condition throughout.
£9,000–11,000 **COR**

1989 Chevrolet Corvette, 6-speed gearbox, acrylic roof panels, air conditioning.
£12,000–14,000 **COR**

1991 Chevrolet Corvette, 5.7 litre V8, automatic transmission, leather interior, air conditioning.
£16,000–18,000 **COR**

Auction Prices

Miller's only includes cars declared sold. Our guide prices take into account the buyer's premium, VAT on the premium, and the extent of any published catalogue information relating to condition and provenance. To identify cars sold at auction, cross-refer the source codes at the ends of photo captions with the Key to Illustrations on page 330.

Chrysler

1961 Chrysler 300G Coupé, 6.7 litre V8, ram-induction intake pipes, 375bhp, push-button Torque-Flite automatic transmission, servo-assisted brakes, restored 1990, finished in white with ivory and black leather upholstery.
£10,000–12,000 BKS

The 300G, with its dramatic Virgil Exner styling incorporating slanted twin headlamps and soaring tailfins, was the last true flowering of the limited-production Chrysler 'letter' series.

Citroën

1932 Citroën Moteur Flottant enamel sign, rare, 28½in (72.5cm) diam.
£450–550 GIRA

1950 Citroën 11BL, 1910cc, 4 cylinder in-line engine, 46bhp at 3,800rpm, 3-speed gearbox, independent front suspension, hydraulic drum brakes, 120km/h top speed.
£2,000–3,000 Pou

◀ **1955 Citroën 11B Normale,** 1911cc, new master cylinder, good mechanical condition, bodywork fair.
£1,750–2,500 BRIT

Undoubtedly one of the most successful automotive designs of all time, the Traction Avant Citroën was introduced in 1934. It set new standards with its excellent handling and exceptionally roomy interior. So successful was the design that it remained in production until 1957, two years after Citroën launched the DS19.

CITROËN Model	ENGINE cc/cyl	DATES	CONDITION 1	2	3
A	1300/4	1919	£4,000	£2,000	£1,000
5CV	856/4	1922–26	£7,000	£4,000	£2,000
11	1453/4	1922–28	£4,000	£2,000	£1,000
12/24	1538/4	1927–29	£5,000	£3,000	£1,000
2½ Litre	2442/6	1929–31	£5,000	£3,000	£1,500
13/30	1628/4	1929–31	£5,000	£3,000	£1,000
Big 12	1767/4	1932–35	£7,000	£5,000	£2,000
Twenty	2650/6	1932–35	£10,000	£5,000	£3,000
Ten CV	1452/4	1933–34	£5,000	£3,000	£1,000
Ten CV	1495/4	1935–36	£6,000	£3,000	£1,000
11B/Light 15/Big 15/7CV	1911/4	1934–57	£9,000	£5,000	£2,000
Twelve	1628/4	1936–39	£5,000	£3,000	£1,000
F	1766/4	1937–38	£4,000	£2,000	£1,000
15/6 and Big Six	2866/6	1938–56	£7,000	£4,000	£2,000

CITROËN Model	ENGINE cc/cyl	DATES	CONDITION 1	2	3
2CV	375/2	1948–54	£1,000	£500	£250
2CV/Dyane/Bijou	425/2	1954–82	£1,000	£800	£500
DS19/ID19	1911/4	1955–69	£5,000	£3,000	£800
Sahara	900/4	1958–67	£5,000	£4,000	£3,000
2CV6	602/2	1963 on	£750	£500	£250
DS Safari	1985/4	1968–75	£6,000	£3,000	£1,000
DS21	1985/4	1969–75	£6,000	£3,000	£1,000
DS23	2347/4	1972–75	£6,000	£4,000	£1,500
SM	2670/ 2974/6	1970–75	£9,000	£6,000	£4,500

Imported (USA) SM models will be 15 per cent less.

◄ **1971 Citroën DS21 Berline,** five-seater coachwork by Chapron, 2175cc, 4 cylinders, electronic fuel injection, 139bhp at 5,250rpm, 5-speed gearbox, servo-assisted disc brakes, hydro-pneumatic suspension, left-hand drive, finished in black, good condition.
£11,000–13,000 Pou

Miller's Starter Marque

Citroën: *2CV, 1948–91*

- In 1935, Citroën managing director Pierre-Joules Boulanger visited the French market town where he was born, returning to Paris with an attack of conscience and a great idea. He decreed, 'Design me a car to carry two people and 50 kilos of potatoes at 60km/h, using no more than 3 litres of fuel per 100km. It must be capable of running on the worst roads, of being driven by a débutante and must be totally comfortable.' The project *Toute Petite Voiture* also had to be like 'a settee under an umbrella,' and capable of 'crossing a field carrying a basket of eggs without breaking any.' From its launch in 1948 to the end of production in 1991, over seven million examples of the 2CV and its derivatives have hit the road.
- It's an undeniable classic, yet a frugal utility vehicle at the same time; fun too. The fabric roofs rolls right back like a sardine can, and you can take the seats out for a family picnic. All the body panels unbolt. In fact, the main bodyshell is only held in place by 16 bolts. That means it's easy to repair rust or crash-damaged panels, but it also means that fresh panels can hide serious rot on the old-style separate chassis.
- Inspect sills – especially at the base of the B-posts – front floorpan, chassis members and chassis rails running to the rear of the car. Wide gaps around the triangular body section in front of the doors are indicators of chassis trouble.
- In most cases, you'll be looking at a car with the 602cc engine, and this needs an oil change at every 3,000 miles or so. Neglect here will be revealed by big-end knocking.
- There are two types of gearbox: one for drum-braked cars up to 1982, the other for later disc-braked models. The former is very robust, and only if it sounds like a lorry will there be any trouble with the bearings. The disc box is a little more fragile, with a tendency to unwind the second-gear selector ring – and that may mean a new unit. Again, listen for excessive noise.
- Brakes are usually trouble-free, but on disc-braked cars, open up the reservoir to see if its filled with the correct Citroën LHM clear green fluid. If not, the master cylinder rubbers will soon go, and that's £300–400 to rectify.
- Parts and spares are plentiful, supply being aided by a number of 2CV specialists and a healthy club network.

1975 Citroën DS23 Safari Estate, 1985cc, semi-automatic transmission, self-levelling hydro-pneumatic suspension, power-operated brakes, clutch and steering, finished in maroon, retrimmed in grey velour, excellent condition.
£3,750–4,500 BKS

Daimler

Although part of Jaguar since 1960, Daimler has the distinction of being the oldest surviving British marque. Formally established in 1896, the company derived its name from the acquisition, in 1890, of UK patents and rights to Gottleib Daimler's pioneering petrol engines. The first British Daimler motor car appeared in March 1897, and through the company's early decades, Daimler's bespoke luxury motor basked in the reflected glory of royal patronage.

After WWII, Daimler began to lose direction in a changing world, and the failure of the dramatic fibreglass-bodied SP250 sports car to earn vital US dollars propelled it into Jaguar's hands. In the 1960s, Daimler and Jaguar products converged, and in today's market, the Daimler variants can often be significantly cheaper than their Jaguar counterparts. Instead of a Mk II Jaguar, you might consider a Daimler 250 V8 saloon, or a Daimler Sovereign as an alternative to a Jaguar 420. The last distinct true Daimler model was the DS420 limousine (1968–92), but Daimler's fluted radiator surround still stands out as a badge of distinction, carried by the luxury flagship of the Jaguar marque.

1912 Daimler Open-Drive Landaulette, 2.6 litre, 4 cylinder sleeve-valve engine, 3-speed gearbox, shaft drive, beaded-edge wire wheels, Lucas acetylene headlamps, oil sidelamps and carriage lamps, finished in black, original.
£19,500–22,000 BKS

This particular car once belonged to the Sultan of Trengganu in Malaysia.

1951 Daimler Limousine, 4095cc, Lucas P100 headlamps, original condition.
£5,000–5,500 PC

1951 Daimler Special Sports 2.5 Drophead Coupé, coachwork by Barker, 2522cc, 6 cylinders, 4-speed manual pre-select gearbox, restored 1995, resprayed in maroon and grey, new grey leather interior, excellent condition.
£12,000–14,000 H&H

1957 Daimler Conquest, 2433cc, finished in dark blue with grey leather interior, mechanics in very good condition.
£2,000–2,500 BRIT

The Conquest was introduced in 1953 to replace the Consort and was powered by a 2.5 litre engine mated to the Daimler pre-selector transmission with a fluid flywheel.

DAIMLER Model	ENGINE cc/cyl	DATES	CONDITION 1	2	3
Veteran (Coventry built)	var/4	1897–1904	£75,000	£60,000	£30,000
Veteran	var/4	1905–19	£35,000	£25,000	£15,000
30hp	4962/6	1919–25	£40,000	£25,000	£18,000
45hp	7413/6	1919–25	£45,000+	£30,000	£20,000
Double Six 50	7136/12	1927–34	£40,000	£30,000	£20,000
20	2687/6	1934–35	£18,000	£14,000	£12,000
Straight 8	3421/8	1936–38	£20,000	£15,000	£12,000
Value is dependent on body style, coachbuilder and condition of the sleeve-valve engine.					

DAIMLER DATES

1896	On January 14, the Daimler Motor Company Ltd is registered as a company.
1897	On October 2, a Daimler sets off from John O'Groats to Land's End, successfully completing the 929 miles at an average speed of just under 10mph.
1900	The Prince of Wales takes delivery of a 6hp Daimler to begin half a century of royal patronage.
1901	Shaft-drive introduced on Daimlers; early cars had been chain-driven.
1904	Daimler fluted radiator surround appears for the first time.
1910	Birmingham Small Arms (BSA) buys Daimler.
1921	3.3 litre TT420 is the last four-cylinder Daimler. In 1922, it is replaced by a 3 litre six.
1923	Daimler's first use of four-wheel brakes.
1926	The 7.1 litre Double Six becomes Britain's first production V12 engine.
1939–45	As part of the war effort, Daimler builds nearly 10,000 Dingo scout cars and armoured cars.
1960	BSA sells Daimler to Jaguar on June 18 for £3,400,000.
1962	Daimler 250 V8 saloon is the final appearance of a powerplant unique to Daimler. This Mk II Jaguar look-alike lasted until 1969. Thereafter, all Daimler's were powered by Jaguar engines.
1966	New Daimler Sovereign is based on Jaguar 420.
1968	Daimler's last pre-Jaguar shapes, the Majestic Major and DR450 limousine, are phased out.
1968	Daimler's DS420 Limousine introduced.
1972	Daimler Double Six name revived for the first time since the 1930s. This time, Double Six refers to Jaguar 5.3 litre V12.
1992	After a production run of nearly 5,000, the Daimler DS420 Limousine bows out.
1996	Limited production run of 200 Daimler Centuries to commemorate 100 years of the oldest British marque.

1961 Daimler Dart SP250, 2548cc V8, 4-speed manual gearbox, stainless steel exhaust, rebuilt front suspension, bodywork craze-free, finished in white with red interior, rim and upholstery, 87,000 miles from new, history file.
£10,500–13,000 H&H

1965 Daimler V8 250, automatic transmission, wire wheels, finished in Opalescent silver-grey with red leather interior, fair condition, some body damage.
£1,800–2,200 CGC

1968 Daimler Sovereign 420, 4235cc, 6 cylinder Jaguar engine, 3-speed automatic transmission, complete mechanical overhaul late 1980s, resprayed in Willow green, matching green interior.
£7,000–8,000 H&H

1965 Daimler 2.5 V8 Saloon, finished in metallic grey with red interior, good condition.
£3,750–4,750 BRIT

Built 1962–69, the 2.5 V8 utilised the excellent engine from the SP250 sports car, albeit with a redesigned sump to clear the Jaguar suspension. The model was a great success, later examples receiving the title V8 250 and being distinguished by revised slimline bumpers.

1968 Daimler V8 250, 2548cc V8, finished in Golden Sand with red interior, brightwork in good condition, original.
£5,000–6,000 BRIT

1968 Daimler Sovereign 420, 4235cc, 6 cylinders, 235bhp at 5,500rpm, automatic transmission, servo-assisted disc brakes, left-hand drive, Sable metallic with black roof.
£5,000–7,000 Pou

DAIMLER Model	ENGINE cc/cyl	DATES	CONDITION 1	2	3
DB18	2522/6	1946–49	£6,000	£3,000	£1,000
DB18 Conv S/S	2522/6	1948–53	£14,000	£7,000	£2,000
Consort	2522/6	1949–53	£5,000	£3,000	£1,000
Conquest/Con.Century	2433/6	1953–58	£4,000	£2,000	£1,000
Conquest Roadster	2433/6	1953–56	£12,000	£7,000	£4,000
Majestic 3.8	3794/6	1958–62	£5,000	£2,000	£1,000
SP250	2547/8	1959–64	£12,000	£10,000	£4,500
Majestic Major	4561/8	1961–64	£6,000	£4,000	£1,000
2.5 V8	2547/8	1962–67	£8,000	£5,250	£2,500
V8 250	2547/8	1968–69	£8,000	£4,000	£2,000
Sovereign 420	4235/6	1966–69	£6,500	£3,500	£1,500

1969 Daimler Sovereign 420, 4235cc, 6 cylinders, mechanical components in good condition, new exhaust system, finished in dark blue, original dark blue leather interior, 36,600 miles from new.
£8,000–9,000 BRIT

1974 Daimler Double Six Vanden Plas, 5343cc V12, finished in Silver Sand, black vinyl covered roof, rust-proofed from new, good mechanical condition, air conditioning and front electric windows in need of attention.
£2,250–2,750 BRIT

1976 Daimler 4.2 Litre Saloon, restored, excellent condition throughout.
£4,500–5,500 WILM

Dealer Prices

Miller's guide prices for dealer cars take into account the value of any guarantees or warranties that may be included in the purchase. Dealers must also observe additional statutory consumer regulations that do not apply to private sellers. This is factored into our dealer guide prices. To identify dealer cars, cross-refer the source codes at the ends of photo captions with the Key to Illustrations on page 330.

1987 Daimler Double Six Series III, finished in maroon with beige interior, air conditioning, very good condition throughout.
£2,000–2,500 BKS

Outwardly distinguishable from the Jaguar XJ6 only by its fluted radiator surround and different badging, the Daimler Sovereign was, in effect, a top-of-the-range model with a high specification. In 1972, V12-engined versions appeared, the Double Six name evoking memories of a great car from Daimler's past.

◄ **1979 Daimler DS420 Limousine,** good condition throughout.
£4,500–5,500 BLE

Datsun

This company's origins as a car maker date back to 1912, long before the Datsun name became known in world markets. In that year, the Kwaishinsha Motor Works produced its very first prototype. The first production model emerged around 1914 and was known as the DAT 31, taking its name from the initials of the company founders. A later model was named Datson – literally son of DAT – but the name was changed to Datsun in 1932 to make reference to Japan's national symbol. At the time, the company was building a range of models based on the British Austin 7. In 1937, the company changed its name to Nissan Motor Company, although the Datsun name continued to be used in export markets until the 1980s.

◄ **1982 Datsun Leopard Four-Door Saloon,** 2753cc, fuel-injection, 125bhp, automatic transmission, self-levelling rear suspension, power steering, restored 1991, finished in silver with black vinyl roof, red leather interior, rear-view mirrors equipped with wipers.
£1,000–1,500 BKS

In 1980, Datsun introduced the Leopard, a top-of-the-range luxury saloon with a choice of engines: a 1770cc 4 cylinder in-line; a 2753cc, overhead-camshaft straight-6; and a 2960cc turbocharged V6. Aimed at the young executive, it was not generally available in the UK.

De Dion Bouton

1904 De Dion Bouton 8hp Rear-Entrance Tonneau, radiator rebuilt, rewired, finished in red with black and gold lining, Lucas King's Own brass sidelamps, double-twist and Pompe horns, deep-buttoned red upholstery, good condition.
£30,000–35,000 BKS

The names De Dion and Bouton are linked inextricably with the pioneering days of the motor car. From 1895, their company was known for high-speed internal-combustion engines. Engineer Bouton's engines developed a significantly greater output than their contemporaries from Daimler and Benz, yet matched them for reliability. Small wonder that they were adopted by many other manufacturers.

c1906 De Dion Bouton 6hp Two-Seater, older restoration in need of cosmetic attention, Ducellier oil sidelamps, single centre-mounted acetylene headlamp, finished in yellow with deep-buttoned brown upholstery, original, in need of recommissioning.
£11,500–13,000 BKS

The 6hp De Dion Bouton performed almost as well as the 8hp model, although it lacked the latter's 'grunt' on steeper hills. Nevertheless, it proved extremely reliable, and later models were offered with a choice of 2- or 3-speed gearboxes.

Delage

◄ **1930 Delage DM Four-Seater Sports Tourer,** Vanden Plas-style coachwork by Tony Robinson, 3180cc, 6 cylinders, restored, *Les Hommes Gentils* two-tone 'town and country' horn, Marchal headlamps, Le Nivex barometric fuel gauge.
£27,000–30,000 BKS

The DM was born out of an uncompromising specification set by Louis Delage himself: 'I want a car virtually as luxurious as the GL... I want an absolutely pure line, I want absolute silence and I want an oil-tight sump...' This car started life as a Weymann-bodied saloon and was one of the last DM chassis built.

Delahaye

◀ **1939 Delahaye 135 MS Drophead Coupé,** coachwork by Mayfair, restored, original, very good condition.
£28,000–33,000 BKS

Launched at the 1938 Paris Salon, the Delahaye 135 MS *Modifiee Speciale* was the top-of-the-range model following discontinuation of the limited-production, short-wheelbase 135 Competition. Although its 3557cc engine had similar dimensions to the preceding model, it was a new unit with a larger head and cylinder block, bigger valves, 14mm spark plugs instead of 18mm, three inlet tracts and six exhaust ports. The power output was 125–130bhp.

DeLorean

There's more than a touch of irony in the fact that the 1985 movie *Back to the Future* featured a DeLorean in the fantasy time-trip back to 1955. For not only was the ill-fated DeLorean DMC 12 old before its time, but also it ranks with the Ford Edsel as one of the auto industry's greatest failures. John Zachary DeLorean launched his venture in 1974 with a formidable track record. In the 1960s, he'd fathered the muscle car movement with the Pontiac GTO and, before setting up on his own, had risen to the rank of Vice President of General Motors. By 1982, his reputation was in tatters; the company he'd founded was caught in a tangled web of legal wrangles; and the short flight of his gullwinged sports car was over. With styling by Giorgetto Giugiaro's Ital Design, chassis and manufacturing development by Lotus, a unique brushed stainless

steel body and fancy gullwing doors, the DeLorean was intended as a glimpse of the future. But with a complex series of capital-raising exercises that eventually saw the company settle in Northern Ireland, production only finally got under way early in 1981. By then, the design was outdated, and those who did buy DeLoreans found a litany of quality control problems – doors that wouldn't always open, windows that fell out, electrical failures, knobs that fell off, and a body that was well-nigh impossible to keep clean. Performance was also disappointing. Like the Edsel before it, the DeLorean bombed against wildly optimistic sales forecasts, and DeLorean Motor Cars foundered in a mire of court cases. Yet today, there is a small cult of DeLorean devotees, who find the fascinating story behind the car almost worth the frustration of owning one.

DeLorean DMC 12 (1981–82)

Construction: Y-shaped backbone chassis, fibreglass body with brushed stainless steel outer skin.
Engine: Overhead-camshaft V6, 2849cc.
Power output: 130bhp at 5,500rpm.
Transmission: Five-speed manual gearbox or three-speed automatic.
Maximum speed: 130mph claimed.
0–60mph: 8.5 seconds claimed.
Production: 8,800

1982 DeLorean DMC-12, 2849cc, fuel-injected V6, 5-speed gearbox, independent suspension and disc brakes all-round, one of only 12 right-hand drive models made, excellent condition.
£15,000–17,000 COYS

Designed by Giugiaro, the DMC-12 had gullwing doors and a brushed stainless steel finish. Originally, it was to have had a chassis made from a lightweight composite material known as ERM. However, this was dropped and the chassis constructed by a patented Lotus vacuum moulding process.

De Tomaso

◄ **1970 De Tomaso Mangusta,** coachwork by Ghia, 4.7 litre Ford V8, 306bhp, 5-speed ZF gearbox, 4-wheel disc brakes, backbone chassis, finished in yellow with black interior, restored 1990, 48,500km from new, excellent condition.
£21,000–24,000 BKS

Alejandro de Tomaso competed successfully in a variety of motor races before deciding to create his own marque. From 1960, he built single-seaters, and several prototype road cars. One of these, the Vallelunga, aroused the interest of major manufacturers and led to a relationship with Ford, which sold de Tomaso cars through its agencies in the USA. The Mangusta was one of the first mid-engined supercars, only 400 examples being made between 1967 and 1971.

Dodge

1915 Dodge Brothers Model 30–35 Five-Passenger Tourer, electric lighting, opening windscreen, varnished wooden wheels, finished in black, deep-buttoned black upholstery, left-hand drive, unused for some time, in need of recommissioning.
£7,000–8,000 BKS

The first Dodge Brothers car left the production line in November 1914, and the formula was right from the start. Powered by a 3474cc, 35hp side-valve engine, driving through a 3-speed gearbox, the Dodge was distinctive in having an all-steel welded body and 12 volt electrics.

1955 Dodge Kingsway Convertible, finished in red with white interior, restored, very good condition throughout.
£8,750–10,000 BKS

At the beginning of the 1950s, Dodge had a stodgy image, but by the time the Kingsway appeared, the marque had been transformed through its successes in NASCAR racing. The secret was Chrysler's hemi-head V8. By 1955, Dodge cars displayed sharp styling thanks to the legendary Virgil Exner. With 175+bhp and levels of equipment found only on the most exclusive European cars, Dodges of the period were exceptional.

Duesenberg

Duesenberg's legendary, almost mythic, reputation is out of all proportion to the small number of cars built and the company's brief spell as a car manufacturer, a little over 1,000 passenger cars being produced between 1920 and 1937. Fred and August Duesenberg first made a name for themselves by building racing cars and – with the onset of WWI – producing aero engines. The first passenger car, the Model A – announced in 1920 and available in 1922 – was received favourably, but the car for which Duesenberg will forever be remembered is the immortal Model J and its variants. Exquisite, extremely expensive and tremendously rapid, these motor cars were favoured by the rich and famous, among them the film stars Clark Gable and Gary Cooper. Although car production ceased in 1937, such was – and remains – the reputation of Duesenberg that the phrase 'It's a Duesy' remains an American colloquial expression for anything superlative.

◄ **1930 Duesenberg Type J,** coachwork by Derham, 6882cc, 8 cylinder in-line engine, excellent condition.
£400,000+ BLK

Restored Values

The cost of a professional restoration will have an influence on, but no direct relation to, a car's market value. A restored car can have a market value lower than the cost of its restoration.

1929 Duesenberg Berline, coachwork by J. Bohman & Schwartz, restored, finished in gold, concours winner.
£400,000+ **BLK**

1926/33 Duesenberg Model A Boat-Tailed Speedster, overhead-camshaft, 8 cylinder in-line engine, new chromed wire wheels, Woodlite headlamps and sidelamps, 1934 Oldsmobile rear lamps, twin-faceted reversing light, cowl-mounted auxiliary control panel, body restored, bare-metal respray in white and grey, upholstered in scarlet hide.
£47,000–52,000 **BKS**

This amazing speedster, on a shortened Duesenberg Model A chassis, was built during 1933–34 in the Los Angeles bodyshop of Bud Lyons.

1931 Duesenberg Roadster, coachwork by J. Murphy, rare disappearing-top model, restored, excellent condition.
£600,000+ **BLK**

1932 Duesenberg Convertible Coupé, coachwork by J. Murphy, finished in red, excellent condition.
£500,000+ BLK

Excalibur

◀ **1973 Excalibur Two-Door Phaeton,** 5001cc V8, 3-speed automatic transmission, tubular chassis, independent front suspension, servo-assisted 4-wheel disc brakes, chromed wire wheels, finished in white with beige interior.
£9,750–11,000 Pou

Facel Vega

Haute 'car-ture' never came much higher than Facel Vegas. These boulevard supercars were once the height of fashion, owned and driven by the rich and famous, like Tony Curtis, Joan Fontaine, Ava Gardner, Ringo Starr, Danny Kay, Stirling Moss and Pablo Picasso. But fashion fades and so did Facel, its ten-year flirtation with car making finally crippling the company in 1964. What remains is a legacy of a little over 2,000 cars, which stand as a fascinating footnote in the history of luxury motoring.

Facel was the first car maker to blend American V8 power with European chassis engineering and styling. In 1954, the first Facel Vega, the FVS, emerged. It was a beautiful Chrysler V8-powered, two-door grand tourer. But grander things were to come in 1958 with the aptly named Excellence, a 17ft, four-door pillarless saloon. It was an exquisite beast with a thumping great 6.3 litre V8 and interior appointments to rival the finest French château. Next was the HK500 two-door coupé, but the favourite and most expensive Facel is the Facel II, a revised HK500 with proper brakes to halt that thunderous 390bhp V8. There are small Facels, too: the Facellia with Facel's own unreliable engine, and its successor, the Facel III, powered by Volvo's rugged and reliable engine from the P1800. In the late 1980s, the big Facel Vegas came back into fashion strongly as values soared and encouraged many a costly restoration. In today's market, many such cars are available for considerably less than the cost of their restoration.

◀ **1960 Facel Vega HK500,** 6286cc V8, automatic transmission, body restored 1990/93 at a cost of £32,000, finished in metallic blue, grey leather interior.
£17,000–20,000 BRIT

The Facel Vega HK500 was virtually unsurpassed in terms of elegance. Its styling was complemented by a formidable technical specification, which included a 6.2 litre Chrysler V8 engine and a choice of 3-speed automatic transmission or 4-speed manual gearbox. Disc brakes were fitted all round on later models, and equipment levels were lavish.

Ferrari

Enzo Ferrari had been involved in racing long before any road car carried his name. Born in 1898, he was driving by his early teens and went on to race Alfa Romeos with considerable success during the 1920s. In 1929, he set up Scuderia Ferrari, which became, in effect, the Alfa Romeo factory team. The decisive moment in Enzo's career came in 1938, when Alfa took back control of its racing activities. In 1940, Ferrari built a Fiat-based racer of his own; although it did not bear his name, there is no doubt that it was the first Ferrari car. In late 1946, he began work on a series of road racers, this time bearing his name, which led to the first true Ferrari production road car, the 166 of 1948. Like the road racers on which it was based, the 166 employed a V12 engine, a feature that would become a hallmark of the make.

Throughout the 1950s and into the 1960s, Ferrari road cars were essentially handmade and dressed with beautiful bodies by the finest Italian stylists. In 1969, Fiat took a 50 per cent interest in the company, and the range broadened throughout the 1970s with a corresponding increase in volume, production approaching 3,000 cars a year by 1980. When Enzo Ferrari died, in 1988, Fiat took complete control, but to this day, cars bearing the marque of the Prancing Horse still set pulses racing, even when they're sitting at the kerb.

1952 Ferrari 340 America, coachwork by Vignale, 4.1 litre V12, 220bhp at 6,000rpm, 5-speed synchromesh gearbox, wishbone/transverse-leaf-spring front suspension, semi-elliptic leaf-sprung rear, restored, excellent condition. £200,000+ RM

1960 Ferrari 250 GT Coupé, coachwork by Pininfarina, engine, transmission and suspension rebuilt, rewired, bodywork restored, bare-metal respray in original Nero Tropicale, interior retrimmed in light tan leather, beige carpets, concours condition. £47,000–52,000 BKS

Launched in 1956, the 250 GT was progressively refined to make it a practical road car. It retained, however, the sporting heritage and broad outline of the sports racing cars from which it was derived.

1961 Ferrari 250 GT Cabriolet Series II, coachwork by Pininfarina, 3 litre V12, 240bhp, finished in red with black upholstery and hood, good condition throughout. £50,000–55,000 BKS

By 1961, Ferrari road cars were being built at a rate of nearly one a day. Thus, the 250 GT became the first volume production Ferrari. This particular car received distinctive modifications, presumably after delivery, the nose being similar to the later 330 GTC/S, while the tail treatment is reminiscent of the Princess de Rethy 330 GTC Speciale.

◄ 1961 Ferrari 250 GTE 2+2 Coupé, coachwork by Pininfarina, 4-wheel disc brakes, finished in Gunmetal grey, new beige leather upholstery, 137mph top speed, 37,000 miles from new, very good condition. £31,000–35,000 BKS

FERRARI Model	ENGINE cc/cyl	DATES	CONDITION 1	2	3
250 GTE	2953/12	1959–63	£32,000	£22,000	£20,000
250 GT SWB (steel)	2953/12	1959–62	£300,000	£185,000	-
250 GT Lusso	2953/12	1962–64	£85,000	£65,000	£50,000
250 GT 2+2	2953/12	1961–64	£32,000	£24,000	£18,000
275 GTB	3286/12	1964–66	£120,000	£80,000	£70,000
275 GTS	3286/12	1965–67	£90,000	£70,000	£50,000
275 GTB 4–cam	3286/12	1966–68	£170,000+	£150,000	£100,000
330 GT 2+2	3967/12	1964–67	£27,000+	£18,000	£11,000
330 GTC	3967/12	1966–68	£55,000	£40,000	£25,000
330 GTS	3967/12	1966–68	£80,000+	£70,000+	£60,000
365 GT 2+2	4390/12	1967–71	£30,000	£20,000	£15,000
365 GTC	4390/12	1967–70	£40,000	£35,000	£30,000
365 GTS	4390/12	1968–69	£150,000+	£90,000	£80,000
365 GTB (Daytona)	4390/12	1968–74	£70,000	£50,000	£40,000
365 GTC4	4390/12	1971–74	£45,000+	£38,000	£30,000
365 GT4 2+2/400 GT	4823/12	1972–79	£25,000	£20,000	£10,000
365 BB	4390/12	1974–76	£45,000	£35,000	£25,000
512 BB/BBi	4942/12	1976–81	£50,000+	£40,000	£28,000
246 GT Dino	2418/6	1969–74	£38,000	£30,000	£15,000
246 GTS Dino	2418/6	1972–74	£50,000	£32,000	£20,000
308 GT4 2+2	2926/8	1973–80	£15,000	£10,000	£8,000
308 GTB (fibreglass)	2926/8	1975–76	£25,000	£18,000	£12,000
308 GTB	2926/8	1977–81	£22,000	£16,000	£10,000
308 GTS	2926/8	1978–81	£22,000	£18,000	£11,000
308 GTBi/GTSi	2926/8	1981–82	£24,000	£17,000	£10,000
308 GTB/GTS QV	2926/6	1983–85	£21,500	£16,500	£9,500
400i manual	4823/12	1981–85	£12,000	£11,000	£10,000
400i auto	4823/12	1981–85	£12,000	£11,000	£8,000

1965 Ferrari 275 GTS Spyder, coachwork by Pininfarina, chassis no. 6889GT, engine no. 6889GT, finished in Giallo Fly with original burgundy leather interior, good condition.
£85,000–100,000 BKS

The pretty 275 GTS was introduced in 1964 as a replacement for the long-running Spyder California. Styled by Pininfarina, the new open-topped car featured the same 3.3 litre V12 engine as the contemporary 275 GTB, although the GTS was altogether a more refined car designed with regular use in mind. None the less, it was capable of 240km/h thanks to its 260bhp, and was blessed with good road manners courtesy of the latest independent suspension. Only 200 were built between 1964 and 1966.

◄ **1965 Ferrari 275 GTS Spyder,** coachwork by Pininfarina, 3.3 litre V12, 260bhp at 7,000rpm, 5-speed transaxle, independent rear suspension, multi-tubular chassis, restored 1993/94, finished in Rosso Corsa with black Connolly hide upholstery, 65,000km from new, very good condition throughout.
£75,000–80,000 BKS

Restored Values

The cost of a professional restoration will have an influence on, but no direct relation to, a car's market value. A restored car can have a market value lower than the cost of its restoration.

1966 Ferrari 275 GTB Berlinetta, coachwork by Pininfarina, 3.3 litre V12, 280bhp at 7,600rpm, 5-speed transaxle, independent rear suspension, multi-tubular chassis, restored, 3,000km covered since, finished in Giallo Fly, tan Connolly hide interior, new Borrani wire wheels, concours condition.
£100,000–120,000 BKS

1967 Ferrari 275 GTB/4, 20,000 miles from new, excellent condition.
£200,000+ HEND

1967 Ferrari 330 GT 2+2 Series II, 4 litre V12, 300bhp at 6,600rpm, 5-speed synchromesh gearbox, power steering, electric windows and hood, engine rebuilt, resprayed Rosso Chiaro 1996, new Connolly magnolia interior, all mechanical components in good condition.
£25,000–28,000 RM

1967 Ferrari 330 GTC Berlinetta, coachwork by Pininfarina, 3960cc V12, 5-speed transaxle, independent suspension all-round, 4-wheel disc brakes, centre-lock alloy wheels, 150mph top speed, engine, transmission and driveshafts overhauled, suspension rebuilt, finished in Midnight blue with black leather interior, good condition.
£43,000–48,000 COYS

Only about 600 examples of the 330 GTC were built before it was superseded by the larger-engined 365 GTC in 1968.

1968 Ferrari 275 GTB/4 Berlinetta, chassis no. 10711, 3.3 litre V12, 300bhp, 5-speed transaxle, independent rear suspension, 160mph top speed, body-off restoration 1997, finished in yellow, standard alloy wheels plus Borrani wire wheels, electric windows, 'as-new' condition.
£200,000+ BKS

1967 Ferrari 330 GTC Coupé, coachwork by Pininfarina, 4 litre V12, 300bhp, finished in black with black leather interior, 29,000km from new, unrestored, good condition.
£40,000–45,000 BKS

The 330 GTC shared its chassis with the 275 GTB, the first production Ferrari with all-independent suspension and the first to use a five-speed transaxle. Disc brakes were fitted all-round. From the 330 GT, it took the 4 litre version of Colombo's classic V12, which produced 300bhp. These ingredients were wrapped in an elegant two-seat coupé body by Pininfarina. The 330 GTC was probably the most sophisticated road car Ferrari had made at that stage, and is often referred to as the best all-round V12 Ferrari.

1968 Ferrari 365 GT 2+2, coachwork by Pininfarina, 4390cc V12, 320bhp at 6,600rpm, 5-speed gearbox, all-independent suspension, 4-wheel disc brakes, 240km/h top speed, finished in metallic grey, good condition.
£16,500–19,000 Pou

FERRARI 365 GTB/4 DAYTONA (1968–74)

Engine: Double-overhead-camshaft V12, six Weber carburettors, 4390cc.
Power output: 325bhp at 7,500rpm.
Transmission: Five-speed manual.
Brakes: Four-wheel discs.
Maximum speed: 174mph.
0–60mph: 5.4 seconds.
Production: 1,412 (including 165 in right-hand drive and 127 Spyders).

There's no doubt about it, the Ferrari Daytona is a beautiful dinosaur, for even at its debut in 1968, the tide of supercar design was shifting toward mid-engined machinery, yet with the 365 GTB/4, Ferrari persisted with the old, reliable front-engined layout. However, with its fearsome 4.4 litre V12 up front, pushing 325bhp through its fat rear tyres, the Daytona was the world's fastest production car. Its chisel-nosed, Pininfarina styling was also luxuriantly extravagant, without crossing the boundary into the dubious automotive netherworld of brutal machismo, chest wigs and medallions. Who cared if the Daytona guzzled fossil fuel at the rate of 14mpg – certainly not your average mature, super-rich Daytona driver with a hectic 'breakfast-in-Paris, dinner-in-Monte Carlo' social timetable. Of course, that was until the fuel crisis of October 1973. After that, the Daytona wasn't quite so *de rigueur* among diamond-studded jetsetters with gnawing social consciences, and one of the most beautiful Ferraris ever faded away in the following year. But the Daytona theme just won't lie down and die. Witness the 1994 launch of the Ferrari 456 – front-engined, V12, 5.4 litres, 13mpg in town...

Daytona data: Ferrari never officially called the car 'Daytona'. The name was adopted by the Press following Ferrari's outright victory in the 1967 24-hour Daytona race. Mel Blanc, creator of cartoon voices for Bugs Bunny, Daffy Duck and Porky Pig, owned two Ferrari Daytona Spyders, one of which sold at auction recently for £304,000.

1970 Ferrari 365 GTB/4 Daytona Berlinetta, coachwork by Pininfarina, chassis no. 12853, engine no. 251, 4390cc V12, 5-speed transaxle, tubular chassis, restored by Ferrari, finished in Rosso Corsa with black leather interior, 'as new' condition throughout.
£75,000–85,000 COYS

A natural development of the earlier 275 GTB/4, the larger-engined 365 GTB/4 was commonly known as the Daytona after Ferrari's 1-2-3 victory in the 24-hour race of 1967. The aggressive shape, styled by Pininfarina, and the uncompromising mechanical specification ensured its success in the demanding sports car market. This particular example is a very early car, featuring the striking wrap-around Perspex nose band that encloses the headlamps and indicators. This design quirk was deleted on later cars, as it did not comply with US headlamp height requirements.

1970 Ferrari 365 GTB/4 Daytona Competition Berlinetta, coachwork by Pininfarina, chassis no. 13213, engine no. 13213, 4390cc V12, dry-sump lubrication, 5-speed transaxle, all-independent wishbone/coil-spring suspension, twin fuel tanks, race-prepared, Group 4-style bodywork with riveted aluminium bonnet, flared wings, front spoiler, Perspex headlamp covers, side exhausts, finished in Rosso Corsa with tricolour bonnet stripe, bucket seats trimmed in Ferrari blue cloth, racing harnesses.
£75,000–85,000 BKS

1972 Ferrari 365 GTB/4, finished in red with black interior, centre-lock alloy wheels, very good condition.
£75,000–85,000 TALA

> A known continuous history can add value to and enhance the enjoyment of a car.

1973 Ferrari 365 GT4 2+2, chassis no. 17371, 4390cc V12, 5-speed manual gearbox, new clutch and exhaust, finished in silver with black leather trim, 55,000 miles from new, history file.
£8,500–11,000 H&H

1978 Ferrari 400 GT Coupé, coachwork by Pininfarina, body restored late 1980s, finished in metallic blue with light tan leather interior, 42,900km from new, full service history, excellent condition.
£12,000–14,000 BKS

Introduced in 1972 as the 365 GT4, this model remained in production until 1988, having the longest run of any Ferrari. It received many mechanical changes, but its classic lines were largely unaltered. Originally fitted with a 340bhp, quad-cam, 4.4 litre (later 4.8 litre) V12, the model received fuel-injection in 1979, which robbed it of 30bhp. Automatic transmission was a popular option. Although it was the world's most desirable four-seat car, with a top speed of almost 150mph, it did not sell in huge numbers because Ferrari refused to adapt its V12 to suit the American market.

▶ **1981 Ferrari 400i Coupé,** coachwork by Pininfarina, 4.8 litre V12, fuel-injection, automatic transmission, self-levelling rear suspension, power-assisted steering, electric windows, finished in Anthracite grey with beige leather interior, air conditioning, unrestored, good condition.
£8,500–10,000 BKS

1972 Ferrari 365 GTC/4, coachwork by Pininfarina, engine top-end overhauled, finished in Rosso Dino, original beige leather upholstery in very good condition.
£22,000–25,000 BKS

The Ferrari 365 GTC/4 was in production for only two years, but during that time, it accounted for half of Ferrari's output of front-engined cars. Contemporary buyers rated it highly, but only 500 were built, making it one of the most exclusive Ferraris of the last 30 years. With all-independent suspension, the 365 GTC/4 had a chassis that was almost identical to that of the Daytona, except that instead of a transaxle, a conventional 5-speed gearbox was mated directly to the 320bhp, 4.4 litre, quad-cam V12 engine. Top speed was comfortably in excess of 150mph.

1980 Ferrari 400i Coupé, finished in red with beige interior, 40,000 miles from new, good condition throughout.
£16,000–18,000 WCL

Affordable Ferraris

Affordable Ferraris may sound like a contradiction in terms, but it's not. However, if you really want a budget Ferrari, you must remember that ownership costs are among the highest. Most of them have 12 spark plugs for a start; and structural rust is no respecter of Italian pedigree. Moreover, you'll have to like the colour red – the choice of more than 70 per cent of Ferrari fanciers.

The beat-all budget Ferrari is the 308 GT4, produced from 1973 to 1979 with a 3 litre V8. The angular 2+2 styling, Bertone's first attempt for Ferrari, is nobody's favourite, but 255bhp and 155mph spell a lot of fun for not much money. In fact, two recently sold for less than £14,000 at auction, and no current price guide pitches them above £20,000. (For current market values please refer to our price table.)

Another to consider is the 308 GT4's successor, the much prettier and softer natured Mondial, produced from 1980 to 1985, along with the 365 GT4 2+2, made from 1972 to 1976, and the follow-on 400 and 412, which were produced in various guises into the early 1990s. In all cases, you get a glorious V12, of at least 4390cc, in a car the size of an XJ6 Jaguar, but which actually looks a lot smaller.

If you want to spend a little more on a 2+2 Ferrari, the models from the 1960s offer a lot more style. The 330 GT 2+2 (1964–67) and 365 GT 2+2 (1967–71) are exquisite Pininfarina grand tourers of flowing finesse and 150mph luxury. The 3967cc 330 GT 2+2 is a common car, by Ferrari standards, and consequently slightly cheaper than the 4390cc, 320bhp 265 GT 2+2.

Of course, the real downside of these 'budget' Ferraris is horrific fuel mileage, as bad or even worse than 12mpg in some cases. In today's market, however, that's another reason why they're so affordable.

FERRARI DINO 246 GT (1969–74)

Engine: Double-overhead-camshaft V6, 2418cc.
Power output: 195bhp at 7,600rpm.
Transmission: Five-speed manual.
Brakes: Four-wheel discs.
Top speed: 142–148mph.
0–60mph: 7.1 seconds.
Production: Dino 246 GT, 2,732; Dino 246 GTS (Spyder), 1,180.

In its day, the pretty little Dino was the cheapest Ferrari ever marketed, a budget supercar that was pitched directly at the Porsche 911. It rang changes in other ways, too, for in place of Ferrari's traditional V12 up front, the Dino had a V6 mounted transversely amidships. In fact, it seems that the Dino was intended as a cheaper 'companion' marque in its own right, as initially it was completely bare of Ferrari script and Prancing Horse insignia. Even so, despite a mere 2.4 litres, its near-150mph performance was very Ferrari-like, with brilliant handling to match. As for the Pininfarina shape, many rate it as one of the prettiest and purest of all Ferraris: lithe, lean and free of the steroid strakes and brutal Rambo garnish that have infected Ferraris since the 1980s.

1969 Ferrari Dino 246 GT Berlinetta, coachwork by Pininfarina, chassis no. 02556, 2418cc, double-overhead-camshaft V6, 195bhp, 5-speed transaxle, tubular chassis, wishbone independent suspension, knock-off alloy wheels, restored, new engine, excellent condition throughout.
£43,000–47,000 COYS

This classic Ferrari was named after Enzo Ferrari's son, Alfredino, who died in 1956, aged 24. Dino had acquired an engineering degree and had presented his arguments for a high-performance V6 engine. Enzo Ferrari commented, 'For reasons of mechanical efficiency he finally came to the conclusion that the engine should be a V6 and we accept his decision.' Thus was born the famous *Tipo* 156. Ferrari was determined to honour his son, and subsequently 'Dino' was the name given to a line of mid-engined V6 coupés, which went on sale in 1969.

1971 Ferrari Dino 246 GT Berlinetta, coachwork by Pininfarina, 2.4 litre, double-overhead-camshaft V6, 5-speed transaxle, restored, finished in Rosso Corsa with black leather upholstery, 46,000 km from new, good condition.
£28,000–32,000 BKS

1972 Ferrari Dino 246 GTS Spyder, coachwork by Pininfarina, 2.4 litre V6, 195bhp, 5-speed transaxle, near 150mph top speed, Targa top, finished in metallic silver with red leather interior, 66,000 miles from new original, good condition.
£31,000–35,000 BKS

1973 Ferrari 246 GTS Spyder, 2.4 litre V6, finished in red with black interior, good condition throughout.
£43,000–48,000 TALA

1973 Ferrari Dino 246 GTS Spyder, coachwork by Pininfarina, 2418cc V6, 5-speed transaxle, wishbone independent suspension, Targa top, £16,000 body restoration, engine rebuilt, very good condition.
£45,000–50,000 COYS

The definitive 246 Dino appeared in late 1969, and fewer than 4,000 were built (about 1,200 being the detachable-roof Spyder variant) before the slightly larger, and completely restyled, V8-engined 308 Dino appeared in 1973.

1975 Ferrari Dino 308 GT4, chassis no. 08900, engine no. 08900, 2926cc V8, mechanical components overhauled, new headlamps, bare metal respray in red, new black leather trim, approximately 66,000 miles from new.
£10,500–12,500 BRIT

Introduced in 1973, the 308 GT4 replaced the 246. Offering 2+2 seating, its body was styled and constructed by Bertone. The V8 power unit was also new, being mounted transversely behind the seats, while the wheelbase was increased by just over 8in. The 308 GT4 remained in production until 1980, when it was displaced by the Mondial.

1980 Ferrari 308 GTS, 2926cc V8, 43,000 miles from new, good condition.
£27,000–30,000 KHP

By Numbers

Most Ferrari model numbers represent the capacity of one engine cylinder. Thus, the Ferrari 365 GTB/4 was so called because the capacity of each of its 12 cylinders was approximately 365cc. Overall capacity was 4390cc. One obvious exception is the F40 of 1987, so named to celebrate 40 years of the famous Prancing Horse marque from Maranello.

1981 Ferrari 308 GTBi Berlinetta, coachwork by Pininfarina, 2926cc V8, fuel injection, 5-speed transaxle, tubular chassis, all-independent coil-spring/wishbone suspension, 4-wheel disc brakes, finished in Rosso Corsa, trimmed in black leather with matching carpets, air conditioning, electric windows, 71,000km from new.
£17,000–19,000 BKS

1983 Ferrari 308 GTB QV, 2926cc, restored, finished in navy blue, good condition.
£27,000–30,000 TALA

1981 Ferrari Mondial 8, 2927cc V8, Bosch K-Jetronic fuel injection, 214bhp, 5-speed gearbox, all-independent suspension, 4-wheel disc brakes, 220km/h top speed.
£11,500–14,000 Pou

1984 Ferrari Mondial QV Cabriolet, 30,303 miles from new, good condition.
£22,000–25,000 KHP

1984 Ferrari Mondial QV, 2926cc V8, fuel injection, good condition throughout.
£17,000–21,000 TALA

1988 Ferrari 328 GTS Spyder, left-hand drive, finished in Rosso Corsa with magnolia leather interior, 16,400km from new, very good condition throughout.
£37,000–42,000 BKS

Ferrari's line of successful V8-engined road cars began with the 308 GT4 of 1973. Its wedge-shaped styling – by Bertone rather than the customary Pininfarina – was not universally acclaimed, but the performance of its mid-mounted, double-overhead-camshaft, 3 litre V8 certainly was. Built on a shorter wheelbase, the beautiful 308 GTB of 1975 marked a return to Pininfarina styling. Further developments included a GTS version with Targa-style removable roof, the adoption of Bosch fuel injection, and cylinder heads with four valves per cylinder. The next stage of engine development was enlargement to 3.2 litres for the 328 GTB/GTS in 1986, maximum power rising to 270 bhp with a significant gain in torque.

1990 Ferrari 348 TS, 3.4 litres, 29,000 miles from new, full service history, good condition.
£43,000–47,000 PARA

1991 Ferrari 348 TS, coachwork by Pininfarina, 3.4 litres, left-hand drive, Targa top, finished in red with black interior 48,000km from new, very good condition.
£27,000–32,000 BKS

The 348 entered production in 1989, replacing the 328 GTB/GTS. Mid-engined like the latter, the 348 differed by mounting the 32-valve V8 engine longitudinally, allowing it to be placed lower in the chassis. Initially typed TS and TB – *transversale berlinetta* and *transversale spyder* – the 348 reverted to the traditional GTB/GTS nomenclature part way through production. with around 300bhp on tap and a top speed of 170mph, the 348 gave little away in terms of outright performance to its larger siblings. Production ceased in 1994 after 8,745 examples of all types had been built.

1985 Ferrari 288 GTO Berlinetta, coachwork by Pininfarina, twin IHI turbochargers, 400bhp, finished in Rosso Corsa with black leather upholstery, 20,000km from new, well maintained, excellent condition throughout.
£150,000–160,000 BKS

When unveiled in 1984, the 288 GTO was the fastest production car in the world. It was built primarily for Group B competition, but Group B was cancelled in 1986, although not before the requisite 200 GTOs had been built for homologation. Although it bore a resemblance to the 308 GTB, its engine was mounted longitudinally and well forward; indeed, the front four cylinders were actually ahead of the rear screen line. Ferrari claimed a top speed of 190mph and 0–62mph in under 5 seconds.

1985 Ferrari 288 GTO, chassis no. 55717, engine no. 167, 2855cc, double-overhead-camshaft V8, twin turbochargers, 400bhp at 7,000rpm, dry-sump lubrication, 5-speed transaxle, all-independent suspension, 4-wheel ventilated disc brakes, left-hand drive, 17,662km from new, tracker alarm system, good condition.
£140,000–150,000 C

1997 Ferrari 512BB, 4.9 litre flat-12 engine, 340bhp, dry-sump lubrication, one of 98 right-hand drive models built, 23,000 miles from new, excellent condition throughout.
£47,500–52,500 HEND

Cross Reference
See Colour Review

1977 Ferrari 512BB, coachwork by Pininfarina, chassis no. 20693, engine no. 20693, 4824cc flat-12, finished in Rosso Corsa with cream leather upholstery, little recent use.
£40,000–45,000 COYS

Losing sales to the mid-engined Maserati Bora and Lamborghini Miura, Ferrari developed a new mid-engined car, the Boxer, based on a 4.4 litre flat-12 derived from the company's F1 programme. The coachwork was a sleek and aggressive Berlinetta design. In 1976, a revised model, the 512BB, was introduced, with a 4.9 litre version of the original engine.

1981 Ferrari 512BB *Competizione*, race-prepared flat-12 engine, forged racing pistons, lightened and balanced con-rods, 420bhp, twin oil coolers, Group 4 exhaust system, lightened tubular steel chassis, uprated suspension and brakes, magnesium alloy wheels, twin side-mounted fuel tanks, aluminium and fibreglass body, finished in Rosso Corsa, Perspex windows, roll-cage, competition harness, 186+mph top speed, excellent condition.
£47,000–52,000 BKS

Although not a factory competition model, this car was prepared to a similar specification.

1985 Ferrari Testarossa, coachwork by Pininfarina, finished in red with cream leather interior, air conditioning, electrically adjustable seats, 13,000 miles from new, excellent condition, history file.
£41,000–45,000 BKS

A next-generation Berlinetta Boxer, the Testarossa was announced in 1984. It retained its predecessor's mid-mounted, 5 litre flat-12 engine, but fitted with four-valve cylinder heads to give 390bhp at 6,300rpm. Despite the power increase, smoothness and driveability were enhanced, the car possessing excellent top-gear flexibility allied to a maximum speed of 180mph. A larger car than the 512BB, the Testarossa managed to combine high downforce with a low coefficient of drag, its body being notable for the absence of extraneous spoilers and other devices.

1983 Ferrari 512BBi, 4824cc flat-12 engine, good condition.
£47,000–52,000 TALA

1986 Ferrari Testarossa, coachwork by Pininfarina, 4942cc flat-12, 4 valves per cylinder, dry-sump lubrication, 390bhp at 6,300rpm, 5-speed gearbox, 0–60mph in 5.4 seconds, tubular steel chassis, all-independent suspension, 4-wheel ventilated disc brakes, finished in Anthracite with grey leather interior, 22,000km from new, well maintained, concours condition.
£36,000–40,000 COYS

1986 Ferrari Testarossa, coachwork by Pininfarina, 5 litre flat-12, 4 valves per cylinder, Bosch fuel injection, 390bhp, 5-speed gearbox, finished in Rosso Corsa, black leather interior, 36,000km from new, excellent condition.
£32,000–36,000 BKS

Fiat

The name of Fiat may not be one that sets the pulse racing, but the company's significance goes far beyond the cars that carry its own name. Fiat controls Ferrari, Lancia and Alfa Romeo, and one can only speculate on the fate of these great names had Fiat not stepped in to take them over. As for the cars bearing the Fiat badge, there's no doubt that the company's contribution to motoring is on a global scale, with mass-market milestones including the brilliantly packaged Fiat 500 Nuova; the 600 Multipla, which served as an early blueprint for the modern people carrier; desirable mainstream sports cars like the 124 Spyder; and the occasional exotic, such as the beautiful Fiat Dino Spyder. Remarkably, the company, which was founded in 1899 by Giovanni Agnelli, is still in family control.

1937 Fiat Topolino, 570cc, 4 cylinder engine, 4-speed manual gearbox, finished in red with black wings, full roll-back sunroof, restored, very good condition.
£3,000–4,000 H&H

1954 Fiat 8V Coupé, coachwork by Vignale, 2 litre V8, restored, finished in red with beige interior, excellent condition.
£130,000–150,000 BLK

Fiat stunned the audience at the 1952 Geneva Motor Show with the company's first V8 engine in a new racing machine. Only 114 were built, and they were shipped to Italy's great coachbuilders: Zagato, Ghia and Vignale, the designer of this coupé. Those custom-built 8Vs are considered by many to be the best performing, and the most beautiful of post-war Fiats.

◀ **1962 Fiat Osca 1500S Coupé,** coachwork by Pininfarina, 1568cc Osca engine, Dunlop front disc brakes, left-hand drive, restored 1984/92, finished in red with tan leather upholstery, in need of recommissioning.
£5,000–7,000 BKS

In 1947, the three surviving Maserati brothers founded Osca, and their sports racing cars became very successful during the 1950s. Osca's superb alloy-block, double-overhead-camshaft engine was adopted by Fiat and put into production by former Ferrari designer Aurelio Lampredi. He restricted the power to 120bhp, but that still gave 105mph (0–60mph in 10.6 seconds) in a coupé with a very pretty body by Pininfarina.

FIAT Model	ENGINE cc/cyl	DATES	CONDITION 1	2	3
500B Topolino	569/4	1945–55	£5,000	£2,000	£750
500C	569/4	1948–54	£4,000	£1,700	£1,000
500 Nuova	479, 499/2	1957–75	£3,000	£1,500	£750
600/600D	633, 767/4	1955–70	£3,000	£2,000	£1,000
500F Giardiniera	479, 499/2	1957–75	£3,000	£1,500	£1,000
2300S	2280/6	1961–68	£3,000	£1,700	£1,000
850	843/4	1964–71	£1,000	£750	-
850 Coupé	843, 903/4	1965–73	£1,500	£1,000	-
850 Spyder	843, 903/4	1965–73	£3,000	£2,000	£1,000
128 Sport Coupé 3P	1116/4				
	1290/4	1971–78	£2,500	£1,800	£1,000
130 Coupé	3235/6	1971–77	£5,500	£4,000	£2,000
131 Mirafiori Sport	1995/4	1974–84	£1,500	£1,000	£500
124 Sport Coupé	1438/4				
	1608/4	1966–72	£3,000	£2,000	£1,000
124 Sport Spyder	1438/4				
	1608/4	1966–72	£5,500	£2,500	£1,500
Dino Coupé	1987/6				
	2418/6	1967–73	£8,000	£5,500	£2,500
Dino Spyder	1987/6				
	2418/6	1967–73	£10,000	£7,000	£5,000
X1/9	1290/4				
	1498/4	1972–89	£4,000	£2,000	£1,500

1967 Fiat 1100R Saloon, restored 1997, resprayed in white, very good condition.
£1,200–1,500 BARO

1968 Fiat Samantha Coupé, coachwork by Vignale, engine rebuilt, chassis restored, resprayed in red, interior retrimmed, electrics in need of attention, good general condition.
£1,000–1,500 CGC

Only 25 Samantha Coupés were produced.

1968 Fiat Dino Spyder, coachwork by Pininfarina, 2 litre V6, 160bhp, 5-speed gearbox, 4-wheel disc brakes, finished in red with black interior, good condition throughout.
£8,500–10,000 BKS

A longer-wheelbase coupé version of the Dino, with Bertone coachwork, appeared in 1967, and in 1969, the V6's capacity was increased to 2418cc, using the iron block from the Fiat 130. Maximum power went up to 180bhp, and there was a commensurate increase in torque.

1987 Fiat X1/9 Bertone, 13,000 miles from new, excellent condition throughout.
£4,500–5,000 Mot

Miller's Starter Marque

Starter Fiats: *Fiat 500, 1957 onwards; Fiat 600; Fiat X1/9; Fiat 124 Coupé and Spyder.*

- Four-wheeled fun doesn't come in a much smaller package than the Fiat 500 – 9ft 9in to be precise. But forget this baby Fiat if you want to hack down to the country for the weekends. In 1957, *The Motor* tested an early 479cc-engined 500 and could only eke out 53mph. Mind you, the fuel-consumption was a fantastic 55mpg.
- The best 500 to go for is the later and slightly peppier 499cc-engined car. In both cases, you'll be served by a crash gearbox, which means you'll have to double-declutch on the way down through the gears. The buzzing, high-revving, air-cooled twin-cylinder engine in the back of the car has a good reputation though, and if anything should go wrong, it can be removed in under an hour.
- These Fiats do fray, however. You'll want to prod any places on the underside and wheel arches where road muck can collect, particularly the structural steel member that runs across the car, beneath the front seats. The floors can rust from the inside and outside, too; also inspect the welded-on front wings and door bottoms.
- With over four million 500s having been made up to 1975, this baby Fiat has a strong network of parts suppliers and club support, making it a viable starter classic that's more distinctive – on British roads at least – than a Mini.
- If the 500's too tight a squeeze, you could always move up – by exactly a foot – to the slightly more commodious 600. It handles well and will even top 60mph. It doesn't have quite the cult following of the 500, and that means it's generally slightly cheaper, but harder to find.
- The Fiat X1/9 offers fresh air, fine handling and Italian flare in a pint-sized, affordable sporting package. Top speed is only just over 100mph, but it will get you there with sure-footed finesse. The X1/9's greatest feature is its mid-mounted engine, which provides optimum weight distribution for the kind of handling and adhesion normally associated with mega-money sports car thoroughbreds. In short, it's just about the only truly affordable and practical, volume produced, mid-engined sports car.
- Unfortunately, this little Fiat funster tends to reinforce the once-popular notion that when you buy an Italian car of this period, you pay for the engine and get the body thrown in free.
- The only thing that doesn't rust on the Fiat X1/9 is the detachable roof – and that's because it's made of plastic. The rule of thumb is to buy the very best you can afford, as body repairs could rapidly outstrip the value of this bargain-basement sports car. The electrics are also fragile, but the engine – either 1300 or 1500cc – is a little gem, being reliable and generally good for 100,000 miles or more.
- More substantial sporting Fiats are the 124 Coupé and Spyder. They've got the looks, performance and handling – and an invitingly modest price tag. Unfortunately, the 124 Spyder was never officially imported to Britain, which means that you are likely to be confronted by a left-hooker. But that's an advantage, too, as it may well have come from a rust-free area of the United States. For an MGB alternative with a touch of Italian flare, the 124 Spyder is definitely worth considering.

A known continuous history can add value to and enhance the enjoyment of a car.

FORD

FORD IN ENGLAND

In 1872, when young Henry Ford, the son of an Irish immigrant farmer, was only nine years old, he fell from a horse. As Ford folklore has it, that little mishap sparked his determination to develop a form of transport that was a little safer and more reliable than the four-legged kind.

After serving an apprenticeship to a machinist, his vision began to take shape in the winter of 1893, when he built an internal-combustion engine on the kitchen table of the Detroit home he shared with his wife, Clara, and new-born son, Edsel. In 1896, his first motorised vehicle took to the streets of Detroit. The Quadricycle was a lightweight buggy powered by a twin-cylinder, four-stroke engine producing all of 4hp. However, with no reverse gear and no brakes, any journey in the machine must have been an adventure.

Other vehicles followed, including racers, and on June 16, 1903, the Ford Motor Company was incorporated in Detroit. A month later, the first Ford Model A runabout was sold. Two of those early two-seaters came to Britain, and in 1904, the Central Motor Car Company was set up to sell Fords in London's Covent Garden.

With the launch of the Model T in 1908, sales began to take off in the UK, and in 1911, The Ford Motor Company (England) Limited was incorporated to handle sales. By October, Ford had set up its first overseas assembly plant in an old tram works at Trafford Park, Manchester.

From 1908 to 1927, over 16 million Model Ts were built, a record that was only overtaken in 1971 by the Volkswagen Beetle. In America, the rugged Model T mobilised the masses. It

was a hit in the UK, too, alongside rivals like the more costly Bullnose Morris, which appeared in 1913. In that year, Ford was producing over 7,000 'British' models a year, making it our number-one car producer. From then until the outbreak of WWII, Ford held a prominent position among the top six British car firms.

The Model T also pioneered mass production in the UK. Before WWI, Ford had already introduced Britain's first moving production line at Trafford Park, where 60 men could assemble 21 chassis an hour. But as Ford's UK sales increased, the company soon began to outgrow the old tram factory. In 1924, Ford paid £150,000 for 500 acres of low-lying, marshy land on the banks of the Thames near the village of Dagenham, and in May, 1929, Edsel Ford cut the first sod with a silver spade. The first Dagenham-produced car, a Model A truck, rolled off the production line in 1931.

The earliest cars produced at Dagenham were British in the sense that they were built here, using British-made components, but the first true British Ford was the Model Y 8hp of 1932. Not only was it built here, but it was also designed specifically to meet British and European motoring needs.

By 1934, the Model Y claimed 34 per cent of the British market for vehicles up to 8hp, but by 1935, that had fallen to 22 per cent. Ford hit back by announcing a £100 Popular version of the Model Y at the end of 1935. It was the first fully equipped saloon to be offered at such a low price and immediately put Ford back at the top of the sales charts. In fact, the humble Model Y established Dagenham as the largest Ford plant outside the USA.

Ford Milestones

1863	Henry Ford born on July 30 in Wayne County, Michigan.
1903	Ford incorporated in the USA; first two Ford cars in Britain were Model As imported from the USA.
1911	Ford Motor Company (England) Limited incorporated. Assembly plant set up at Trafford Park, Manchester.
1918	Ford produces its first British truck, a 1 ton vehicle.
1925	The 250,000th British Ford, a Model T, produced.
1929	Henry's son, Edsel, cuts the first sod on marshy Dagenham site.
1931	First vehicle produced at Dagenham, a 30cwt Model A truck.
1947	Henry Ford dies on April 7 after a brain haemorrhage.
1950	Transatlantic styling of the new Mk I Consul, Zephyr and Zodiac is a highlight of the 1950 London Motor Show.
1961	Parent company buys outstanding British Ford shares at a price of £119,595,645 12s.
1962	Cortina introduced.
1963	New plant at Halewood on Merseyside opens.
1966	Ford GT40 wins Le Mans; victory repeated for next three years.
1968	Escort launched.
1969	Capri introduced.
1971	Millionth Escort built, less than four years after launch.
1976	Millionth Transit built.
1981	Escort voted Car of the Year.
1982	Sierra replaces Cortina.
1987	Ford buys Aston Martin Lagonda.
1989	Ford acquires majority shareholding in Jaguar Cars.
1992	Ford regains position of UK best-seller with 121,140 Escort registrations.
1993	Mondeo launched as world car.

1909 Ford Model T Tourer, brass radiator, folding brass windscreen, finished in black with white coachlines, upholstered in deep-buttoned black leatherette, oil and acetylene lighting, acetylene generator, double-twist bulb horn.
£9,500–11,000 BKS

Henry Ford's Model T was introduced in 1908 and remained in production until 1927, by which time some 16 million had been built. It had a powerful and reliable 4 cylinder engine, and once mastered, the planetary gearbox – operated by two pedals and two levers – was simplicity itself. The Model T boasted a 45mph top speed and 25mpg fuel economy, with remarkably flexible top-gear performance.

1911 Ford Model T Tourer, 4 cylinder engine, 2-speed epicyclic gearbox, transverse-leaf-spring suspension, artillery wheels, acetylene generator and lamps, left-hand drive, restored, finished in black with black leather upholstery, very good condition.
£11,000–13,000 S

The Model T was imported to the UK from 1909, assembly beginning at Ford's Trafford Park factory in 1911. Over 20 styles of bodywork were available.

1914 Ford Model T Speedster, open two-seater bodywork, 2892cc, 4 cylinders, monocle screen, wire wheels.
£11,000–13,000 TUC

1914 Ford Model T 15hp Tourer, 4 cylinder engine, 3-speed manual gearbox, side-mounted spare wheel, restored, finished in black with black leather upholstery, matching hood, brasswork in good condition.
£10,000–12,000 H&H

Auction Prices

Miller's only includes cars declared sold. Our guide prices take into account the buyer's premium, VAT on the premium, and the extent of any published catalogue information relating to condition and provenance. To identify cars sold at auction, cross-refer the source codes at the ends of the photo captions with the Key to Illustrations on page 330.

◄ **1917 Ford Model T Tourer,** 2892cc, 4 cylinders, 2-speed epicyclic gearbox, finished in black with black upholstery, black hood, paraffin lights, artillery wheels, good condition.
£4,500–6,000 H&H

FORD Model	ENGINE cc/cyl	DATES	CONDITION 1	2	3
Model T	2892/4	1908–27	£12,000	£7,000	£4,000
Model A	3285/4	1928–32	£8,500	£6,000	£3,500
Models Y and 7Y	933/4	1932–40	£5,000	£3,000	£1,500
Model C, CX & 7W	1172/4	1934–40	£4,000	£2,000	£1,000
Model AB	3285/4	1933–34	£10,000	£8,000	£4,500
Model ABF	2043/4	1933–34	£9,000	£6,000	£4,000
Model V8	3622/8	1932–40	£8,500	£6,000	£4,500
Model V8–60	2227/8	1936–40	£7,000	£5,000	£2,000
Model AF (UK only)	2033/4	1928–32	£9,000	£6,000	£3,500

A right-hand-drive vehicle will always command more interest in the UK than a left-hand-drive model. Coachbuilt vehicles, and in particular tourers, achieve a premium at auction. Veteran cars (manufactured before 1919) will often achieve a 20 per cent premium.

1923 Ford Model T Centre-Door Saloon,
2892cc, 4 cylinders, left-hand drive, finished
in black, running, in need of restoration.
£6,000–7,000 TUC

1926 Ford Model T Camionette, 2892cc, 4 cylinders,
French coachbuilt body, finished in yellow with orange
wings, twin side-mounted spares, left-hand drive.
£7,000–8,000 TUC

1929 Ford Model A Tourer, 3285cc, 4 cylinders,
restored, finished in green with black wings, new black
hood, new tan leather interior, very good condition.
£8,500–10,000 H&H

1929 Ford Model A Roadster, dickey seat,
finished in yellow with black wings and top,
left-hand drive, restored, good condition.
£6,000–8,000 PALM

1930 Ford Model A Cabriolet, 4 cylinder, side-valve
engine, 3-speed manual gearbox, 4-wheel brakes,
dickey seat, left-hand drive, restored, finished in
yellow over blue, good condition throughout.
£6,000–7,000 S

**The Model A was launched in 1928 in a choice
of body styles: Tudor and Fordor Saloons,
Coupé, Phaeton, Roadster and Pick-up. Later,
a Cabriolet and Doctor's Coupé were added.
Its arrival monopolised the headlines of
all the city newspapers in America,
and it proved an instant success.**

1932 Ford Model B Fordor Saloon, restored,
finished in dark red with black wings, original black
leather seats, interior in need of reburbishment,
otherwise very good condition.
£4,500–6,000 S

**A sophisticated version of its forebear, the
Model A, the B used the 24hp, 4 cylinder engine
of the former in the V8's chassis.**

Ford at War

During WWII, Ford's
contribution to the war effort
included 360,000 military
vehicles and 34,000
Rolls-Royce Merlin engines,
which powered aircraft like the
Spitfire, Hurricane, Lancaster
and Mosquito.

1934 Ford V8 Cabriolet, 3621cc, side-valve V8, 85bhp at
3,800rpm, 3-speed manual gearbox, 4-wheel hydraulic drum
brakes, left-hand drive, finished in ivory with black hood.
£12,000–14,000 Pou

POST-WAR MODELS AND FIFTIES GLITZ

With the return to peacetime production after WWII, the first new model was the beefy, V8-powered Pilot, introduced in 1948. Today, devotees love its gutsy 3622cc side-valve V8, but its styling owed much to pre-war practices. In 1950, the new Consul and Zephyr shook off any pre-war trappings. They were thoroughly modern in looks with full-width, slab-sided styling. Under the skin, they were also up to the minute, being the first Fords to use an integral chassis-body construction. In addition, they featured advanced McPherson-strut independent front suspension, while the four- and six-cylinder engines had overhead valves for the first time.

These new Fords were elegant and even glamorous, being decorated with just enough chrome to give a little transatlantic dash. In 1954, the Zodiac topped the range with two-tone paint and whitewall tyres. In 1956, the Mk II models of the Consul, Zephyr and Zodiac appeared. They were bigger, bolder, brasher and dripped with chrome. To British eyes at least, they were American.

Lower down the range, the Prefect, Popular, Escort and Anglia models of the 1940s and 1950s provided dependable budget motoring for millions. If the British thought the big flashy saloons were a slice of American apple pie on wheels, the small, modest Fords were as British as Morris, Austin and roast beef.

They were generally conservative, too. In fact, the 'sit-up-and-beg' Popular 103G that finally ceased production in 1959 was not much more than a gentle blow-over of the 1932 model, yet it provided excellent basic transport. Even the more-modern looking small Fords of the period, the slab-sided Anglia and Prefect 100E, were still powered by stone-age side-valve engines.

1953 Ford Anglia Saloon, 993cc, 4 cylinder, side-valve engine, 3-speed manual gearbox, finished in Bristol fawn with beige and red interior, 64,500 miles from new, excellent condition.
£2,400–2,800 H&H

► **1953 Ford Prefect Four-Door Saloon**, 1172cc, side-valve engine, 3-speed gearbox, fewer than 67,000 miles from new, original in all major respects.
£1,500–2,000 BKS

1948 Ford Prefect Four-Door Saloon, 1172cc, 4 cylinders, stainless steel exhaust, restored, finished in black with brown leather and leatherette interior trim, concours winner, excellent condition.
£4,750–5,250 BRIT

Launched with a flourish in 1938, and billed as 'the Ten at the head of its class', the Prefect was the first Ford model to be given a name instead of a simple series letter. Its styling was very much in the modern idiom, with thrust-forward radiator grille and sloping rear panel.

┌─────────────────────────────┐
│ **Cross Reference** │
│ See Colour Review │
└─────────────────────────────┘

◄ **1955 Ford Zephyr 6 Mk I**, 2.2 litre, 6 cylinder, in-line engine, period accessories, restored.
£3,300–3,800 FORD

FORD (British built) Model	ENGINE cc/cyl	DATES	CONDITION 1	CONDITION 2	CONDITION 3
Anglia E494A	993/4	1948–53	£2,000	£850	£250
Prefect E93A	1172/4	1940–49	£3,500	£1,250	£900
Prefect E493A	1172/4	1948–53	£2,500	£1,000	£300
Popular 103E	1172/4	1953–59	£1,875	£825	£300
Anglia/Prefect 100E	1172/4	1953–59	£1,350	£625	£250
Prefect 107E	997/4	1959–62	£1,150	£600	£200
Escort/Squire 100E	1172/4	1955–61	£1,000	£850	£275
Popular 100E	1172/4	1959–62	£1,250	£600	£180
Anglia 105E	997/4	1959–67	£1,400	£500	£75
Anglia 123E	1198/4	1962–67	£1,550	£575	£150
V8 Pilot	3622/8	1947–51	£7,500	£5,000	£1,500
Consul Mk I	1508/4	1951–56	£2,250	£950	£400
Consul Mk I DHC	1508/4	1953–56	£6,000	£3,500	£1,250
Zephyr Mk I	2262/6	1951–56	£3,000	£1,250	£600
Zephyr Mk I DHC	2262/6	1953–56	£7,000	£4,000	£1,300
Zodiac Mk I	2262/6	1953–56	£3,300	£1,500	£700
Consul Mk II/Deluxe	1703/4	1956–62	£2,900	£1,500	£650
Consul Mk II DHC	1703/4	1956–62	£5,000	£3,300	£1,250
Zephyr Mk II	2553/6	1956–62	£3,800	£1,800	£750
Zephyr Mk II DHC	2553/6	1956–62	£8,000	£4,000	£1,500
Zodiac Mk II	2553/6	1956–62	£4,000	£2,250	£750
Zodiac Mk II DHC	2553/6	1956–62	£8,500	£4,250	£1,800
Zephyr 4 Mk III	1703/4	1962–66	£2,100	£1,200	£400
Zephyr 6 Mk III	2552/6	1962–66	£2,300	£1,300	£450
Zodiac Mk II	2553/6	1962–66	£2,500	£1,500	£500
Zephyr 4 Mk IV	1994/4	1966–72	£1,750	£600	£300
Zephyr 6 Mk IV	2553/6	1966–72	£1,800	£700	£300
Zodiac Mk IV	2994/6	1966–72	£2,000	£800	£300
Zodiac Mk IV Est.	2994/6	1966–72	£2,800	£1,200	£300
Zodiac Mk IV Exec.	2994/6	1966–72	£2,300	£950	£300
Classic 315	1340/4 1498/4	1961–63	£1,400	£800	£500
Consul Capri	1340/4 1498/4	1961–64	£2,100	£1,350	£400
Consul Capri GT	1498/4	1961–64	£2,600	£1,600	£800

1956 Ford Consul Mk II, 1700cc, 4 cylinder engine, in need of minor restoration.
£1,700–2,000 FORD

1958 Ford Zodiac Mk II, 2.5 litre, 6 cylinder engine, 74,000 miles from new, original, excellent condition.
£4,000–5,000 FORD

1963 Ford Zephyr 4 Mk III, 1700cc, 4 cylinders, finished in dark green, 58,000 miles from new, good condition throughout.
£2,600–2,900 FORD

TOWARD THE WORLD CAR

A revolution in small Fords took place in 1959 with the introduction of the striking Anglia 105E, with its voguish rear fins and full-width chromium grin. But a more important Ford was to follow the Anglia. In the late 1950s, Ford's research had revealed a gap in its product line between the basic models and the big saloons. In 1962, that gap was filled with the Cortina, which rapidly became Britain's best-selling car. Although there was nothing revolutionary about its styling or engineering, the Cortina scored in two areas: first, its mean price-tag of £639, which undercut rivals; and second, the fact that the profit had been designed in.

The Mk I Cortina became the first British car to sell more than a million in less than four years. Through the Mk II, Mk III and Mk IV, it remained a best-seller until it was replaced in 1982 by the Sierra. Meanwhile, there was a slightly less sensible Ford, the 2+2 fastback Capri, launched in 1968. The Capri was Ford's European interpretation of the American Mustang 'pony-car' theme, which had sold a million in its first year. Early UK adverts billed the Capri as 'the car you always promised yourself', and by the end of production in 1987, nearly two million motorists had treated themselves to one.

In fact, it's difficult to think of a Ford failure, unless you count failure as selling less than a million, in which case, there are a few contenders. The ungainly Consul Classic of 1961–63 struggled to pass 100,000. Its sporting sister, the original two-door Consul Capri, was a pretty thing with its pillarless, tear-drop window. However, with the exception of the rare GT version (of which only 2,002 were built), it was a gutless machine, and production tailed off at 20,000. Another contender is the square-cut, Mk IV Zephyr/Zodiac of 1966–72, with a bonnet you could land a Harrier jump-jet on. Production totalled under 200,000.

In fact, the breeze-block Mk IV Zephyrs and Zodiacs were the last all-British Fords. Since then, each subsequent model has been increasingly European in design and production, and lately even global with the Mondeo.

Yet as the company presses on with its 'world car' policy, I wonder if there will ever be a Ford to match the remarkable global achievement of the Model T, the American Ford that became a British car and led to the creation of Ford UK.

1963 Ford Cortina Lotus Mk I, 1558cc, 4 cylinders, double overhead camshafts, 3,955 miles from new, very good original condition.
£35,000–40,000 COYS

The very high value of this car is explained by its colourful history. It was originally owned by Bruce Reynolds, mastermind of the infamous Great Train Robbery, and was used by him as a getaway car. Introduced in April 1963, the Cortina Lotus sported white paintwork, green side-flashes and discreet Lotus badging. The bonnet, boot lid and doors were in alloy. The MacPherson-strut front suspension was lowered and stiffened, while at the rear, the standard leaf springs were replaced by an A-bracket, coil springs and trailing arms. With 105bhp from its Lotus twin-cam engine and close-ratio gears, the car could top 106mph and cover 0–60mph in 10.5 seconds.

1968 Ford Anglia 105E Deluxe, 997cc, overhead-valve, 4 cylinder engine, restored, good condition throughout.
£1,800–2,200 FORD

Starter Fords: *Anglia, Prefect, Popular models from 1948 onwards; Mk I, II, III, Consul, Zephyr and Zodiac, Mk IV Zephyr/Zodiac; Consul Classic 315/Consul Capri; Cortina Mk I, II, III;.Corsair, Capri, Escort.*

- Whatever your taste, there's a Ford you can afford – in fact, more than we have space to mention. Their list of virtues as starter classics is almost as long as the list of models to choose from. Importantly, many were made in millions, which means that generally there's a ready stock of cars and spares, backed by a healthy network of clubs and specialists.

- The Consul, Zephyr and Zodiac (Mk I, II and III) are what you might term lifestyle Fords – there's one to match your taste in clothes and music. The Mk I and II models are favoured as Brit-sized chunks of Americana for the retro crowd. For Mk I models, read early Elvis, rockabilly rather than rock 'n' roll. They are also ideal for post-war swing spivs with Cesar Romero pencil moustaches, double-breasted suits and nylons to sell. The Mk II is mainstream Elvis, structurally reinforced quiffs, pedal pushers, bowling shirts and Levi 501s. As for the Mk III, that's Elvis at Vegas, teddy-boy drape-coats, long sideburns and a tub of Swarfega in the hair. All are eminently viable for the DIY enthusiast. While performance is hardly shattering by today's standards, they are fast enough to go with the flow of modern traffic without causing a tail-back.

- The Anglia of 1959 represented the shape of fins to come: a pretty little saloon that was an instant hit with buyers who might otherwise have opted for something drearily and domestically familiar, like an Austin A40 or Morris Minor. The Anglia 105E was a stylish device with a miniature, full-width version of the 'dollar-grin' grille up front and voguish US-hand-me-down rear fins. Under the skin, there was a little innovation, too, with the first overhead-valve engine for a small Ford and – wonder of wonder – four gears. The Anglia was a worthy and peppy workhorse that went on to sell more than a million before making way for the Escort in 1967. **Pick of the bunch:** The Anglia Super 123E, which has an 1198cc engine compared to the 997cc of the 105E, so you'll get to 60mph in 22 seconds rather than 29, and eventually nudge 85mph instead of running out of puff at 75mph.

- The Cortina appeared late in 1962, and soon you couldn't miss it on Britain's roads as sales soared. It undercut rivals on price and, in many cases, offered a lot more. **Pick of the bunch:** The 1500GT, which gave a creditable 13 second 0–60mph and 95mph top speed; and the Lotus Cortina, which with a 1558cc, 105bhp, Lotus twin-cam engine and uprated suspension scorched its way to 108mph. There were only 4,012 genuine Mk I Lotus Cortinas. They're highly prized, so watch out for fakes – there are plenty.

- The theme of Ford's American hot-selling Mustang fastback resurfaced in Europe in 1969 as the Capri. For medallion men who favoured curved-collared suits tailored from static-sparking petro-chemical by-products and splashed on Old Spice to mask the odour, a Capri was the next best thing to sex – and a lot more likely. The Capri offered kaleidoscopic customer choice, from the sheep-in-wolf's clothing, 89mph 1300 to rorty V6-engined RS, GT and injected models, some with130+mph performance. Essentially, if you added the right stick-on goodies, you could make your Dagenham donkey mimic a road-burning RS – in fact, over the years, there were an astonishing 900 variants on the Capri theme. Today, though, with the rediscovery of the dubious styles and values of the 1970s, the Capri is emerging as a New Lad's icon. **Pick of the bunch:** V6-engined models, including RS, GT and E designations. Avoid troublesome V4 engines; ordinary 1300 and 1600 models are pretty lame, but the 1600GT is an option in the go-less-slowly stakes.

1965 Ford Cortina 1500 GT, 1500cc, 4 cylinders, restored, finished in dark blue, very good condition.
£2,300–2,700 FORD

1968 Ford Cortina 1600E, 1600cc, 4 cylinders, 4-speed manual gearbox, left-hand drive, finished in Saluki bronze with tan interior trim, 81,000km from new, excellent condition throughout.
£3,500–4,000 H&H

1968 Ford Cortina Mk II, 1600cc, finished in white, wide steel wheels, good condition.
£1,300–1,500 CGC

1971 Ford Escort Mexico Mk I, 1600cc, 4 cylinders, restored, finished in yellow, quarter bumpers, excellent condition throughout.
£2,500–3,000 FORD

1978 Ford Escort RS2000 Mk II, 2 litre 4 cylinder engine, 4-speed manual gearbox, completely restored to original condition, finished in red, sunshine roof, alloy road wheelsl, excellent condition throughout.
£3,000–4,000 FORD

> **Cross Reference**
> See Colour Review

Ford Cortina Mk II (1966–70)

Body styles: Two- and four-door saloon, estate, Crayford convertible.
Engine: Four-cylinder; 1297cc, 1498cc, 1599cc (Lotus, 1558cc).
Power output: 53.5–88bhp (Lotus, 105bhp).
Transmission: Four-speed manual, optional automatic.
Brakes: Front discs, rear drums.
Maximum speed: 80–98mph (Lotus, 105mph).
0–60mph: 12.5–24 seconds (Lotus, 9 seconds).
Production: 1,010,580.
Prices in 1968: Two-door 1300, £792; 1600GT, £939; 1600E, £1,073; Lotus, £1,163.
The Mk I Cortina was a hard act to follow: not only was it Britain's best-selling car in its day, but it was also the first British car to top a million sales in four years. As fins faded from automotive fashion, Ford remodelled the Mk I into the square-cut Mk II, which continued the company's domination of middle-market family and professional motoring.

As with the Mk I, there was nothing revolutionary about the styling or engineering of the Mk II, yet once more its mean price undercut rivals and made it difficult to resist. What's more, the Cortina was not so much a single model as a whole model range, with versions to match your wallet, aspirations and need for speed – from the plain Standard and DeLuxe versions to the sporty 95–100mph two-door GT or, for £130 more, the 1600E. The 'E' stood for Executive, the model being based on the 1600GT with extra luxury trim, fancy wheels and two more doors. The fastest and most expensive variant was the rare Cortina Lotus.
Cortina Fact: In 1970, the millionth export Cortina was helicoptered from Ford's Dagenham plant to its buyer in Belgium, achieving a record for the fastest million in overseas sales and the fastest delivery to an export customer.

1969 Ford Cortina Lotus Mk II, 1558cc, double-overhead-camshaft, 4 cylinder engine, Minilite wheels, restored, good condition.
£5,250–5,750 WILM

1972 Ford Cortina Mk III 2000 GXL, finished in red with white vinyl roof, 60,000 miles from new, original, excellent condition.
£2,000–2,400 FORD

FORD (British built) Model	ENGINE cc/cyl	DATES	CONDITION 1	2	3
Cortina Mk I	1198/4	1963–66	£1,550	£600	£150
Cortina Crayford Mk I	1198/4	1963–66	£3,500	£1,800	£950
Cortina GT	1498/4	1963–66	£1,800	£1,000	£650
Lotus Cortina Mk I	1558/4	1963–66	£10,000	£7,500	£4,500
Cortina Mk II	1599/4	1966–70	£1,000	£500	£100
Cortina GT Mk II	1599/4	1966–70	£1,200	£650	£150
Cortina Crayford Mk II DHC	1599/4	1966–70	£4,000	£2,000	£1,500
Lotus Cortina Mk II	1558/4	1966–70	£6,000	£3,500	£1,800
Cortina 1600E	1599/4	1967–70	£4,000	£2,000	£900
Consul Corsair	1500/4	1963–65	£1,100	£500	£250
Consul Corsair GT	1500/4	1963–65	£1,200	£600	£250
Corsair V4	1664/4	1965–70	£1,150	£600	£250
Corsair V4 Est.	1664/4	1965–70	£1,400	£600	£250
Corsair V4 GT	1994/4	1965–67	£1,300	£700	£250
Corsair V4 GT Est.	1994/4	1965–67	£1,400	£700	£350
Corsair Convertible	1664/ 1994/4	1965–70	£4,300	£2,500	£1,000
Corsair 2000	1994/4	1967–70	£1,350	£500	£250
Corsair 2000E	1994/4	1967–70	£1,500	£800	£350
Escort 1300E	1298/4	1973–74	£1,900	£1,000	£250
Escort Twin Cam	1558/4	1968–71	£8,000	£5,000	£2,000
Escort GT	1298/4	1968–73	£3,000	£1,500	£350
Escort Sport	1298/4	1971–75	£1,750	£925	£250
Escort Mexico	1601/4	1970–74	£4,000	£2,000	£750
RS1600	1601/4	1970–74	£5,000	£2,500	£1,500
RS2000	1998/4	1973–74	£4,500	£2,200	£1,000
Escort RS Mexico	1593/4	1976–78	£3,500	£2,000	£850
Escort RS2000 Mk II	1993/4	1976–80	£6,000	£3,500	£2,000
Capri Mk I 1300/ 1600	1298/ 1599/4	1969–72	£1,500	£1,000	£550
Capri 2000/ 3000GT	1996/4 2994/6	1969–72	£2,000	£1,000	£500
Capri 3000E	2994/6	1970–72	£4,000	£2,000	£1,000
Capri RS3100	3093/6	1973–74	£6,500	£3,500	£2,000
Cortina 2000E	1993/4	1973–76	£2,500	£550	£225
Granada Ghia	1993/4	1974–77	£3,000	£900	£350

◀ **1968 Ford Corsair,** 1700cc V4, restored, finished in pale green, good condition. **£1,600–2,000 FORD**

1963 Ford Consul Classic 315, 1340cc, 4 cylinders, finished in blue with white roof, poorly restored. **£1,100–1,500 FORD**

1970 Ford Capri Mk I 1600GT, finished in metallic blue, Rostyle wheels, good condition. **£1,700–2,000 FORD**

◀ **1971 Ford Sbarro GT40,** 4.7 litre V8, correct Weber carburettors, rebuilt ZF transaxle, restored, finished in red with black leather interior 3,000km from new, excellent condition. **£48,000–53,000 BKS**

This machine was originally manufactured by Franco Sbarro as one of a limited production run, paying homage to Ford's double Le Mans-winning design from the 1960s. Some original GT40 components were used in the process.

Ford GT40

Henry Ford's grandson, Henry Ford II, was determined to win Le Mans, and when his offer to buy Ferrari was rebuffed, his resolve strengthened still further. The result was a Le Mans legend, the awesome GT40, a joint Anglo-American project. After a Le Mans 1–2 in 1966, GT40s won the 24-hour classic for the next three years. Henry Ford II had proved his point emphatically with an achievement that perhaps even surpasses Jaguar's string of Le Mans laurels in the mid-1950s.

Ford – USA

1960 Ford Thunderbird Convertible, 5763cc V8, automatic transmission, power steering, brakes, windows and seats, Kelsey-Hayes wire wheels, continental kit, restored, finished in Flamingo pink, new black and white interior, black Haartz cloth top, excellent condition.
£15,000–18,000 RM

The four-seater 'squarebird', as the 1958–60 Thunderbird was known, was very popular and sold in numbers almost doubling those of the earlier two-seater 'baby bird'. The 1960 version had similar styling to the 1959 model, but with a new grille, new triple tail-light clusters, and minor trim changes.

1967 Ford Mustang Convertible, 4.7 litre V8, finished in dark red with white interior and top, left-hand drive, excellent condition.
£7,500–9,000 PALM

1973 Ford Mustang Convertible, 4949cc V8, finished in green with cream vinyl hood, major mechanical components in good condition.
£5,000–6,000 BRIT

1964 Ford Thunderbird Convertible, 6400cc V8, restored, new rubber window, top and boot seals, bare-metal respray in Arcadian blue, light blue metallic interior trim and matching power-assisted hood, 31,352 miles from new, excellent condition throughout.
£12,000–14,000 H&H

1966 Ford Mustang Convertible, 4.7 litre V8, finished in white with blue interior trim and top, alloy wheels, left-hand drive, good condition.
£5,500–7,000 PALM

1968 Ford Shelby Mustang GT350 Convertible, 4949cc V8, 4-speed manual gearbox, alloy wheels, left-hand drive, restored early 1990s, finished in Apple red with black interior and power hood, very good condition.
£20,000–23,000 COYS

Keen to take on the Corvettes of rival Chevrolet in SCCA events, Ford commissioned Carroll Shelby to work his magic on the Mustang, launched in 1964. The result was the GT350, with 306bhp, 4727cc V8, uprated suspension and brakes, and a heavy-duty Galaxie rear axle. The package could top 124mph and cover 0–60mph in 6.8 seconds.

FORD (American built) Model	ENGINE cu in/cyl	DATES	CONDITION 1	2	3
Thunderbird	292/8				
	312/8	1955–57	£18,500	£13,500	£9,000
Edsel Citation	410/8	1958	£9,000	£4,500	£2,500
Edsel Ranger	223/6–				
	361/8	1959	£6,000	£3,500	£2,000
Edsel Citation convertible	410/8	1958	£12,000	£6,000	£4,000
Edsel Corsair convertible	332/				
	361/8	1959	£10,500	£7,000	£4,500
Fairlane 2-door	223/6–				
	352/8	1957–59	£8,000	£4,500	£3,000
Fairlane 500 Sunliner	223/6–				
	352/8	1957–59	£12,000	£8,000	£6,500
Fairlane 500 Skyliner	223/6–				
	352/8	1957–59	£14,000	£10,000	£8,000
Mustang FHC/Conv.	289/8	1964–66	£9,000	£4,000	£2,000
Mustang GT350	289/8	1966–67	£15,000	£10,000	£6,000
Mustang hardtop	260/6–				
	428/8	1967–68	£6,000	£4,000	£3,000
Mustang GT 500		1966–67	£20,000	£14,000	£6,000

Frazer Nash

1935 Frazer Nash TT Replica, 1500cc, Meadows 4ED engine, restored 1992, engine rebuilt with new counterbalanced crank, forged rods, modified Omega pistons (9.5:1), new timing gears and original Brooklands camshaft, magneto, starter and wheels rebuilt, transmission overhauled, rewired, bucket seats retrimmed, many original Electron parts retained, excellent condition.
£44,000–48,000 BKS

Known as the 'Electron Nash', this car was described by Jenkinson in his standard work as being 'raced extensively by owner.' He was referring to its first owner, H. Porter-Hargreaves, but the description aptly summarises its 63-year history.

1954 Frazer Nash Le Mans Coupé, 1971cc, 6 cylinder Bristol engine, 4-speed gearbox with overdrive, transverse-leaf-spring/wishbone front suspension, torsion-bar rear, BMW rack-and-pinion steering, Alfin brake drums, restored late 1980s, resprayed in dark green, red interior, excellent condition.
£50,000–55,000 COYS

The Le Mans Coupé was the first closed car made by Frazer Nash, and it came about when cycle wings were banned for Le Mans. Since an enveloping body had to be built, the company decided to exploit the aerodynamic advantage of a closed car. The body was based on the Targa Florio, but had a distinctive radiator grille that became standard on all subsequent Frazer Nash models. Only nine examples were made.

Gilbern

A known continuous history can add value to and enhance the enjoyment of a car.

◄ **1966 Gilbern GT,** 1798cc, 4 cylinder MG engine, space-frame chassis, fibreglass body, restored, finished in white, good condition.
£4,000–5,000 GILB

In all, 197 examples of the Gilbern GT were built between 1962 and 1966.

Graham

1925 Graham Five-Seater Tourer, 3673cc, 4 cylinders, manual gearbox, right-hand drive, serpent horn, finished in blue with black wings, black hood and black spoked wheels, black interior in good condition, large history file.
£8,500–10,000 H&H

1935 Graham 68 Notchback Four-Door Saloon, 3670cc, 6 cylinder in-line engine, 3-speed manual gearbox, finished in burgundy with brown interior, chrome trim and bodywork in good condition.
£4,000–5,000 H&H

Cross Reference
See Colour Review

Healey

The total output of The Healey Motor Company between 1946 and 1954, when it was absorbed into BMC, amounted to little more than 1,100 cars. Their engines were proprietary units from Riley and, later, Nash and Alvis; the bodies were not always beautiful, but all Healey-produced cars were truly sporting in character with performance to match. The most sought-after Healey is the Silverstone, a pared to the bone road car that proved a favourite among club racers. Today, the name of Donald Mitchell Healey is possibly better known for the true-Brit Austin-Healey breed of sports cars. At the 1952 Earls Court Motor Show in London, he debuted his new Austin-engined Healey Hundred, and

such was its impact that Austin's Leonard Lord quickly decided that he wanted to build it. However, long before Donald Healey set up his own car company, he had made a very significant contribution to motoring in Britain. In 1931, he had driven an Invicta to outright victory in the 1931 Monte Carlo Rally. In 1933, he joined Riley's experimental team, and in 1935 moved across Coventry to become experimental manager and technical director at Triumph, where he remained until the company collapsed in 1939. Donald Healey died in 1988, and it's no exaggeration to say that he was one of the most influential figures in the British motor industry.

◀ **1950 Healey Silverstone,** restored, engine rebuilt, fewer than 100 miles covered since, fibreglass wings. **£23,000–27,000 BKS**

The Donald Healey Motor company's first offering was a 2.4 litre Riley-powered sports saloon with welded chassis and Healey's own trailing-arm independent front suspension. For the clubman racer, there was the Silverstone, which was equally at home on road and track. This retained the saloon's engine and basic underpinnings, but it had a shorter frame and stiffer springing. Lightweight aluminium bodywork was complemented by cycle wings, while the headlamps were mounted behind the radiator grille.

Hillman

Hillman was one of many British firms based in the Midlands that made the transition from bicycles to motor cars. The company built its first cars in 1907, and in 1928 came under the control of Humber and the Rootes Group. During the 1930s, the Hillman Minx was more refined and luxurious than offerings from rivals. In many ways, these were Hillman's glory days; in 1939, the company was ranked fourth in Britain, and in the last complete model year

before the outbreak of war, more than 55,000 Minxes were built, amounting to more than a third of all Hillman production up to that point. Immediate post-war offerings were equally stylish, but in the 1950s, an epidemic of badge engineering saw Hillmans lose their identity, differing only in matters of detail and powerplant from the Singer Vogue and Sunbeam Rapier. By 1964, Chrysler had taken control of Rootes, and in 1976 the Hillman name vanished for good.

1936 Hillman Aero Minx, 1185cc, 4 cylinder side-valve engine, 4-speed manual gearbox, semi-elliptic leaf-spring suspension, mechanical drum brakes, 72+mph top speed, interior restored, radiator surround in need of replating, very good condition, comprehensive history file.
£5,750–7,000 C

The Aero Minx was introduced in 1932.

1954 Hillman Minx Mk VII Drophead Coupé, 1265cc, side-valve engine, restored, bare-metal respray in maroon, trimmed in brown leathercloth, new leathercloth hood, excellent condition throughout.
£4,500–5,000 BRIT

The first Minx made its appearance in 1932 and soon established itself as a worthy competitor in the popular 10hp category.

Starter Hillmans: *Californian; Minx models and variants from 1956; Imp; Avenger.*

- One of the most attractive traits of post-war Hillmans is their price. They're affordable and generally reliable, and if you're into budget top-down motoring, there's a wide choice from the company that persisted with convertibles when lots of other makers didn't bother.
- The 1950s Californian offers a suggestion of transatlantic glamour with straight-forward Rootes underpinnings. The problem lies in finding one, because as with later Hillmans, its low value has lured many a salvageable car to the scrapyard.
- The Super Minx convertible of 1962–66 makes an interesting four-seat, fresh-air alternative to cars like the Triumph Herald. It has a more substantial body and a bigger engine.
- The Imp was a real might-have-been – if only the Mini hadn't appeared three years before, and if only it had been built better. They're redeemed, though, by a lovely engine, super gearbox and sheer entertainment value when behind the wheel.
- During the 1970s, the Hillman Avenger tilted against Morris Marinas, Ford Escorts and Vauxhall Vivas. The GT model was surprisingly nimble and offered 100mph performance. The very rare Tiger derivative was capable of exceeding 110mph and enjoyed a successful rallying career.

1964 Hillman Super Minx Convertible, restoration project, engine rebuilt, underside refurbished, in need of cosmetic attention, sound condition.
£400–600 BARO

1967 Hillman Californian, 875cc, 4 cylinders, rear-mounted engine, finished in blue with blue upholstery 15,400 miles from new, original, good condition throughout.
£3,250–3,750 BKS

The Hillman Californian was built to the same basic mechanical specification as the Imp, having a rear-mounted, 875cc, overhead-camshaft, aluminium engine driving the rear wheels. The most obvious difference was the stylish coupé coachwork, but the Californian also had a higher specification and featured fully reclining front seats, divided rear seating, a heater blower, carpets, twin-tone horn and wheel trims. Like the basic Imp, it offered generous luggage space, with ample room at the front of the car and additional space behind the rear seats.

Dealer Prices

Miller's guide prices for dealer cars take into account the value of any guarantees or warranties that may be included in the purchase. Dealers must also observe additional statutory consumer regulations, which do not apply to private sellers. This is factored into our dealer guide prices. To identify dealer cars, cross-refer the source codes at the ends of photo captions with the Key to Illustrations on page 330.

HILLMAN Model	ENGINE cc/cyl	DATES	CONDITION 1	2	3
Minx Mk I–II	1184/4	1946–48	£1,750	£800	£250
Minx Mk I–II DHC	1184/4	1946–48	£3,500	£1,500	£250
Minx Mk III–VIIIA	1184/4	1948–56	£1,750	£700	£350
Minx Mk III–VIIIA DHC	1184/4	1948–56	£3,750	£1,500	£350
Californian	1390/4	1953–56	£2,000	£750	£200
Minx SI/II	1390/4	1956–58	£1,250	£450	£200
Minx SI/II DHC	1390/4	1956–58	£3,500	£1,500	£500
Minx Ser III	1494/4	1958–59	£1,000	£500	£200
Minx Ser III DHC	1494/4	1958–59	£3,750	£1,500	£400
Minx Ser IIIA/B	1494/4	1959–61	£1,250	£500	£200
Minx Ser IIIA/B DHC	1494/4	1959–61	£3,750	£1,250	£500
Minx Ser IIIC	1592/4	1961–62	£900	£500	£200
Minx Ser IIIC DHC	1592/4	1961–62	£3,000	£1,500	£500
Minx Ser V	1592/4	1962–63	£1,250	£350	£150
Minx Ser VI	1725/4	1964–67	£1,500	£375	£100
Husky Mk I	1265/4	1954–57	£1,000	£600	£200
Husky SI/II/III	1390/4	1958–65	£1,000	£550	£150
Super Minx	1592/4	1961–66	£1,500	£500	£100
Super Minx DHC	1592/4	1962–64	£3,500	£1,250	£450
Imp	875/4	1963–73	£800	£300	£70
Husky	875/4	1966–71	£800	£450	£100
Avenger	var/4	1970–76	£550	£250	£60
Avenger GT	1500/4	1971–76	£950	£500	£100
Avenger Tiger	1600/4	1972–73	£2,000	£1,000	£500

Hispano-Suiza

1913 Hispano-Suiza 15T Alfonso XIII Two-Seater Sports, 3.6 litres, restored, engine rebuilt, new gearbox and differential internals, chassis realigned, new road springs and hubs, bare-metal respray in French blue with dark blue wings, reupholstered in leather, original specification.
£75,000–85,000 BKS

In the 1910 *Coupe de l'Auto* race at Boulogne, Zuccarelli finished first in a 2.6 litre Hispano-Suiza. The T-head engine design of this winning voiturette was the inspiration for the 3620cc 15T. Spanish monarch Alfonso XIII was a loyal supporter of Hispano-Suiza and, impressed by the 75mph guarantee offered with each car, bought several examples, giving his name to the model. The 15T engine featured massive 60mm valves and pressure lubrication, being built in unit with the gearbox. The output was 64hp at 2,300rpm.

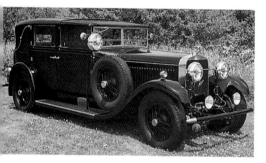

◀ **1928 Hispano-Suiza H6B Sedanca de Ville,** coachwork by Freestone & Webb, 6.6 litre, overhead-camshaft engine, fabric-covered scuttle and panelling, Grebel headlamps and matching pillar-mounted spotlamp, twin side-mounted spare wheels, dummy pram irons, finished in black, older restoration.
£59,000–64,000 BKS

Freestone & Webb produced the Sedanca de Ville coachwork on this H6B for 'Diamond Harry', Sir Harry Oakes, who had a grand estate in Bar Harbour and was murdered in Nassau in the 1930s, prompting the book, *Who Killed Sir Harry Oakes?*.

Horch

1938 Horch 855 Special Roadster, coachwork by Erdmann & Rossi, bulletproof windscreen, restored, finished in silver over black, excellent condition, concours winner.
£1,250,000+ BLK

One of three Special Roadsters known to exist, this particular Horch 855 was once owned by the wartime German Field Marshal, Hermann Goering.

Hudson

◄ **1935 Hudson Straight-Eight Saloon,** 4200cc, 8 cylinders, 3-speed manual gearbox, original right-hand drive model, restored, finished in red with beige trim and upholstery, very good condition throughout.
£7,000–9,000 H&H

This Straight-Eight was imported for the Earls Court Motor Show and has many special features and extras.

Humber

From bicycles to motorcycles, cyclecars, motor cars and even aeroplanes, the early decades of the Midlands company founded by Thomas Humber were extremely diverse. In 1928, Humber took over nearby Hillman, then in turn came under the control of the Rootes Group in the early 1930s, a decade during which the imposing six-cylinder Pullmans and Super Snipes enjoyed official patronage. In the late 1940s and into the 1950s, the Super Snipe and gargantuan Pullman and Imperial limousines were imposing machines with considerable presence, if a little funereal. Design was reinvigorated in 1957 with the transatlantic-influenced four-cylinder Hawk, which was soon joined by the plusher and chromier six-cylinder Super Snipe. For many fans, these fine cars rate as the last true Humbers. In 1964, Chrysler took over the Rootes Group, and the Humber's distinction as a marque was speedily devalued, the name being used for upmarket Hillmans with a little extra garnish. In 1976, it was dropped completely.

◄ **1926 Humber 12/25hp Five-Seater Tourer,** front wheel brakes, Barker lever-operated dipping headlamps, sidescreens and weather equipment, traditional Humber 'mole' livery with black wings, brown leatherette upholstery, correct period instrumentation, little recent use, engine free, original, in need of refurbishment and recommissioning.
£9,500–11,000 BKS

While Morris and Austin favoured side-valve engines, Humber produced an altogether more sophisticated inlet-over-exhaust valve unit, which was used in the 12/25hp introduced for 1925. Essentially, the engine was a development of the earlier 11.4hp unit, but bored out to 69mm and displacing 1795cc. Sturdy and reliable, the Humber's build quality was superb, with fittings reminiscent of the Edwardian era and a distinctive V-windscreen that continued until 1928. A particularly neat feature of the 12/25hp and other 1925 models was the fold-away stowage of the sidescreens in the door and body side panels.

A known continuous history can add value to and enhance the enjoyment of a car.

HUMBER Model	ENGINE cc/cyl	DATES	CONDITION 1	2	3
Veteran	var	1898			
		1918	£25,000	£20,000	£14,000
10	1592/4	1919	£7,000	£5,000	£3,000
14	2474/4	1919	£8,000	£6,000	£4,000
15.9–5/40	2815/4	1920–27	£9,500	£7,000	£4,000
8	985/4	1923–25	£7,000	£5,000	£2,500
9/20–9/28	1057/4	1926	£7,000	£5,000	£4,000
14/40	2050/4	1927–28	£10,000	£8,000	£5,000
Snipe	3498/6	1930–35	£8,000	£6,000	£4,000
Pullman	3498/6	1930–35	£8,000	£6,000	£4,000
16/50	2110/6	1930–32	£9,000	£7,000	£5,000
12	1669/4	1933–37	£7,000	£5,000	£3,000
Snipe/Pullman	4086/6	1936–40	£7,000	£5,000	£3,000
16	2576/6	1938–40	£7,000	£5,000	£3,000

Pre-1905 and Brighton Run cars are very popular.

1938 Humber Pullman Limousine, coachwork by Thrupp & Maberly, 4086cc, 6 cylinders, finished in black and fawn, engine and ancillary components in good condition, structurally sound, original upholstery with fawn cloth to the rear and black leather to front, in need of cosmetic attention.
£3,000–4,000 BRIT

Flagship of the Rootes range, the Pullman was produced between 1936 and 1940, effectively being a derivative of the Snipe and Snipe Imperial. Coachwork offered on the 132in-wheelbase chassis comprised a Limousine, Landaulette and Sedanca de Ville. These models of Humber are probably best remembered today for their popular role as military staff cars during WWII.

Hupmobile

◀ **1923 Hupmobile Model R City-to-City Racer,** two-seater coachwork, restored, good condition throughout.
£6,500–8,000 BKS

Londoner H.P. Rose arrived in Cape Town, in 1910, intending to market Panhard-Levassor motor cars, but he soon switched his allegiance to Hupmobile. In South Africa, motor sport was relatively new, and the fashion in the early 1920s was for city-to-city dashes against the clock. Rose exploited these stunts to the full, developing a standard Model R Hupmobile into a full-blown racer. This was the car he used to challenge the 42 hour, 32 minute time set by Hunt's Chevrolet for the 1,507km journey from Cape Town to Johannesburg. On 9/10 October 1924, Rose achieved his aim, in a record 38 hours, 28 minutes.

Invicta

Founded in Cobham, Surrey in 1925, Invicta had been effectively killed off by the late 1930s, despite abortive efforts to revive the marque both before and after WWII. What was left was a legacy of a mere 1,000 cars, most of them exquisite and none more revered than the rare 4½ Litre S-Type low-chassis tourer, dubbed 'the 100mph Invicta'.

In fact, the S-Type is so fabled that it's surrounded by its own mythology, for even today there's lively debate in vintage circles concerning the number made: some say 77; others, always in quotes for some reason, say 'around 50'. Either way, the rumbustious S-Type was a quintessentially British device – spare, unfussy and unadorned.

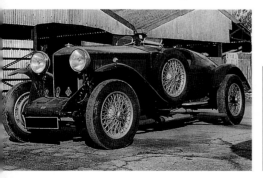

◀ **1930 Invicta 4½ Litre High-Chassis Special,** Meadows engine, handbuilt sporting body, wire wheels, finished in green with red upholstery.
£20,000–23,000 S

1932 Invicta 4½ Litre S-Type, coachwork by Carbodies, 4467cc, 6 cylinder, overhead-valve engine, twin SU carburettors, 115bhp at 3,200rpm, 4-speed manual gearbox, semi-elliptic leaf-spring suspension, front beam axle, mechanical 4-wheel drum brakes, finished in Royal blue with red leather interior, very good condition.
£130,000–140,000 C

ISO

The original name of the Italian company founded by Renzo Rivolta in 1939 was Isotheromos, and as the name suggests, it produced fridges. After the war, the name was changed to Iso Automotoveicoli and the company began producing motor scooters, followed in 1953 by bubble cars marketed as Isettas (later, these were built under licence by BMW). Iso ceased making bubble cars in 1956 and today is best remembered for its exclusive sports cars, which blended Chevrolet V8 power with Italian design. They were produced between 1963 and 1978.

◄ **1965 Iso Grifo,** coachwork by Bertone, 5359cc, Chevrolet V8 engine, 4-speed manual gearbox, left-hand drive, finished in red with black leather upholstery, bodywork and interior in fair condition, otherwise good condition.
£8,000–11,000 BKS

Iso joined the supercar constructors in 1962 with the Giotto Bizzarrini-designed Rivolta coupé. Styled by Bertone and powered by a 5.4 litre Chevrolet V8, the Rivolta featured independent front suspension, De Dion rear and disc brakes all-round. Developments included the Ghia-styled Fidia four-door saloon, the Rivolta-replacement Lele, and the short-wheelbase Grifo – the most successful Iso with 504 examples built.

1971 Iso Grifo, coachwork by Bertone, 5.7 litre Chevrolet V8, automatic transmission, 150mph top speed, restored, 15,000km covered since, transmission overhauled, new driveshafts, finished in red with light tan interior.
£19,000–23,000 BKS

aguar

he first 'Jaguar' – although it was many years
efore the company adopted the name – was
ot a car at all, but a motorcycle sidecar
roduced in 1922. The company's founder,
Villiam Lyons, was an enthusiastic
motorcyclist, who went into partnership
with William Walmsley to form the Swallow
idecar Company. In 1927, they switched
o four wheels, producing a stylish sporting
model based on the popular Austin 7. The
akish SS1 followed in 1931, and in 1934, the
aguar name appeared for the first time. Among
he pre-war models, the beautiful and fast

SS100 is the most prized. Yet Jaguar's glory
years really began after WWII, with the 1948
launch of the XK120. Virtually all Jaguars
produced since have been enthusiasts' motor
cars, enjoyed by those lucky enough to own
them, and coveted by those who can only
admire them. The best news is that in today's
market, all manner of classic Jaguars are at
their most affordable for years, particularly
Mk 2 models and E-Types, both of which
have fallen back dramatically from their over-
inflated peak values of the late 1980s and
early 1990s.

938 Jaguar SS100 Drophead Coupé, 2663cc, 6 cylinder engine, 100bhp, restored 1992/93, finished in Old English
vhite, upholstered in red leather, new interior veneers, one of only 279 built, excellent condition.
29,000–34,000 BKS

Jaguar SS100 (1936–40)

Engine: Six-cylinder, 2663 or 3485cc.
Power output: 103bhp (2663cc), 125bhp (3485cc).
Price new: £395
At the 1935 Olympia Motor Show, William Lyons'
Swallow Sidecar and Coachbuilding Company
debuted the first true Jaguars, for that was the
model name he had chosen for his new range.
Most stunning of all was the 2½ litre Jaguar
SS100 open two-seater. These days, the
glorious SS100 stands out as the quintessential
traditional pre-war sports car. Back then, there
was nothing traditional about it at all. In a word,
it was flash. These early Jaguars were often
dismissed by the old guard of the Bentley, Lagonda
and Invicta brigade as 'Wardour Street Bentleys';
in other words, the kind of cars that would appeal
to cigar-chomping theatrical agents with a
penchant for astrakhan coats. Nevertheless, the
SS100 was a sparkling performer. The '100' in
its name was barely an exaggeration, for the car

could reach 96mph and sprint from a standstill
to 60mph in 12.8 seconds. In 1938, a 3½ litre
version of the SS100 appeared, and that took
the top speed to just over the ton, with 0–60mph
in just over 10 seconds. By the outbreak of WWII,
only 309 SS100s had been built.
Pick of the bunch: 3½ litre models from 1938.
They can make the magic ton, but are rarer
(only 116 built) and more expensive.
What to watch: Many an SS saloon has been cut
down and passed off as an original SS100 sports
two-seater.
SS associations: With the onset of WWII,
'SS' gained rather unfortunate connotations,
and at the end of the war, William Lyons'
company became Jaguar Cars. The SS100
name had previously been used as a model
name for Brough Superiors, then the
'Rolls-Royce' of motorcycles and a rather
more positive association.

JAGUAR Model	ENGINE cc/cyl	DATES	CONDITION 1	2	3
SSI	2054/6	1932–33	£26,000	£18,000	£12,000
SSI	2252/6	1932–33	£22,000	£17,000	£13,500
SSII	1052/4	1932–33	£18,000	£15,000	£11,000
SSI	2663/6	1934	£26,000	£22,000	£15,000
SSII	1608/4	1934	£18,000	£15,000	£12,000
SS90	2663/6	1935	£60,000+	-	-
SS100 (3.4)	3485/6	1938–39	£90,000+	-	-
SS100 (2.6)	2663/6	1936–39	£90,000+	-	-

Very dependent on body styles, completeness and originality, particularly original chassis to body.

1949 Jaguar Mk V Four-Door Saloon, 3.5 litres, finished in black with brown interior, good condition.
£8,500–10,000 BKS

Jaguar Cars – as William Lyons' SS concern had been renamed in 1945 – began post-war production with a range of essentially pre-war designs. Work on a new advanced saloon would not bear fruit until the launch of the Mk VII in 1950, but elements of the car were incorporated in other Jaguars: the double-overhead-camshaft engine in the XK120 sports car, and the chassis design in the interim Mk V saloon, both appearing in 1948. The Mk V's cruciform-braced chassis featured torsion-bar independent front suspension and all-round hydraulic brakes. The existing Standard-based, 6 cylinder engine was continued in both 2.5 and 3.5 litre forms in the Mk V, the bodywork of which maintained the pre-war tradition.

1951 Jaguar XK120 Roadster, double-overhead camshaft, 6-cylinder engine, finished in white with black leather interior, tonneau cover, original, 30,000 miles from new, not used since 1973, in need of refurbishment and recommissioning.
£17,000–20,000 S

The XK120 created tremendous interest when introduced in 1948. It was available in roadster, drophead and fixed-head coupé form, and at its heart was the new 3442cc, double-overhead-camshaft XK engine, equipped with twin SU carburettors and producing 160bhp – sufficient for 126mph and 0–60mph in 10 seconds. This car once belonged to the cartoonist Giles and was immortalised in his famous cartoons in *The Daily Express*. It is thought to have been a gift from the newspaper's proprietor, Max Beaverbrook.

1952 Jaguar XK120 Fixed-Head Coupé, fitted with later 3781cc XK engine and 4-wheel disc brakes, left-hand drive finished in red with tan upholstery, very good condition throughout.
£17,000–20,000 COYS

1954 Jaguar XK120 SE Drophead Coupé, 3422cc, 6 cylinder engine, 180bhp at 5,200rpm, 4-speed manual gearbox, independent wishbone/torsion-bar front suspension, semi-elliptic leaf-sprung rear, drum brakes, left-hand drive, very good condition throughout.
£21,000–24,000 C

From September 1952, Special Equipment models were offered on the XK120. These had high-lift camshafts, centre-lock wire wheels and stiffer front torsion bars.

1954 Jaguar XK120M Drophead Coupé, 3.4 litres, 190bhp, left-hand drive, gearbox refurbished, rewired, bodywork restored, finished in British Racing green, beige leather interior, excellent condition.
£30,000–34,000 BKS

In the USA, the special equipment (SE) version of the XK120 was sold as the XK120M (for modified).

1955 Jaguar XK140SE Drophead Coupé, 3.4 litre, 6 cylinder engine, rack-and-pinion steering, left-hand drive, restored 1989, finished in pastel blue with grey-piped blue leather upholstery.
£37,000–40,000 BKS

Launched in 1954, the XK140 was broadly similar to the XK120, major engineering changes being confined to moving the engine 3in further forward and adopting rack-and-pinion steering. The XK140 was built in three versions: roadster, coupé and drophead coupé, the last two offering extra interior space. Outwardly, the newcomer was distinguishable by its revised radiator grille, rear lights incorporating flashing indicators and larger bumpers. The power unit remained Jaguar's well-tried 3.4 litre, twin-cam six, which produced 190bhp in standard trim. Special Equipment XK140s came with wire wheels, Lucas foglamps, and a 210bhp engine courtesy of the C-Type cylinder head.

1955 Jaguar XK140 Coupé, 3.4 litre, 6 cylinder engine, 190bhp, matching numbers, manual gearbox with overdrive, restored 1993, finished in British Racing green with matching leather interior, excellent condition throughout.
£21,000–24,000 BKS

Jaguar XK120 (1949–54)

Body styles: Two-seater roadster, fixed-head coupé and drophead coupé.
Engine: Double-overhead-camshaft, six-cylinder, twin SU carburettors, 3442cc.
Power output: 160bhp at 5,100rpm.
Maximum speed: 126mph.
0–60mph: 10 seconds.
Production: 12,055.
A car-starved Britain, still trundling around in perpendicular, pre-war motors, glimpsed the future at the 1948 Earls Court Motor Show in the lithe form of the Jaguar Super Sports. It was sensational to

look at, with a purity of line that didn't need chrome embellishment. It was sensationally fast, too: in production form, as the XK120, it would show that '120' really did stand for 120mph, making it the fastest standard production car in the world.
As for 'XK', that stood for the double-overhead-camshaft, six-cylinder XK engine, which debuted in the XK120 and went on to power Le Mans-winning C- and D-Type racing Jags, the 1961 E-Type and Jaguar saloons until 1986. Yep, the XK120 was a consummate Cat, more sensational in 1948, I'd venture, than the E-Type was in 1961.

JAGUAR Model	ENGINE cc/cyl	DATES	CONDITION 1	2	3
XK120 Roadster aluminium	3442/6	1948–49	£50,000+	£28,000	£15,000
XK120 Roadster	3442/6	1949–54	£30,000	£20,000	£15,000
XK120 DHC	3442/6	1953–54	£25,000	£17,000	£12,000
XK120 Coupé	3442/6	1951–55	£16,000	£12,000	£10,000
C-Type	3442/6	1951	£150,000+	-	-
D-Type	3442/6	1955–56	£500,000+	-	-
XKSS (original)	3442/6	1955–57	£400,000+	-	-
XK140 Roadster	3442/6	1955–58	£32,000	£23,000	£16,000
XK140 DHC	3442/6	1955–58	£28,000	£22,000	£15,000
XK140 Coupé	3442/6	1955–58	£18,000	£12,000	£7,500
XK150 Roadster	3442/6	1958–60	£35,000	£22,000	£15,000
XK150 DHC	3442/6	1957–61	£28,000	£18,000	£10,000
XK150 Coupé	3442/6	1957–60	£16,000	£10,000	£6,000
XK150S Roadster	3442/6 3781/6	1958–60	£40,000	£26,000	£20,000
XK150S DHC	3442/6 3781/6	1958–60	£36,000+	£22,000	£18,000
XK150S Coupé	3442/6 3781/6	1958–61	£22,000	£18,000	£10,000

D-Type with competition history considerably more.
Watch out for left-hand to right-hand-drive conversions in the XK series of cars.

1956 Jaguar XK140MC Roadster, rebuilt C-Type cylinder head with high-performance camshafts, left-hand drive, restored, finished in cream with red interior, new black hood, concours condition. **£32,000–36,000 BKS**

1958 Jaguar XK150 Drophead Coupé, 3.4 litres, matching numbers, manual gearbox with overdrive, rack-and-pinion steering, Dunlop 4-wheel disc brakes, restored 1992/97, finished in red with matching leather upholstery, excellent condition in most respects. **£35,000–38,000 BKS**

1958 Jaguar XK150 Drophead Coupé, manual gearbox with overdrive, original right-hand drive model, older restoration, good condition. **£22,000–25,000 TWY**

Introduced in 1957 and, at first, available only in fixed-head coupé form, the XK150 sported a restyled, roomier body with a higher front wing line, one-piece wrap-around windscreen and broad radiator grille. The chassis remained much as before, as did the 3.4 litre, 6 cylinder engine and 4-speed Moss gearbox. Overdrive and automatic transmission were options, as was the new B-Type cylinder head, which boosted maximum power from 190bhp to 210bhp. For 1960, the 3.8 litre XK engine, first seen in the Mk IX saloon, was offered. Production ceased the following year with the arrival of the E-Type.

Auction Prices

Miller's only includes cars declared sold. Our guide prices take into account the buyer's premium, VAT on the premium, and the extent of any published catalogue information relating to condition and provenance. To identify cars sold at auction, cross-refer the source codes at the ends of photo captions with the Key to Illustrations on page 330.

1958 Jaguar XK150S Roadster, restored 1995, finished in original British Racing green with Suede green hide upholstery.
£48,000–52,000 BKS

S-designation cars had tuned suspension and 250bhp, which meant that Jaguar still made the world's fastest production car.

1959 Jaguar XK150S Fixed-Head Coupé, 3.8 litres, triple carburettors, 265bhp, one of only 111 right-hand-drive models built, resprayed, history file.
£30,000–33,000 TWY

1959 Jaguar XK150 Roadster, 3442cc, 6 cylinders, 4-speed manual gearbox, left-hand drive, restored, finished in red with black interior trim and upholstery, history file.
£27,000–30,000 H&H

1960 Jaguar XK150 Coupé, 3.8 litre, 6 cylinder engine, 4-speed manual gearbox with overdrive, Dunlop 4-wheel disc brakes, left-hand drive, restored 1993 at a cost of around £18,000, finished in red with matching leather interior, excellent condition throughout.
£15,000–17,000 BKS

1960 Jaguar Mk II 3.8 Saloon, 3781cc, 6 cylinders, overdrive, excellent condition.
£12,000–14,000 WILM

Jaguar Mk I (1956–60)

Construction: Unitary.
Engine: Double-overhead-camshaft, six-cylinder, 2483 or 3442cc.
Power output: 112bhp at 5,750rpm (2.4); 210bhp at 5,500rpm (3.4).
Transmission: Four-speed manual with optional overdrive; optional automatic.
Maximum speed: 101mph (2.4); near 120mph (3.4).
0–60mph: 14.5 seconds (2.4); 10.7 seconds (3.4).
Production: 36,740.
Prices when new: £1,344 (2.4); £1,672 (3.4).
Everybody remembers the tyre-squealing Mk II Jaguar, once beloved of tonic-suited villains and latterly finding favour on the right side of the law as the TV wheels of the opera-loving Inspector Morse. In the late 1980s, the Mk II was virtually standard issue for Soho advertising executives along with red-rimmed specs and an expense account at *L'Escargot*, but the car that paved the way for it has almost been forgotten. In the early 1950s, Jaguar was riding high, winning at Le Mans and in the home and export markets with the XK120 sports car and the gargantuan Mk VII saloon. In 1955, the company added its first unitary-built car, the new compact 2.4 litre saloon – known retrospectively as the Mk I – to create its most complete model range ever. On first sight, you'd think that someone had customised a Mk II, filling in the rear wheel arches and glass area to create something that looked more menacing than its better-known successor. Even though the engine was a downsized 2483cc version of the famed XK six-cylinder unit, the Mk I was still considered sporting with its 100mph performance, and its keen pricing introduced a new group of motorists to Jaguar ownership. In 1957, Jaguar added a 3.4 litre version, while optional disc brakes were offered shortly after. By the end of production, in 1960, the Mk I had become the biggest-selling Jaguar ever. The Mk II was certainly a more capable car, not least because its widened rear wheel track overcame the Mk I's uncertain handling on the limit, but without the Mk I there would have been no Mk II, and today, the unsung Mk I is both cheaper and more distinctive.

1960 Jaguar Mk II 2.4 Saloon, 2484cc, 6 cylinder engine, twin carburettors, 120bhp at 5,750rpm, 4-speed manual gearbox with overdrive, 4-wheel disc brakes, left-hand drive, finished in Old English white.
£4,500–6,000 Pou

1961 Jaguar Mk II 3.4 Saloon, 3442cc, manual gearbox with overdrive, restored engine overhauled and fitted with lightened flywheel, finished in original dark blue with pale blue leather interior.
£13,500–16,000 BKS

A development of the Mk I, Jaguar's popular Mk II debuted in 1959. Slimmer windscreen pillars and deeper side windows enlarged the car's glass area, while the deletion of its predecessor's rear-wheel spats enabled the rear track to be widened, improving roll resistance and stability. Otherwise, the running gear remained much as before, with independent front suspension by wishbones and coil springs, a leaf-sprung live rear axle and Dunlop disc brakes all-round. The Mk II could be had with the 3.8 litre XK twin-cam engine, in addition to the 2.4 and 3.4 litre units of the Mk I.

1961 Jaguar Mk II 3.4 Saloon, 3442cc, manual gearbox with overdrive, wire wheels, restored, bare-metal respray, engine and gearbox overhauled, steering, suspension and rear axle overhauled, brakes upgraded, stainless steel exhaust, red hide interior, very good condition.
£9,500–11,000 BRIT

1961 Jaguar Mk II 3.8 Saloon, 3781cc, 6 cylinder engine, twin SU carburettors, 220bhp at 5,500rpm, Borg-Warner 3-speed automatic transmission, 4-wheel disc brakes, chromed wire wheels, finished in white with matching Connolly hide interior.
£9,500–11,000 Pou

1962 Jaguar Mk II 3.8 Saloon, 3781cc, 6 cylinder engine, 4-speed manual gearbox with overdrive, engine rebuilt, finished in metallic maroon with red leather interior.
£9,000–11,000 H&H

1962 Jaguar Mk II 3.8 Saloon, 3781cc, restored, finished in British Racing green.
£18,000–20,000 DHAM

1963 Jaguar Mk II 3.4 Saloon, 3442cc, 6 cylinder engine, automatic transmission, restored, resprayed in dark blue, grey leather upholstery in good condition, largely original, good mechanical condition.
£7,000–9,000 BRIT

1965 Jaguar Mk II 3.4 Saloon, 3442cc, 6 cylinder engine, automatic transmission, wire wheels, finished in white with new red leather interior, wood trim refurbished, non-functioning heater, otherwise good condition.
£7,000–8,000 BRIT

1966 Jaguar Mk II 3.8 Saloon, 3781cc, 4-speed manual gearbox with overdrive, completely restored, engine, gearbox and overdrive balanced, twin 2in SU carburettors, stainless steel exhaust system, strengthened chassis, competition suspension, power steering, chrome wire wheels, louvred bonnet, rear wheel spats removed and arches moulded, Webasto sunroof, finished in British Racing green, air conditioning, XJ6 reclining seats, tan leather upholstery, woodwork refurbished, excellent condition throughout.
£13,500–16,000 H&H

◄ **1969 Jaguar 240 Saloon,** 2483cc, 6 cylinder engine, 3-speed automatic transmission, good condition throughout, history file.
£3,000–4,000 H&H

JAGUAR Model	ENGINE cc/cyl	DATES	CONDITION 1	2	3
1½ Litre	1775/4	1945–49	£8,500	£5,500	£2,000
2½ Litre	2663/6	1946–49	£10,000	£7,500	£2,000
2½ Litre DHC	2663/6	1947–48	£17,000	£11,000	£8,000
3½ Litre	3485/6	1947–49	£12,000	£6,000	£4,000
3½ Litre DHC	3485/6	1947–49	£19,000	£13,500	£5,500
Mk V 2½ Litre	2663/6	1949–51	£8,000	£5,000	£1,500
Mk V 3½ Litre	3485/6	1949–51	£11,000	£7,000	£1,800
Mk V 3½ Litre DHC	3485/6	1949–51	£20,000	£17,000	£8,500
Mk VII	3442/6	1951–57	£10,000	£7,500	£2,500
Mk VIIM	3442/6	1951–57	£12,000	£8,500	£2,500
Mk VIII	3442/6	1956–59	£8,500	£5,500	£2,000
Mk IX	3781/6	1958–61	£9,000	£7,000	£2,500
Mk X 3.8/4.2	3781/6	1961–64	£7,500	£3,500	£1,500
Mk X 420G	4235/6	1964–70	£6,000	£3,000	£1,200
Mk I 2.4	2438/6	1955–59	£7,000+	£5,500	£2,000
Mk I 3.4	3442/6	1957–59	£9,000	£6,000	£2,500
Mk II 2.4	2483/6	1959–67	£7,000	£5,000	£2,000
Mk II 3.4	3442/6	1959–67	£10,000+	£6,500	£3,000
Mk II 3.8	3781/6	1959–67	£12,000+	£6,000	£4,000
S-Type 3.4	3442/6	1963–68	£9,000	£6,500	£2,000
S-Type 3.8	3781/6	1963–68	£10,000	£6,500	£2,000
240	2438/6	1967–68	£9,000	£6,000	£2,500
340	3442/6	1967–68	£8,000	£7,000	£3,000
420	4235/6	1966–68	£6,000	£3,000	£2,000

Manual gearboxes with overdrive are at a premium.
Some concours examples make as much as 50 per cent over Condition I.

1965 Jaguar S-Type Saloon, 3781cc, 6 cylinder engine, manual synchromesh gearbox with overdrive, all-independent suspension, wire wheels, finished in grey with red leather interior and trim, bodywork in need of attention, otherwise good condition.
£3,500–4,500 H&H

1961 Jaguar E-Type 'Flat Floor' Roadster, 3.8 litres, restored, finished in Old English white with black interior, concours condition.
£25,000–28,000 BKS

Introduced in 1961, the E-Type caused a sensation with its classic lines and 140+mph top speed. Its design owed much to the racing D-Type, a monocoque tub forming the main structure, while a tubular space-frame extended forward to support the engine. The latter was the 3.8 litre unit first offered as an option on the XK150. The E-Type's performance did not disappoint, firstly because it weighed around 500lb less than the XK150, and secondly because it had one of the most aerodynamically efficient shapes ever to grace a motor car. Tall drivers, though, could find the interior somewhat cramped, a criticism addressed by the introduction of footwells early in 1962. But of all the versions of the E-Type, it is the very early 'flat floor' models that, for many, remain the most desirable.

▶ **1965 Jaguar E-Type Series I Roadster,** 4.2 litres, unrestored, stainless steel exhaust, finished in golden beige metallic with beige interior and black hood, very good condition.
£15,000–18,000 BKS

The 4.2 litre E-Type was launched in 1964. Along with the bigger, torquier engine came a gearbox with synchromesh on first gear and a superior Lockheed brake servo. The car's external appearance was unchanged, but under the skin there were many detail improvements. Top speed remained the same, the main performance gain being improved acceleration.

1965 Jaguar Mk X Saloon, automatic transmission, restored, all mechanical components renewed or rebuilt, bare-metal respray, chrome plating in excellent condition, interior retrimmed in beige leather.
£11,500–13,000 BKS

When launched in October 1961, the Mk X was the most technically advanced Jaguar to date. A unitary-construction bodyshell replaced the separate chassis of its predecessors, and for the first time on a Jaguar saloon there was independent rear suspension. Built at first with the 3.8 litre XK engine, the Mark X gained the torquier 4.2 litre unit in October 1964.

◀ **1967 Jaguar 420 Saloon,** 4235cc, 6 cylinder engine, dual-circuit brakes, older restoration, good condition.
£4,000–5,000 BRIT

This 420 saloon was originally owned by Lord Louis Mountbatten.

1962 Jaguar E-Type Coupé, 3.8 litres, finished in Old English white with black interior, coachwork, interior and transmission in good condition, otherwise fair condition.
£10,000–13,000 BKS

Aerodynamically, the E-Type Coupé was superior to the Roadster and the better grand tourer, enjoying a marginally higher top speed and the convenience of a generously-sized luggage platform accessed through the side-hinged rear door.

1962 Jaguar E-Type Roadster, 3781cc, 6 cylinder engine, 4-speed manual gearbox, genuine right-hand drive model, finished in red, new black leather interior trim, 54,000 miles from new, very good condition throughout.
£23,000–27,000 H&H

Jaguar E-Type (1961–74)

Engine: Double-overhead-camshaft, six-cylinder, 3781 or 4234cc; V12, 5343cc.
Power output: 265–272bhp.
Maximum speed: 143–150mph.
0–60mph: 7–7.2seconds.
Production: 75,520.
Price when new: £2,098 (roadster).

The E-Type was a sensational showstopper at the 1961 Geneva Motor Show. British motoring magazines had produced road tests of pre-production models to coincide with the launch – and yes, the fixed-head coupé really could do 150.4mph (149.1mph for the roadster), although most owners found 145mph more realistic. The stunning, svelte sports car wasn't matched by anything within £1,000 of its price – Astons and Ferraris were more than double the money. E-Types took off again in the late 1980s as grasping speculators drove prices into orbit, nudging a stratospheric £100,000 before the gravitational pull of the market brought them down to earth in a big way. That's good news for today's buyer, who stands a chance of owning an E-Type for less than will have been lavished on its restoration.

What to watch: The trade calls them 'Yuppie blow-overs', hastily tarted-up cars sold to impressionable types at inflated prices during the boom. By now, many bodges will be showing through, but there are still plenty of smart paint jobs concealing the touch of a cack-handed cowboy.

1966 Jaguar E–Type Series I Roadster, 4.2 litres, restored 1992, converted to right-hand drive, engine rebuilt, finished in red with black interior, factory hardtop.
£20,000–23,000 BKS

1968 Jaguar E-Type Series 1½ Roadster, 4.2 litres, wire wheels, finished in cream, black leather interior, good condition.
£15,000–18,000 BKS

The Series 1½ retained the matchless charisma of the Series I, but benefited from numerous detail improvements. It can be recognised by its open headlamps, teamed with the slimmer bumpers and dainty side and rear lamps of the Series I.

▶ **1970 Jaguar E-Type Series II Roadster,** 4235cc, 6 cylinder engine, 265bhp, 4-speed gearbox, all-independent suspension, 4-wheel disc brakes, finished in pale metallic blue with blue upholstery, very good condition.
£27,000–30,000 COYS

This car was once owned by Bill Heynes, chief engineer of Jaguar Cars and co-designer of the XK engine.

1969 Jaguar E-Type Series II Roadster, 4235cc, restored, finished in red, new black leather upholstery and black cloth hood.
£17,000–20,000 BRIT

The Series II E-Type appeared in October 1968. Various detail improvements were incorporated, the most obvious being the larger air intake and wider grille bar, together with improved side and flasher lamps located beneath the bumpers. The 4.2 litre engine was retained.

1970 Jaguar E-Type Coupé, 4235cc, 6 cylinders, left-hand drive, finished in black, original black interior trim, good condition.
£10,500–13,000 BRIT

1970 Jaguar E-Type Series II Roadster, 4235cc, 6 cylinders, wire wheels, restored, new bodyshell, doors, boot lid and bonnet, finished in silver-grey metallic with black leather interior, excellent condition throughout.
£20,000–23,000 BRIT

1970 Jaguar E-Type Series II 2+2 Coupé, finished in Signal red with black leather interior, 82,000km from new, good original condition throughout.
£11,000–13,000 BKS

In 1966, Jaguar introduced a stretched version of the E-Type to cater for the family man, adding 9in to the wheelbase, raising the roofline and fitting two extra seats. Later, it would become the basis on which all the V12 models were manufactured.

1971 Jaguar E-Type Series III Roadster, 5343cc V12, automatic transmission, restored, 'as-new' condition.
£38,000–44,000 HEND

1971 Jaguar E-Type Series III 2+2, 5343cc V12, restored, stainless steel exhaust system, new bonnet, rear door, sills and floor panel, finished in original Old English white, maroon leather interior, excellent condition.
£11,000–13,000 BRIT

The final version of the E-Type, the Series III powered by the 5.3 litre V12 engine, appeared in 1971 and remained in production until 1975. Built in two-seater roadster and 2+2 coupé versions, it continued Jaguar's tradition of offering a level of performance and luxury unrivalled at the price.

◄ **1971 Jaguar E-Type Series III 2+2,** V12, automatic transmission, refurbished, new engine, gearbox and torque converter, new wheels and hubcaps, finished in light blue with dark blue interior, regularly serviced, bodywork fair, otherwise very good condition.
£9,000–10,500 BKS

1972 Jaguar E-Type Series III Roadster, V12, unrestored, 52,000 miles from new, original, excellent condition. **£32,000–35,000 THOR**

1973 Jaguar E-Type Series III 2+2, V12, manual gearbox, sunroof, restored, finished in Primrose yellow with tan leather interior, good condition. **£8,000–10,000 BKS**

The 5.3 litre, overhead-camshaft V12 engine's 272bhp provided a top speed of 140mph, while the 0–100mph time was around 16 seconds. Externally, the Series III was easily identified by an enlarged radiator intake with grille, flared wheel arches, wider tyres and V12 badging.

◄ **1973 Jaguar E-Type Series III Roadster,** 5343cc V12, manual gearbox, hardtop, finished in green, good condition throughout. **£20,000–23,000 BRIT**

1975 Jaguar XJ6 Saloon, 3442cc, 6 cylinder engine, 3-speed automatic transmission, finished in lavender with navy interior, 41,700 miles from new, original, good condition throughout. **£1,750–2,250 H&H**

JAGUAR Model	ENGINE cc/cyl	DATES	CONDITION 1	2	3
E-Type 3.8 flat floor Roadster (RHD)		1961	£40,000	£30,000	£22,000
E-Type SI 3.8 Roadster	3781/6	1961–64	£30,000	£19,000	£15,000
E-Type 3.8 FHC	3781/6	1961–64	£20,000	£13,000	£10,000
E-Type SI 4.2 Roadster	4235/6	1964–67	£28,000	£18,000	£14,000
E-Type 2+2 manual FHC	4235/6	1966–67	£16,000	£11,000	£9,000
E-Type SI 2+2 auto FHC	4235/6	1966–68	£14,000	£10,000	£9,000
E-Type SII Roadster	4235/6	1968–70	£30,000	£21,000	£14,000
E-Type SII FHC	4235/6	1968–70	£18,000	£12,000	£10,000
E-Type SII 2+2 manual FHC	4235/6	1968–70	£15,000	£10,000	£8,000
E-Type SIII Roadster	5343/12	1971–75	£40,000+	£26,000	£17,000
E-Type SIII 2+2 manual FHC	5343/12	1971–75	£19,000	£14,000	£10,000
E-Type SIII 2+2 auto FHC	5343/12	1971–75	£17,000	£12,000	£9,000
XJ6 2.8 Ser I	2793/6	1968–73	£3,000	£1,500	£1,000
XJ6 4.2 Ser I	4235/6	1968–73	£3,500	£2,000	£1,000
XJ6 Coupé	4235/6	1974–78	£8,000	£5,000	£3,500
XJ6 Ser II	4235/6	1973–79	£3,500	£2,000	£750
XJ12 Ser I	5343/12	1972–73	£3,500	£2,250	£1,500
XJ12 Coupé	5343/12	1973–77	£9,000	£5,000	£3,000
XJ12 Ser II	5343/12	1973–79	£3,000	£2,000	£1,000
XJS manual	5343/12	1975–78	£6,000	£4,500	£2,500
XJS auto	5343/12	1975–81	£4,500	£3,000	£2,000

Jaguar E-Type Series III Commemorative Roadster fetches more than SIII Roadster – only 50 of the limited-edition model were built.

Jaguar XJ6 Series 1 (1968–73)

Engine: Double-overhead-camshaft, six-cylinder, 2792 or 4235cc.
Power output: 140bhp (2.8); 180bhp (4.2).
Transmission: Four-speed manual with optional overdrive; optional automatic.
Maximum speed: 113mph (2.8); 120–127mph (4.2).
0–60mph: 12.6 seconds (2.8); 8.7 seconds (4.2).
Production: 78,218.
Prices in 1969: £1,797 (2.8); £2,397 (4.2).

Although the late Sir William Lyons retired as Jaguar's boss in 1972, his vision lives on in today's generation of XJ saloons. The original XJ6 of 1968 was the last car on which he exercised his styling touch. Into the 1980s, the shape was flat-ironed, folded and creased into a less harmonious fusion of the traditional and merely voguish, but in 1994, the evolution came full circle with the return of the sensuous curves. In fact, so familiar is the essence of the XJ, that it's easy to overlook the classic credentials of the original; especially as the Series 1 XJ6s descended from executive expresses to become cheap jewellery for sheepskin-coated bookies until, finally, they were carted off to the breakers when the cost of a new exhaust outstripped the price of a tax ticket. In 1968 though, the XJ6 was a sensation, the press gushing with praise for the way it blended luxury, refinement, comfort and silence with performance and handling that bettered most sports cars. What's more, it was very keenly priced. It sounded too good to be true, and it was. First, the XJ6 was built down to a price, and second, under the demoralised mess of British Leyland, quality went downhill, tarnishing Jaguar's reputation at home and abroad. Now, that's all long forgotten, and the first-of-breed purity is becoming increasingly admired.

1976 Jaguar XJ6C Coupé, 4235cc, 6 cylinders, finished in Indigo blue, alloy wheels, 67,000 miles from new, good condition.
£2,300–2,700 RCC

1977 Jaguar XJ6C Coupé, 4235cc, 6 cylinders, refurbished, bare-metal respray in black, retrimmed, mechanically sound.
£3,750–4,250 BRIT

1988 Jaguar Sovereign V12 Series III, 5343cc, automatic transmission, cruise control, electric sunroof, finished in Silver Birch, Desert Sand leather interior, 41,000 miles from new.
£7,000–8,000 BKS

Built on the longer wheelbase of the Series II, but subtly restyled by Pininfarina, the Series III Sovereign debuted in 1979. It became known as the Sovereign V12 between 1983 and 1989, after which the XJ designation was restored.

1984 Jaguar XJS Coupé, 5343cc V12, 4-speed automatic transmission, refurbished, finished in British Racing green with tan and cream leather interior, good condition.
£2,750–3,500 H&H

◄ **1986 Jaguar XJS Coupé,** 5343cc V12, stainless steel exhaust system, alloy wheels, American twin-headlight conversion, TWR rear spoiler, finished in Claret with Doeskin leather interior, full service history, 38,000 miles from new, very good condition.
£10,000–11,000 H&H

ensen

From the 'drastic plastic' fibreglass-bodied 541 and CV8 to the growling, but refined, Interceptor with its Italian-designed elegance and pioneering four-wheel drive in the FF versions, Jensens were always, at the very least, interesting. In fact, such is the charisma of the marque that although the West Bromwich company closed its doors in 1976, there have been several attempts to revive it. Brothers Richard and Allen Jensen started out as coachbuilders, but began producing their own cars in 1936. The original Interceptor of 1950–57 used an Austin 4 litre engine, which was also employed in the dramatic 541 of 1954. From 1962, with the launch of the CV8, Jensen adopted Chrysler V8 power. The car that really made Jensen a household name, however, was the 1967 Interceptor, which combined the massive American V8 engine with elegant Italian coachwork to create a formidable high-performance GT. Sadly, the gas-guzzling Interceptor's heyday was cut short by two oil crises and a worldwide recession.

1954 Jensen Interceptor, 3993cc, 6 cylinders, refurbished, bare-metal respray, original red leather interior in good condition.
£7,500–9,000 BRIT

Following success as coachbuilders in the early 1930s, the Jensen brothers began producing their own vehicles in 1935. These were of a high quality and well styled, using both Nash and Ford power. Immediately after WWII came the PW, a large, well-equipped saloon powered by a Meadows engine. It was followed by the Interceptor, equipped with a 4 litre, 6 cylinder Austin engine. This offered exceptional quality and value for money, being an ideal long-distance machine, with its high gearing and, from 1952, overdrive.

1964 Jensen CV8, 6.3 litre, Chrysler V8, partially restored, finished in red, blue leather interior in excellent condition, chassis, bodywork and engine in good condition, poor electrics and transmission.
£1,500–2,000 BKS

By the late 1950s, the need to offer automatic transmission in luxury cars, even those of a nominally sporting nature, signalled the end of Jensen's reliance on Austin's 4 litre six, which was deemed insufficiently powerful. Thus, the company turned to Chrysler's 5.9 litre V8 and Torque-Flite automatic transmission. The package debuted in the all-new CV8 in October 1962, and while the car's styling was not to everyone's taste, there were no complaints about its 136mph maximum speed and outstanding acceleration. The model was revised through Mk II and III versions, Chrysler's 6.3 litre V8 becoming standard issue part way through Mk II production.

1957 Jensen 541, 3993cc, 6 cylinder Austin engine, finished in silver with red interior trim, new carpets, concours winner.
£8,000–10,000 BRIT

Jensen Motors were among the pioneers of fibreglass coachwork with the 541. A handsome car, it was very much in the *Gran Turismo* idiom.

1965 Jensen CV8 Mk II, 5916cc V8, Salisbury Powr-Lok differential, restored, engine, suspension and braking systems overhauled, chassis refurbished, new sills, finished in blue with red leather interior.
£8,500–10,000 BRIT

1969 Jensen FF Mk I, 6276cc V8, engine overhauled, new transmission, good condition.
£9,500–11,000 BRIT

The 4-wheel-drive **FF Mk I** boasted a comprehensive specification that included anti-lock brakes, Salisbury Powr-Lok differential, automatic transmission and power-assisted steering. Only 320 examples were produced.

1971 Jensen Interceptor SP, new stainless steel exhaust, finished in mid-metallic blue with black vinyl roof, very good condition.
£5,000–6,000 BARO

The fifth of only 232 Interceptor SPs made, this car was displayed by Jensen at the Scottish Motor Show in 1971.

1973 Jensen Interceptor III, 7212cc V8, restored, finished in silver with burgundy interior trim, good condition.
£7,000–8,000 BRIT

1973 Jensen Interceptor III, 7212cc V8, 3-speed automatic transmission, finished in metallic blue with magnolia leather interior, 49,000 miles from new, good condition throughout.
£2,000–3,000 H&H

1973 Jensen Interceptor III, 7212cc V8, automatic transmission, stainless steel exhaust, restored, finished in blue with cream hide interior, 50,000 miles from new, detailed history file, excellent condition throughout.
£9,000–11,000 Mot

A known continuous history can add value to and enhance the enjoyment of a car.

1974 Jensen Interceptor III Convertible, 7212cc V8, automatic transmission, power hood, finished in Rolls-Royce Regale red, light tan interior, lambswool seat inserts, electric windows, air conditioning, 62,000 miles from new, excellent condition throughout.
£11,500–14,500 H&H

This car once belonged to the actor David Prowse, familiar for his roles as the Green Cross Code Man and Darth Vader in the film *Star Wars*.

JENSEN Model	ENGINE cc/cyl	DATES	CONDITION 1	2	3
541/541R/541S	3993/6	1954–63	£13,000	£7,000	£4,500
CV8 Mk I–III	5916/8				
	6276/8	1962–66	£14,000	£7,000	£6,000
Interceptor SI–SIII	6276/8	1967–76	£11,000	£8,000	£6,000
Interceptor DHC	6276/8	1973–76	£25,000	£16,000	£10,000
Interceptor SP	7212/8	1971–76	£13,000	£9,000	£5,000
FF	6766/8	1967–71	£17,000	£11,000	£7,000
Healey	1973/4	1972–76	£5,000	£3,000	£1,500
Healey GT	1973/4	1975–76	£6,000	£3,000	£2,000

The Jensen CV8 and 541 are particularly sought after.

1974 Jensen Interceptor III, 7.2 litre V8, automatic transmission, power steering, finished in Electric blue with cream leather upholstery, air conditioning, brightwork and wheels in need of refurbishment.
£1,000–13,000 S

1976 Jensen Interceptor III Convertible, 7212cc V8 engine, automatic transmission, power-operated hood, left-hand drive, refurbished, stainless steel exhaust system, finished in gold with brown leather interior trim and upholstery, electric windows, air conditioning, 26,000 miles from new, excellent condition throughout.
£12,000–15,000 H&H

ensen-Healey

1975 Jensen-Healey Mk II, 1973cc, 4 cylinder engine, 5-speed manual gearbox, new stainless steel exhaust, new hood, finished in Copper gold with black interior trim, 38,000 miles from new, unused for 14 years, recently recommissioned, excellent condition throughout.
£4,000–5,000 H&H

Jowett

'By Jupiter,' or more likely, 'By 'eck!' That's what Yorkshiremen must have thought when the old-established Bradford firm produced its first sports car. Since 1913, the Jowett company, founded by brothers Benjamin and William Jowett, had built its reputation on a range of small, durable, flat-twin-engined cars and tradesmen's vehicles. That all changed in 1947 with the genuinely innovative and very capable Javelin saloon. Then, in 1950, came the Jupiter three-abreast sports car, prompted in part by the Javelin's competition success – including a class win in the 1949 Monte Carlo Rally – and the lure of Yankee dollars. *The Motor* magazine rate the Jupiter as the fastest post-war 1.5 litre car it had tested. On the downside, it was highly priced – considerably more than a 2.1 litre Morgan Plus Four – suffered early on from unreliable engines, and had those curious looks If Noddy had asked Big Ears for a Jaguar XK120 this is what he would have got. When America adverts asked, 'Can you really handle a race-bred European car?', the question unfortunately possessed more irony than Jowett intended. The brave Bradford company's 50 years of car manufacture ceased at the end of 1953.

1927 Jowett 7hp Type C Two-Seater with Dickey, finished in black with black upholstery, hood in good condition, sidescreens, rear luggage rack, Brolt electric headlamps, Miller sidelamps, footscraper on nearside running board, museum displayed for many years, in need of recommissioning.
£5,000–6,000 BKS

Marketed with the slogan, 'the little engine with the big pull', the Jowett 7hp was essentially an Edwardian design. Developed in 1910, its horizontally-opposed, twin-cylinder engine would remain in production, in only mildly modified form, right through to the Jowett Bradford vans of the 1950s. The backbone of vintage production was the charismatic two-seater with dickey, which could carry three adults up the steepest of gradients and, on the open road, at a very comfortable 35–40mph.

1952 Jowett Javelin Four-Door Saloon, finished in black with dark red interior, original, some body/chassis repairs needed, otherwise good condition in most respects, in need of recommissioning.
£2,500–3,000 BKS

Jowett caused a sensation when it launched the Javelin in 1947. All-steel, unitary body construction, independent front suspension, torsion-bar springing, and rack-and-pinion steering were all features of a very advanced design. The horizontally-opposed, 4 cylinder engine displaced 1.5 litres and developed 50bhp, sufficient to give a top speed of around 80mph. It had a 4-speed manual gearbox with column change and Girling hydro-mechanical brakes which were replaced by a fully hydraulic system in 1952. Production ceased just before Jowett's demise in 1954.

Kaiser Darrin

1954 Kaiser Darrin Roadster, 2.6 litre, 6 cylinder, Continental F-head engine, 90bhp, 3-speed gearbox with overdrive, restored , finished in original Pine Tint with white interior, lacking original top, good condition.
£23,000–28,000 BKS

Newcomer Kaiser-Frazer stole a march on the Detroit establishment with the launch of an all-new range in 1947. The fledgling marque prospered briefly, producing a number of novel designs. By 1949, however, sales were in decline, and to remedy matters, gifted designer Howard Darrin was hired. As well as restyling the Kaisers for 1951, Darrin began development of a two-seater sports car. Based on the chassis and running gear of Kaiser's Henry J compact, Darrin's handsome design featured electrically-powered doors that slid forward into the wings. Darrin production ceased at the end of June 1954 after 435 had been built.

Lagonda

In the early 1930s, if you were British, young and fashionably idle, there were three fast and certain ways to lighten the burden of the hefty inheritance burning a hole in your plus-fours. For the mere price of a none-too-pokey working-man's house, the sporting automobilist could choose between a Bentley, Invicta and Lagonda, but which one? For those who considered the Bentley a little obvious, the choice was between Invicta and Lagonda, but as Invicta's fortunes waned, Lagonda's short period of bloom began with the glorious M45, which adopted the powerful six-cylinder Meadows engine also used by Invicta. Less dreadnought dour than the Bentley, and not as rakish as the Invicta, the M45 Lagonda possessed a rough,

tough elegance with a substantial, stiff and sturdy chassis, firm suspension and a series of graceful saloon and open bodies. Even the heaviest-bodied models could top 90mph, while the tuned, short-chassis M45 Rapide versions were good for a ton and more.

In 1935, a Lagonda M45 won outright at Le Mans, averaging 77.85mph; but in the same year, the company also foundered and fell briefly into receivership, before being revived with W.O. Bentley as designer and technical director. He refined the six-cylinder M45, then produced a magnificent V12, considered by some as his crowning achievement. In 1947, David Brown, who'd just acquired Aston Martin, added Lagonda to his portfolio.

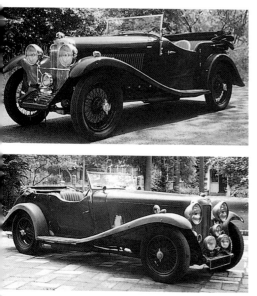

◀ **1934 Lagonda Rapier Four-Seater Tourer,** coachwork by E.D. Abbott, 1104cc, double-overhead-camshaft engine, pre-selector gearbox, restored 1990, finished in British Racing green with tan leather upholstery, black weather equipment complete with sidescreens, excellent condition.
£33,000–37,000 BKS

For its engine size, the Rapier was in a class of its own. Revving comfortably at 5,500rpm, it offered impressive acceleration and a top speed of around 75mph.

1935 Lagonda M45R Drophead Coupé, three-position coachwork by Freestone & Webb, original Jackall jacking system, central chassis lubrication system, older restoration, finished in silver and blue with blue hood, blue leather upholstery, sidelamps wired for indicators.
£60,000–65,000 BKS

1935 Lagonda 3½ Litre T9 Tourer, fitted with Vokes air, oil and fuel filters, running gear sound, chassis and suspension in good condition, bodywork in need of some restoration, front seats recovered in vinyl, all other upholstery original leather, last used 1962, running.
£30,000–35,000 BKS

The final incarnation of Lagonda's 6 cylinder engine arrived in 1934 in the 3½ Litre. Displacing 3619cc, the 7-bearing, overhead-valve unit was fitted to a short-wheelbase (10ft 3in) version of the 3 litre chassis. The car offered respectable performance, 90mph being within the tourer's reach. However, it was a rarity, only 85 or so being completed before production ceased at the end of 1935. This car once belonged to the late C.G. Vokes, founder of the Vokes group of companies, pioneers in the science of high-efficiency filtration.

Lagonda M45 (1934–36)

Body styles: Saloon, drophead coupé, tourer.
Engine: Six-cylinder, 4467cc.
Power output: 115–130bhp.
Transmission: Four-speed manual, non synchromesh.
Maximum speed: 95–105mph.
Production: M45, approximately 410; M45R, approximately 53.

LAGONDA Model	ENGINE cc/cyl	DATES	CONDITION		
			1	2	3
12/24	1421/4	1923–26	£14,000	£10,000	£8,000
2 Litre	1954/4	1928–32	£28,000	£25,000	£19,000
3 Litre	2931/6	1928–34	£35,000	£30,000	£22,000
Rapier	1104/4	1934–35	£15,000+	£9,000	£5,000
M45	4429/6	1934–36	£50,000+	£30,000	£20,000
LG45	4429/6	1936–37	£45,000	£32,000	£22,000
LG6	4453/6	1937–39	£40,000	£28,000	£20,000
V12	4480/12	1937–39	£75,000+	£50,000	£25,000

Prices are very dependent upon body type, dhc or saloon, originality and competition history.

Lamborghini

In the early 1960s, upstart supercar maker Ferruccio Lamborghini, who'd made his fortune out of tractors and air conditioning, was on a mission, and with the debut of the mesmerisingly beautiful Miura, he achieved his goal – to 'out-Ferrari' Ferrari. In fact, the unveiling of the Miura at the 1966 Geneva Salon did more than that; it set the supercar standard with technical sophistication, shattering near-180mph performance, and race-derived engineering that left rivals floundering in its wake. Not only was the Miura the fastest true road car of its day – no question, but it also made Ferrari's best efforts of the period look old-fashioned and even mundane. Some of the

Miura's inspiration came from the looks and layout of the mid-engined Ford GT40 road racer that dominated Le Mans. The difference was that the Miura was never meant to go racing, merely to be the supreme road car. So what if early models were plagued by chronic unreliability and an alarming tendency (later sorted with the S version) for the nose to lift at around 125mph, and occasionally for the front wheels to leave the ground completely at 170mph? Many reckon that the exquisitely beautiful lines penned by Carrozzeria Bertone make the Miura the most beautiful Lamborghini there's ever been; some say the most beautiful car of all time.

1970 Lamborghini Espada SII, coachwork by Bertone, 3929cc V12, all-independent suspension, dual-circuit, servo-assisted disc brakes, finished in silver with burgundy hide interior, 61,000km from new, good condition. **£8,000–10,000 COYS**

Lamborghini introduced the Espada in 1968. It was powered by the 4 litre, quad-cam V12 engine from the 400 GT, mated to a 5-speed gearbox. The engine's 320bhp could propel the car's four occupants to over 150mph. In 1970, the improved SII appeared. It featured ventilated brakes from the Miura S, halfshafts with CV joints and 350bhp from a higher compression ratio.

1982 Lamborghini Countach LP400S Berlinetta, coachwork by Bertone, left-hand drive, finished in original Tahiti blue with white leather upholstery, 21,000km from new, excellent condition throughout. **£30,000–40,000 BKS**

From the moment production began in 1974, the Countach set the supercar standard for a generation. It retained Lamborghini's quad-cam V12, but unlike the Miura, this was installed longitudinally. To achieve optimum weight distribution, the gearbox was placed ahead of the engine, and the differential at the rear. In 1978, the Countach S appeared.

LAMBORGHINI Model	ENGINE cc/cyl	DATES	CONDITION 1	2	3
350 GT fhc	3500/12	1964–67	£55,000	£45,000	£25,000
400 GT	4000/12	1966–68	£45,000	£40,000	£25,000
Miura LP400	4000/12	1966–69	£60,000	£50,000	£30,000
Miura S	4000/12	1969–71	£75,000	£60,000+	£40,000
Miura SV	4000/12	1971–72	£90,000+	£75,000	£60,000
Espada	4000/12	1969–78	£18,000	£14,000	£10,000
Jarama	4000/12	1970–78	£22,000	£15,000	£11,000
Urraco	2500/8	1972–76	£18,000	£11,000	£8,000
Countach	4000/12	1974–82	£60,000+	£40,000	£30,000

Countach limited editions are sought after, as well as Miura SV.

Lanchester

◄ **1933 Lanchester 15/18hp Four-Door Saloon,** coachwork by Carbodies, restored 1990, engine rebuilt, finished in black over maroon, burgundy leather interior, sunroof, good condition. **£5,000–6,000 BKS**

Powered by a 2504cc, overhead-valve six, producing 55bhp, the 15/18 combined Daimler's fluid flywheel with a Wilson 4-speed pre-selector gearbox. Servo-assisted hydraulic brakes were another advanced feature. The model received a shorter-stroke, 2390cc engine for 1935. When production ceased at the end of that year, around 2,100 cars had been built.

► **1953 Jensen 541 Prototype Sports Saloon,** 3993cc, 6 cylinders, 4-speed manual gearbox with overdrive, completely restored over 9 years, finished in red with cream interior upholstery and trim.
£16,000–18,000 H&H

This car was the prototype for the Jensen 541 range and is the only model built with an aluminium body. It was displayed at the 1953 Earls Court Motor Show and caused a sensation when it was unveiled. The boot lid is the only fibreglass panel on the car; all production 541s had fibreglass bodywork.

◄ **1933 Lagonda 16/80 Sports Tourer,** Crossley 1600cc engine, 4-speed manual gearbox, original right-hand-drive model, stored 1949–97, professionally restored, finished in black enamel with red chassis, wheels, apron and fuel tank, red interior, oil temperature gauge unserviceable, original, very good condition throughout.
£24,000–26,000 H&H

Although Lagonda began by building light cars, in the 1920s the company switched to the fast sporting cars and tourers that characterise the marque.

◄ **1933 Lagonda M45 T7 Tourer,** 4553cc, 6 cylinders, T7 factory coachwork with driver and passenger doors, restored late 1980s, finished in green with matching upholstery and carpets, well maintained, original.
£65,000–70,000 COYS

Handsome, rugged and fast, the expensive Lagonda M45 caught the rich sporting fraternity's imagination. The build was to a very high standard and sturdy specification, and the power came from Henry Meadows' 4.5 litre engine. Straightforward and untemperamental, this had 'earned its spurs' in marine applications, gaining an enviable reputation for power and reliability.

► **1969 Lamborghini Miura S Berlinetta,** coachwork by Bertone, 3929cc V12, carburettor rebuilt, brakes and steering overhauled, rewired, leather interior, good condition.
£42,000–48,000 BKS

Ferruccio Lamborghini's bold challenge to Ferrari began in 1964 with the 350GT, but it was the Miura – arguably the founder of the supercar class – that established Lamborghini as a major manufacturer of luxury sporting cars. Introduced in 1969, the Miura S featured a more powerful (375bhp) engine and was distinguishable from its predecessor by its wider tyres and chromed window surrounds.

◀ **1992 Lamborghini Diablo Berlinetta,** engine updated by factory in 1993, VT-style carbon-fibre engine bay shrouding, electrics and transmission overhauled, fitted with 'Valeo 98' clutch, new brake discs, sports exhaust, resprayed in yellow, 6-point competition harnesses, telephone, tailored car cover, 23,500km from new, excellent condition throughout.
£55,000–60,000 BKS

1933 Lincoln KB Willoughby Panel Brougham, restored, finished in Cardinal red with wicker side panels, front compartment finished in black, rear in beige, inter-compartment telephone, sterling silver vanity case, smoking set, hassocks, throw pillows, assist loops, award winner.
£120,000–130,000 BLK

This car is one of only two Willoughby Panel Broughams built in 1933.

▶ **1962 Lotus Elite Series II SE,** 1216cc, overhead-camshaft, 4 cylinder engine, 85bhp, 5-speed gearbox, 3,573 miles from new, original.
£23,000–26,000 COYS

The Elite boasted a fibreglass bodyshell, 4-wheel disc brakes and all-independent suspension by wishbones and coil springs at the front, and Chapman struts, lower wishbones and radius arms at the rear. Revised rear suspension, with triangulated wishbones in place of the two radius arms, appeared on the Series II of 1961.

◀ **1973 Lotus Elan Sprint Coupé,** 1558cc, 4 cylinders, 126bhp, 121mph top speed, 1,599 miles from new, excellent condition.
£24,000–27,000 COYS

Launched in 1962, the Elan was powered by a 1498cc Ford engine with Lotus twin-cam head and twin Weber 40DCOE carburettors, but this soon grew to 1558cc. Various improvements were made through S2, S3 and S4 models. In 1970, the Sprint appeared with improved driveshafts, camshafts and inlet valves.

▶ **1991 Lotus Elan M200 Speedster Concept Car,** 1588cc, 4 cylinders, Recaro seats, modified centre console, good condition.
£13,500–16,000 COYS

Based on the standard Elan, the M200 Speedster sported individual canopy screens for the twin cockpits. Other features included 'projector' headlamps, larger engine and brake cooling ducts, a deeper front spoiler and a new rear spoiler.

► **1960 Maserati 3500 GT Spyder Vignale,** 3485cc, 6 cylinder in-line engine, triple Weber carburettors, 220bhp at 5,500rpm, 5-speed ZF gearbox, front disc brakes, 230km/h top speed, mechanics and electrics overhauled, resprayed 1990, excellent condition throughout.
£47,000–52,000 Pou

◄ **1967 Maserati Quattroporte,** coachwork by Frua, double-overhead-camshaft V8, 260bhp, 5-speed ZF gearbox, boxed tubular frame, 140mph top speed, 0–60mph in 8 seconds, finished in blue with black interior, good condition throughout.
£3,500–5,000 BKS

The Maserati Quattroporte had a racing pedigree and was the fastest four-door car in the world during the 1960s. Its engine was a milder version of a power unit that had been commissioned for Indianapolis. In all, 679 Quattroporte's were built between 1963 and 1970.

► **1975 Maserati Merak SS Coupé,** coachwork by Ital, 2965cc V6, recent extensive restoration, excellent condition.
£12,500–14,000 COYS

Based on the company's flagship, the Bora, the Merak was powered by a 90° V6, initially developing 190bhp for a top speed of 240km/h. Roadholding and handling were excellent. In 1975, the SS appeared, weighing less and with an extra 30bhp. Only 250 SS versions of the Merak were produced.

◄ **1991 Maserati Biturbo Spyder,** coachwork by Zagato, 2.8 litre V6, 250bhp, automatic transmission, body enhancement kit, 48,000 miles from new, excellent condition.
£14,000–16,000 BKS

The first production road car to employ twin turbochargers, the Biturbo saloon debuted in 1982. Built initially with a 2 litre, quad-cam, 3-valves-per-cylinder V6, producing 180bhp, the Biturbo gained 2.5 and 2.8 litre units as the model range expanded to include four-door and open variants; the Spyder arrived in 1984.

1938 Maybach SW38 Cabriolet, 4-door convertible coachwork by Glaser, short chassis, completely restored.
£180,000–200,000 BLK

The first of the SW range of cars appeared in 1935, initially with the 3.5 litre, 6 cylinder, overhead-camshaft engine. With the introduction of the SW38 in 1936, the capacity was increased to 3.8 litres. This particular example was owned by Joachim von Ribbentrop, who was Ambassador to the Court of St James before the onset of WWII.

1929 Minerva AK Faux Cabriolet, coachwork by Labourdette, 5.9 litre, Knight 6 cylinder sleeve-valve engine, restored, excellent condition.
£160,000–180,000 **BLK**

Sylvian de Jong, a Dutchman, emigrated to Brussels in 1883. At first, he built pedal and motorised bicycles, but switched to cars in 1904. In 1909, he decided to adopt Charles Yale Knight's sleeve-valve engine. Quiet, efficient, trouble-free and durable, the Knight was the perfect powerplant for the 'Grand Luxe' carriage.

▶ **1969 Mini Countryman Estate,** 998cc, 4 cylinders, 4-speed manual gearbox, completely restored, engine rebuilt, new clutch and fuel floats, all wood cappings replaced, 78,466 miles from new, excellent condition.
£2,000–2,500 **H&H**

◀ **1992 Mini 'British Open Classic' Limited Edition,** Minilite alloy wheels, full-length folding sunroof, front and rear chromed nudge bars, finished in British Racing green with gold logos and coachlines, Cooper-style interior, half leather seats.
£2,500–3,000 **CARS**

Developed to commemorate the British Open Classic golf tournament, a total of 1,000 of these limited-edition Minis were built.

1921 Morgan 8hp Deluxe Two-Seater Sports, twin-cylinder enclosed MAG engine, 2-speed gearbox, finished in maroon with red interior trim, stored for many years, in need of recommissioning, good condition throughout.
£5,000–6,000 **H&H**

c1932 Morgan Super Sports, Matchless MXA twin-cylinder, water-cooled engine, completely restored, finished in bright red with black interior and tonneau cover, excellent condition throughout.
£15,000–16,000 **FHD**

1980 Morgan 4/4, 1600cc,
cylinder, Ford crossflow engine,
-speed gearbox, completely
estored, finished in British Racing
reen with red interior, serviceable
lack hood, wire wheels, rear-
ounted luggage rack, very good
ondition throughout.
14,000–16,000 BHM

936 Morris 10/4 Series II, 1292cc, 4 cylinders, engine
onverted to unleaded fuel, finished in black, 40,614 miles
om new, good condition.
4,000–5,000 BRIT

1969 Morris Minor Four-Door Saloon, restored,
finished in green with matching interior, 52,000 miles
from new, excellent condition throughout.
£2,000–2,500 ESM

**1948 Oldsmobile Dynamic 76 Two-Door
oupé,** 4.2 litre, 6 cylinder in-line engine,
-speed manual gearbox, 78,000km from
ew, original, excellent condition throughout.
15,000–17,000 BKS

he Olds 76 displays the influence of GM
tylist Harley Earl's legendary 1938 'Y-Job'
oncept car in the treatment of its pontoon
vings and the rounded front with its wide
rille. This particular example once belonged
o the Birkigt family of Hispano-Suiza fame.

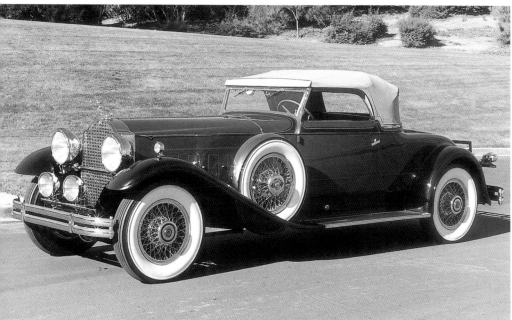

930 Packard Series 745 Custom Eight Derham Roadster, 6309cc, 8 cylinder in-line engine, 106bhp, 3-speed
manual gearbox, dickey seat, older restoration, chromed wire wheels, twin side-mounted spares, Pilot Ray steering
ghts, rear luggage rack, one of only three existing, good condition.
110,000–120,000 BLK

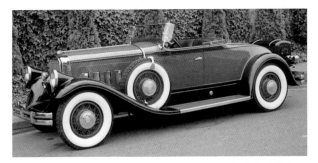

◀ **1930 Pierce-Arrow Model B Sport Roadster,** 5998cc, 8 cylinder in-line engine, 134in wheelbase, dickey seat, original paintwork and brightwork, replated radiator shell, correct Archer mascot, finished in red with black wings and coachlines, original fawn top, original black leather upholstery, Pierce rubber floor mats, toolkit and owner's manual. **£33,000–37,000 BKS**

The Sport Roadster is one of the rarer variants of the complex 1930 model range.

▶ **1954 Plymouth Belmont,** standard Plymouth chassis, fibreglass roadster body, only example built. **£200,000+ BLK**

A concept car for Chrysler's Plymouth division, the Belmont was highly publicised and well received at the various major car shows where it was displayed. It was styled by Briggs, whose aim had been to create a car that not only was practical, but also displayed sweeping beauty.

◀ **1957 Porsche 356A Carrera GS,** fitted with pushrod 356 engine, 90bhp, Porsche Rudge centre-lock wheels, restored, engine rebuilt, finished in Aquamarine, factory sunroof, tan leather upholstery, oatmeal carpets, beige overmats, original 1600cc four-camshaft Carrera engine included on display stand. **£34,000–37,000 BKS**

Porsche adopted the name 'Carrera' after two 550 Spyders finished third and fourth in the 1954 Carrera Panamericana, sandwiched between Ferraris of three times the engine capacity. The early 356 Carrera GS had a 1500cc roller-bearing quad-cam engine, but some owners substituted the plain-bearing 1600cc Carrera unit introduced in the following year.

▶ **1957 Porsche 356A Speedster,** 1600cc, Zenith instead of Solex carburettors, left-hand drive, completely restored 1993/98, leather interior, excellent condition. **£44,000–48,000 BKS**

In 1952, Porsche built a small batch of 356 roadsters; their success in the USA led to the introduction of the Speedster in 1954. The following year marked the arrival of the 356A, distinguished by its rounded windscreen; 1300 and 1600cc engines were available.

1971 Porsche 911S, 2195cc, fitted with later-type hydraulic chain tensioners and Weber carburettors, 180bhp, engine, clutch, transmission, suspension, brakes and steering rebuilt, 500 miles covered since, Fuchs alloy wheels, bare-metal respray excellent condition. **£11,500–13,000 H&H**

► 1973 Porsche 911RS Carrera GT, 2.7 litres, Bosch mechanical fuel injection, 210bhp, 4-speed manual gearbox, front air dam, lightweight seats, inertia-reel safety belts, electric windows, 149mph top speed, 0–60mph in around 6 seconds, excellent condition. £28,000–32,000 **BKS**

◄ 1973 Porsche 914, modified by MVR Sport of Belgium, engine enlarged to 2.2 litres, sports camshafts, 2 twin-choke carburettors, twin-pipe exhaust system, 5-speed gearbox, 4-wheel disc brakes, original Porsche 5-spoke wheels and body kit, targa roof, 50,000km from new, very good condition. £5,000–6,000 **BKS**

The first Porsche was a VW special, while Porsche has long provided technical expertise to VW, in 1969 came the first public expression of that relationship, the mid-engined 914 targa-top sports car.

► 1985 Porsche 959 Factory Prototype, 2.9 litre, flat-6 engine, titanium con-rods, forged aluminium pistons, 4 valves per cylinder, double overhead camshafts per cylinder bank, twin 2-stage turbochargers, 450bhp at 6,500rpm, programmable 4-wheel drive, 4-wheel ventilated disc brakes, full ABS. £50,000–55,000 **BKS**

Porsche's typically cultivated and refined high-performance counterpart to Ferrari's F40 supercar of the late 1980s was the magnificent 959, which positively bristled with sophisticated technical features. This particular example is factory prototype 007.

◄ 1908 Renault AX 6.9hp Two-Seater Transformable Coupé, 1060cc, 2 cylinders, magneto ignition, 3-speed gearbox, semi-elliptic leaf springs all-round, 2-wheel drum brakes plus transmission brake, detachable coupé roof, Continental detachable-rim wheels, older restoration, repainted, fitted with boot, refurbished brass coil horn, scuttle-mounted headlights and tail-lamp, original upholstery in reasonable condition. £11,500–13,000 **C**

In 1902, Renault began to make 4 cylinder engines, and later singles and twins, although De Dion units were also used until the end of 1903. In 1904, the radiator was moved behind the 'coal-scuttle' bonnet, and although it was a feature copied by many other manufacturers at the time, none kept it as long as Renault, who retained this distinguishing feature until 1928. Annual production had reached 2,100 cars by 1905, when the first of the 1060cc twin-cylinder models was introduced, the most famous being the AG and AX.

► 1968 Renault-Alpine A110 Berlinette, 1300cc, 4 cylinders, restored 1993, finished in metallic blue with black interior, good condition. £10,000–12,000 **COYS**

Société Automobiles Alpine was formed in 1955, the first model being the A106, which was based on modified Renault 4CV running gear. Variants with up to 950cc engines followed. In 1963, the most familiar body style appeared in the form of the A110, using Renault R8 components. It went on to gain an enviable competition record, excelling in international rallying.

◄ **1949 Riley RMC Roadster,** 2443cc,
4 cylinder engine, 4-speed manual gearbox,
folding windscreen, spotlamps, completely
restored 1989, 3,000 miles covered since,
finished in Ming blue with black hood, interior
trim and upholstery, very good condition
throughout, history file.
£10,000–12,000 H&H

**Only approximately 500 examples of the
RMC roadster were built.**

▶ **1926 Rolls-Royce 20hp Woodgrain
Cabriolet De Ville,** coachwork by Barker,
3.1 litre, 6 cylinder engine, new stainless steel
silencer box and tail pipe, dipping Lucas
headlamps, split-rim wheels, boa constrictor
horn, 'diver's helmet' rear lamps, nickel-
finished fittings, original oak woodgrain
painted finish, original leather roof covering
and leather upholstery.
£35,000–40,000 BKS

**The Barker Cabriolet de Ville (Prince of
Wales) coachwork can be set in any of
three positions to provide a fully-enclosed
limousine, a sedanca de ville arrangement
or an open cabriolet.**

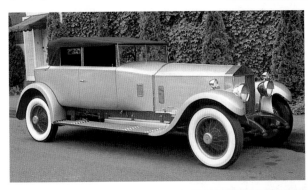

◄ **1927 Rolls-Royce Phantom I Two-Door
Light All-Weather Tourer,** coachwork by
Connaught, 7.7 litres, 6 cylinders, boat-tail
coachwork, wind-up side windows,
mechanically overhauled, bodywork
completely restored.
£38,000–43,000 BKS

**This particular car was exported to India,
where it became part of a large stable
maintained 'regardless of cost' by His
Highness the Maharajah of Dhenkanal. Its
folding top disappears into the rounded
stern of the bodywork, being concealed
beneath clamshell-type hatch covers.**

▶ **1935 Rolls-Royce 20/25
Brougham de Ville,** coachwork by
Windover, 3699cc, 6 cylinder in-line
overhead-valve engine, 4-speed
gearbox with synchromesh on upper
2 ratios, semi-elliptic leaf springs all-
round, servo-assisted 4-wheel
mechanical drum brakes, Marchal
headlamps, central driving lamp,
fold-away rear luggage rack, basket
weave to rear of bodywork, restored,
reupholstered passenger
compartment, occasional seat,
writing desk and smoker's
companion, speaking tube, leather
upholstery to driving compartment.
£40,000–45,000 C

◄ **1930 Rolls-Royce Phantom II Dual-Cowl
Tourer,** coachwork by Woodall Nicholson,
long-wheelbase chassis, blade wings,
fully demountable weather equipment,
very good condition.
£38,000–43,000 COYS

**Around 1,770 Phantom IIs were made
between 1929 and 1935, long- and short-
wheelbase models being available. It was
a greatly improved car that could hold its
own against the increasing competition by
luxury cars from American and other
European manufacturers.**

1933 Rolls-Royce Phantom II Continental, coachwork by Barker, 7668cc, 6 cylinders, P100 headlamps, mechanical refurbishment, original, very good condition.
£125,000–135,000 COYS

This car once belonged to the well-known vintage racer, the late Kenneth Neve. It features in his autobiography, *A Bit Behind the Times*, in which he documents its purchase and use as everyday transport, long-distance tourer, tow car for his 1914 TT Humber racing car, and concours entrant.

1933 Rolls-Royce Phantom II Continental Four-Door Sports Saloon, coachwork by Freestone & Webb, short-wheelbase chassis, Stephen Grebel driving light, sliding steel sunroof, low-rake steering column, white ivory steering wheel and knobs, silvered instrument faces, over £100,000 spent on restoration, Jaguar V12 fuel pump mounted in boot, well maintained, excellent condition.
£70,000–80,000 BKS

1934 Rolls-Royce Phantom II Continental Cabriolet, three-position coachwork by Kellner, rear-mounted spare wheel, restored, finished in beige and brown with brown interior, low mileage, award winner.
£250,000+ BLK

◄ **1950 Rover 75,** 2103cc, carburettors and braking system overhauled, finished in British Racing green, interior retrimmed in red leather, good condition.
£2,000–2,500 BRIT

Rover's venerable P3, finally yielded to the P4 in 1949. With its American-inspired styling, the new model met with criticism from more traditional Rover customers, yet it went on to achieve great success, spawning a line of cars that remained in production until 1964 with comparatively few styling changes. Early models were immediately recognisable by their central 'Cyclops' driving lamp, which was deleted in 1952.

1967 Sunbeam Tiger, 4735cc Ford V8 engine, 4 barrel Holley carburettor, Edelbrock inlet manifold, 200bhp at 4,500rpm, 4-speed gearbox, 4-wheel disc brakes, Minilite-type alloy wheels, hard top, left-hand drive, 118mph top speed, one of last built, restored 1991/93, very good condition throughout.
£13,000–15,000 Pou

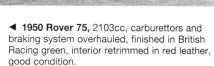

1904 Talbot 12/16hp CT4VB Side-Entrance Tonneau, 2724cc, 4 cylinders, T-head, magneto ignition, drip-feed lubrication, 4-speed and reverse gearbox, shaft drive, semi-elliptic leaf-spring suspension, internal expanding brakes on rear wheels and transmission, full undertrays, wooden wheels, period windscreen and hood, older restoration.
£50,000–55,000 C

In 1904, the Talbot range ran from a 1 litre twin to a large, 4.9 litre 4 cylinder car. A mid-range 12/16hp model, with a long chassis for side-entrance coachwork, was introduced later that year.

▶ **1935 Talbot BA110 Drophead Coupé,** concealed-hood coachwork by James Young, 3.4 litre, overhead-valve 6 cylinder engine, 120bhp, partially restored, £7,000 spent, cylinder head overhauled, finished in blue over grey, interior retrimmed in blue leather, one of only 41 BA-chassied 110s built, good condition throughout, history file.
£22,000–24,000 BKS

◀ **1947 Triumph 1800 Roadster,** 1799cc, 4 cylinder Standard engine, dickey seat, complete body-off restoration, engine rebuilt, bare-metal respray in red, interior retrimmed in tan leather, original tools under bonnet, excellent condition throughout.
£11,000–13,000 H&H

▶ **1954 Triumph TR2,** 2138cc, 4 cylinder engine, 4-speed manual gearbox, original right-hand drive model, complete body-off restoration, 2,000 miles covered since, engine rebuilt, new starter motor, dynamo, clutch and radiator core, rewired, new crown wheel, resprayed in British Racing green, interior retrimmed in Stone with new matching hood, very good condition throughout.
£7,000–8,000 H&H

◀ **1961 Triumph Italia Coupé,** coachwork by Vignale, 1991cc, 4 cylinders, twin SU H6 carburettors, 95bhp at 5,000rpm, 4-speed gearbox with overdrive, good condition.
£7,500–9,000 Pou

Stylist Michelotti combined his talent with that of Vignale to produce the pretty Italia on Triumph's TR3A chassis. The prototype was shown in 1958, production beginning in mid-1959 and continuing until 1962.

1966 Triumph TR4A, 2138cc, 4 cylinders, bare-metal respray in Signal red, wire wheels, good condition.
£6,000–7,000 BRIT

When introduced in 1961, the TR4 was very much in the modern idiom and quite advanced compared to its predecessors. It featured hitherto unknown refinements for a sports car in its price bracket, including wind-up windows and a heater. The crisp Michelotti styling ensured that the TR4 was a best-seller. For 1965, it evolved into the TR4A, which incorporated a number of improvements, the most significant being a new independent rear suspension system for home-market cars that gave a more comfortable ride and better handling.

1978 Triumph Stag Mk II, 2997cc, manual gearbox with overdrive, completely restored early 1990s, all mechanical components rebuilt, finished in magenta, excellent condition throughout, concours winner.
£9,000–11,000 BRIT

1968 Volvo 122S, 1780cc, 4 cylinders, new radiator and brake pipes, finished in red.
£1,750–2,500 BRIT

1966 Wolseley Heinz 57 Hornet, 997cc, restored, very good condition.

Concours	£10,000
Very good	£5,000
Wreck	£1,000 CRAY

The Wolseley Heinz 57 Hornet was commissioned by H.J. Heinz Ltd in 1966. Only 57 were created, being given away as prizes in a competition based around the company's varieties of canned soup. The cars were turned into full convertibles by Crayford Engineering. Several accessories were added, including built-in insulated food cabinets, front and rear seat belts, an electric kettle, a tartan rug, Brexton picnic hamper, radio and built-in make-up tray fitted by Max Factor. They were offered in two colour choices: Toga grey and Birch grey with Cardinal red leather seats.

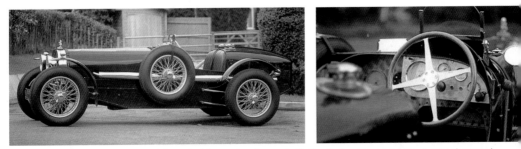

Teal Bugatti Type 59 Replica, 4.2 litre, double-overhead-camshaft, 6 cylinder Jaguar engine, 4-speed manual gearbox, disc brakes, chromed wire wheels, aluminium bodywork, finished in navy blue with dark red interior, well maintained, excellent condition.
£17,000–19,000 COYS

Bugatti's pre-war Grand Prix cars were some of the greatest and best-loved of all time, and models such as the immortal Type 35 have had more than their fair share of imitators. Among the better replicas are those built by Thistledown Engineering Automotive Ltd, under the acronym Teal. The standard model replicates the Type 35 and uses very mundane British Leyland mechanical components, ensuring inexpensive, reliable and practical sports motoring. This Teal is rather different, emulating the Type 59, famously raced by the likes of the Hon. Brian Lewis.

▶ **JZR Morgan SS Replica,** 499cc Honda CX500 twin-cylinder engine, 5-speed sequential gearbox, shaft drive to rear wheel, assembled using all new or reconditioned parts, hazard and high-density rear lights, 15in MGA wire wheels, full-width laminated Perspex windscreen, finished in British Racing green, walnut veneer dashboard, very good condition.
£4,500–5,500 BRIT

◀ **Sbarro BMW 328 Replica,** 2 litre, 4 cylinder overhead-camshaft BMW 320 engine two-seater fibreglass bodywork, finished in white with black interior, used exclusively for exhibition purposes, good condition.
£11,000–13,000 BKS

Since the early 1970s, the exotic one-offs made by Franco Sbarro have been major attractions at the Geneva Motor Show. In the mid-1970s, BMW's legendary pre-war sports car, the 328, was revived in replica form by Sbarro, the German firm's contemporary 300-series saloon providing the running gear.

Jaguar C-Type Replica, 3442cc, 6 cylinder XK engine, Moss gearbox with overdrive, tubular-steel space-frame chassis, solid rear axle, servo-assisted disc brakes all-round, 16in wheels, aluminium bodywork, engine overhauled and converted to unleaded fuel, fewer than 1,000 miles covered since, well maintained, excellent condition throughout.
£35,000–40,000 COYS

With an uprated XK engine, lightweight tubular chassis and aerodynamic alloy body, the C-Type won the world's greatest sports car race at Le Mans, repeating the victory in 1953. This particular replica was built from components supplied by Proteus, a company that has been replicating Jaguars since 1983.

◄ **Porsche 550RS Spyder Replica,** 1585cc, air-cooled VW flat-4 engine, 4-speed manual gearbox with synchromesh, tubular chassis, independent suspension all-round, GRP body, finished in silver with red interior, left-hand drive, Porsche 356 instruments.
£9,500–11,000 COYS

Built by Technic, this 550RS replica is finished as a copy of the car raced by screen idol James Dean in America.

► **Tri-Tech Autocraft Messerschmitt Cabriolet Replica,** Honda CN250 engine, automatic transmission, finished in red, built at a cost of approximately £10,000, excellent condition throughout.
£4,750–5,750 BKS

Introduced in 1953 as the Fend, the 148cc Messerschmitt microcar soon took its maker's name, the change coinciding with the adoption of a 174cc unit. Rear-mounted, the single-cylinder two-stroke produced 9bhp, enough to propel the KR175 to 55mph. This replica features a far more refined engine/transmission package than the original.

◄ **Ford GT40 Replica,** 3528cc Rover V8 engine, 5-speed manual gearbox, alloy wheels, finished in red with grey interior trim and upholstery, professionally built from GTD kit, correct in every detail, only used for promotional work, 1,000 miles from new, excellent condition throughout.
£13,000–14,000 H&H

1950 Austin Sheerline 125, roof damaged, complete and original.
£500–600 CGC

1960 Austin-Healey Sprite Mk I, 948cc, Lilywhites hardtop, finished in maroon, poor condition throughout.
£650–900 LF

◄ **1925 Bentley 3 Litre Light Tourer,** coachwork by Vanden Plas, complete in all major respects, factory optional luggage grid, Barker dipping headlamps, stored for almost 20 years, running order when laid up, engine regularly turned since, coachwork in sound condition, original interior well preserved, all cosmetics in need of refurbishment, comprehensive history file.
£55,000–60,000 BKS

The Light Tourer was built on a Speed Model chassis, but was designed to sell for less than £1,000 to help boost sales and cash flow. This particular car was the Bentley Motors showroom demonstrator.

▶ **1928 Rolls-Royce Phantom I Huntington Limousine,** 7668cc, 6 cylinder engine, left-hand drive, correct and complete, stored for many years, last used in 1956, running order, in need of major restoration.
£15,000–17,000 RCC

Developed as a successor to the Silver Ghost, the Phantom appeared in 1925. It had a 6 cylinder bi-block power unit, although both blocks shared a common cylinder head with pushrod-operated overhead valves, which produced 100bhp.

1927 Stutz Model AA Seven-Passenger Brougham, unrestored, correct and complete, original paintwork and upholstery, tools and accessories, 46,000 miles from new.
£12,000–14,000 BKS

Designed by gifted Belgian engineer Paul Bastien, the Stutz Vertical Eight was one of the outstanding American luxury cars of the late 1920s. It was powered by a 4.7 litre overhead-camshaft straight-8 engine, which developed 92bhp at 3,200rpm, and was capable of 75mph in standard trim. The speedster Black Hawk variant was a match for the best that Europe could offer – a Status finished a close second behind a 4½ litre Bentley at Le Mans in 1928 – endorsing the company's proud boast that 'the car which is safest has the right to be fastest.'

◀ **1926 Sunbeam 3 Litre Super Sports,** 2920cc, 6 cylinders, originally finished in ivory and green with matching Jaeger instrumentation, green hide trim, requiring complete restoration.
£15,000–18,000 COYS

This car was built for Sir Henry Segrave, and it went with him to the USA in 1927 when he set a new record in the Sunbeam. He refers to it in his biography, *The Lure of Speed,* recalling the trip to Daytona and his companion's awe at its performance: 'This type of car is non-existent in America. I had beside me Mr Frank Pierson the Secretary of the Daytona Beach Chamber of Commerce, and his remarks, interspersed with plenty of "Gees", were themselves worthy of a separate volume...'

▶ **1936 Talbot 105 Sports Tourer,** 'barn discovery', dry-stored for 40 years, original, mechanically sound in all respects, engine turns, inboard-mounted headlamps, chrome fittings, maroon paint, leather upholstery and canvas hood reflect age, original screen, 62,000 miles from new, Talbot handbook.
£15,000–17,000 S

Talbot scored many successes in the touring and sporting fields, and under chief engineer George Roesch built superbly engineered and understated cars of great integrity. The 3 litre Type 105 was introduced in 1931.

Lancia

Although Lancia never consistently sought competition glory with the same commitment as Maserati, Alfa Romeo and, later, Ferrari, the character of the marque has always been essentially sporting. Indeed, before setting up his own company in late 1906, Vincenzo Lancia had pursued a racing career, starting in 1900, while working for Fiat. The beginnings of Lancia's company were hardly auspicious, as its first automobile was destroyed by fire, but after that setback, Lancias soon earned a reputation for inspired innovation and technical excellence, often married to stunning shapes. The Lambda, of 1922, was tremendously advanced, having a monocoque structure, independent front suspension and a compact, narrow, overhead-camshaft V4 engine. At the lower end of the market, in the late 1930s, the Aprilia was a little jewel. In the 1950s, Lancia made some able and beautiful machines, but could never offer a line-up that was comprehensive enough to compete with Alfa Romeo and Fiat. By 1969, long after Lancia family interest in the company had ceased, Fiat had taken control. Shortly after, in 1973, the awesome Lancia Stratos was born and blazed a trail on the international rally circuit.

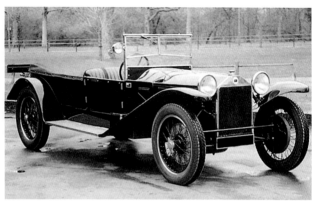

▶ **1926 Lancia Lambda 7th Series *Lungo* Torpedo Tourer,** restored 1994, finished in black with red leather upholstery, driver's swivelling spotlamp, adjustable footrests for rear passengers, full weather equipment.
£29,000–34,000 BKS

Lancia's Lambda of 1922 broke new ground with the introduction of monocoque construction, independent sliding-pillar front suspension and a pioneering 2.1 litre narrow V4 engine. By 1926, the 7th Series cars were powered by a 2370cc engine developing 59bhp, while the 8th Series engine (as fitted to this car) was further enlarged to 2570cc, giving 69bhp at 3,500rpm.

1926 Lancia Lambda 7th Series Short-Chassis Torpedo Tourer, 2570cc V4, 4-speed gearbox, independent front suspension, monocoque bodyshell, engine overhauled, fitted with coil as well as magneto ignition, original leather interior apart from reupholstered front seat, full weather equipment, good condition.
£29,000–34,000 BKS

1949 Lancia Aprilia Drophead Coupé, coachwork by Stabilimenti Farina,1487cc, overhead-camshaft V4, 4-speed gearbox, original right-hand drive model, older restoration, original maroon leather upholstery in very good condition.
£25,000–28,000 BKS

One of the most outstanding small cars of its day, the Aprilia was the final Lancia model to be developed under the personal supervision of the company's founder, Vincenzo Lancia, who died, aged 56, shortly before it was launched in 1937.

Miller's Starter Marque

Starter Lancias: *Fulvia, Beta Coupé and Spyder, Beta HPE, Monte Carlo·*

- Betas and Monte Carlos rate as affordable classics, drivers' cars with interesting engineering, but flawed by a sadly deserved reputation for rusting. The rule is to buy the best available – a later model if you can find one, and one that's as complete as possible. In some cases, trim and fittings can be very difficult to track down. Body panels can also be pricey.
- The reasons for buying any Lancia are its styling and performance, and if it's a Beta you're after, the best bets are the two-door coupé, Spyder and the HPE – that's the high-performance estate. The four-door saloon has the same Lancia virtues, but it just doesn't look sporting.
- One of the chief virtues is the Fiat-derived double-overhead-camshaft engine, which proved so successful in the Fiat 124. Over the engine's lifetime, customers were offered a choice that ran from 1300cc to 2000cc, and all of them, even when inserted in the humblest saloon, were good for a genuine 100+mph.
- The Beta Monte Carlo was a separate car from the rest of the Beta family; it was an automotive may-be, so right in concept, sadly lacking in execution. The concept was pure Fiat, a mid-engined, grown-up X1/9. In fact, it was even going to be called the X1/20.
- A tough-looking car with plenty of attitude, the Monte Carlo looked faster than it was, having a top speed of only 120mph or so. The early models had servoed front brakes, which caused heart-stopping front lock-up in the wet. The Monte Carlo was suspended in 1978, but came back in 1980 as a revised and improved model with better braking, and it's these cars that fetch a premium. The trouble is there just aren't many around – some say as few as 200 in the UK – and that means there isn't much choice. Even so, the Monte Carlo does rate highly as an affordable, exclusive and exotically engineered mid-engined sports car.
- From an earlier era, there's the Fulvia, and all but the saloon are as sharp as any Italian suit. Sharpest of all these V4-engined cars is the Zagato coupé. Some think it ugly, but it's definitely striking – and correspondingly pricey. Best mid-price compromise is probably the second-series 1.3 litre Fulvia coupé of 1970–76, or, if you've got the money, the uprated 1.6HF. The Fulvia has a strong following, though, because Fulvias simply spell four-wheeled fun in big dollops.

1966 Lancia Flaminia Zagato Supersport 'Double Bubble' Coupé, coachwork by Zagato, 2775cc V6, 152bhp, de Dion rear transaxle with inboard brakes, new clutch and shock absorbers, new chrome, resprayed in metallic grey, red leather interior.
£27,000–30,000 BKS

This striking Lancia features Zagato's renowned 'double bubble' body form, in which low overall lines and a rounded streamlined shape were achieved by creating a bulge in the roof above each front seat to provide head clearance. Only 150 Zagato Supersports were made.

1969 Lancia Fulvia HF1600 Coupé, rebuilt 1992, approximately 4,000 miles covered since, 10/6 camshafts, 45mm Weber carburettors, Group 4 exhaust system, 136bhp, finished in red with black interior, one of 20 right-hand-drive cars built, excellent condition.
£6,500–8,000 BKS

Introduced in 1963, the Fulvia saloon featured an overhead-camshaft, narrow-angle V4 engine, front-wheel drive, double-wishbone independent front suspension and disc brakes all-round. A 2+2 coupé was launched in 1965 and came with an 80bhp, 1216cc engine. Tuned HF versions formed the basis of the highly successful works rally programme.

▶ **1960 Lancia Flaminia Coupé,** 2458cc, 6 cylinders, new stainless steel exhaust, finished in silver with black interior trim and upholstery, 46,072km from new, very good condition throughout.
£4,000–5,000 H&H

LANCIA Model	ENGINE cc/cyl	DATES	CONDITION 1	2	3
Theta	4940/4	1913–19	£24,000	£16,500	£8,000
Kappa	4940/4	1919–22	£24,000	£16,000	£8,000
Dikappa	4940/4	1921–22	£24,000	£16,000	£8,000
Trikappa	4590/4	1922–26	£25,000	£18,000	£10,000
Lambda	2120/4	1923–28	£40,000	£20,000	£12,000
Dilambda	3960/8	1928–32	£35,000	£16,000	£10,000
Astura	2604/8	1931–39	£30,000	£20,000	£10,000
Artena	1925/4	1931–36	£9,000	£5,000	£2,000
Augusta	1196/4	1933–36	£9,000	£4,000	£2,000
Aprilia 238	1352/4	1937–39	£10,000	£5,000	£3,000

Coachbuilt bodywork is more desirable and can increase prices.

LANCIA Model	ENGINE cc/cyl	DATES	CONDITION 1	2	3
Aprilia 438	1486/4	1939–50	£11,000	£6,000	£3,000
Ardea	903/4	1939–53	£10,000	£5,000	£3,000
Aurelia B10	1754/6	1950–53	£9,000	£6,000	£3,000
Aurelia B15–20–22	1991/6	1951–53	£15,000+	£10,000	£8,000
Aurelia B24–B24 Spyder	2451/6	1955–58	£40,000+	£17,000	£12,000
Aurelia GT	2451/6	1953–59	£18,000+	£11,000	£9,000
Appia C10–C105	1090/4	1953–62	£6,000	£3,000	£2,000
Aurelia Ser II/IV	2266/6	1954–59	£11,000	£6,000	£4,000
Flaminia Zagato	2458/6	1957–63	£18,000+	£10,000	£7,000
Flaminia Ser	2458/6	1957–63	£18,000	£10,000	£5,000
Flavia 1500	1500/4	1960–75	£6,000	£4,000	£2,000
Fulvia	1091/4	1963–70	£3,000	£2,000	£1,000
Fulvia S	1216/4	1964–70	£5,000	£4,000	£1,500
Fulvia 1.3	1298/4	1967–75	£6,000	£4,000	£2,000
Stratos	2418/6	1969–71	£45,000	£20,000	£10,000
Flavia 2000	1991/4	1969–75	£3,000	£2,000	£1,000
Fulvia HF/1.6	1584/4	1969–75	£9,000	£5,000	£2,000
Beta HPE	1585/4	1976–82	£3,000	£1,500	£500
Beta Spyder	1995/4	1977–82	£4,000	£1,500	£800
Monte Carlo	1995/4	1976–81	£6,000	£3,000	£1,000
Gamma Coupé	2484/4	1977–84	£2,500	£1,500	£500
Gamma Berlina	2484/4	1977–84	£2,500	£1,200	£300

Competition history and convertible coachwork could cause prices to vary.

Land Rover

◀ **1948 Land Rover Series 1**, 2 litres, 80in wheelbase, pre-production type bulkhead with remote body-mounted gear lever, concealed brake fluid reservoir and square bell housing cover, original differentials and hydromatic brake shoes, finished in green, largely original, good condition. **£5,000–6,000 S**

Rover's bosses, the Wilks brothers, saw the need for a tough, 4-wheel-drive utility vehicle to serve the agricultural community in the immediate post-war years. Inspired by the Jeep, the Land Rover became an instant success. Its aluminium panels, necessitated by a shortage of steel, became a virtue in its sphere of operation, while the use of existing parts – including the P3 saloon's 1595cc, 4 cylinder engine – cut production costs and development time.

Lea-Francis

◀ **1930 Lea-Francis 1½ Litre Supercharged Hyper TT Replica**, 1.5 litre Meadows engine, twin-port head, 3-piece roller crankshaft, tubular con-rods, later self-contained supercharger, Ki-Gass starter, aero screens, full windscreen, hood and tonneau cover, finished in maroon with cream wheels, black leather bucket seats, Jaeger instruments. **£15,000–18,000 BKS**

The Hyper was the first supercharged British production car, being distinguishable from Lea Francis touring models by its sloping radiator and sporting two-seater coachwork. This car was built by Lea-Francis Cars in the 1990s, using an original saloon chassis and period parts.

LEA-FRANCIS Model	ENGINE cc/cyl	DATES	CONDITION 1	2	3
12hp	1944/4	1923–24	£10,000	£5,000	£3,000
14hp	2297/4	1923–24	£10,000	£5,000	£3,000
9hp	1074/4	1923–24	£7,000	£4,000	£2,000
10hp	1247/4	1947–54	£10,000	£5,500	£3,000
12hp	1496/4	1926–34	£12,000	£6,000	£4,000
Various 6 cylinder models	1696/6	1927–29	£13,500	£9,500	£5,000
Various 6 cylinder models	1991/6	1928–36	£10,500	£8,750	£5,000
14hp	1767/4	1946–54	£10,000	£6,000	£4,000
1.5 Litre	1499/4	1949–51	£11,000	£6,000	£3,000
2.5 Litre	2496/4	1950–52	£14,000	£8,000	£4,000

Lincoln

1927 Lincoln Model L Aero-Phaeton, coachwork by LeBaron, 6308cc side-valve V8, Winfield carburettor, 90bhp, restored, polished aluminium finish with green wings, retains all original features.
£140,000–150,000 BKS

The sensation of the 1928 New York Hotel Commodore Automobile Salon, the unique Lincoln Aero-Phaeton was the most expensive car Ford had built up to that point, bearing a price tag of $10,000. The front wings carried aircraft landing lights instead of side lights, the headlamps were bullet-shaped, and the original radiator mascot (since lost) was a stylised aeroplane. The polished aluminium body had a pointed tail, complete with aircraft-type tail and running light. Even the fuel tank was aerofoil-shaped. The instrument panel incorporated an altimeter and compass, in addition to more conventional instruments, while an aircraft-style deflector cowl was set in front of the rear cockpit.

1933 Lincoln KB Four-Door Convertible Sedan, coachwork by Dietrich, V-windscreen, suicide doors, divider window, restored late 1980s, well maintained, concours winner.
£90,000–100,000 BKS

Ford's flagship marque introduced its first V12-powered model – the KB – for 1932. The 7.3 litre, 7-bearing engine produced 150bhp at 3,400rpm. It had a forged-steel crankshaft, L-head valve gear and 'knife-and-fork' con-rods, allowing opposing cylinders to be directly opposite one another for a shorter block.

1938 Lincoln Model K Seven-Passenger Convertible Brougham, coachwork by Brunn & Co, 6784cc V12, 150bhp, engine rebuilt, new cylinder heads, original interior, wind-up glass division, 2 folding occasional seats, silk blinds, 34,000 miles from new.
£15,000–18,000 BKS

1947 Lincoln Continental, 5 litre V12, finished in dark blue with blue/grey interior trim, power windows, period radio, very good condition.
£10,000–12,000 BKS

Created as a one-off personal car for Edsel Ford, the original 1939 Continental attracted so much attention that it was put into production for 1940. Always exclusive, for it was essentially hand-built, the Continental was put back into production after WWII virtually unchanged. Only 5,324 were built before the end of production in 1948.

1947 Lincoln Continental, 4998cc V12, 130bhp at 3,600rpm, 3-speed gearbox, independent front suspension, hydraulic brakes, finished in black and blue with grey interior.
£12,000–14,000 Pou

LINCOLN Model	ENGINE cu in/cyl	DATES	CONDITION 1	2	3
Premiere Coupe	368/8	1956–57	£6,000	£4,000	£2,000
Premiere Convertible	368/8	1956–57	£14,000	£8,000	£5,000
Continental Mk II	368/8	1956–57	£10,000	£6,000	£4,000
Continental 2-door	430/8	1958–60	£6,000	£4,000	£2,000
Continental Convertible	430/8	1958–60	£18,000+	£10,000+	£7,000+

Lotus

From the humblest beginnings with an Austin 7-based trials special built in a North London lock-up, Colin Chapman's Lotus has amassed a remarkable collection of motor racing trophies and produced a string of road cars. The latter, at their very least, were always innovative and sometimes quite brilliant.

1969 Lotus 7 SIII, 1600cc, 4 cylinder Kent engine, Lotus Holbay cylinder head, polished aluminium body with yellow wings and green nose-cone, correct alloy wheels, full weather equipment, 3 miles from new, unregistered, 'as-new' condition.
£13,500–15,000 COYS

This Lotus 7 was originally supplied in component form, but was not completed until recently.

1962 Lotus Elite S2, 1216cc, 4 cylinder, overhead-camshaft Coventry-Climax engine, 75bhp at 6,100rpm, 112mph top speed, finished in white with black interior, 78,500 miles from new, original.
£19,000–22,000 COYS

▶ **1967 Lotus Elan S3,** 1558cc, double overhead camshafts, 4 cylinders, engine rebuilt, new Lotus chassis, running gear overhauled and renewed as necessary, finished in Gold Leaf Elan Sprint colours, black interior.
£9,500–11,000 H&H

The development programme for the Elan led Colin Chapman to evolve the 'twin-pontoon' F1 Lotus 25 chassis, which ultimately introduced the modern age of monocoque racing car construction.

1960 Lotus Elite SE, 1216cc, 4 cylinder, all-aluminium, overhead-camshaft Coventry-Climax engine, 4-wheel disc brakes, 112mph top speed, finished in red with original tan interior, very good condition throughout.
£19,000–22,000 BRIT

Designed during the mid-1950s, the striking Lotus Elite achieved wide acclaim. It was the first production car to use monocoque fibreglass construction.

1964 Lotus Elan S1, 1558cc, 4 cylinders, left-hand drive, restored, little use since, in need of running in.
£12,000–14,000 BRIT

Of advanced specification with superlative handling, the Elan was a worthy successor to the original Elite, being introduced in 1962. It was built upon a rigid backbone chassis, which proved very effective. The Elan evolved through several forms before its eventual demise in 1973.

Lotus Elite (1957–63)

Body style: Two-door, two-seater sports coupé.
Construction: Fibreglass monocoque.
Engine: Overhead-camshaft, four-cylinder Coventry-Climax, 1216cc.
Power output: 75–105bhp at 6,100–6,800rpm.
Transmission: Four-speed MG or ZF gearbox.
Suspension: Independent all-round: front by wishbones and coil springs; rear by MacPherson-type Chapman struts.
Brakes: Discs all-round (inboard at rear).
Maximum speed: 118mph.
0–60mph: 11.1 seconds.
Average fuel consumption: 35mpg.
Production: 988 approximately.

The Elite was the first Lotus designed for road use rather than out-and-out racing, paving the way for a string of stunning sports and GT cars that, at least, were always innovative. However, the first Elite was much more than that; its all-fibreglass construction – chassis as well as body – was a bold departure which, coupled with many other innovations, made the car truly exceptional. What's more, its Lotus race-breeding endowed it with phenomenal handling. This, together with an unparalleled power-to-weight ratio, brought an almost unbroken string of racing successes. The Elite also happens to be one of the prettiest cars of its era, in short, a superb GT in miniature.

1971 Lotus Elan Sprint, 126bhp 'big-valve' engine, 120+mph, 0–60mph in 6.7 seconds, rebuilt 1990, finished in yellow with black interior, very good condition throughout.
£7,500–9,000 BKS

1971 Lotus Elan Sprint, 1600cc, double-overhead-camshaft engine, finished in Gold Leaf Team Lotus colours, some surface micro-blistering of bodywork, interior worn, engine bay in need of tidying.
£8,000–9,000 BKS

1968 Lotus Elan 2+2, finished in pale blue with black interior trim and upholstery, fibreglass bodywork showing signs of micro-blistering, interior worn, unrestored, original.
£3,250–4,250 BKS

► **1972 Lotus Elan +2,** 1558cc 'big-valve' engine, restored, engine rebuilt, new clutch and Lotus servo, finished in red with black interior, 85,000 miles from new, good condition.
£4,000–5,000 H&H

◄ **1972 Lotus Elan +2S 130/5,** 1558cc, finished in Tawny gold with metallic silver roof, original, excellent condition throughout.
£14,500–17,000 BRIT

This +2S 130/5 (the '5' denoting a 5-speed gearbox) was fitted with all the Lotus extras and prepared for the late Colin Chapman's own use. He retained the car until it had covered only 6,777 miles, at which point it was placed in the Lotus museum.

LOTUS Model	ENGINE cc/cyl	DATES	CONDITION 1	2	3
Six		1953–56	£13,000+	£7,000+	£5,000+
Seven S1 Sports	1172/4	1957–64	£12,000+	£9,000+	£5,000+
Seven S2 Sports	1498/4	1961–66	£10,000+	£8,000+	£5,000+
Seven S3 Sports	1558/4	1961–66	£10,000+	£8,000+	£5,000+
Seven S4	1598/4	1969–72	£8,000	£5,000	£3,000
Elan S1 Convertible	1558/4	1962–64	£12,000+	£8,000	£4,500
Elan S2 Convertible	1558/4	1964–66	£12,000+	£7,000	£4,000
Elan S3 Convertible	1558/4	1966–69	£12,000+	£8,000	£5,000
Elan S3 FHC	1558/4	1966–69	£13,000	£7,000	£5,000
Elan S4 Convertible	1558/4	1968–71	£14,000+	£9,500	£7,000
Elan S4 FHC	1558/4	1968–71	£10,000+	£7,500	£5,000
Elan Sprint Convertible	1558/4	1971–73	£15,000+	£8,500+	£7,000
Elan Sprint FHC	1558/4	1971–73	£10,000+	£7,000	£6,000
Europa S1 FHC	1470/4	1966–69	£4,000+	£3,500	£2,000
Europa S2 FHC	1470/4	1969–71	£5,500+	£3,000	£2,000
Europa Twin Cam	1558/4	1971–75	£8,000	£6,000	£4,000
Elan +2S 130	1558/4	1971–74	£8,000	£5,000	£4,000
Elite S1 FHC	1261/4	1974–80	£3,500	£2,500	£1,500
Eclat S1	1973/4	1975–82	£3,500	£3,000	£1,500
Esprit 1	1973/4	1977–81	£6,500	£5,000	£3,000
Esprit 2	1973/4	1976–81	£7,000	£4,000	£2,500
Esprit S2.2	2174/4	1980–81	£7,000	£5,500	£3,000
Esprit Turbo	2174/4	1980–88	£10,000	£7,000	£4,000
Excel	2174/4	1983–85	£5,000	£3,000	£2,500

Prices vary with some limited-edition Lotus models and with competition history.

1975 Lotus Europa Special, 1558cc, 4 cylinders, finished in black with gold coachlines, 82 miles from new, very good original condition throughout.
£20,000–22,000 COYS

Launched in 1966, the mid-engined Type 46 Europa was based on a steel backbone chassis, bonded to a fibreglass body, and housing an alloy 1470cc Renault engine and 4-speed transaxle. Suspension was all-independent, while the brakes were a combination of front discs and rear drums. The Type 46 was superseded by the Type 74 Twin Cam in 1971. This was equipped with the 1558cc, 105bhp twin-cam engine from the Elan. The Europa Special came in 1972 and had the Elan Sprint's 126bhp engine and Lotus 5-speed gearbox. This 123mph Europa could sprint to 60mph in just 6.8 seconds.

◄ **1972 Lotus Elan +2,** restored, new chassis, finished in red with black vinyl roof.
£7,500–9,000 WILM

1972 Lotus Europa, 1600cc, double-overhead-camshaft engine, 105bhp, 4-speed gearbox, restored, 'as-new' condition.
£11,000–14,000 PC

1980 Lotus Esprit S2 2.2, 2174cc, 4 cylinders, finished in bronze with tan leather interior, ski rack, 19,070 miles from new, used in the film *For Your Eyes Only*.
£26,000–30,000 COYS

The Esprit was launched in 1975. Based on Vauxhall's 1973cc alloy block, its motor sported a Lotus twin-cam cylinder head and twin Dell'Orto carburettors, producing 160bhp, which was good for 0–60mph in 7.5 seconds and 135mph. The S2, with wider wheels, larger radiator and vents behind the rear windows, followed in August 1978, and in May 1980, capacity rose to 2174cc. Only 88 2.2 litre S2 models were built before being replaced by the S3 in 1981.

◄ **1985/91 Lotus Eclat Excel Active Suspension,**
2174cc, 4 valves per cylinder, Dell'Orto carburettors,
160bhp at 5,500rpm, rebodied as an SE model in 1991,
finished in dark blue, good condition.
£9,000–10,000 COYS

**This Excel was used by Lotus as a research vehicle.
It is fitted with an active suspension system using
hydraulics and springs.**

Lotus Elan (1962–73)

Engine: Double-overhead-camshaft, four-cylinder
Ford, 1588cc.
Power output: Up to 126bhp (Elan Sprint).
Transmission: Four- or five-speed manual.
Brakes: Discs all-round.
Maximum speed: 121mph (Elan Sprint).
0–60mph: 6.7 seconds (Elan Sprint).
Production: 12,224.
For: Sublime handling finesse; gutsy Ford-based
double-overhead-camshaft engine that's as lively as
many a 16-valve GTi unit; poise and suppleness
that make an MGB or Triumph TR feel like a
clapped-out tractor.
Against: Build quality was indifferent. Neither does

it help that many Elans were home-built from kits.
They also appealed to hard-charging, string-
backed-glove types, who would fiddle with and
tune their cars until eventually they broke, crashed
or caught fire.
Best buy: The Elan you want is either an unrestored
warts-and-all car, or a first-class restoration that's
been properly stripped, refurbished and repainted.
The key to the engine is careful and regular
maintenance, so make sure you study the bills and
service history. By now, most cars will have had a
replacement backbone chassis – galvanised if it
was made after 1980. Even if it hasn't, you can buy
a galvanised replacement.

Mallalieu

◄ **1979 Mallalieu Barchetta ,** 4257cc, 6 cylinders,
left-hand drive, finished in white with tan leather interior
trim, mechanically sound.
£13,000–15,000 BRIT

While in America, the late Derry Mallalieu
constructed a special based on a Mk VI Bentley,
which was so admired by fellow enthusiasts that
upon his return to Britain, he set up a business to
build similar cars. In the 1970s, Mk VI Bentleys
requiring major surgery were not difficult to come by,
and donor cars were acquired with ease. Following
removal of the bodywork, the chassis and all
mechanical components were reconditioned before
being fitted with four-seat (Barchetta) or two-seat
(Oxford) open touring coachwork.

Marcos

**Miller's is a price GUIDE
not a price LIST**

◄ **1996 Marcos Montana,**
4 litres, finished in dark blue,
6,000 miles from new.
£20,000–23,000 WILM

MARCOS Model	ENGINE cc/cyl	DATES	CONDITION 1	2	3
1500/1600/1800	1500/1600/1800/4	1964–69	£8,000	£5,000	£2,500
Mini-Marcos	848/4	1965–74	£3,500	£2,500	£1,500
Marcos 3 Litre	3000/6	1969–71	£9,000	£6,000	£4,000
Mantis	2498	1970–71	£10,000	£4,500	£1,500

Maserati

Although it wasn't until 1926 that the first car to bear the Maserati name appeared – the 1.5 litre Tipo 26 racer – the five Maserati brothers had been very closely involved with engineering and building racing cars for some time. The company's automotive activities are split between two distinct eras: the racing years and the period of wonderful road cars. The first Maserati road car, the A6 of 1946, was really a racer dressed in street clothes. However, in 1957, as Maserati abandoned Grand Prix racing, the company committed to building true road-going sports cars and a line of luxury GTs.

1962 Maserati 3500GT Coupé, coachwork by Touring, 3500cc, double-overhead-camshaft, 6 cylinder engine, twin spark plugs, fuel injection replaced by earlier triple-Weber set-up, 5-speed all-synchromesh gearbox, tubular chassis, independent coil-spring/wishbone front suspension, leaf-sprung rear axle, 4-wheel disc brakes, 144mph top speed, finished in green with tan leather interior, 11,000km from new, good original condition.
£16,000–18,000 COYS

The 3500GT was the first true production Maserati, previous models having been little more than revamped racers manufactured in limited numbers.

1962 Maserati 3500GT Sebring Series I, coachwork by Vignale, double-overhead-camshaft, 6 cylinder engine, fuel injection, 235bhp, 5-speed gearbox, 4-wheel disc brakes, tubular chassis, restored at a cost of £25,000, finished in red with tan hide interior, excellent condition
£24,000–26,000 BKS

1964 Maserati Mistral Spyder, coachwork by Frua, 245bhp, 5-speed ZF gearbox, 4-wheel disc brakes, restored, finished in light metallic green with black leather upholstery, concours condition.
£43,000–47,000 BKS

The Mistral was based on a short-wheelbase, square-tube version of the 3500GT chassis, and it was the stiffest frame of the line. The car's 3.5 litre, twin-cam, straight-6 engine was a first cousin to the 250F unit that powered Fangio to the World Championship in 1957.

Maserati Ghibli (1967–73)

Body styles: Two-door sports coupé; open Spyder.
Construction: Steel body, separate tubular chassis.
Engine: Double-overhead-camshaft, 90-degree V8, 4719cc or 4930cc (SS).
Power output: 330bhp at 5,000rpm (4719cc); 335bhp at 5,500rpm (4930cc).
Transmission: Five-speed ZF manual or three-speed Borg-Warner automatic.
Suspension: Independent front by wishbones and coil-springs; rigid rear axle with radius arms and semi-elliptic leaf springs.
Brakes: Girling discs all-round.
Maximum speed: 154mph or 168mph (SS).
0–60mph: 6.6 seconds or 6.2 seconds (SS).
0–100mph: 15.7 seconds.
Average fuel consumption: 10mpg.
Production: 1,274.

Many reckon that the Ghibli is the greatest of all road-going Maseratis. It was the sensation of the 1966 Turin Show, and 30 years on is widely regarded as Maserati's ultimate front-engined road car, a supercar blend of luxury, performance and stunning good looks that never again came together so sublimely on anything bearing the three-pointed trident. Pitched squarely against the Ferrari Daytona and Lamborghini Miura, it outsold both. Its engineering may have been dated, but it had the perfect pedigree, with loads of grunt from its throaty V8 engine, especially low down, and roadholding bred of a long racing heritage. Add the flawless Ghia design and five-star interior appointments that were a cut above contemporary Lambo and Ferrari interiors in finish, detail and layout, and you've got something very special.

1968 Maserati Mistral Coupé, coachwork by Frua, 3 litres, 6 cylinders, 260bhp, 5-speed ZF gearbox, 4-wheel disc brakes, Borrani wire wheels, 140mph top speed, restored 1992/93 finished in light metallic blue with red leather interior, excellent condition throughout.
£16,000–18,000 BKS

1971 Maserati Indy, 4719cc V8, 320bhp at 5,500rpm, 5-speed ZF gearbox, independent front suspension, 4-wheel disc brakes, 250km/h top speed.
£9,500–11,000 Pou

◄ **1979 Maserati Kyalami,** coachwork by Frua, manual gearbox, all independent suspension, left-hand drive, finished in metallic sable with cream cloth/leather upholstery, unrestored, good original condition.
£6,750–8,000 BKS

Parent company Citroën's financial crisis led to Maserati changing hands in 1975, its saviour being Alessandro De Tomaso. One of the revitalised company's first products was the Kyalami saloon, effectively a revised De Tomaso Longchamp fitted with a Maserati V8 engine.

MASERATI Model	ENGINE cc/cyl	DATES	CONDITION 1	2	3
AG-1500	1488/6	1946–50	£30,000+	£20,000	£10,000
A6G	1954/6	1951–53	£50,000+	£35,000	£22,000
A6G-2000	1985/6	1954–57	£45,000+	£35,000	£20,000
3500GT FHC	3485/6	1957–64	£20,000	£14,000	£10,000
3500GT Spyder	3485/6	1957–64	£35,000	£22,000	£15,000
5000GT	4935/8	1960–65	£60,000	£20,000	£15,000
Sebring	3694/6	1962–66	£20,000	£15,000	£10,000
Quattroporte	4136/8	1963–74	£11,000	£9,000	£7,000
Mistral	4014/6	1964–70	£15,000	£11,000	£9,000
Mistral Spyder	4014/6	1964–70	£30,000+	£18,000	£12,000
Mexico	4719/8	1965–68	£15,000	£12,000	£9,000
Ghibli	4719/8	1967–73	£20,000	£15,000	£12,000
Ghibli-Spyder/SS	4136/8	1969–74	£50,000	£40,000	£25,000
Indy	4136/8	1969–74	£18,000	£13,000	£10,000
Bora	4719/8	1971–80	£25,000	£18,000	£11,000
Merak/SS	2965/6	1972–81	£16,000	£14,000	£9,000
Khamsin	4930/8	1974–81	£16,000	£11,000	£9,000

Early cars with competition/berlinetta coachwork, eg. Zagato, command a premium.

Maxwell

◄ **1911 Maxwell Model AB 14hp Two-Seater Runabout,** horizontally-opposed, twin-cylinder engine, epicyclic gearbox, folding brass windscreen, Maxwell No. 27 brass headlamps and lighting, restored 1990, engine and differential rebuilt, finished in blue and black with deep-buttoned black upholstery, original.
£11,000–13,000 BKS

With backer Benjamin Briscoe, Jonathan D. Maxwell set up the Maxwell-Briscoe Motor Company in Tarrytown, New York, Initially, the company produced a twin-cylinder car with 2-speed epicyclic gearbox and shaft drive. A European touch was the forward mounting of the engine and radiator, at a time when many American manufacturers insisted on leaving the engine where you really had to 'get out and get under'.

Maybach

◄ **1938 Maybach SW38 Spohn Sports Cabriolet,** 3.8 litre, overhead-camshaft, 6 cylinder in-line engine, older restoration, excellent condition throughout.
£500,000+ BLK

Maybach built respected and costly cars, the company's roots extending back to the very first self-propelled vehicles. The first of the SW range appeared in 1935.

McLaren

1994 McLaren F1, 6.1 litre, double-overhead-camshaft, 48-valve BMW V12, 627+bhp at 7,500rpm, 6-speed transverse gearbox, central driving position, 2 passenger seats, windscreen with heater membrane and ultra-violet filter, finished in black with beige leather upholstery, 500km from new, 'as-new' condition.
£380,000+ BKS

The McLaren F1 incorporates much technology from the world's premier racing class, including ground-effect aerodynamics. A TAG electronic chassis control unit monitors the car's behaviour, deploying a rear spoiler to enhance stability under heavy braking and operating cooling ducts to ensure optimum brake temperature at all times. The F1's hull is formed from carbon fibre, offering enormous advantages in rigidity, safety, and weight reduction. This particular example was the seventh car built.

Mercedes-Benz

Germany's largest industrial concern is now an even bigger global player after recently teaming up with Chrysler. It's all a very long way from 1886, when Karl Benz and Gottleib Daimler, working independently of each other, produced petrol-engined road vehicles. In 1894, Benz's Velo became the world's first true production automobile. The name Mercedes was first used on a Daimler in 1899.

In 1926, the two concerns merged to form Daimler-Benz, the cars being called Mercedes-Benz. In the 1930s, the range of road cars was comprehensive, and from 1934 to the outbreak of war, Mercedes-Benz dominated the Grand Prix scene along with its compatriot, Auto Union. Following post-war reconstruction, Mercedes-Benz signalled to the world that it was back on top with the gorgeous 300SL Gullwing, the forerunner of modern supercars. Since then, the company has concentrated on producing upmarket executive saloons, sporting coupés and cabriolets, all formidably engineered. And now, with the A-class, Mercedes' product range is the broadest it's ever been.

1924 Mercedes 24/100/140 PS Sports Phaeton, 6.3 litre, overhead-camshaft, 6 cylinder engine, Roots-type supercharger, 80mph top speed, twin side-mounted spares, Bosch headlamps, centre-lock wooden artillery wheels, finished in white with black leather interior trim. **£60,000–70,000 BKS**

Built under the direction of Ferdinand Porsche, who had been appointed chief engineer at Mercedes in 1923, the 24/100/140 was the forebear of the legendary line of supercharged Mercedes cars that included the mighty SSK and SSKL. Approximately 395 chassis were produced between 1924 and 1929.

Tony Upson, large mural of a Mercedes-Benz, acrylic on board, framed, 96x48in (244x122cm). **£400–450 BKS**

▶ **1954 Mercedes-Benz 300SL Gullwing,** fuel injection, synchromesh gearbox, brakes overhauled, original undertrays, finished in metallic silver with black upholstery, excellent condition throughout. **£150,000–170,000 BKS**

Gullwings were only made until 1957, the fuel-injected, 3 litre engine being sufficiently powerful to make the 300SL the fastest car on the road during the 1950s. This example was only the eighth car built. Its first owner was Prince Sadruddin Aga Khan, one of the world's wealthiest young men, who took delivery of it while studying at Harvard.

1930 Mercedes-Benz 630K Town Car, coachwork by Million Guiet, 6.25 litre, supercharged, 6 cylinder engine, left hand drive, finished in navy blue with red coachlines, black leather-trimmed driver's compartment, tan upholstery to passenger compartment, older restoration, good condition. **£95,000–110,000 BKS**

During 1926, a shortened version of the 630 Mercedes-Benz was launched. This was the 630K (the 'K' standing for *kurz*, German for short). Powered by a supercharged 6.25 litre engine, it was capable of speeds in excess of 90mph.

1957 Mercedes-Benz 220S, 2195cc, 6 cylinders, new kingpins and trunnions, new exhaust, finished in grey, largely original, good condition. **£2,000–2,500 BRIT**

The twin-carburettor 220S saloon was capable of reaching a speed of 100mph.

1956 Mercedes-Benz 300SL Gullwing, 2996cc, 6 cylinders, space-frame chassis, restored, engine rebuilt at a cost over $12,000, braking system, front hubs and rear axle overhauled, finished in silver with blue leather interior, excellent condition throughout.
£110,000–125,000 COYS

The 300SL was originally created by Mercedes-Benz as a racing car to pave the way for a return to F1. There was no intention to build it as a road car, until the American importer, Max Hoffman, guaranteed an order for a thousand.

Nicholas Watts, Carrera Panamericana 1952, showing the winning Mercedes-Benz 300SL driven by Karl Kling, limited-edition print, signed by Karl Kling. 24¾x33in (63x84cm).
£90–100 MPG

Tony Upson, large mural of the 1955 Mille Miglia-winning Mercedes-Benz 300SLR, inset showing Stirling Moss and Dennis Jenkinson, acrylic on board, 48x96in (122x244cm).
£600–700 BKS

1956 Mercedes-Benz 300SL Gullwing, 3 litre, 6 cylinder engine, fuel-injection, dry-sump lubrication, tubular space-frame chassis, aluminium doors, bonnet and boot lid, restored, finished in Eggshell white with dark green leather upholstery, 33,000km from new.
£110,000–125,000 BKS

A known continuous history can add value to and enhance the enjoyment of a car.

MERCEDES-BENZ Model	ENGINE cc/cyl	DATES	CONDITION		
			1	2	3
300ABCD	2996/6	1951–62	£15,000	£10,000	£8,000
220A/S/SE Ponton	2195/6	1952–60	£10,000	£5,000	£3,000
220S/SEB Coupé	2915/6	1956–59	£11,000	£7,000	£5,000
220S/SEB Cabriolet	2195/6	1958–59	£28,000+	£18,000	£7,000
190SL	1897/4	1955–63	£20,000+	£15,000+	£10,000
300SL Gullwing	2996/6	1954–57	£120,000+	£100,000	£70,000
300SL Roadster	2996/6	1957–63	£110,000+	£90,000	£70,000
230/250SL	2306/6				
	2496/6	1963–68	£14,000+	£10,000+	£7,000
280SL	2778/6	1961–71	£16,000	£12,000	£9,000
220/250SE	2195/6				
	2496/6	1960–68	£10,000	£7,000	£4,000
300SE	2996/6	1961–65	£11,000	£8,000	£6,000
280SE Convertible	2778/6	1965–69	£25,000	£18,000	£12,000
280SE V8 Convertible	3499/8	1969–71	£30,000+	£20,000	£15,000
280SE Coupé	2496/6	1965–72	£12,000	£8,000	£5,000
300SEL 6.3	6330/8	1968–72	£12,000	£7,000	£3,500
600 & 600 Pullman	6332/8	1964–81	£40,000+	£15,000	£8,000

1957 Mercedes-Benz 300SL Roadster, 3 litre, 6 cylinder engine, fuel injection, dry-sump lubrication, tubular space-frame, finished in silver-grey, new black leather trim, black top, good condition throughout.
£80,000–90,000 COYS

A roadster version of the 300SL was launched in 1957. In addition to the same basic mechanical specification as the Gullwing, it had a soft top that could be concealed beneath a hinged metal cover, and revised rear axle location to improve roadholding. More than 1,800 were delivered in the course of the following six years.

1966 Mercedes-Benz 230SL Coupé, 2306cc, manual gearbox, finished in white with red interior, good condition.
£9,000–11,000 LF

1966 Mercedes-Benz 230SL, 2306cc, 6 cylinder engine, manual gearbox, later alloy wheels, restored, engine rebuilt, many new panels, resprayed in metallic red, hardtop in need of restoration, Oatmeal leather trim, excellent condition throughout.
£14,000–16,000 H&H

> **Miller's is a price GUIDE not a price LIST**

Mercedes-Benz 230/250/280SL (1963–71)

Body style: Two-door, two-seat convertible with detachable hardtop.
Construction: Pressed-steel monocoque.
Engines: Six-cylinder, in-line, 2281cc, 2496cc and 2778cc.
Power output: 150bhp (230 and 250SL), 170bhp (280SL).
Transmission: Four-speed manual, optional five-speed manual or four-speed automatic.
Brakes: Servo-assisted front discs and rear drums (230SL); discs all-round (250 and 280SL).
Maximum speed: 115-125mph.
0–60mph: 9.3–11 seconds.
Production: 230SL, 19,831; 250SL, 5,196; 280SL, 23,885.
In 1963, the new SLs took over the sporting mantle of the ageing 190SL. In its place, the new 230SL, which evolved through the 250SL to the 280SL, was strikingly modern, with uncluttered, clean-shaven good looks, which endured until 1971 and still look crisp today. In fact, you can still pick out some of the styling motifs on today's sporting Mercs. Underneath the elegant sheet metal, they were based closely on the earlier 'fintail saloons',

sharing even the decidedly unsporting, recirculating-ball steering. Suspension, too, was on the soft side for string-backed-glove types. Yet it's the looks that really mark this Merc out as something special, and that enduring design, with its distinctive 'pagoda roof', is down to Frenchman Paul Bracq. It's certainly not the most hairy-chested of sports cars, yet this well-manicured Merc is a beautifully-built boulevardier that will induce a sense of supreme self-satisfaction on any journey.
Market comment: There's little to choose between the 230 and 250SL, either in price or performance – the 250SL offered no more power, but a little more torque. Expect to pay at least £6,000–8,000 for something safe and drivable – cars offered for less should be subjected to the closest scrutiny – to around £15,000 and more for really cracking cars. The 280SL was appreciably more powerful and today is the most prized model, commanding a premium of £2,000 or more for better cars.
SL jargon: In Mercedes code speak, the 'S' stood for Sport or Super, 'L' for *Leicht* (light) and sometimes *Luxus* (luxury), although at well over 3000lb, the 280SL certainly wasn't particularly light.

1968 Mercedes-Benz 250SL, 2496cc, 6 cylinders, power steering, 4-wheel disc brakes, new hood, finished in white with blue interior, good condition throughout.
£9,000–11,000 COYS

In March 1963, the new generation of SL sports cars was launched with the debut of the 230SL. Mercedes engineering, together with elegance and practicality, made the 'pagoda-roof' SL one of the most distinctive designs of its era.

1968 Mercedes-Benz 280SL, 2778cc, automatic transmission, restored, bare-metal respray in white, black interior trim and upholstery, history file.
£24,000–26,000 H&H

1969 Mercedes-Benz 280SL, 2778cc, overhead-camshaft, 6 cylinder engine, fuel injection, 170bhp, automatic transmission, 4-wheel disc brakes, left-hand drive, restored 1994, finished in Sable with cream trim, good condition throughout.
£13,000–15,000 BKS

The 280SL was launched late in 1967. The ultimate version of the celebrated 'pagoda-roof' sporting two-seaters, it could cruise effortlessly at 99mph and had a top speed of over 121mph. Well received, it remained in production until 1971.

◀ 1981 Mercedes-Benz 280SL, 2778cc, finished in Inca red with beige interior, good condition.
£13,000–15,000 BRIT

1968 Mercedes-Benz 600 Pullman Limousine, 6332cc, overhead-camshaft V8, Bosch fuel injection, 300bhp at 4100rpm, 4-speed automatic transmission, hydro-pneumatic, self-levelling independent suspension, 4-wheel disc brakes, left-hand drive, lockable safes beneath rear seats, CCTV camera trained through rear window, refrigerator in boot.
£16,000–20,000 C

With its sophisticated engineering and all-embracing levels of equipment, the 600 outpaced any competitor. It was available as a four-door limousine, Pullman six-door limousine or Pullman landaulette.

1969 Mercedes-Benz 600 Limousine, 6.3 litre, fuel-injected V8, 4-speed automatic transmission, hydro-pneumatic, self-levelling suspension, 4-wheel disc brakes, power steering, separate heating/ventilation systems for front and rear compartments, 78,000km from new, finished in metallic burgundy with cream leather upholstery, very good condition.
£22,000–25,000 BKS

1968 Mercedes-Benz 280SE, 2778cc, overhead-camshaft, 6 cylinder in-line engine, automatic transmission, finished in silver with black interior, good condition throughout.
£3,750–4,500 LF

> **Cross Reference**
> See Colour Review

1969 Mercedes-Benz 280SE Cabriolet, 2778cc, overhead-camshaft, 6 cylinder engine, fuel injection, 160bhp at 5,500rpm, automatic transmission, restored, engine overhauled, finished in Sable with matching hood and beige upholstery, very good condition.
£19,000–22,000 BKS

Mercedes' 15 'new generation' models went on sale in January 1968. However, although the 280SE saloon shared its bodyshell with the new 280S, the coupé and cabriolet retained the elegant looks of the outgoing 250SE, which they replaced.

1970 Mercedes-Benz 280SE Cabriolet, 3.5 litre, overhead-camshaft V8, fuel injection, 200bhp at 5,800rpm, 120mph top speed, 0–60mph in under 10 seconds, restored 1989, finished in Smoke silver with tan interior, excellent condition.
£30,000–34,000 COYS

◄ **1972 Mercedes-Benz 280SE Four-Door Saloon,** 3.5 litre, overhead-camshaft V8, cast-iron block and aluminium cylinder heads, 200bhp at 5,800rpm, Bosch electronic fuel injection, automatic transmission, 125mph top speed, finished in metallic blue with blue leather interior, good condition throughout.
£1,400–1,800 BKS

1972 Mercedes-Benz 250CE, 2496cc, 6 cylinders, 8,000 miles from new, 'as-new' condition throughout. £7,000–8,000 BRIT

1972 Mercedes-Benz 350SL, 3499cc V8, manual gearbox, finished in white with tan interior trim, black cloth hood, good mechanical condition. £8,500–10,000 BRIT

1973 Mercedes-Benz 350SL, 3.5 litre V8, very good condition. £10,000–12,000 WILM

1978 Mercedes-Benz 350SL, restored, engine rebuilt, new body panels, bare-metal respray, little recent use, comprehensive history. £9,500–11,000 BARO

1979 Mercedes-Benz 450SE Saloon, 4250cc V8, 3-speed automatic transmission, new brake discs, shock absorbers and exhaust, finished in blue with magnolia upholstery, 89,419 miles from new, very good condition. £2,500–3,000 H&H

1979 Mercedes-Benz 450SEL, 6.9 litres, 3-speed automatic gearbox, stainless steel exhaust, resprayed in silver, blue velour trim, 82,870 miles from new, very good condition throughout. £4,000–5,000 H&H

1979 Mercedes-Benz 450SL Convertible, 4.5 litre V8, hard and soft tops, finished in dark blue, good condition. £6,000–8,000 WILM

1979 Mercedes-Benz 450SLC, 4520cc V8, electric sunroof, air conditioning, cruise control, 15,700 miles from new, excellent condition.
£16,000–18,000 BRIT

The 450SLC combined luxury with performance. Its robust 4.5 litre V8 made it an ideal long-distance tourer.

1979 Mercedes-Benz 450SL, 4520cc V8, finished in bronze with contrasting cream leather interior, air conditioning, very good condition throughout.
£10,500–12,000 BRIT

1980 Mercedes-Benz 380SLC, 3818cc V8, finished in silver with blue velour interior, good condition throughout.
£3,500–4,500 BRIT

1988 Mercedes-Benz 300SL, hard and soft tops, finished in red, excellent condition.
£19,000–21,500 SJR

1988 Mercedes-Benz 300SL Convertible, 2962cc, overhead-camshaft, 6 cylinder engine, 188bhp, 3-speed automatic transmission, hard and soft tops, finished in white with black leather interior trim and upholstery, black carpets, good condition throughout.
£16,000–18,000 LF

▶ **1987 Mercedes-Benz 190E Cosworth,** high-performance, 2.3 litre, 16-valve engine, 5-speed manual gearbox, alloy wheels, electric sunroof, finished in black metallic, black leather interior upholstery and trim, excellent condition throughout.
£8,000–9,000 Mot

◀ **1990 Mercedes-Benz 190 Evo II Saloon,** 2463cc, 4 cylinders, 373 miles from new.
£30,000–34,000 COYS

With ever stiffer competition in touring car racing, Mercedes sought to revise the Cosworth-developed 190E 2.3. The result was the 2.5 litre Evolution II, a homologation special built in limited numbers and sold at vast cost. The engine produced 235bhp, permitting an artificially-limited top speed of 155mph and 0–100mph in 14 seconds.

Mercury

967 Mercury Cougar, 4736cc, V8 engine, 225bhp, automatic transmission, good condition throughout.
4,500–5,000 COUG

MG

In the beginning, the famous initials 'MG' stood for Morris Garages. The marque was born in 1923, when Cecil Kimber, general manager of the Oxford garage, attached a stylish two-seater sporting body to a Morris chassis. Since then, those two letters have spelled affordable sports car fun for literally millions of enthusiasts. Throughout much of its history, MG has been starved of resources and been close to oblivion.

Since 1935, when it became part of the Morris empire, the MG marque has had to endure a succession of owners who were, at times, both apathetic and completely disinterested. Yet somehow, through the good years and the lean times, MG has mostly managed to retain an individual sporting identity. Today, the mantle of MG magic has passed to BMW through its ownership of the Rover Group.

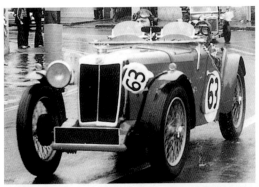

◄ **1933 MG J2 Midget,** 847cc, overhead-camshaft, 4 cylinder engine, 36bhp at 5,500rpm, 4-speed manual gearbox, 4-wheel hydraulic drum brakes, semi-elliptic leaf spring suspension, finished in red with black fabric interior, good condition.
£10,000–12,000 C

The J2 Midget was a true driver's machine, embodying the essential aspects of sports car design, including a fold-flat windscreen, external Le Mans-type slab petrol tank, and a remote gear-change. The high-revving, overhead-camshaft engine produced 36bhp at 5,500rpm. The car had a top speed of 83mph and lively acceleration, ensuring competition success.

1933 MG Magna L1 Four-Seater, 1087cc, 6 cylinders, original specification, full weather equipment, older restoration, finished in navy blue with black interior trim, very good condition throughout.
£20,000–22,000 S

One of the lowest four-seater cars ever built, the F-Type Magna was introduced toward the end of 1931. The F2 and F3 followed in 1932, and total production of F-Types approached 1,300. The series continued in 1933 with the improved L-Type, employing the same engine design as the renowned Magnette. It was available in Tourer, Saloon or Continental Coupé form.

► **1946 MG TC Midget,** race-tuned 1500cc engine, 130bhp, competition clutch, strengthened gearbox, stiffened suspension, alloy drum brakes, uprated steering box, lightweight body, full weather equipment, aero screens, restored, finished in Carmen red, Brooklands-type steering wheel, racing seats trimmed in beige Connolly hide, competition history, good condition.
£10,500–13,000 S

The engine fitted to this Midget was originally prepared by Jack Newton for one of Harry Lester's 1955 Le Mans entries, but never used.

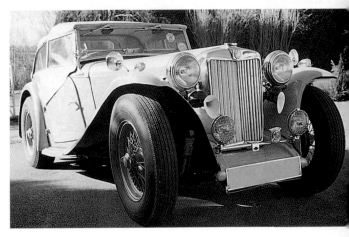

1946 MG TC Midget, 1303cc, full weather equipment, chassis-up restoration, finished in cream with red interior trim, excellent condition throughout.
£13,000–15,000 H&H

1947 MG TC Midget, 1250cc, overhead-valve 4 cylinder engine, twin SU carburettors, 54bhp at 5,200rpm, 4-speed manual gearbox, semi-elliptic leaf-spring suspension, 4-wheel drum brakes, in need of recommissioning, otherwise good condition throughout.
£10,500–12,500 C

Although unashamedly old-fashioned when it appeared in 1946, the TC Midget captured hearts all over the world and became MG's best-seller.

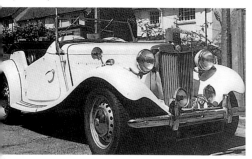

1952 MG TD Midget, finished in cream with black leather interior, good condition.
£6,500–8,000 BKS

A larger car than its predecessors, the TD appeared in 1949. It retained the looks of the traditional MG sports car and used the TC's well-tried 1250cc XPAG engine. However, it shared many other mechanical components with the Y-Type saloon, including independent front suspension and rack-and-pinion steering. The TD was the most successful of the T-series MGs, over 29,000 being built between 1949 and 1953.

1953 MG TD Midget Mk II, 1250cc, 4 cylinders, independent front suspension, rack-and-pinion steering, 15in disc wheels, restored, converted to right-hand drive, finished in red, excellent condition throughout.
£9,500–11,000 BRIT

1956 MGA Roadster, 1489cc, 4 cylinders, original right-hand-drive model, restored, finished in Orient red, correct in every respect.
£13,500–15,500 BRIT

1953 MG TF Midget, 1250cc, 4-speed manual gearbox, wire wheels, luggage rack, finished in Old English white with red leather interior, 95,700 miles from new, excellent condition.
£13,000–15,000 H&H

Of the T-series Midgets, the TF was the last and arguably the best. There were two engine sizes: 1250cc and 1500cc.

Restored Values

The cost of a professional restoration will have an influence on, but no direct relation to, a car's market value. A restored car can have a market value lower than the cost of its restoration.

1956 MGA Roadster, completely restored, converted to right-hand drive, finished in Old English white, interior trimmed in red leather, concours condition.
£14,000–15,000 BRIT

The MGA appeared in 1955 as the successor to the TF Midget. Its curvaceous styling was well received and it proved a tremendous success, remaining in production until 1962.

1959 MGA Twin Cam Roadster, 1588cc, double-overhead-camshaft engine, 108bhp, 110mph top speed, 0–60mph in 9.1 seconds, 4-wheel disc brakes, body-off restoration, corroded panels replaced, new floor, engine and ancillaries overhauled, finished in navy blue with red leather upholstery.
£14,000–16,000 BKS

1959 MGA Twin Cam Roadster, 1680cc, twin 45DCOE Weber carburettors, competition camshafts, rods and pistons, 150bhp, close-ratio gearbox, 4-wheel disc brakes, originally modified for racing, but returned to road use, finished in Sage green with black interior, good condition.
£18,000–20,000 PC

MG	ENGINE	DATES	CONDITION		
Model	cc/cyl		1	2	3
14/28	1802/4	1924–27	£26,000	£18,000	£10,000
14/40	1802/4	1927–29	£25,000	£18,000	£10,000
18/80 Mk I/Mk II/Mk III	2468/6	1927–33	£40,000	£28,000	£20,000
M-Type Midget	847/4	1928–32	£11,000	£9,000	£7,000
J-Type Midget	847/4	1932–34	£15,000	£12,000	£10,000
J3 Midget	847/4	1932–33	£18,000	£14,000	£12,000
PA Midget	847/4	1934–36	£13,000+	£10,000	£8,000
PB Midget	936/4	1935–36	£15,000	£10,000	£8,000
F-Type Magna	1271/6	1931–33	£22,000	£18,000	£12,000
L-Type Magna	1087/6	1933–34	£26,000	£18,000	£12,000
K1/K2 Magnette	1087/6	1932–33	£35,000	£30,000	£20,000
N Series Magnette	1271/6	1934–36	£30,000	£28,000	£20,000
TA Midget	1292/4	1936–39	£13,000+	£12,000	£9,000
SA 2 litre	2288/6	1936–39	£22,000+	£18,000	£15,000
VA	1548/4	1936–39	£12,000	£8,000	£5,000
TB	1250/4	1939–40	£15,000	£11,000	£9,000

Value will depend on body style, history, completeness, racing history, the addition of a supercharger and originality.

1961 MGA Mk I Roadster, 1600cc, restored, finished in blue with red interior, immaculate condition.
£12,000–13,000 SJR

1960 MGA Mk I Roadster, 1600cc engine, original right-hand-drive model, completely refurbished 1998, very good condition throughout.
£14,500–15,500 SJR

1980 MG Midget, 1491cc, 4 cylinder engine, 4-speed manual gearbox, roll-over bar, boot rack, spare set of wire wheels and hubs, finished in blue with tan interior trim, 56,390 miles from new, excellent condition throughout.
£3,750–4,500 H&H

1962 MG Midget Mk I, 948cc, 4 cylinders, brakes overhauled, finished in Ice blue, original-pattern blue PVC hood, tonneau cover in good condition, original, very good mechanical condition.
£3,500–4,000 BRIT

1967 MGB Roadster, 1798cc, overdrive, wire wheels, restored, new sills, floorpans, wings and trim, finished in British Racing green, good mechanical condition.
£6,000–7,000 BRIT

1968 MGB Roadster, 1798cc, restored, excellent condition throughout.
£7,000–8,000 WILM

> A known continuous history can add value to and enhance the enjoyment of a car.

Miller's Starter Marque

Starter MG: *Midget 1961 onwards.*

- The Midget is a compelling classic cocktail for the cost conscious – in fact, about the only cheaper way of enjoying fresh air on four wheels is to buy a skateboard. Midgets have a massive following, more than 200,000 having been built up to 1979, and that means there's tremendous club support, a well-established and competitive spares and remanufacturing industry, and a mature network of marque specialists.

- Better still, the 'Spridget', as the Midget/Sprite models are often called, is a BMC parts-bin special, based on the mechanics and running gear of the likes of the million-selling Morris Minor and Austin A35. If the body's riddled with rust, you can buy a new bodyshell from Rover subsidiary British Motor Heritage.

What to watch: Particular points include the inner and outer sills. Be wary of ill-fitted replacement sills, and check the closing action of the doors. If they bind or snag, someone may have welded on new sills without supporting the car in the middle to ensure the frame maintains its correct shape. Another trouble area is the door pillar. Shake each door firmly in this area to reveal any flexing. The engines are generally reliable and long-lasting, but check for fluid leaks. Gearboxes can be noisy, but are similarly robust, and the rear axle rarely gives trouble.

Pick of the bunch: For classic credibility, the Sprite Mk IV and Midget Mk III (1966-70) are probably the best bet, with better performance from the 1275cc engines than earlier cars. They are still chrome-era classics, however, with all the visual appeal of the older versions. If performance matters more, the 1500cc Triumph Spitfire-engined Midgets from 1974 will touch 100mph, but they have the vast black plastic bumpers that some people loathe.

1969 MGB GT, 1798cc, wire wheels, resprayed, new carpets and front seat covers, 67,000 miles from new, good condition.
£4,000–5,000 BRIT

1970 MGB GT, 1798cc, 4 cylinder engine, refurbished, reconditioned engine, many new body panels, finished in Trafalgar blue, good condition throughout.
£3,000–4,000 BRIT

Miller's Starter Marque

Starter MGs: *MGA; MGB; MGB GT.*
- The MGB has to be one of the most practical, affordable and enjoyable classic sporting packages to be found. For a start, it's the most popular British sports car ever made, a winning formula based on rugged reliability, simple clean lines, fine road manners and adequate performance. For sheer classic credentials, models before the 1974 introduction of rubber-bumper cars with higher ride height are favoured, but later models can be even more affordable. They're also a great way to make 50,000 friends, for that's how many members belong to the MG Owners' Club, the world's largest one-make car club. There is also a superb parts and specialist network – even brand-new bodyshells are made on original tooling. The fixed-head MGB GT is cheaper than the roadster, yet it offers additional practicality and comfort.
What to watch: Few worries with engines and mechanicals, but MGBs can rot. Because of their unitary construction, pay particular attention to sills and other structural members.
- The MGA is the separate-chassised forerunner of the MGB. However, it wasn't made in anything like the numbers of the MGB: 101,000 MGAs were built between 1956 and 1962, and a staggering 81,000 of those were exported to America. Although that makes the MGA rare compared with the MGB, the sports car is still eminently practical and usable. One good reason for this is that so many parts – including the unburstable BMC B-series engine – were shared with other vehicles under the Morris-BMC-Nuffield banner.

1969 MGB Roadster, restored, engine bored out to 1950cc, manual gearbox with overdrive, stainless steel exhaust system, converted to right-hand drive, finished in Tartan red with Autumn Leaf interior, excellent condition.
£7,000–8,000 BKS

The MGB enjoyed an 18-year production life and world-wide sales in excess of 500,000 cars. Conceived in the late 1950s as a replacement for the MGA, it dispensed with its predecessor's separate chassis in favour of unitary construction. The existing B-series engine was stretched to 1798cc, and the MGB's aerodynamically efficient lines made the most of the 95bhp available to achieve a top speed of just over the magic 'ton'.

1970 MGB GT, 1798cc, restored early 1990s, fewer than 24,000 miles covered since converted to unleaded fuel, stainless steel exhaust system, finished in British Racing green with black interior trim.
£3,000–4,000 H&H

1971 MGB Roadster, 1798cc, 4 cylinders, wire wheels, completely restored 1995, finished in red with black leather interior, good condition.
£12,000–13,000 SJR

1972 MGB GT, completely restored, engine bored out to 1950cc and tuned, gearbox rebuilt, front and rear anti-roll bars, Minilite alloy wheels, Britax folding sunroof, finished in Glacier white, very good condition.
£5,000–6,000 BKS

MG Model	ENGINE cc/cyl	DATES	CONDITION 1	2	3
TC	1250/4	1946–49	£13,000	£11,000	£7,000
TD	1250/4	1950–52	£13,000	£9,000	£5,000
TF	1250/4	1953–55	£15,000	£13,000	£8,000
TF 1500	1466/4	1954–55	£16,000	£14,000	£9,000
YA/YB	1250/4	1947–53	£5,500+	£2,750	£1,500
Magnette ZA/ZB	1489/4	1953–58	£3,500	£2,000	£500
Magnette Mk III/IV	1489/4	1958–68	£3,500	£1,200	£350
MGA 1500 Roadster	1489/4	1955–59	£12,000+	£7,000	£4,000
MGA 1500 FHC	1489/4	1956–59	£8,000	£6,000	£3,000
MGA 1600 Roadster	1588/4	1959–61	£13,000	£9,000	£4,500
MGA 1600 FHC	1588/4	1959–61	£7,000	£5,000	£3,000
MGA Twin Cam Roadster	1588/4	1958–60	£18,000	£12,000	£9,000
MGA Twin Cam FHC	1588/4	1958–60	£14,000	£9,000	£7,000
MGA 1600 Mk II Roadster	1622/4	1961–62	£13,000	£10,000	£4,000
MGA 1600 Mk II FHC	1622/4	1961–62	£9,000	£7,000	£3,000
MGB Mk I	1798/4	1962–67	£7,000	£4,000	£1,200
MGB GT Mk I	1798/4	1965–67	£5,000	£3,500	£1,000
MGB Mk II	1798/4	1967–69	£7,500	£4,000	£1,500
MGB GT Mk II	1798/4	1969	£4,500	£2,500	£850
MGB Mk III	1798/4	1969–74	£6,500	£4,000	£1,100
MGB GT Mk III	1798/4	1969–74	£4,500	£2,500	£1,000
MGB Roadster (rubber bumper)	1798/4	1975–80	£6,000	£4,500	£1,200
MGB GT	1798/4	1975–80	£5,000	£3,000	£1,000
MGB Jubilee	1798/4	1975	£5,000	£3,000	£1,200
MGB LE	1798/4	1980	£8,500	£4,750	£2,250
MGB GT LE	1798/4	1980	£6,000	£3,750	£2,000
MGC	2912/6	1967–69	£8,000	£6,500	£4,000
MGC GT	2912/6	1967–69	£7,000	£5,000	£2,000
MGB GT V8	3528/8	1973–76	£9,000	£6,000	£3,000
Midget Mk I	948/4	1961–62	£4,000	£2,000	£850
Midget Mk II	1098/4	1962–66	£3,000	£2,000	£850
Midget Mk III	1275/4	1966–74	£3,200	£2,000	£850
Midget 1500	1491/4	1975–79	£3,000	£2,000	£850

All prices are for British right-hand-drive cars. Deduct 10–15 per cent for left-hand-drive varieties, even if converted to right-hand drive.

◄ **1972 MGB Roadster,** 1798cc, 4 cylinders, overdrive gearbox, new engine, all brightwork replaced or replated, new hood and interior trim, resprayed, good mechanical condition. **£5,500–7,000 BRIT**

1973 MGB Roadster, 1798cc, 4-speed manual gearbox with overdrive, restored, new chromed wire wheels, resprayed in Blaze red, new black interior, 74,699 miles from new, concours condition throughout. **£7,500–8,500 H&H**

1975 MGB GT, 1798cc, 4 cylinder engine, 4-speed gearbox with overdrive, restored, many new panels, finished in maroon, new black cloth interior trim, excellent condition throughout. **£4,500–5,000 H&H**

1976 MGB GT, 1798cc, overhead-valve engine, finished in British Racing green with beige cloth interior, last used 1992, bodywork good for age, sills in need of attention.
£900–1,200 BKS

1976 MGB Roadster, 1798cc 4 cylinders, 4-speed manual gearbox with overdrive, refurbished, new sills, carpets and seats, finished in blue with black leather interior trim, good condition.
£4,000–5,000 H&H

1978 MGB GT, 1798cc, 4 cylinders, overdrive gearbox, vinyl sunroof, slightly over 23,000 miles from new, excellent original condition.
£5,000–6,000 BRIT

1979 MGB Roadster, 1798cc, finished in white with beige leather interior, good condition.
£2,500–3,000 H&H

◄ **1979 MGB GT,** 1798cc, 4-speed manual gearbox with overdrive, finished in yellow with black interior trim and upholstery, 80,894 miles from new, good condition.
£1,300–1,800 H&H

1979 MGB GT, 1798cc, Rostyle wheels, sunshine roof, finished in yellow, excellent condition throughout.
£4,500–5,000 WCL

1979 MGB Roadster, 1798cc, 4 cylinder engine, 4-speed manual gearbox with overdrive, completely restored, new body panels, stainless steel exhaust, finished in blue with black leather interior trim.
£5,500–7,000 H&H

MGB GT, 1798cc, restored 1997, finished in Tahiti blue, body in very good condition.
£2,000–2,500 BRIT

1979 MGB Roadster, 1798cc, finished in Inca yellow, original in all respects, slightly over 40,000 miles from new, very good condition.
£4,750–6,000 BRIT

1980 MGB Roadster, 1798cc, 4 cylinder engine, brakes overhauled, finished in Russet brown, 53,000 miles from new, totally original, unused for 12 years, good condition.
£4,000–5,000 BRIT

1980 MGB Roadster, 1798cc, Rostyle wheels, finished in blue, excellent condition.
£6,500–7,500 WCL

◄ **1981 MGB GT Limited Edition,** 1798cc, 4 cylinders, resprayed in original shade, good condition.
£3,750–4,500 BRIT

Although production of the MGB finished in October 1980, it was not until February 1981 that the Limited Edition model was announced to commemorate the end of the great line. A thousand vehicles were produced, split equally between Roadsters and GTs. The former were finished in metallic bronze, and the latter in Pewter with distinctive side stripes.

1982 MGB Roadster, 1798cc, restored, finished in Blaze orange with black and grey interior, concours condition.
£10,000–12,500 PORT

1968 MGC Roadster, 2912cc, 6 cylinder engine, 4-speed manual gearbox with overdrive, wire wheels, completely restored, engine, gearbox, rear axle, suspension, steering and brakes rebuilt, finished in white, new black interior trim and upholstery, good condition throughout.
£11,000–12,000 H&H

1968 MGC GT, 2912cc, 6 cylinders, Minilite wheels, very good condition.
£6,500–7,500 WILM

◀ **1968 MGC Roadster,** 2912cc, 6 cylinders, overdrive gearbox, wire wheels, chromed luggage rack, restored, little use since, finished in Tartan red, original, 'as-new' condition.
£13,000–14,000 BRIT

MGC and MGC GT (1967–69)

Engine: Overhead-valve, six-cylinder, 2912cc.
Power output: 145bhp at 5,250rpm.
Transmission: Four-speed manual with optional overdrive; optional three-speed automatic.
Maximum speed: 120–122mph.
0–60mph: 10 seconds.
Production: MGC, 4,552; MGC GT, 4,457.
Prices in 1968: MGC (roadster), £1,145; MGC GT (fixed-head), £1,299.

Misunderstood, that's the MGC, and some cruel critics might also say misbegotten. In the second half of the 1960s, BMC's no-nonsense MGB was soaring up the sales charts, while time was fast catching up with the characterful Austin-Healey 3000, the oldest sports car in BMC's portfolio. At the time, BMC was also reworking the Austin-Healey's six-cylinder engine for the upcoming Austin 3 Litre saloon, and thus the MGC was born, a parts-bin hybrid that looked like an MGB, but wasn't man enough to carry the mantle of the Austin-Healey. The C was slower than the Austin-Healey 3000, lacked its handling and sports car exuberance, and for the short period of model overlap was more expensive than the butch old Healey. Gone, too, were many of the MGB's virtues. The six-cylinder engine, 200lb heavier than the B's four-pot, was levered in by using the crow-bar approach, with a bonnet bulge, increased ride height and revised front suspension. The result was a front-heavy understeerer that lacked the MGB's lively handling. The Press panned the car, and in a little over two years of dismal sales, it disappeared. Certainly, part of the MGC's burden was the weight of unfair comparison, because in reality, the MGC was not so much a true sports car, but rather a pleasant, long-legged cruiser, more at home on motorways and *routes nationales* than either the MGB or Austin-Healey.

1969 MGC Roadster, 2912cc, restored, engine rebuilt, suspension overhauled, new steering rack and braking system, many new body panels, all brightwork replaced or replated as necessary, resprayed in original Mineral blue, new hood and interior trim, excellent condition.
£8,000–9,000 BRIT

1969 MGC GT, finished in blue with black leather interior, one owner, original, excellent condition throughout.
£4,500–5,500 BKS

Restored Values

The cost of a professional restoration will have an influence on, but no direct relation to, a car's market value. A restored car can have a market value lower than the cost of its restoration.

1973 MGB GT V8, 3528cc, 4-speed manual gearbox with overdrive, completely restored, resprayed in Teal blue, excellent condition.
£7,000–8,000 H&H

◀ **1975 MGB GT V8,** older conversion from a 4 cylinder model, 3528cc aluminium V8 engine, 4-speed manual gearbox with overdrive, Rostyle wheels, completely restored 1990/91 at a cost of over £6,500, finished in Snowberry white with black interior upholstery and trim, full-length Webasto sunroof, good condition throughout.
£3,000–4,000 H&H

1976 MGB GT V8, 3528cc, finished in black with tan interior, excellent condition throughout.
£7,000–8,000 WCL

1994 MG RV8, alloy wheels, full and half tonneau, finished in Le Mans green pearlescent metallic with tan leather interior, maplewood dashboard, door cappings, air conditioning, 11,000 miles from new.
£16,000–19,000 CARS

The RV8 was produced in a limited edition of 2,000, most of which were exported to the Far East, notably Japan. Following the 1997 financial crisis in the Pacific rim, some found their way back to the UK.

Michelotti

1968 Michelotti Shellette Beach Car, DAF chassis and running gear, 2-speed, constantly-variable transmission, finished in white with orange hood, wicker seats and dashboard, original, excellent condition throughout.
£14,000–15,000 BKS

It is believed that this car was built to the special commission of Aristotle Onassis, who kept it on his yacht and used it to ferry Jackie Kennedy around various resorts when he was courting her.

Don't Throw Away A Fortune!
Invest In
Miller's Price Guides

Please send me the following editions

❏ **Miller's Collectables Price Guide 1999/2000** – £17.99

❏ **Miller's Chinese & Japanese Antiques Buyer's Guide** – £19.99

❏ **Miller's Clocks & Barometers Buyer's Guide** – £18.99

❏ **Miller's Antiques Price Guide 2000** – £22.50

❏ **Miller's Classic Motorcycles Price Guide 1999/2000** – £14.00

If you do not wish your name to be used by Miller's or other carefully selected organisations for promotional purposes, please tick this box ❏

I enclose my cheque/postal order for £.................post free (UK only)
Please make cheques payable to *'Octopus Publishing Group Ltd'*
or please debit my Access/Visa/Amex/Diners Club account number

Expiry Date............/............

*NAME Title   Initial   Surname*_____

*ADDRESS*_____

*Postcode*_____

*SIGNATURE*_____

Minari

◄ **1991 Minari Road Sport,** 1.7 litre, 16-valve Alfa Romeo engine, 150bhp, 130mph top speed, left-hand drive, finished in silver with blue interior, air conditioning original, 'as-new' condition in most respects.
£7,000–8,000 BKS

Built during 1990–94, the Road Sport utilised Alfa Romeo 33 components in a fibreglass monocoque shell. The engine, transmission, front suspension and steering were carried on a steel subframe, while the Alfa rear suspension was bolted directly into the tub.

Minerva

1908 Minerva 28hp Type-N Two-Seater, 4060cc, 4 cylinder, T-head engine, poppet valves, brass accessories, hood, windscreen, restored, good condition throughout, history file.
£15,500–18,000 BKS

Minerva's history can be traced back to a cycle business run in Antwerp by Dutchman, Sylvain de Jong. The first Minerva motor car appeared around the turn of the century. It featured a twin-cylinder engine and chain drive. The cars enjoyed singular success in their home country and in their principal export market, Britain.

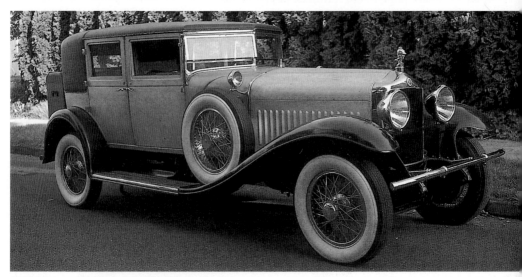

1927 Minerva 30CV Seven-Passenger Sedan-Limousine, coachwork by LeBaron, 6 litre, sleeve-valve engine, dual side-mounted spare wheels, finished in silver, partially restored, wiring, interior fittings and paintwork in need of attention.
£50,000–55,000 BKS

1902 Mors Type Z 60hp Paris–Vienna City-To-City Racing Two-Seater, 9.2 litre engine, short-wheelbase chassis, third car built.
£300,000+ BKS

The city-to-city format of major road races prevailed from the pioneering Paris–Bordeaux event of 1895 until the tragedies of the notorious Paris–Madrid in 1903. When that event was stopped by Government edict at Bordeaux, first place was held by the next development of this very car – Fernand Gabriel's 70hp Mors. There is evidence that this 60hp model was employed as a team tender in that Paris–Madrid race.

1908 Hutton Racing Two-Seater 'Little Dorrit', 7.8 litres, 4 cylinder engine, bi-block, L-head, dual ignition, 4-speed gate-change gearbox, multi-plate clutch, shaft drive, pressed-steel chassis, semi-elliptic leaf-spring suspension, internal expanding brakes on rear wheels and transmission, Rudge-Whitworth wire wheels, bolster tank, finished in British Racing green with black leather seats.
130,000–150,000 C

This particular car won the 1908 Tourist Trophy race.

1908 Mors Grand Prix Two-Seater, 12.5 litre engine, pushrod-actuated overhead-valve induction, copper-jacketed cylinder barrels, restored, repainted, new wooden wheels with original-style quick-detachable rims.
£425,000+ BKS

1912 Bugatti 5 Litre Chain-Driven Racing Car, 5027cc, overhead-camshaft, 4 cylinder engine, 3 valves per cylinder, 4-speed gearbox plus reverse, chain drive, rear wheel and transmission brakes, wire spoke wheels, finished in black with black leather seat.
£350,000+ C

In 1912, Bugatti drove this 5 litre, chain-driven car, fitted with aerodynamic, cowled two-seater bodywork – distinguishable by its pointed tail – in a race at Le Mans and later at the Mont Ventoux Hill Climb, where he won his class and finished fourth overall.

1932 Talbot-Darracq Two-Seater Racing Special, French Talbot Pacific 8 cylinder, overhead-valve, in-line engine, 4-speed pre-selector gearbox, semi-elliptic leaf-spring suspension, 4-wheel mechanical drum brakes, shortened British Talbot Type 65 chassis, period headlamps, engine-turned aluminium dashboard, Jaeger instruments,
£50,000–60,000 C

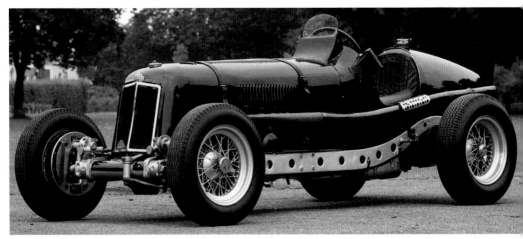

1935 ERA D-Type 2 Litre Single-Seater Racer, completely restored, excellent condition throughout.
£400,000+ BKS

For many years the fastest of the 'Old English' upright ERAs, this car was built to spearhead English Racing Automobiles' international programme, being tailor-made for company-founding, number-one driver Raymond Mays. His subsequent successes in the car included a class victory in the Brighton Speed Trials, FTD at Shelsley Walsh Hill Climb, and a new lap record on the Brooklands Mountain Circuit. In 1938, after a South African tour, the car was rebuilt on a new, stiffer D-Type chassis to become the last word in ERAs.

1936 Alta Supercharged Offset Single-Seater Grand Prix Car, 1488cc, 4 cylinders, underslung chassis, offset rear axle on quarter-elliptic leaf springs, finished in British Racing green, engine in need of rebuild, otherwise in excellent mechanical condition, FIA papers.
£58,000–65,000 COYS

Alta was the brainchild of avid enthusiast Geoffrey Taylor. The company's roots were founded in the manufacture of go-faster cylinder heads and other parts for Austin 7s, but Taylor was keen to produce a Riley Nine-derived sports special, thus the first Alta was born. Such was the interest generated by its appearances that Taylor decided to produce a batch. By 1935, his interests had progressed and he began developing his own out-and-out racing cars.

1936 Lagonda M45 Le Mans Replica, coachwork by Rod Jolly, 4554cc, 6 cylinder engine, hydraulic brakes, restored 1986/91, finished in black with black upholstery, extensive history file, FIA papers and VSCC blue form.
£65,000–70,000 COYS

The original firm of Lagonda Ltd was replaced in 1935 by LG Motors, a new company with Alan Good as chairman and W.O. Bentley as technical director and designer. They faced two immediate tasks: to put the M45 model back into production, and to build the best car in the world. The result was the great 12 cylinder car. The M45 received some cosmetic treatment, then was replaced by the LG45 in September. In May 1937, Alan Hess covered over 104 miles in the hour at Brooklands in a standard LG45.

1957 Cooper-Climax T43, ex-Roy Salvadori, 1960cc, 4 cylinders, fully race prepared, finished in dark blue with white stripes, well-proven race record, regular competitor on the historic racing scene, full FIA papers.
£57,000–65,000 COYS

Based on the highly accomplished, very light and nimble Bobtail/Manx sports car, Cooper's T43 F2 car was powered by a 1.5 litre, twin-cam, alloy Coventry Climax engine mated to a Citroën-ERSA 4-speed transaxle. It offered superb roadholding and stability at speed, and was so effective that by the time the 1957 season got under way, most of the grid comprised T43s. This particular car was used by the works team in 1957.

1957 Lotus 12 Monoposto, ex-Graham Hill/Cliff Allison, 1960cc, 4 cylinders, modified gearbox with Hewland internals, space-frame chassis, undertray, double-wishbone front suspension, Chapman-strut rear suspension, 4-wheel disc brakes, cast magnesium wheels, engine rebuilt 1997, FIA and VSCC papers, only remaining example in race-ready condition.
£87,000–97,000 COYS

The 12 was the first Lotus single-seater, and it gave full expression to Colin Chapman's preoccupation with lightness and minimal dimensions. This car was the third Lotus 12 to be built, and the first to race. In 1958, Graham Hill raced it twice, at Toima and Brands Hatch.

1985 Alfa Romeo 185T Formula 1 Grand Prix Single-Seater, chassis no. 03, fitted with experimental V6 engine, carbon fibre and Kevlar bodywork, unused since 1996, good condition throughout.
£50,000–60,000 BKS

The last F1 car to race under the Alfa Romeo name, the 1985 185T, was an evolution of the previous season's 184T, it was based on an aluminium honeycomb monocoque and had an unusual suspension layout, with pull-rods at the front and pushrods at the rear.

1953 Fiat 750 Barchetta Sport, enlarged Fiat 500 engine with overhead-camshaft conversion and water cooling, tubular frame, Fiat suspension components, aluminium body, restored 1992, excellent mechanical condition.
£30,000–35,000 BKS

This Fiat is typical of the lightweight sports cars that raced in Italy during the early 1950s and gave rise to a generation of special builders, among them Nardi, Moretti, Ermini, Stanguellini and Bandini.

1955 Ferrari 410 Sport, restored, excellent condition throughout.
£2,000,000+ TALA

◀ **1956 Aston Martin DB3S,** 3 litre, double-overhead-camshaft, 6 cylinder engine, restored, finished in white with blue stripes, 'as new' condition.
£300,000+ BKS

1956 Lister Jaguar, 2400cc, 6 cylinders, genuine early Lister retaining almost all original components, restored, finished in mid-green with broad yellow stripe.
£75,000–85,000 COYS

1960 Maserati Tipo 60/61 'Birdcage', chassis no. 2462, canted 2 litre engine, chrome-moly tubular chassis, Kamm-type rear end, second Tipo 60 constructed, competition history.
£650,000+ RM

Maserati managing director Omer Orsi's post-war sanction of racing car production began in 1955 with the 150 S. The legendary 250 S, 300 S, 350 S and 450 S sports racers followed. In 1959, Orsi approved the construction of the Tipo 60, a 2 litre, front-engined sports racer of advanced design. Only six were produced during 1959–60.

c1964 Lotus 23B, 1594cc, double-overhead-camshaft, 4 cylinder engine, 5-speed Hewland transaxle, tubular space-frame, front suspension by unequal-length double wishbones and coil-spring/damper units, rear by lower wishbones, upper lateral links, coil-spring / damper units and parallel arms, disc brakes, fibreglass body, excellent condition.
£27,000–33,000 COYS

Launched in 1962, the Lotus 23 was essentially a two-seater version of the all-conquering 1961 Lotus 20 Formula Junior, but featuring the improvements that saw the latter evolve into the 22.

1970 Abarth 2000 SE19, 2 litre, double-overhead-camshaft, 4 cylinder engine, iron block, alloy cylinder head, twin-choke Weber carburettors, 250bhp at 8,000rpm, 5-speed gearbox, space-frame with stressed sills, front suspension by coil springs and double wishbones, rear by coil springs, horizontal links and radius arms, 4-wheel disc brakes, alloy wheels, restored, race-ready.
£48,000–56,000 BKS

1975 Toj SC205, ex-Jo Gartner, 2000cc, 16 valve, 4 cylinder engine, 308bhp at 9,250rpm, 5-speed gearbox with oil cooler, aluminium monocoque, double-wishbone suspension with coil springs and adjustable shock absorbers, 4-wheel disc brakes, chassis and engine rebuilt 1996, race-ready.
£42,000–47,000 COYS

In 1972, Norfolk-based GRD produced the successful 573 sports racing car. Conflicts within the company saw production of all models cease in 1974, but construction of the promising 2 litre 573 was resumed by the Austrian Toj Racing Cars, under the designation SC205.

In the late 1960s and early 1970s, one of the most closely contested racing classes was for 2 litre Group 5 sports racers. It was natural that Carlo Abarth would join in, since his 1 litre and 1300cc cars had dominated their classes in the Sports Car World Championship for some years. In 1970, Abarths were right on the pace in circuit racing and performed well at a wide variety of circuits. Abarth finished third in the European 2 litre Sports Car Championship in 1970 and 1971, but won it outright in 1972.

1937 Adler Rennlimousine Competition Coupé, 1.5 litres, front-wheel drive Trumpf chassis, restored to original specification, only remaining example of 3 competition Adlers built, concours winner.
£400,000+ BLK

◀ **1957 Arnott-Climax 1.1 Litre GT Competition Coupé,** ex-Jim Russell/Dennis Taylor, overhead-camshaft, Coventry-Climax 4 cylinder engine, undertrays to improve airflow, restored.
£26,000–29,000 BKS

1965 Ferrari 250 Le Mans Berlinetta, 3.3 litre, overhead-camshaft V12 engine, 6 Weber downdraught carburettors, twin distributors, overhung 5-speed transaxle, tubular chassis frame, all-independent suspension, original.
£1,000,000+ BKS

This is the only 250LM to have been fitted as original with fibreglass body panels instead of aluminium. It also has a slightly more pronounced rear spoiler. It achieved the European auction record price in 1998.

1965 Alfa Romeo TZ2 Berlinetta Corsa, coachwork by Zagato, 1570cc, 4 cylinder engine, dry-sump lubrication, 170bhp, 5-speed all-synchromesh gearbox with magnesium casing, limited-slip differential, tubular frame, Campagnolo alloy wheels, fibreglass body panels, original, history file.
£575,000+ BKS

1967 Ford GT Mk IV, 7 litre V8, 520bhp, honeycomb-aluminium monocoque chassis tub, originally a back-up car and not completed until early 1980s, engine rebuilt 1989, actively campaigned since.
£250,000+ BKS

A development of the Ford GT and GT40 line, the GT Mk IV presented a completely new departure in road racing design. In 1967, driven by Dan Gurney and A.J. Foyt, the model took Ford to victory at Le Mans.

◀ **1987 Porsche 962C,** ex-Kremer team, 2649cc, flat-6 engine, turbocharged, Thompson honeycomb monocoque, factory long-tail body, race-ready condition.
£115,000–130,000 COYS

1956 AC Ace, ex-works, 2553cc, 6 cylinder Ford engine, dry-sump lubrication, all-independent suspension, rebuilt to competition specification, race-quality fuel tank, roll-over bar, full safety harness, finished in midnight blue, excellent condition.
£39,000–46,000 COYS

This car was a works entry in the 1957 Sebring 12-hour race, being driven by the team of Fernandez and Droulers. It came home 17th to achieve a class win.

1961 Jaguar E-Type Competition Roadster, ex-Bruce McLaren/David Hobbs/Peter Berry, 3781cc, 6 cylinders, JL-series close-ratio gearbox, bronze-brushed suspension, lightweight E-Type aluminium wheels, aluminium hardtop, restored to period road race specification.
£190,000–210,000 COYS

The majority of the first batch of E-Types were sold to prominent racing exponents and a variety of celebrities. A considerable number of these early cars found their way on to the circuits, establishing the E-Type's reputation as a true GT car with racing potential. To reinforce this, Jaguar prepared seven right-hand-drive roadsters to an uprated competition specification, allocating them to prominent private racing teams.

1972 Ferrari 246 GT Dino Competition Berlinetta, coachwork by Pininfarina, 2.4 litre, double-overhead-camshaft V6, 195bhp at 7,600rpm, lightweight aluminium body panels.
£55,000–65,000 COYS

1967 Abarth 1000 TC, 5-speed gearbox, genuine car, not raced since 1974.
£17,000–20,000 BKS

Abarth versions of small Fiats have passed into legend. Their trademark was a permanently raised engine cover, supported on a tubular frame. This was widely thought to be an aid to engine cooling, but in fact, it served as an aerodynamic device. The 1000 TC (*Turismo Competizione*) was loosely based on the Fiat 850.

◄ **1976 Lancia Stratos Group IV Rally Car,** 2.4 litre Ferrari Dino engine, in need of overhaul.
£18,000–23,000 BKS

► **1950s Hispano-Suiza Dragster,** overhead-camshaft, 4 cylinder Hispano-Suiza engine, Howe crankcase, magnesium wheels.
£12,000–14,000 BKS

When pioneer hot rodders stumbled upon the potential of the WW1 Hispano-Suiza aero engine, the main attraction was its overhead-camshaft valve gear. Sometimes, the engine would be halved, as in this car, to produce a relatively low-line slant-4 power unit, Although the resulting open crankcase was often sealed by a simple bolt-on plate, in this case it has a purpose-made crankcase from Howe Machine Co.

Nicholas Watts, The Calm Before The Storm, depicting the Alfa Romeo Monzas of Scuderia Ferrari prior to a race, limited-edition print.
£70–80 MPG

Nicholas Watts, Archie and the Lister Jaguar – A Dedication, depicting Archie Scott-Brown driving the Lister Jaguar in the Aintree 200 to record his final major victory, limited-edition print, signed by Brian Lister.
£90–100 MPG

Nicholas Watts, The End of an Era, depicting von Brauchitsch and Nuvolari racing in close company through the streets of Belgrade on the day WW2 broke out, limited-edition print, signed by Manfred von Brauchitsch.
£110–130 MPG

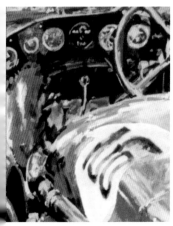

Helen Taylor, an Alfa Romeo 8C Monza, showing the rear and dash areas, acrylic on board, 30x19¾in (76x50cm).
£350–400 BKS

Dion Pears, Le Mans 1953, depicting the C-Type Jaguar of Rolt/Hamilton, signed by the artist, mounted and framed, 23½x35½in (60x90cm).
£900–1,000 BKS

Nicholas Watts, Schumacher Reigns Supreme, depicting
Michael Schumacher driving the Ferrari F310B to victory during
a rain-soaked 1997 Monaco Grand Prix, limited-edition print,
signed by Michael Schumacher.
£375–425 MPG

Roy Nockolds, J.M. Hawthorn –
Cooper 1952, watercolour and
gouache with chalk and charcoal
on board, wooden title plaque,
inscribed 'Presented to Mike
Hawthorn by the Esso Petroleum Co.
Ltd', signed and dated 1952,
30¼x25¼in (77x64.5cm).
£1,600–1,750 S

Nicholas Watts, Monaco Grand Prix 1961, depicting Stirling Moss in the Rob Walker Lotus 18 leading the Ferraris of
Ginther and Hill as they round Gasworks Hairpin, limited-edition print, signed by Stirling Moss and Rob Walker.
£110–120 MPG

Georges Hamel, Monte Carlo Rally 1955, depicting
Sunbeam Talbot No. 201 during a snowstorm in
the Alps, watercolour and gouache, signed,
11x18in (28x46cm).
£3,000–3,500 C

Nicholas Watts, The Power and the Glory – A Tribute,
depicting a Porsche 917 leading a Ferrari 512 at Le
Mans, limited-edition print, signed by Brian Redman,
Richard Attwood, David Piper, Jacky Ickx and Derek Bell.
£175–200 MPG

Helen Taylor, Maserati 250F, depicting Juan Manuel Fangio at Monaco in 1957, acrylic on canvas, 28x36in (71x91.5cm).
£525–575 **BKS**

Michael Wright, 1936 Mille Miglia, depicting the 8C-2900A Alfa Romeo of Antonio Brivio and Carlo Ongaro passing through Ferrara, mixed media on paper, signed and inscribed, 26½x24½in (67x62cm).
£1,000–1,200 **S**

Nicholas Watts, The Cobra Strikes – Le Mans 1964, depicting the Daytona Cobra Coupé driven by Gurney and Bondurant accelerating past a Triumph Spitfire as it exits Tertre Rouge, limited edition print, signed by Carroll Shelby.
£125–140 **MPG**

Walter Gotschke, Grosser Preis Von Deutschland, Nürburgring, 25 July 1937, depicting the winner, Rudolf Caracciola, in his Mercedes leading from Bernd Rosemeyer (Auto Union), Manfred von Brauchitsch (Mercedes) and Tazio Nuvolari (Alfa Romeo), watercolour and gouache, signed and dated, 17¼x23½in (44x60cm).
£3,500–4,000 **S**

John W. Burgess, 3 images illustrating a design that Burgess never built, inscribed 'A-F-16 Fronty, Designed For A Dual Positive Displacement Intercooled Supercharger Installation', a later design also featured on a similar publication 'Automobile Quarterly' 1988 Vol.26, mixed media, signed and dated 1934, 13x21in (33x53.5cm).
£780–830 **BKS**

Tony Upson, mural depicting Monza Grand Prix of 1961, acrylic on board, 48x96in (122x244cm).
£900–1,000 BKS

After Meffes, a 1958 Dutch Grand Prix poster, depicting Alberto Ascari at the wheel of his Ferrari 500 F2.
£375–425 BKS

1931 Rockingham Auto Races poster, featuring 8 portraits of notable drivers, some fold marks, framed and mounted, 28x44in (71x112cm).
£1,275–1,375 BKS

1954 *Daily Express* International Trophy Meeting at Silverstone, coloured poster, 20x30in (51x76.5cm).
£275–325 LE

Renault poster with all 16 car scrutineering tickets from the 1996 World Championship season, signed by Damon Hill, framed.
£3,500–4,000 BKS

Toschi Ferrari 500 F2 die-cast alloy and tinplate model, original unused rubber band, geared drive and winding assembly, original set of instructions, original box, no windscreen.
£1,275–1,375 **BKS**

A scratch-built 1:4 scale model of the Ferrari 512M by Daniel Stöckli, detailed V12 engine, fibreglass body, Perspex screen, riveted aluminium monocoque chassis, cast-alloy racing wheels, solid rubber slick tyres, fully detailed suspension,
£10,000–12,000 **BKS**

A 1:43 scale model of a 1991 BMW M3 E30 Ravalier/Grohs racing car.
£60–70 **DRAK**

A scratch-built model of the Fronty Special by John W. Burgess, exposed engine, 15in (38cm) long, mounted.
£570–630 **BKS**

A highly-detailed model of the McLaren MP4/6 driven by Ayrton Senna in the German Grand Prix of 1991, mounted on polished wood and velvet base, with applied brass plaque inscribed 'Ayrton Senna Hockenheim 1991, McLaren MP4/6 Honda V12', signed by Ayrton Senna, 14½in (37cm) long.
£3,800–4,200 **BKS**

A collection of 67 model Ferrari F1 cars and hand-built miniatures, including many rare versions, all in 1:43 scale.
£10,000–13,000 **BKS**

Doug Nye, *Theme Lotus 1956–1986*, signed by Doug Nye, and drivers Andretti, Allison, Geltini, Ireland, Leston, Parnell and Piper, 1986.
£145–155 GPCC

Anthony Pritchard, *Grand Prix Reflections, From the 2½-Litre Formula Era 1954–60*, signed by Jose Gonzalez.
£90–100 GPCC

Christopher Hilton, *Alain Prost*, signed by Prost, Hilton, René Arnou and Jacques Laffite.
£70–75 GPCC

James Hunt and Eoin Young, *Against All Odds*, signed by Lord Alexander Hesketh, James Hunt and Eoin Young, 1977.
£90–95 GPCC

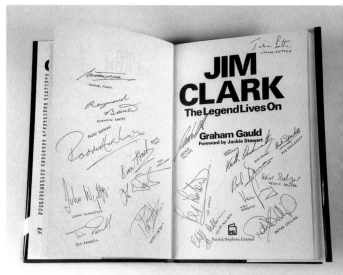

Graham Gauld, *Jim Clark, The Legend Lives On*, 3rd edition, signed by 38 of Jim Clark's contemporaries, including his girlfriend, sisters, Colin Chapman's widow, Innes Ireland, Raymond Baxter, Jackie Oliver, Brian Hart, Les Leston, Paddy Hopkirk, Cliff Allison and Tom Walkinshaw, 1989.
£150–160 GPCC

Timothy Collings, *The New Villeneuve, The Life of Jacques Villeneuve*, signed by Villeneuve and Heinz-Harald Frentzen, 1997.
£60–65 GPCC

Alan Henry, *Damon Hill, On Top Of The World*, signed by Damon Hill, 1996.
£40–45 GPCC

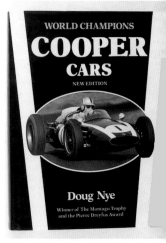

Doug Nye, Cooper Cars, 2nd edition, signed by John Cooper and Doug Nye, 1987.
£55–65 GPCC

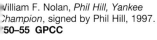

William F. Nolan, *Phil Hill, Yankee Champion*, signed by Phil Hill, 1997.
£50–55 GPCC

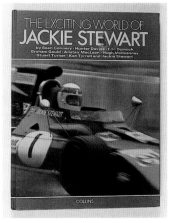

The Exciting World of Jackie Stewart, signed by Jackie, Helen, Paul and Mark Stewart, 1974.
£55–65 GPCC

A pair of Jim Clark's Les Leston flameproof two-piece racing overalls, used during the 1966 season, some staining and wear to material.
£4,600–5,200 S

An OMP racing suit worn by Johnny Herbert during 1997, signed on right breast, driver's name and national flag embroidered on belt.
£2,000–2,500 S

A Footwork Arrows team shirt, 1989.
£15–20 GPT

A race suit worn by James Hunt during the 1976–77 F1 season.
£750–850 BKS

A TAG-McLaren race suit worn by Niki Lauda during the 1984 period.
£4,500–5,500 BKS

A Jordan Team shirt, 1996.
£55–60 GPT

A pair of Graham Hill's Gold Leaf Team Lotus racing overalls, used during the 1968 World Championship-winning season, white Nomex by Les Leston, elasticated cuffs and ankles.
£7,500–8,500 S

A Stand 21 blue Nomex race suit worn by Alain Prost during the 1982 season.
£1,750–2,250 BKS

Ayrton Senna's Stand 21 racing suit and helmet, last worn at the 1986 French Grand Prix, still in race condition, radio-equipped.
£30,000–35,000 BKS

◄ A pair of OMP gloves worn by Michael Schumacher during the 1996 season while driving for Ferrari, signed and dated 1996 on the left palm, mounted in a framed and glazed display case.
£900–1,000 BKS

A blue and white Sparco race suit worn by Jacques Villeneuve during the 1996 French Grand Prix, patch bearing driver's name and national flag, together with a Williams certificate of authenticity.
£3,000–3,500 S

A replica of Johnny Herbert's 1994 helmet, worn while driving for Lotus, signed by Herbert.
£600–800 GPT

A 1993 Bell helmet worn by Mario Andretti during his last winning season, complete with microphone, earphones, cable system and plugs, pop-off valve, signed by Mario Andretti.
£6,000–7,000 **BKS**

A 1996 Bell helmet worn by Emerson Fittipaldi, visor with tear-off strip, full radio equipment.
£3,000–4,000 **BKS**

A Bell helmet worn by Niki Lauda during his World Championship-winning 1984 season with McLaren, original visor, fittings on right for radio system, radio not present.
£8,000–9,000 **BKS**

◄ A helmet worn by Mika Häkkinen in 1992, extensive range of logos, G-strap D-ring on each side.
£7,500–8,500 **BKS**

A helmet visor used by Damon Hill in 1996, signed by Hill.
£350–400 **GPT**

A 1973 Griffin helmet worn by Graham Hill, London Rowing Club colours, detachable sun peak on visor, life-support system on left side, significant dent on right.
£7,500–8,500 **BKS**

◄ A Bell helmet worn by James Hunt during his World Championship winning year of 1976, Velcro strip around neck for fire-protective mane, small hole to the right of the chin for water supply, microphone, together with newspaper cuttings and an invitation to Hunt's commemorative service in 1993.
£10,000–11,000 **BKS**

A Jordan helmet worn by Eddie Irvine in 1995, visor with tear-off, radio equipment, together with a signed racing suit.
£4,000–5,000 BKS

A Bell helmet worn by Alan Jones during his World Drivers' Championship-winning 1980 season, dark visor with driver's name in centre, airline attachment, together with a file of letters and ephemera relating to the provenance of this helmet.
£7,000–8,000 S

An Arai helmet worn by Nigel Mansell during his 1987 season with Williams, clear visor with later 1990-season Ferrari logostrip, microphone lead attached.
£3,000–4,000 S

A GPA helmet worn by Nelson Piquet during his World Championship-winning 1983season, special SJ shutting system, good post-race condition, signed by Nelson Piquet.
£7,000–8,000 BKS

An Arai helmet worn by Alain Prost during the 1990 British Grand Prix, which he won for Ferrari, original visor and radio system, signed 'Silverstone 90, Per il ricordo della stagione 1990 Prost' (In remembrance of the 1990 season Prost).
£20,000–23,000 BKS

A 1979 Simpson helmet worn by Keke Rosberg while racing for team Wolf.
£6,700–7,700 BKS

◀ A Bell helmet worn by Michael Schumacher at the Italian Grand Prix during his Championship-winning 1995 season with Benetton, tinted visor with two tear-offs, evidence of microphone fittings, one forehead air-vent cover missing, dated '95.16 Monza'.
£12,500–14,000 S

◀ An Arai helmet worn by Jacques Villeneuve during the 1995 IndyCar World Series, which he won, visor with tear-off, full radio system.
£8,000–9,000 B

Mini

At long last, it seems that the Mini's amazing lease of life is about to come to an end, with a brand-new replacement due within the next year or so. The revolutionary, front-wheel-drive Mini, with its east-west engine layout and brilliant compact packaging, was launched in 1959. Offered originally as an Austin 7 Mini or Morris Mini Minor, this pocket-sized wonder car had achieved its own identity by 1970, becoming simply the Mini. The Austin Metro of 1980 was supposed to replace the Mini, but wasn't up to the task. The Mini was so right at its launch that it's actually benefited from being left pretty much alone.

It was all down to Alec Issigonis, who had earlier created the Morris Minor. The Minor was Britain's first million-selling car, but the Mini went on to eclipse it many times over, production now totalling more than five million. With its modest aspirations as an affordable, compact family runabout, it has become so much more: a racing and rallying giant-killer; a chic fashion accessory and icon of the swinging sixties; and film star, most notably in the movie, *The Italian Job*, starring Michael Caine and Noel Coward.

1959 Morris Mini Minor DeLuxe, left-hand drive, completely restored, finished in Old English white. £3,500–4,500 **S**

This car is the 40th Mini Minor built. It was auctioned by Sotheby's in 1987, being bought by the *Today* newspaper and offered as a competition prize in 1988.

1961 Austin Mini 'Claustrophobia', engine bored out to 1300cc, twin SU carburettors, customised bodywork, Triumph Herald sills, Austin Allegro rear lights, Hillman Avenger instruments, full working order. £3,300–4,000 **BKS**

Featured in *The Guinness Book of Records* in 1988 as the lowest car on the road, this unique vehicle was created by Andy Saunders of Poole in Dorset. Saunders chopped no less that 14½in from the body and roof pillars, leaving a 'letterbox' windscreen just 6in deep.

1964 Morris Mini Countryman, 848cc, 4 cylinder in-line engine, 34bhp at 5,500rpm, 4-speed manual gearbox, alloy wheels, left-hand drive, finished in cream. £4,200–4,800 **Pou**

1959 Morris Mini Minor, restored, good condition. £5,000–5,500 **MIN**

1962 Morris Mini Cooper, 997cc, 4 cylinders, optional twin fuel tanks, finished in Almond green with an Old English white roof, interior trimmed in Porcelain green and Dove grey, original, very good mechanical condition. £5,500–6,000 **BRIT**

MINI Model	ENGINE cc/cyl	DATES	CONDITION 1	2	3
Mini	848/4	1959–67	£3,500	£1,200	–
Mini Countryman	848/4	1961–67	£2,500	£1,200	–
Cooper Mk I	997/4	1961–67	£8,000	£5,000	£2,500
Cooper Mk II	998/4	1967–69	£6,000	£4,000	£1,500
Cooper S Mk I	var/4	1963–67	£7,000	£5,000	£2,000
Cooper S Mk II	1275/4	1967–71	£6,000	£5,000	£2,000
Innocenti Mini Cooper	998/4	1966–75	£4,500	£2,000	£1,000

Starter Minis: *All models.*

* Whether yours is a 1959 car with sliding windows, cord door-pulls and external hinges, or a 1995 model, all Minis are classics. Even though modern Minis are still closely related to the 1959 original, the early cars have an extra, subtle charm. Parts are rarely a problem, but the Mini's major enemy is rust.

* Before looking underneath, inspect the roof panel, guttering and pillars supporting the roof. If they are rusted or show that filler has been used, the rest of the structure may be in similar, or worse, shape.

* Examine floorpans from above and below, joints with the inner sills, front and rear bulkheads, crossmember and jacking points. If the subframe has welded plates, check that they've been properly attached. Look inside the parcel compartment on each side of the rear seat, beneath the rear seat, and in all corners of the boot, spare-wheel well and battery container. These are all common rust spots.

* Clicking from beneath the front of the car indicates wear in the driveshaft constant-velocity joints – not easy or cheap to rectify.

* Rear radius-arm support bearings deteriorate rapidly unless regularly lubricated; check the grease points ahead of each rear wheel for signs of recent attention.

* The A-series engine is generally reliable and long-lived. However, expect timing-chain rattle on older units; burnt exhaust valves may be evident on high-mileage examples, as may exhaust smoke under hard acceleration, indicating cylinder/piston wear.

* Mini Coopers can be worth more than double the ordinary classic Minis. Consequently, fakes abound. It's not just a question of checking the uprated specification – twin carbs, disc brakes, badges and the like – but also of unravelling engine and chassis numbers, and subtle tell-tale signs that you'll only learn about from club experts and professionals. First join the club (see Directory of Clubs), then go shopping.

Pick of the bunch: Of the original generation of Coopers, the best all-round performer is the 1275S, 60mph coming up in 10.9 seconds, and puff running out just shy of the ton. As usual, the aficionados prefer the first-of-breed purity of earlier cars with sliding windows, etc.

1964 Austin Mini Cooper S, 1275cc, completely restored, 1,000 miles covered since, engine rebuilt stainless steel exhaust, twin fuel tanks, reclining seats, finished in ivory with black roof, excellent condition. **£11,000–12,000 COYS**

1965 Austin Mini Cooper S, 1365cc high-performance engine, restored 1997 at a cost of £22,000, finished in ivory with dark green interior, sunroof, concours condition. **£7,000–8,000 BKS**

Racing car manufacturer John Cooper already knew quite a bit about tuning BMC's A-series engine before a test drive in a prototype Mini convinced him of the car's competition potential. The result, launched in 1961, was the Mini Cooper. With a tuned 997cc engine, it soon established its credentials as a rally and race winner. The 1071cc Mini Cooper S of 1963 took engine development a stage further and provided the basis for the 970 S and 1275 S of 1964. The latter pumped out 76bhp and was good for a genuine 100mph.

1968 Austin Mini Cooper, 998cc, 4 cylinder engine, 4-speed manual gearbox, rebuilt 1995, finished in original beige with white roof, black interior trim and upholstery, original factory specification, excellent condition throughout, Heritage Trust certificate. **£3,400–4,000 H&H**

1969 Austin Mini Moke, finished in dark green, canvas roof, unused for some time, recommissioned 1998, 6,142 miles from new, canvas seats in fair condition, one of only six built to special order for military use, good condition. **£5,500–6,500 S**

Did You Know?

Mini designer Alec Issigonis didn't approve when John Cooper approached him with plans for a hot Mini. The creator of the miniature marvel stuck to his vision of a car that would provide 'everyman transport', but Cooper went over his head, got the go-ahead to breathe magic on the Mini and created an unlikely sporting legend.

1970 Morris Mini Cooper S, Wood & Pickett conversion, 1275cc, knock-off Minilite wheels, Webasto sunroof, finished in Sable with beige leather upholstery, leather dashboard, electric tinted windows, 17,286 miles from new.
£13,000–15,000 BKS

The Mini was never more luxurious than when upgraded by Wood & Pickett. This car belonged to film star Lawrence Harvey until his death in 1973.

1970 Morris Mini Cooper, rebuilt, alloy wheels, tinted glass, concours winner.
£5,000–6,000 BARO

1972 Mini Cooper Mk III, Downton tuned dry suspension, original Teal blue paintwork in good condition.
£10,000–12,000 MIN

1975 Morris Mini Clubman, 50,000 miles from new, good condition throughout.
£600–800 BARO

1980 Mini Clubman Estate, 998cc, automatic transmission, finished in Blaze orange with black cloth upholstery, fewer than 18,000 miles from new, excellent original condition.
£1,800–2,200 BKS

British Leyland's corporate strategy for the 1970s saw Austin and Morris dropped as marque names for the Mini. At the same time, a new top-of-the-range variant – the Mini Clubman – was introduced. It featured an extended nose and, along with the rest of the Mk III Minis, had a revised bodyshell with internal door hinges. Wind-up windows were also new.

◄ **1981 Mini Clubman HL Estate,** rustproofed, new rear subframe, 48,000 miles from new.
£1,200–1,500 BARO

Morgan

If ever a car manufacturer was an anachronism, Morgan is it, for to this day, the company's cars are defiantly traditional, post-vintage in appearance and built with little concession to modern production-line practices. It's a curious formula, but one that works; indeed, in the 1960s, when Morgan made a stab at passing modernity with the fibreglass-bodied Plus Four Plus closed coupé, the company's traditional customers failed to bite – only 26 were produced. Ever since then, Morgan has stuck to what it does best, gently refining and improving a car that displays a direct lineage back to the company's first four-wheeler of 1935. Some consider modern Morgans with Rover V8 power and 125mph performance to be 'less classic' than older models, but the company still has trouble in keeping abreast of demand from those who crave high-speed, instant nostalgia. As for the vintage-era three-wheeled Morgans, these were produced from 1910 and soldiered on until 1952. They still enjoy a tremendously enthusiastic following, particularly in historic club racing.

1925 Morgan Grand Prix Three-Wheeler, 885cc V-twin JAP engine, fitted with later carburettor, 2-speed gearbox with chain final drive, electric lighting, hood, rear-mounted picnic hamper, mechanical overhaul 1996, new mainshafts, clutch, pistons and silencers, finished in brown with beige upholstery, good condition throughout.
£10,000–12,000 BKS

The first of the three-wheeler Morgans emerged in 1909, a V-twin-engined machine with chain final drive and independent front suspension. Production began in 1910, and it was not until 1936 that Morgan offered a four-wheel option. This was not surprising, as the three-wheelers were remarkably successful and formidable in competition in Aero and Grand Prix guise, powered by Blackburne, Matchless or JAP engines.

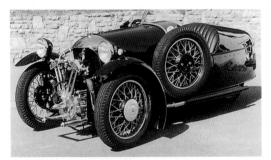

1934 Morgan Super Sports, 1000cc Matchless engine, 80mph top speed, side-mounted spare wheel, low-level exhaust pipes and silencer, restored, engine and gearbox rebuilt, steering, brakes and suspension overhauled, finished in black with matching trim, in need of running in.
£30,000–35,000 BKS

The Super Sports Aero was announced in 1928, being longer, lower and faster than earlier Aeros. In competition, it was all conquering, gaining Morgan international records at Montlhéry and Brooklands, while in trials, its successes continued unabated.

1948 Morgan 4/4 Drophead Coupé, coachwork by Andrews of West Bromwich, 1267cc, rebuilt 1960 with new chassis and bullnose radiator surround, finished in black with navy blue leather interior, one owner from new, stored 10 years, in need of recommissioning, good condition, history file.
£8,000–9,000 BKS

The first four-seat, four-wheel Morgan appeared in 1937, and a special sports model, powered by a 42bhp Coventry-Climax engine, competed at Le Mans in 1938. That year, a Standard engine of 1267cc was offered in the 4/4, and the elegant 2+2 Drophead Coupé was announced. Fewer than 50 of the latter were built between 1938 and 1950.

1966 Morgan Plus 4 Drophead Coupé, completely restored, original engine and twin Stromberg carburettors, concours condition.
£14,000–17,000 RM

Production of Plus 4 Morgans began in the early 1950s and continued until the late 1960s. Starting in 1962, the Plus 4 was powered by the 2.1 litre Triumph TR4 engine, which produced 105bhp. Top speed was slightly over 100mph.

1993 Morgan Plus 4 Two-Seater, Rover 2 litre engine, wire wheels, finished in dark green.
£18,000–22,000 BHM

1977 Morgan Plus 8, 3528cc, Rover V8, 161bhp, 5-speed manual gearbox, limited-slip differential, 125mph top speed, finished in red with grey and brown interior, 19,500 miles from new, leather interior showing some signs of wear, otherwise good condition throughout.
£13,000–15,000 H&H

1982 Morgan Plus 8, 3528cc, Rover V8, alloy wheels, finished in white with black hood.
£16,000–18,000 BHM

A known continuous history can add value to and enhance the enjoyment of a car.

1980 Morgan 4/4, 1599cc, 4 cylinders, wire wheels, finished in yellow, serviceable black canvas hood and sidescreens, black vinyl interior trim, good condition throughout.
£9,500–11,000 BRIT

The post-war 4/4 range utilised Ford power and changed very little in appearance over the years.

1970 Morgan Plus 8, 3528cc, Rover V8, 184bhp at 5,200rpm, 4-speed gearbox, finished in Connaught green with beige sidescreens and hood, Havana interior.
£18,000–20,000 Pou

Morris

Like so many other early British car makers, Morris had its roots in the bicycle boom of the latter half of the 19th century. Born in 1877, the eldest son of an Oxford farm manager, William Morris' only job working for someone else was at an Oxford bicycle shop, where he lasted a year before leaving in a huff when his request for a pay rise was turned down.

Using his £4 savings, Morris set up on his own at home. A fine athlete and trophy-winning cyclist, his local fame boosted his business, and as it expanded, he tinkered with motorbikes and started selling and servicing cars. The first Morris car, the 1 litre 'bull-nose' Morris Oxford, was produced in 1913, and by 1924, Morris was Britain's biggest car manufacturer.

In fact, for 70 years from 1913, the name of Morris stood out as a byword for middle-class motoring. The cars were rarely exciting, but usually deserving of their reputation as no-frills, stoutly dependable machines. By the time the name of Morris was finally dropped from the Austin-Rover inventory in 1984, it had been sadly devalued, becoming in later times more of a byword for mediocrity. Those ungainly Morris Marinas, Itals and the short-lived Morris 1800 and 2200 'cheese wedges' of the 1970s serve as inglorious mementos to a remarkable man and company. A more fitting tribute is the wonderful 1948 Morris Minor, which went on to become Britain's first million-selling motor car.

1914 Morris Oxford 10hp Two-Seater and Dickey, White & Poppe 4 cylinder side-valve engine, 3-speed gearbox, correct gilled tube radiator, electric cooling fan, P&H acetylene headlamps and oil sidelamps converted to electric operation, folding windscreen, beige canvas hood, finished in blue over black.
£9,500–10,500 BKS

After graduating to motor car manufacturing, following his early beginnings as a cycle repairer, William Morris began trading as WRM Motors. He accepted his first order for 400 Morris Oxford cars from Stewart & Ardern. At the time, this was a huge pledge of faith by both parties, particularly as Morris had no proven record of serious motor car production. However, the successful outcome of the arrangement established a long and fruitful relationship for both companies.

1916 Morris Cowley 11.9hp Bullnose Sliding-Door Saloon, finished in dark blue and black with blue buttoned leather upholstery, unused for some years, in need of cosmetic refurbishment and recommissioning.
£6,750–7,750 BKS

This car was originally purchased in chassis form by a Mr Bowden and used as a factory hack with a lash-up body at the front and a flatbed rear. In 1918, Bowden designed a lightweight saloon body for the car from 1in steel tubes covered with aluminium at the bottom and fabric at the top. Quite a few American imports of the period were centre-door models, so he made his in that style, but with a sliding door arrangement.

◄ **1923 Morris Oxford Doctor's Coupé,** Hotchkiss engine, older restoration.
£9,000–10,000 BKS

Morris Milestones

1877 William Richard Morris born on October 10 near Oxford.
1905 William Morris buys his first car.
1913 In Morris' first year, 393 cars are produced.
1917 William Morris receives OBE for war work.
1919 WRM Motors Ltd becomes Morris Motors Ltd.
1924 Morris Motors becomes Britain's largest producer of motor cars.
1926 Morris Motors Ltd becomes a public company.
1927 William Morris personally buys Wolseley with his own money.
1929 Morris Motors employs over 10,000 workers.
1929 William Richard Morris is knighted.
1934 Sir William Morris becomes Baron Nuffield.
1935 Morris Motors takes over MG.
1938 Morris Motors takes over Riley and becomes the Nuffield Organisation.
1938 William Morris becomes Viscount Nuffield of Nuffield in the County of Oxfordshire.
1939 The millionth Morris rolls off production line on May 22.

1948 First Morris Minor built on September 20.
1949 Market share of the Nuffield Organisation is down to one-sixth of total British production – half the share it had in 1939.
1952 Austin and Morris merge to form British Motor Corporation – BMC.
1954 William Morris retires.
1959 Mini launched on 26 August.
1960 On December 10, the millionth Morris Minor is made.
1963 William Morris dies on August 22.
1966 British Motor Corporation becomes British Motor Holdings after merger with Jaguar.
1968 Merger with Leyland results in another name, British Leyland Motor Corporation.
1970 Last Morris Minor built on November 12.
1975 British Leyland nationalised.
1980 British Leyland reorganises under Austin-Rover Group banner.
1984 Morris name disappears from Austin-Rover inventory.
1986 Five-millionth Mini produced on 19 February.

1925 Morris Oxford Bullnose Two-Seater with Dickey, brass-rimmed headlamps and sidelamps, restored to original condition.
£10,000–12,000 PC

1925 Morris Cowley 11.9hp Bullnose Two-Seater with Dickey, front wheel brakes, Gabriel snubbers, wellbase wheels, luggage grid, calormeter, completely restored, unused since, fitted with replica coachwork.
£6,500–7,500 BKS

A staggering 33,913 Morris Cowley chassis were laid down in 1925, testament to the popularity, reliability and competitive pricing of the model.

1925 Morris Cowley Two-Seater with Dickey, finished in yellow with matching wheels and black wings, upholstered in blue leather, last used 1981, reasonable condition.
£4,750–5,750 S

Restored Values

The cost of a professional restoration will have an influence on, but no direct relation to, a car's market value. A restored car can have a market value lower than the cost of its restoration.

1929 Morris Cowley Tourer with Dickey, side-mounted spare wheel, finished in blue over black, black interior trim, completely restored, concours condition.
£6,000–7,000 S

The Morris Oxford light car was joined by the larger Cowley in 1915, and few changes were made to the best-selling cars until the advent of a new range of models distinguished by a flat-fronted radiator.

1930 Morris CMS Special, cable brakes, Lucas headlamps, Rotax sidelamps, aluminium sporting two-seater coachwork, V-screen, steel bonnet, finished in red with grey interior trim, tonneau cover, new wooden floor panel, luggage rack, very good condition.
£4,600–5,200 S

This little Morris was the forerunner of a limited number of special-bodied cars built by CMS between the wars. CMS formed part of Grindlay-Peerless, a company better known for its sidecars and motorcycles between 1923 and 1934.

◀ **1930 Morris Minor Two-Door Saloon,** overhead-camshaft engine, 3-speed gearbox with dry clutch, cable-operated brakes, steel-panelled body, restored 1988/92 at a cost of over £9,000, finished in maroon and black, excellent condition.
£5,750–6,750 BKS

Morris' 1927 acquisition of Wolseley Motors allowed the production of a light car to rival Austin's successful 7. Wolseley's 847cc, overhead-camshaft, 4 cylinder engine powered the new Minor which, with around double the 7's output, offered markedly superior performance. A fabric-bodied saloon and four-seater tourer were offered initially, being joined for 1930 by a steel-panelled saloon and light van.

1934 Morris Minor Two-Seater Tourer, 847cc, side-valve engine, body restored, new leather upholstery, new duck hood and sidescreens, good condition throughout.
£4,500–5,000 Mot

1933 Morris 10/4, 1292cc, 4-speed gearbox, hydraulic brakes, fitted with rare Wilcot direction indicators, good condition throughout.
£6,000–8,000 VIC

1934 Morris 25 Saloon, 3.5 litres, Bendix automatic clutch, freewheel option, sliding roof, trafficators and trafficator interior mirrors, original maroon leather upholstery, inlaid wooden door fittings, lasted used 1971, in need of recommissioning. £4,000–5,000 BKS

Introduced in September 1932, the 25hp was top of the Morris range, and the most expensive model built at the time. Power came from a 6 cylinder engine of 3485cc, which featured an 'air-cleaning and fume-consuming head'. Some considered the latter to be a Morris ruse to make the side-valve engine look like the more fashionable overhead-valve configuration.

Morris, the man

What kind of man was William Richard Morris? Undoubtedly, he was ambitious and hardworking. These virtues are taken for granted and often attributed to the responsibility he held at an early age to support his family. He was also famously frugal at work and at home. But there's much contradiction, too. He was, at times, a hero to the shop-floor workers and a tyrant to his managers. This handsome man said and wrote much about good management, but it seems that in practice, he sometimes lapsed from his high moral stance. He was a philanthropist on a massive scale, giving away an estimated £25 million, much of it to medical charities. He also pioneered employee amenities, like sports clubs, medical centres, profit sharing and paid holidays. Yet he would also sack people at the drop of a hat. Although he became immensely wealthy, he was not a snob; in fact, if anything, he may have been a slightly inverted snob. Once, he was refused membership of an exclusive golf club, but later the club relented as his status grew. William Morris subsequently bought the club.

In his own words:

'It is not always the men who have an expensive education who do things.'
'When I decided to start for myself it was because I felt that no one else would pay me as well as W.R. Morris.'
'Without worry you never get anywhere.'
'There are very few types of business which I would not be prepared to tackle with some hope of success, relying entirely on my own experience.'
'Work is the natural mission of every real man.'
'The one object in life of many makers seems to be to make the thing the public cannot buy. The one object of my life has been to make the thing they can buy.'
'Bad management has the same effect as sand in the bearings of a machine. I have proved on many occasions that by removing someone from the top or the bottom the sand has been removed and production has gone up in consequence.'
'No factory can turn out a cheap car on low wages...A low wage is the most expensive method of producing.'
On his wealth and frugal spending: 'Can you use more than one toothbrush or eat more than one meal at a time?...Happily I have no expensive hobbies. Neither would I care to live anywhere save next door to the works.'
'I can't understand people not using up soap to the last bit. It makes me mad.'
'I could have stopped Hitler if only he had spoken English.'
'I have more money than any man can possibly want, and for what it is worth I have a title, but all that I have dies when I die. That is my personal tragedy.'

By others:

'We all worshipped the ground W.R. Morris walked on.'
At the funeral of one of his managers: 'Why cry? Why cry when you killed him. You worked the poor bugger to death.'
'Autocratic despot.'
By a shopfloor employee: 'I remember he always gave us a chicken at Christmas.'
'To him all life was a challenge. He had a simple minded determination to make his mark in the world.'
'With complete faith in what he wanted to do, he has always had an unwavering faith in his own abilities and judgement.'
'He was an inspiration. Enthusiasm radiated from him.'
'His character made it difficult for him to enjoy close friendships.'

1930s/40s Morris Retail Dealer singled-sided enamel sign, in red and blue on white background, 36in (91.5cm) diam.
£250–300 MSMP

Miller's is a price GUIDE not a price LIST

▶ **1953 Morris Minor Tourer,** 1098cc, 4 cylinder engine, 4-speed manual gearbox, split-screen, finished in green with matching interior, 72,525 miles from new, 'barn discovery', good condition.
£2,750–3,500 H&H

Miller's Starter Marque

Starter Morris: *Minor 1948–71.*
- Designed by Alec Issigonis, the genius who later would pen the Mini, the 1948 Morris Minor went on to become Britain's first million seller, a feat marked in 1960 with a series of 349 livid lilac-hued Morris 'Millions'. The Minor featured unitary construction, and its famed handling finesse and ride comfort more than made up for a lack of power. The combination proved to be just what ordinary people needed from a car.
- Any model is eminently affordable and almost as practical to own now as when in production, owing to ready availability and a blossoming cottage industry that provides everything you need to keep your Minor in fine fettle. The Minor is also generally long-lived and one of the easiest cars for DIY maintenance. Front and rear wings are bolt-on items, and sound wings can conceal horrors underneath. On Travellers, the wood framing is structural and should be examined very carefully.

Pick of the bunch: The first split-screen 'low-light' models, especially convertibles, produced before the headlights were raised to the top of the wings to conform to US regulations.
What to watch: Beware 'rogue rag-tops'. Convertibles are more prized, and although there's a legitimate industry converting saloons to open tops, there are also fast-buck cowboys and inept DIY bodgers. Bodged convertibles are potential killers – literally.
Body styles: Saloon, convertible Tourer, estate Traveller.
Engine: Four-cylinder, 803-1098cc.
Power output: 28-48bhp.
Maximum speed: 62-75mph
Production: 1,619,958.

1949 Morris Minor Saloon, finished in green with beige leather interior, complete and largely original, unused for some time, in need of recommissioning.
£1,400–1,800 BKS

Introduced in 1948, at a time of post-war austerity, the Minor was the work of Alec Issigonis, and although initially it was not a favourite of Lord Nuffield, it proved to be the British equivalent of the German 'People's Car'. Early models used the pre-war side-valve Morris Eight engine, but in 1952, the Minor was equipped with the much livelier overhead-valve Austin A30 unit.

1954 Morris Minor Four-Door Saloon, 803cc, 4 cylinder engine, 4-speed manual gearbox, split screen, finished in Clarendon grey with red interior, 59,848 miles from new, little recent use, good condition throughout, history file.
£1,750–2,250 H&H

1955 Morris Minor Four-Door Saloon, 803cc, split screen, finished in beige with red leather interior, concours condition.
£5,500–6,000 Mot

1962 Morris Minor 1000 Two-Door Saloon, 948cc, 4-cylinder engine, 4-speed manual gearbox, finished in grey with red interior trim, good condition throughout.
£1,400–1,800 H&H

1968 Morris Minor 1000 Four-Door Saloon, completely restored, very good condition.
£1,750–2,250 BARO

1968 Morris Minor 1000 Traveller, fitted with front anti-roll bar and disc brakes, rear drums overhauled, servo installed, halogen headlamps, bodywork restored, new ash sections, bare-metal respray in Moss green, woodwork revarnished, seats recovered, inertia-reel seatbelts fitted, electric aerial, excellent condition throughout.
£2,250–2,750 BKS

This car once belonged to the well-known actor Robbie Coltrane.

1971 Morris Minor 1000 Traveller, 1098cc, restored, finished in maroon, excellent woodwork, very good condition throughout.
£2,250–2,750 BKS

The Traveller estate version of the Minor appeared in 1953. By then, the car was in Series II form, with an 803cc, overhead-valve A-series engine in place of the original 918cc side-valve unit. In 1956, the Minor 1000 appeared, featuring a 948cc engine and improved gearbox. Another capacity increase, to 1098cc, came in 1962. The practical Traveller remained popular right up until the end of production in 1971.

◄ 1969 Morris Oxford Series VI Four-Door Saloon, manual gearbox, finished in grey with red interior, unused for 10 years, in need of recommissioning, good condition throughout.
£500–800 BKS

MORRIS Model	ENGINE cc/cyl	DATES	CONDITION 1	2	3
Minor Series MM	918/4	1948–52	£3,000	£1,600	£800
Minor Series MM Conv	918/4	1948–52	£4,500	£2,200	£1,200
Minor Series II	803/4	1953–56	£2,000	£1,000	£500
Minor Series II Conv	803/4	1953–56	£5,500	£3,500	£1,500
Minor Series II Est	803/4	1953–56	£3,000	£1,250	£800
Minor 1000	948/4	1956–63	£1,750	£925	£250
Minor 1000 Conv	948/4	1956–63	£4,000+	£2,000	£750
Minor 1000 Est	948/4	1956–63	£4,000	£2,200	£1,200
Minor 1000	1098/4	1963–71	£2,000	£950	£250
Minor 1000 Conv	1098/4	1963–71	£4,500	£3,000	£1,500
Minor 1000 Est	1098/4	1963–71	£4,000	£3,000	£1,500
Cowley 1200	1200/4	1954–56	£1,675	£1,000	£300
Cowley 1500	1489/4	1956–59	£1,750	£950	£350
Oxford MO	1476/4	1948–54	£2,000	£850	£250
Oxford MO Est	1476/4	1952–54	£3,000	£1,500	£350
Series II/III	1489/4	1954–59	£2,000	£1,200	£300
Series II/III/IV Est	1489/4	1954–60	£2,250	£1,350	£250
Oxford Series V Farina	1489/4	1959–61	£1,800	£800	£250
Oxford Series VI Farina	1622/4	1961–71	£1,750	£750	£200
Six Series MS	2215/6	1948–54	£2,500	£1,500	£500
Isis Series I/II	2639/6	1955–58	£2,500	£1,300	£450
Isis Series I/II Est	2639/6	1956–57	£2,600	£1,350	£500

Napier

◄ **1911 Napier 15hp Colonial Model Tourer,** 2.9 litre, 4 cylinder engine, brass lighting, acetylene headlamps and oil sidelamps, folding windscreen, five-seater coachwork with additional occasional seating for two, restored, finished in green with black leather upholstery, good condition throughout.
£22,000–25,000 BKS

Introduced in 1910 as a development of an earlier car of the same output, the 15hp Napier became the company's most successful model. It cost £350 in chassis form, to which Napier's own four-seater bodywork added an extra £80 (plus £7 for the windscreen).

Nash

► **1929 Nash Series 430 Tourer,** 3670cc, 6 cylinder engine, older restoration, finished in gold and black with beige interior, very good condition throughout.
£14,500–17,000 BRIT

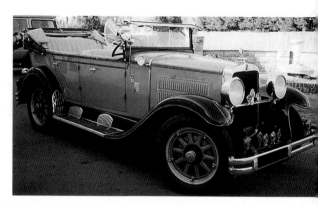

The Nash Motor Company began production in 1917, Through the 1920s, the range increased, all models offering excellent value for money and being of high quality. By 1928, 2.7 per cent of American new-car registrations were Nash products, and in 1931, when most automobile companies lost money due to the deepening depression, Nash Motors showed a profit of $4.8 million.

Oakland

◄ **1930 Oakland Roadster,** 4200cc, 6 cylinder in-line engine, 3-speed gearbox, sem-elliptic leaf-spring suspension, 4-wheel hydraulic drum brakes, 75mph top speed, older restoration, finished in white, little recent use.
£6,500-8,000 Pou

Auction Prices

Miller's only includes cars declared sold. Our guide prices take into account the buyer's premium, VAT on the premium, and the extent of any published catalogue information relating to condition and provenance. To identify cars sold at auction, cross-refer the source codes at the ends of photo captions with the Key to Illustrations on page 330.

Oldsmobile

► **1902 Oldsmobile 5 hp Curved Dash Runabout,** restored, finished in black, bench seat reupholstered in black hide, sold with later 1904 mudguards and unrestored hood.
£13,500–15,000 BKS

The Curved Dash was light, and easy to drive and maintain. It featured tiller steering, unique cantilever-type suspension and a single-cylinder engine that developed 4.5bhp at 600rpm. Its high ground clearance made the Olds ideal for the rutted roads of the day. Estimated production figures for the successful 1902 Curved-Dash model were 2,500 units.

◀ **1903 Oldsmobile 5hp Model R Curved Dash Runabout,** single-cylinder engine, tiller steering, cantilever suspension, brass oil lamps and bugle-type horn, varnished wooden wheels, restored, finished in black with deep-buttoned green leather upholstery, good condition throughout.
£13,500–15,000 BKS

OLDSMOBILE Model	ENGINE cc/cyl	DATES	CONDITION 1	2	3
Curved Dash	1600/1	1901–04	£16,000	£14,000	£12,000
30	2771/6	1925–26	£9,000	£7,000	£4,000
Straight Eight	4213/8	1937–38	£14,000	£9,000	£5,000

Overland

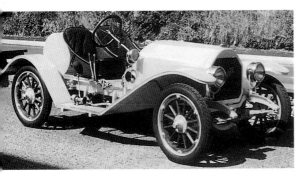

◀ **1916 Overland Model 83 35hp Raceabout,** electric starter, electric headlamps, replica raceabout coachwork, finished in yellow with varnished wooden wheels, monocle driver's windscreen, wicker bucket seats, unused for many years, in need of recommissioning
£12,500–14,500 BKS

For 1916, Overland listed a range of four cars: three 4 cylinder models, ranging from 20 to 40hp, and a 6 cylinder model of 45/50hp. The Model 83, rated at 35hp, was offered in no less than eight body styles.

Packard

Founded by James Ward Packard, in Ohio, the company produced its first motor cars in 1899 and went on to build an envied reputation in the luxury-car field. In 1915, the company built the world's first production V12 engine, and in the 1920s made some magnificent, cost-no-object machines. In the following decade,

with a dwindling luxury market, Packard's salvation came from a move into the middle market with the 120-series. After WWII, Cadillac made severe inroads into Packard's traditional luxury market, and even though Packard bought Studebaker in 1954, the marque disappeared in 1958.

1930 **Packard 745 Convertible Victoria,** coachwork by Proux, Deluxe Eight chassis, completely restored, concours condition throughout.
115,000–130,000 RM

1939 Packard 1705 Coupé Chauffeur, coachwork by Franay, restored, excellent condition, concours winner.
£125,000–135,000 BLK

PACKARD	ENGINE	DATES	CONDITION		
Model	cc/cyl		1	2	3
Twin Six	6946/12	1916–23	£30,000	£20,000	£15,000
6	3973/6	1921–24	£20,000	£15,000	£12,000
6, 7, 8 Series	5231/8	1929–39	£35,000+	£25,000+	£14,000+
12	7300/12	1936–39	£50,000+	£30,000+	£18,000+

Panhard

◄ **1961 Panhard PL17 Tigre,** engine completely overhauled in 1992, body restored and resprayed in 1993, tiger-skin-pattern seats, very good condition throughout. **£3,800–4,200 Pel**

The Tigre model was equipped with a higher-performance engine than the standard PL17. It is much rarer.

Panhard-Levassor

◄ **1925 Panhard-Levassor Model X47 11.2hp Saloon,** coachwork by Driquet Fréres of Paris, 4 cylinder engine, manual gearbox, cone clutch, restored, resprayed in original French blue over black, interior mostly original with cord trim, history file. **£8,500–9,500 H&H**

Dealer Prices

Miller's guide prices for dealer cars take into account the value of any guarantees or warranties that may be included in the purchase. Dealers must also observe additional statutory consumer regulations, which do not apply to private sellers. This is factored into our dealer guide prices. To identify dealer cars, cross-refer the source codes at the ends of photo captions with the Key to Illustrations on page 330.

Panther

1983 Panther Lima, 2.3 litre, 4 cylinder engine, finished in black and red, good condition.
£6,000–6,500 **EPP**

Peugeot

1955 Peugeot 203 Airline Saloon, 1290cc, 4 cylinder engine, finished in black, good condition throughout.
£5,000–5,500 **BC**

1973 Peugeot 304 Cabriolet, 1288cc, new headlamps, radiator and exhaust system, braking system overhauled, finished in ivory with black hood, hardtop, dark tan interior trim.
£3,500–4,000 **H&H**

◄ **1976 Peugeot 604 SL Saloon,** body restored, new front wings and door skins, rustproofed, excellent condition throughout.
£4,000–5,000 **CPUK**

> A known continuous history can add value to and enhance the enjoyment of a car.

PEUGEOT Model	ENGINE cc/cyl	DATES	CONDITION 1	2	3
Bebe	856/4	1912–14	£18,000	£12,000	£8,000
153	2951/4	1913–26	£9,000	£5,000	£3,000
163	1490/4	1920–24	£5,000	£4,000	£2,000
Bebe	676/4	1920–25	£7,000	£6,000	£3,000
156	5700/6	1922–24	£7,000	£5,000	£3,000
174	3828/4	1922–28	£7,500	£5,000	£2,000
172	714/4	1926–28	£4,000	£3,000	£1,500
183	1990/6	1929–30	£5,000	£3,000	£1,500
201	996/4	1930–36	£6,000	£3,000	£1,500
402	2140/4	1938–40	£4,500	£3,000	£1,000

Right-hand-drive cars and tourers will always achieve more interest than left-hand-drive models.

Pierce-Arrow

1934 Pierce-Arrow V12 Seven-Passenger Limousine, 144in wheelbase, new running boards, finished in blue, interior retrimmed in mohair, floor heater, vanity units, 2 occasional seats, approximately 30,000 miles from new, good original condition throughout.
£12,000–14,000 BKS

The mighty V12 Pierce-Arrow made its debut in November 1931. The new engine was a smooth, yet rugged, L-head unit that gave the 2 ton car an 80mph cruising speed. Its potential was amply demonstrated in September 1932, when Ab Jenkins covered 2,710 miles in 24 hours, driving a lightly-stripped V12 Roadster at an average speed of almost 113mph. In the following year, he averaged 117mph for 3,000 miles. During the run, he shaved while driving at 125mph to demonstrate the smooth ride of the Pierce-Arrow.

Plymouth

◄ **1946 Plymouth P15 Deluxe Saloon,** 3000cc, 6 cylinder engine, 3-speed manual gearbox, right-hand drive, body-off restoration 1993, finished in black with brown interior trim and upholstery, 82,000 miles from new.
£4,500–5,000 H&H

Plymouth produced the P15 from 1946 until 1949 in various guises. This four-door saloon was ordered originally by the South African Embassy in the USA, hence the reason for it having right-hand drive.

Pontiac

Although the name Pontiac had been linked to several early American automobile ventures, it wasn't until 1926 that the marque as it is known today really got under way as a new General Motors brand, produced by the Oakland Motor Company. In the General Motors hierarchy, the early Pontiacs slotted in just above Chevrolet. They enjoyed immediate success, outselling the more expensive Oaklands. As a result, in 1932, General Motors dropped the Oakland brand althogether and renamed the division the Pontiac Motor Company.

The Pontiac name derives from the native Indian tribe. It is one of the few subsidiary US marques to have been created rather than acquired. Pontiac is also notable for being the only companion car in the GM line-up to have eclipsed its parent in sales volume.

1976 Pontiac Firebird TransAm, 50th Anniversary Limited-Edition model, 7500cc V8, automatic transmission, left-hand drive, finished in black with gold trim and wheels, matching interior, 44 miles from new, 'as-new' condition throughout.
£15,000–17,000 H&H

Porsche

Few would argue with the classic credentials of any Porsche model, whether the first-of-breed 356 or today's latest super-performers and the lovely retro-styled Boxster. One reason is that current models still display an unbroken linear descent from the very first 356 of 1949, both in styling and concept.

Volkswagen Beetle designer Ferdinand Porsche may have given the world the people's car, but it was his son, Ferry, who, with long-time associate Karl Rabe, created a car that people all over the world would prize from the day the first example rolled off the production line.

1956 Porsche 356A Speedster, 1600cc, air-cooled, flat-4 engine, completely restored, finished in red with tan upholstery, optional comfort seats, very good condition, history file.
£40,000–44,000 COYS

By 1954, Porsche sales in the USA were suffering from the onslaught of MG, Austin-Healey and Triumph, whose cars provided as much exhilaration for a lot less money. As a result, coachbuilder Reutter penned a minimal shell based on the convertible 356, with low wrap-around windscreen, reduced frontal area, removable sidescreens, a lightweight hood and more basic interior. Selling at a competitive $2,995 and available with a 55bhp, 1488cc engine, the 110mph Speedster proved popular on road and track. In 1955, the 356A was introduced with a choice of 1290cc and 1582cc engines, the latter producing 75bhp.

1958 Porsche 356A Speedster, 1600cc, finished in light blue with red leather interior trim, new black hood, excellent condition.
£42,000–48,000 H&H

1960 Porsche 356B Roadster, 1584cc, 4 cylinders, restored 1995/96, engine rebuilt, new Weber carburettors, new kingpins, Koni shock absorbers, finished in ivory with burgundy leather trim and beige carpeting, excellent condition throughout.
£27,000–30,000 BRIT

Porsche 356

The Porsche 356 is the car that started it all, beginning a proud sporting tradition that continues to this day. In many ways, the 356 is the Beetle's athletic son, its concept, rear-engined layout and design descending directly from the parent. It hardly sounds exotic, but the 356 is much more than a Bug in butterfly's clothes. In the 356, the humble Volkswagen genes are miraculously mutated into a true sporting machine, a peppy, pert piece of precision engineering available in myriad combinations, from humble 'cooking' models for less than Mondeo money, to the exotic and very precious Speedsters and quad-cam Carreras.
Pick of the bunch: Ultimate in performance and price is the 356C Carrera II. Some purists favour the earliest split-windscreen, jelly-mould shape, but for all-round drivability and affordability, the last-of-the-line, 1600cc 356C coupés with all-round disc brakes make most sense.

PORSCHE Model	ENGINE cc/cyl	DATES	CONDITION 1	2	3
356	var/4	1949–53	£15,000	£8,000	£5,000
356 Cabriolet	var/4	1951–53	£20,000	£14,000	£10,000
356A	1582/4	1955–59	£13,000	£9,000	£5,000
356A Cabriolet	1582/4	1956–59	£16,000	£10,000	£7,000
356A Speedster	1582/4	1955–58	£25,000	£19,000	£14,000
356B Carrera	1582/ 1966/4	1960–65	£40,000+	£30,000+	£18,000
356C	1582/4	1963–65	£15,000	£11,000+	£5,000
356C Cabriolet	1582/4	1963–64	£25,000+	£16,000	£10,000
911/911L/T/E	1991/6	1964–68	£12,000	£7,000	£5,000
912	1582/4	1965–68	£6,500	£5,000	£2,000
911S	1991/6	1966–69	£12,000	£8,000	£5,500
911S	2195/6	1969–71	£13,000	£9,000	£6,000
911T	2341/6	1971–73	£13,000	£8,000	£6,000
911E	2341/6	1971–73	£12,000+	£8,000	£6,000
914/4	1679/4	1969–75	£4,000	£3,000	£1,000
914/6	1991/6	1969–71	£6,000	£3,500	£1,500
911S	2341/6	1971–73	£16,000	£10,000	£8,500
Carrera RS lightweight	2687/6	1973	£40,000	£28,000+	£16,000
Carrera RS Touring	2687/6	1973	£30,000	£26,000	£17,000
Carrera 3	2994/6	1976–77	£14,000	£9,000	£7,000
924 Turbo	1984/4	1978–83	£5,000	£4,000	£2,000
928/928S	4474/4664/V8	1977–86	£10,000	£7,000	£4,000
911SC	2993/6	1977–83	£13,000	£8,000	£6,000

Sportomatic cars are less desirable.

Tony Upson, a large mural of a 1958 Porsche 356 coupé together with factory logo, acrylic on board, 48 x 96in (122 x 244cm).
£275–300 BKS

1960 Porsche 356B T5 Sunroof Coupé, 1600cc, 15in wheels, left-hand drive, partially restored, over £10,000 spent, finished in red with matching interior, body and chassis in excellent condition, good mechanical condition, interior fair.
£6,000–8,000 BKS

◄ **1973 Porsche 911 Targa,** 2.4 litres, left-hand drive, finished in Aubergine with black and fawn interior, little recent use, good condition throughout.
£5,500–7,000 BKS

Porsche's long-running 911 arrived in coupé form in 1964 as a replacement for the 356. Two years later, a convertible stablemate – the Targa – arrived. Expected US safety legislation prompted Porsche to adopt an ingenious approach to the soft-top 911, the Targa sporting a hefty roll-over bar and removable roof and rear hood sections. For 1969, a quieter and less leak-prone fixed rear window replaced the rear hood. In this form, the ever-popular Targa continued into the 1990s.

Porsche 356B (1959–63)

Body styles: 2+2 fixed-head coupé, cabriolet and Speedster.
Construction: Unitary: steel body with integral pressed-steel platform chassis.
Engine: Air-cooled, flat-four, twin carburettors, 1582cc.
Power output: 90bhp at 5,500rpm (Super 90).
Transmission: Four-speed manual, all-synchromesh, rear-wheel drive.
Suspension: Independent front by trailing arms with transverse torsion bars and anti-roll bar; rear suspension by swing axles, radius arms and transverse torsion bars. Telescopic shock absorbers front and rear.
Brakes: Hydraulic drums all-round.
Maximum speed: 110mph.
0–60mph: 10 seconds.
Average fuel consumption: 30–35mpg.
Production: 30,963 (all types).

1973 Porsche 911 Carrera 2.7 RS, Touring specification, original engine, 153mph top speed, 0–60mph in 5.7 seconds, restored 1992, finished in Signal yellow with black interior, one of last 20 made.
£27,000–32,000 BKS

It was 25 years before Porsche made its first 'homologation special'. The rule book said that if at least 1,000 examples of a car were made in a year, it would qualify as a Group 3 (production sports/GT) car, which is how the 1972/73 Carrera RS came about.

1989 Porsche 911 Carrera Speedster, 3164cc, 6 cylinders, K-Jetronic fuel injection, 231bhp at 5,900rpm, 5-speed manual gearbox, servo-assisted disc brakes all-round, left-hand drive, 152mph top speed, finished in red with black interior and hood.
£23,000–27,000 Pou

1981 Porsche 924 Carrera GT, rebuilt turbocharged engine, multi-spoke alloy wheels, finished in red with red-piped black interior, well maintained, very good condition.
£9,500–11,000 BKS

1985 Porsche 959 Factory Prototype 006, 2.9 litre, double-overhead-camshaft, flat-6 engine, 4 valves per cylinder, twin two-stage turbochargers, 450bhp at 6,500rpm, 4-wheel drive, 4-wheel ventilated disc brakes, ABS, many hand-made parts.
£60,000–70,000 BKS

Porsche's objective was to produce a strictly limited edition of no more than 200 examples of the 959 supercar. Months of painstaking design, testing and development perfected the model. This car was one of the prototypes used in that process.

1982 Porsche 911SC, 2993cc, 6 cylinders, finished in Arrow blue with beige/brown interior, good condition throughout.
£10,000–11,000 BRIT

1973 Porsche 914 Targa, 1679cc, 4 cylinders, alloy wheels, excellent condition.
£5,000–6,000 PALM

Dealer Prices

Miller's guide prices for dealer cars take into account the value of any guarantees or warranties that may be included in the purchase. Dealers must also observe additional statutory consumer regulations, which do not apply to private sellers. This is factored into our dealer guide prices. To identify dealer cars, cross-refer the source codes at the ends of photo captions with the Key to Illustrations on page 330.

Railton

◀ **1935 Railton Saloon,** 4168cc, 8 cylinder in-line engine, 3-speed synchromesh gearbox, Hudson Challenger chassis, new windscreen, bare-metal respray 1995, finished in original black, original blue leather interior, roof in need of recovering.
£3,500–4,500 S

The gifted designer Reid Railton gave his name to a marque which, from 1933, brought prosperity to Noel Macklin's Fairmile Works in Surrey. Around 1,500 were produced before production was wound up in 1939. It is thought that about 250 remain.

Rambler

◀ **1904 Rambler 16hp,** twin-cylinder engine, brass fittings and lamps, wooden spoked wheels, restored, excellent condition throughout.
£40,000–45,000 SVV

Reliant

Reliant began in 1935 by making three-wheeled utility vehicles. From 1952, the three-wheelers were also produced as passenger cars, and a fourth wheel was added with the launch of the Rebel in 1965. Meanwhile, the company had turned its attention to sporting products with the quirky Sabre of 1961–63, which grew into the far more harmonious Sabre Six of 1962–64, then the

ground-breaking Scimitar. Although there was nothing revolutionary in its fibreglass body, the Scimitar GTE created a new class of car, the sports estate. Today, this plastic classic still cuts it as one of that rare breed of sensible sports cars. It's a mark of how enduring the design was that the Scimitar GTE lasted from 1968 to 1986 and still looked fresh at the end of the 16,000 production run.

1967 Reliant Scimitar SE4, 3 litre V6, centre-lock wire wheels, restored, very good condition.
£5,250–5,750 GW

1969 Reliant Scimitar GTE SE5, 2994cc V6, restored, finished in green with black vinyl roof.
£4,500–5,000 GW

RELIANT Model	ENGINE cc/cyl	DATES	CONDITION 1	2	3
Sabre 4 Coupé & Drophead	1703/4	1961–63	£5,500	£2,750	£1,000
Sabre 6 Coupé & Drophead	2553/6	1962–64	£6,000	£3,500	£1,500
Scimitar GT Coupé SE4	2553/6, 2994/V6	1964–70	£4,500	£2,500	£1,000
Scimitar GTE Sports Estate SE5/5A	2994/V6	1968–75	£6,000	£3,000	£750
Scimitar GTE Sports Estate SE6/6A	2994/V6	1976–80	£6,000+	£3,500+	£1,250
Scimitar GTE Sports Estate SE6B	2792/V6	1980–86	£8,000	£5,000	£2,000
Scimitar GTC Convertible SE8B	2792/V6	1980–86	£9,000	£8,000	£5,500

Renault

Louis Renault's first car design, based on a De Dion tricycle, emerged in 1898. In the company's very earliest years, Louis concentrated on racing, until his brother, Marcel, was killed in the 1903 Paris-Madrid race. Thereafter, he devoted his efforts to car production and soon built up a comprehensive model range. By 1913, the company was responsible for around 20 per cent of French automobile production. Renault was nationalised in 1945, shortly after Louis Renault's death. Since then, there have been landmark cars – such as the 4CV of 1947, the Dauphine, and the Renault 4 and 5 – along with some interesting diversions, such as the pretty Floride and Caravelle small sports cars.

1906 Renault 30hp Open Drive Town Car, coachwork by Rothschild & Fils, brass fittings, good condition.
£35,000–40,000 COHN

1908 Renault 8hp, twin-cylinder engine, wooden artillery wheels, hood, finished in white, unused for many years, original, good condition throughout.
£13,000–15,000 SVV

◄ **1936 Renault 17.9hp Vivaquatre Saloon,** left-hand drive, restored late 1980s, finished in maroon with grey upholstery.
£4,750–5,500 BKS

Renault introduced a range of 6 cylinder cars in the late 1920s, but the Monasix proved too heavy for its 1474cc engine, and production ceased in 1931. The Monasix chassis, however, was used for a new 17.9hp car of 2383cc, the Primaquatre, and later the spacious six-seater Vivaquatre.

1956 Renault 4CV Saloon, 747cc, 4 cylinder in-line engine, 21bhp at 4,100rpm, 3-speed manual gearbox, 4-wheel drum brakes, left-hand drive, finished in grey, original.
£2,000–2,500 Pou

1962 Renault 4L, 747cc, 4 cylinders, interior retrimmed in black velour used in later models, 11,500 miles from new, unused for several years, paintwork in need of cosmetic attention, otherwise good original condition.
£1,200–1,400 BRIT

RENAULT Model	ENGINE cc/cyl	DATES	CONDITION 1	2	3
4CV	747/4				
	760/4	1947–61	£3,500	£2,000	£850
Fregate	1997/4	1952–60	£3,000	£2,000	£1,000
Dauphine	845/4	1956–66	£1,500	£1,000	£350
Dauphine Gordini	845/4	1961–66	£2,000	£1,000	£450
Floride	845/4	1959–62	£3,000	£2,000	£600
Caravelle	956/4				
	1108/4	1962–68	£4,500	£2,800	£750
R4	747/4				
	845/4	1961–86	£2,000	£1,500	£350
R8/R10	1108/4	1962–71	£1,800	£750	£200
R8 Gordini	1108/4	1965–66	£8,000	£5,000	£2,000
R8 Gordini	1255/4	1966–70	£8,000	£5,500	£2,500
R8S	1108/4	1968–71	£2,000	£1,200	£400

◄ **1966 Renault Gordini 1300,** 1255cc, 4 cylinder in-line engine, 2 twin-choke Weber 40DCOE carburettors, 105bhp at 6,750rpm, 4-speed manual gearbox, all-independent suspension, 4-wheel disc brakes, alloy wheels, left-hand drive, 180km/h top speed, finished in French blue, original, very good condition throughout.
£9,000–10,000 Pou

Renault-Alpine

1974 Renault Alpine A110, 1300cc engine, alloy wheels, left-hand drive, 100+mph top speed, restored, finished in blue, very good condition throughout.
£10,000–11,000 BKS

One of the great names in post-war French motorsport, Alpine was the brainchild of Jean Redélé, who began in the early 1950s by developing a competition version of the Renault 4CV, which won its class in the Mille Miglia three years running. From this, he developed the first Alpine, with Renault 4CV running gear and a streamlined fibreglass coupé body. In 1963, Alpine launched the A110 *Berlinette*, which became the mainspring of production, its rearward weight bias giving it outstanding cornering characteristics for rallying.

◄ **1977 Renault Alpine A110,** 1397cc, 4 cylinders, tubular backbone chassis, Gottie split-rim alloy wheels, left-hand drive, finished in blue with black interior trim, 59,100km from new, very good condition.
£13,000–14,000 BRIT

The A110 was extensively developed over the years, final versions being powered by a choice of 1400 or 1600cc engines.

Riley

It's rather sad that the once forward-thinking Coventry firm of Riley ended its days as little more than an upmarket badge of dubious distinction on mainstream BMC products. Indeed, when the name died in 1969, some Riley fans, who remembered the fine, sporting RM models of the immediate post-war period, probably thought it a blessed relief. Like many of the early automobile firms, Riley took up car making via bicycle manufacture, producing its first car in 1898. In the 1920s and 1930s, the company produced some very appealing and highly regarded small sporting cars, before being taken over by Morris in 1938. The immediate post-war products, the RM-series cars, were hallmark Riley sporting saloons and managed to retain a distinct identity before the rot set in with the plague of badge-engineering. For many, they were the last true Rileys.

◄ **1933 Riley 9hp Monaco Saloon,** double-overhead-camshaft engine, manual 'crash' gearbox, aluminium-panelled bodywork, fabric-covered top, sunroof, finished in Oxford blue over black, original black leather upholstery, interior woodwork refurbished, unused for several years, in need of recommissioning, very good condition throughout. **£7,500–8,500 BKS**

The Monaco 9hp was introduced in 1927. It was a stylish sporting saloon that became the best-seller of the Riley range.

1936 Riley 12/4 Merlin Saloon, 4 cylinder engine, 4-speed pre-selecter gearbox, sunroof, electric wipers, finished in black over red, dark red leather upholstery, two additional engines and large quantity of spares, service history. **£6,500–7,500 S**

Restored Values

The cost of a professional restoration will have an influence on, but no direct relation to, a car's market value. A restored car can have a market value lower than the cost of its restoration.

1946 Riley RM 1½ Litre Saloon, older restoration, finished in Autumn red with ivory side panels, original brown leather interior and woodwork in good condition, 61,280 miles from new, good mechanical condition. **£4,500–5,500 BRIT**

Introduced in late 1945, the RM was based largely on earlier Riley designs, but boasted such advanced features as torsion-bar front suspension and rack-and-pinion steering. Power came from a slightly modified version of the famous double-overhead-camshaft 12/4 engine. This particular 1½ Litre saloon was used by Victor Riley as his personal transport.

◄ **1949 Riley RMC 2½ Litre Roadster,** double-overhead-camshaft, 4 cylinder engine, completely restored 1995, finished in Old English white with red leather upholstery and light tan hood, full weather equipment including sidescreens, concours condition. **£24,000–27,000 BKS**

The 2½ Litre Roadster was designed very much as a dollar earner and was rated at 100bhp. One of the most elegant cars of the immediate post-war era, it had performance to match its beautiful lines, would cruise at 80mph, and had a top speed of 94mph.

RILEY Model	ENGINE cc/cyl	DATES	CONDITION 1	2	3
9hp	1034/2	1906–07	£9,000	£6,000	£3,000
Speed 10	1390/2	1909–10	£10,000	£6,000	£3,000
11	1498/4	1922–27	£7,000	£4,000	£2,000
9	1075/4	1927–32	£10,000	£7,000	£4,000
9 Gamecock	1098/4	1932–33	£14,000	£10,000	£6,000
Lincock 12hp	1458/6	1933–36	£9,000	£7,000	£5,000
Imp 9hp	1089/4	1934–35	£35,000	£28,000	£20,000
Kestrel 12hp	1496/4	1936–38	£8,000	£5,000	£2,000
Sprite 12hp	1496/4	1936–38	£40,000	£35,000	£20,000
Many Riley 9hp Specials are available and are ideal for VSCC and club events.					

RILEY Model	ENGINE cc/cyl	DATES	CONDITION 1	2	3
1½ Litre RMA	1496/4	1945–52	£6,000	£3,500	£1,500
1½ Litre RME	1496/4	1952–55	£6,000	£3,500	£1,500
2½ Litre RMB/F	2443/4	1946–53	£9,000	£7,000	£3,000
2½ Litre Roadster	2443/4	1948–50	£18,000	£11,000	£9,000
2½ Litre Drophead	2443/4	1948–51	£18,000	£14,000	£10,000
Pathfinder	2443/4	1953–57	£3,500	£2,000	£750
2.6	2639/6	1957–59	£3,000	£1,800	£750
1.5	1489/4	1957–65	£3,000	£2,000	£850
4/68	1489/4	1959–61	£1,500	£700	£300
4/72	1622/4	1961–69	£1,600	£800	£300
Elf I/II/III	848/4	1961–66	£1,500	£850	£400
Kestrel I/II	1098/4	1965–67	£1,500	£850	£400

1950 Riley RMD Drophead Coupé, 2.5 litre, double-overhead-camshaft, 4 cylinder engine, 100bhp, 4-speed synchromesh gearbox, torsion-bar independent front suspension, rack-and-pinion steering, Girling hydro-mechanical brakes, restored 1990/91, finished in blue with cream leather interior, good condition throughout.
£10,500–12,000 BKS

1953 Riley RME Saloon, double-overhead-camshaft, 4 cylinder engine, hydraulic brakes, finished in maroon with original matching leather interior, chassis sound, engine, gearbox and bodywork in good condition, minor paint blemishes, 59,000 miles from new.
£2,000–2,500 BKS

1958 Riley 1.5 Saloon, finished in grey with blue and beige trim, 12,440 miles from new, good condition.
£3,250–3,750 BKS

The Riley 1.5 married the Morris Minor floorpan to a conservatively styled body with Riley's traditional grille. Independent front suspension and rack-and-pinion steering made for good ride and handling, while the 1489cc B-series engine endowed the twin-carburettor saloon with respectable 85mph performance.

1955 Riley 1½ Litre RME Saloon, 1496cc, double-overhead-camshaft, 4 cylinder engine, 4-speed manual gearbox, completely restored, finished in blue and white with blue leather interior trim and upholstery.
£8,500–10,000 H&H

Riley RM Models (1946–55)

Engine: Double-overhead-camshaft, four-cylinder, 1496 or 2443cc.
Power output: 55bhp (1496cc); 90-100bhp (2443cc).
Transmission: Four-speed manual.
Brakes: Drums all-round, hydraulic at front, rod-operated at rear; hydraulic all-round from 1952.
Steering: Rack-and-pinion.
Maximum speed: 75mph (1496cc); 90-95mph (2443cc).
0-60mph: 25–31 seconds (1496cc); 15.2–16.5 seconds (2443cc).
These fine sporting saloons and convertibles were classically British at a time when Britishness was shorthand for a whole catalogue of virtues. As one of the very first new post-war British designs, the RM's elegant styling was pleasingly traditional and reassuring, rather than faddishly modern. On the inside, that whiff of Wilton and leather, and the deep lustre of the walnut dash, said more about you than cash alone ever could. On the road, it offered brisk performance and confident poise. In short, this Riley was sporting in the manner of blazers, cravats and slacks, rather than Nikes, Lycra and steroids.
Which is which? The RM-series had a confusing array of suffixes. The RMA and RME were 1.5 litre saloons; the RMB and RMF were longer-chassised 2.5 litre saloons; the RMC was a three-abreast 2.5 litre roadster; the RMD was a four-seater drophead coupé.
What to watch: Engines have deservedly good reputations. A greater worry is the ash frame, which can all but disintegrate to leave a body with only a sentimental attachment to its chassis.

Rolls-Royce

From the beginning in 1904, Henry Royce and Charles Rolls established Rolls-Royce as a producer of very expensive, superb motor cars of the highest quality. Royce was a Manchester electrical engineer who had built three 10hp, twin-cylinder cars in 1903. Rolls had a business selling foreign cars in London. The company's early reputation was founded on the 40/50, now known universally as the Silver Ghost. It was introduced in 1906 and began the long-established Rolls-Royce practice of evolution rather than revolution, being refined and developed until its replacement in 1925 by the New Phantom. Incidentally, although Rolls had died in a flying accident in 1910, the impact of this tragedy on the company was far from disastrous, as by then he had largely lost interest in cars. The same could not be said of Royce. He died in 1933, three years before the magnificent V12-engined Phantom III, which he'd inspired, went into production.

In 1949, Rolls-Royce entered a new era with the Silver Dawn, the first Rolls-Royce offered complete by the factory rather than as a chassis to be fitted with bespoke coachwork of the owner's choosing. The company continued to offer chassis to coachbuilders alongside its factory-bodied cars until 1965, when the Silver Shadow appeared. This new model was the first to have an integral body and chassis.

In 1971, Rolls-Royce became bankrupt after trouble with the RB211 aircraft engine, and the car division was separated and floated as a public company. In 1980, Rolls-Royce was acquired by Vickers, and the more modern Silver Spirit replaced the ageing Silver Shadow. Today, the company that built the Merlin aero engine for Spitfire fighters is owned by BMW.

1924 Rolls-Royce Silver Ghost Salamanca, coachwork by Brewster, chassis no. 112JH, finished in black with beige cloth to rear, stored for some time, running well, excellent condition throughout.
£80,000–90,000 RCC
The full cabriolet coachwork of this Brewster Salamanca has fold-down pillars, offering a variety of configurations from fully closed to completely open.

Rolls-Royce Ghost 20 Club cuff links, c1950.
£225–275 BRIT

▶ **1923 Rolls-Royce 20hp Hamshaw Tourer,** 3127cc, 6 cylinders, restored, finished in maroon over black, very good condition throughout.
£42,500–47,500 COHN

1924 Rolls-Royce Silver Ghost, 7428cc, 6 cylinders, 4-speed gearbox, dickey seat, restored, good condition.
£150,000–165,000 BLE

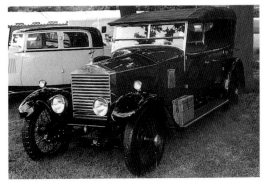

1923 Rolls-Royce 20hp Drophead Coupé with Dickey, coachwork by James Young, chassis no. GA74, engine no. G692, partially restored, bodywork stripped ready for painting, interior and weather equipment in need of restoration.
£16,000–18,000 COYS

The 20hp model was considerably smaller than previous Rolls-Royces, being powered by an all-new, 6 cylinder engine of 3127cc, mated to a 3-speed gearbox. Its sturdy chassis was leaf-sprung at both ends, while brakes were fitted to the rear axle only. Introduced in 1922, and quickly nicknamed the 'Baby Rolls', the 20hp was warmly received and soon became a popular model.

◀ **1926 Rolls-Royce Doctor's Coupé with Dickey,** coachwork by Mullion, chassis no. GYK36, engine no. G1851, 3122cc, 6 cylinder, overhead-valve engine, standard-wheelbase chassis, Barker dipping headlights, restored, finished in blue and black, original matching leather hood and grey headlining, original interior with concealed and secure pill boxes in excellent condition, only known example of this body style.
£29,000–32,000 S

ROLLS-ROYCE Model	ENGINE cc/cyl	DATES	CONDITION 1	2	3
Silver Ghost 40/50	7035/6	pre-WWI	£350,000+	£120,000	£80,000
Silver Ghost 40/50	7428/6	post-WWI	£110,000+	£70,000	£40,000
20hp (3-speed)	3127/6	1922–25	£29,000+	£23,000	£15,000
20hp	3127/6	1925–29	£30,000+	£24,000	£15,000
Phantom I	7668/6	1925–29	£50,000+	£28,000	£22,000
20/25	3669/6	1925–26	£30,000+	£18,000	£13,000
Phantom II	7668/6	1929–35	£40,000+	£30,000	£20,000
Phantom II Continental	7668/6	1930–35	£60,000+	£40,000	£28,000
25/30	4257/6	1936–38	£24,000+	£18,000	£12,000
Phantom III	7340/12	1936–39	£38,000	£28,000	£14,000
Wraith	4257/6	1938–39	£38,000	£32,000	£25,000

Prices will vary considerably depending on heritage, originality, coachbuilder, completeness and body style. A poor reproduction body can often mean that the value will be dependent only upon that of a rolling chassis and engine.

1927 Rolls-Royce 20hp **Four-Door Limousine,** coachwork by Cockshoot, opening V-windscreen, peaked roof, finished in green and black with black leather interior, partial engine rebuild in 1990, new pistons, water pump overhauled, coil rewound, original, in need of minor refurbishment, large history file.
£17,000–20,000 **BKS**

This car is the only six-light version bodied by Cockshoot. It is a rare owner/driver limousine without the customary division between the front and rear compartments. Its first owner was disabled, and to provide wide access, the body features a removable nearside centre-post and tip-up front seat.

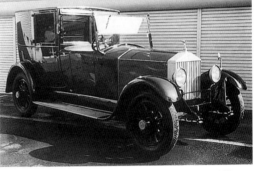

1928 Rolls-Royce 20hp **Two-Door Saloon,** coachwork by Glassbrook, chassis no. GTM6, engine no. N7P, 3127cc, 6 cylinders, older restoration, finished in black with maroon hide interior, large touring trunk, unused for some time, not running, in need of recommissioning, good condition.
£11,500–14,000 **BRIT**

1928 Rolls-Royce 20hp **Open Drive Brougham de Ville,** coachwork by Kellner, chassis no. GFN30, engine no. D6A, 3127cc, 6 cylinder, overhead-valve engine, 4-speed gearbox, servo-assisted 4-wheel mechanical drum brakes, semi-elliptic springs all-round, wooden artillery wheels, original button-pleated rear interior, good condition.
£29,000–32,000 **C**

As the French motor industry flourished, so did Kellner. The company's beautifully balanced four-seater Torpedo tourers on Rolls-Royce Silver Ghost chassis were style leaders in their time, but it was for Brougham de Ville town carriages that Kellner received great acclaim. With gently curving surfaces and razor-edged outlines, they demanded the highest levels of craftsmanship. The body style was intended entirely for town work, usually having neither luggage trunk nor grid.

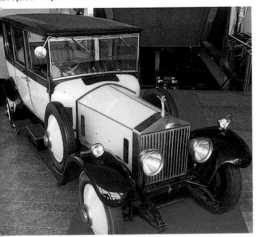

1925 Rolls-Royce 40/50hp **Phantom I Limousine,** coachwork by Barker, chassis no. 61RC, West of England cloth seating, fold-away occasional seats, wooden cappings.
£25,000–28,000 **BKS**

Dealer Prices

Miller's guide prices for dealer cars take into account the value of any guarantees or warranties that may be included in the purchase. Dealers must also observe additional statutory consumer regulations, which do not apply to private sellers. This is factored into our dealer guide prices. To identify dealer cars, cross-refer the source codes at the ends of photo captions with the Key to Illustrations on page 330.

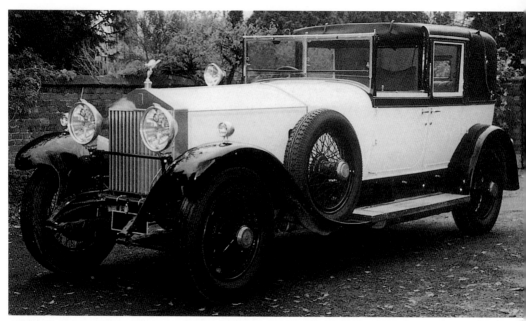

1925 Rolls-Royce 40/50hp Phantom I Sedanca de Ville, coachwork by Barker, largely original, Barker dipping Marchal headlamps, matching spotlamps, finished in pale yellow and black, rear compartment trimmed in original beige Bedford cord, silver-plated occasional seats, quartered walnut veneered woodwork, vanity unit.
£75,000–80,000 BKS

The worthiest of successors to the long-running Silver Ghost, the New Phantom – retrospectively designated Phantom I – was announced in May 1925.

1927 Rolls-Royce Phantom I Tourer, aluminium dual-cowl coachwork, mahogany decking, rear Auster screen, twin side-mounted spares, 'tiger' lamp, polished aluminium wheel discs, brown leather upholstery, restored, good condition.
£60,000–65,000 Mot

1933 Rolls-Royce 20/25 Four-Door Saloon, coachwork by James Young, chassis no. GEX 35, stored for some time, in need of cosmetic attention and respray, original brown leather interior in poor condition, good mechanically.
£11,000–13,000 RCC

A known continuous history can add value to and enhance the enjoyment of a car.

1931 Rolls-Royce Regent Convertible Coupé, coachwork by Brewster, close-coupled body, original, mostly unrestored condition.
£40,000–45,000 RM

By the early 1920s, the Silver Ghost was lagging behind its American counterparts from Cadillac and Lincoln, and European competitors like Hispano-Suiza, Isotta Fraschini and Bentley. This would soon change with the introduction of the Phantom I. It was powered by an overhead-valve six that increased power by 33 per cent to around 100hp. More refined than the Playboy and Piccadilly roadsters, Brewster's Regent body style, on a Springfield-built Phantom I chassis, satisfied those who wanted the elegance of a Rolls-Royce with the sportiness of a convertible coupé.

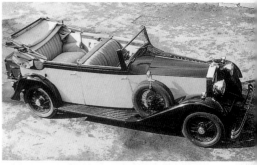

1933 Rolls-Royce 20/25 Four-Door Cabriolet, coachwork by Hooper, chassis no. GSY 68, wind-up windows, collapsible pillars, finished in black and yellow with beige leather interior, original, sound, in need of refurbishment.
£35,000–38,000 RCC

1934 Rolls-Royce 20/25 Limousine, coachwork by
Cooper, 3669cc, 6 cylinder engine, completely restored,
new cream leather upholstery, chassis and structure
sound, all mechanical components in good condition.
£23,000–27,000 **BRIT**

The 20/25 was introduced during 1929 as a replacement
for the successful 20hp model which, although popular
with the owner/driver, proved rather underpowered
when fitted with heavier, more formal coachwork.
The 20/25 benefited from a 3.7 litre engine, giving a
substantial advantage over the earlier car's 3.1 litre unit.

1935 Rolls-Royce 20/25 Sedanca Coupé, coachwork
by Mulliner, chassis no. GHG 26, louvred bonnet and
scuttle, P100 headlamps, finished in black, twin side-
mounted spares, Ace wheel discs, sound condition.
£35,000–38,000 **RCC**

1935 Rolls-Royce 20/25 Limousine, 3669cc, 6 cylinder
engine, finished in black and red, good condition.
£17,000–20,000 **BLE**

◀ **1935 Rolls-Royce 20/25 Sedanca de Ville,**
coachwork by Barker, fitted with Laycock overdrive,
body completely restored and resprayed 1997, roof
rebuilt and covered in black Everflex, front compartment
reupholstered in black Connolly hide, rear compartment
retrimmed in beige West of England cloth, original.
£25,000–28,000 **BKS**

A development of the earlier 20hp model, the 20/25hp
was launched in 1929. It was produced until 1936,
3,827 examples being sold.

1930 Rolls-Royce Phantom II with Dickey, 7668cc,
6 cylinder engine, restored, finished in black with gold
coachlines, good condition.
£47,000–52,000 **BLE**

1930 Rolls-Royce Phantom II Boat-Tail Tourer,
7668cc, 6 cylinders, four-door coachwork, restored,
very good condition.
£40,000–43,000 **BC**

Cross Reference
See Colour Review

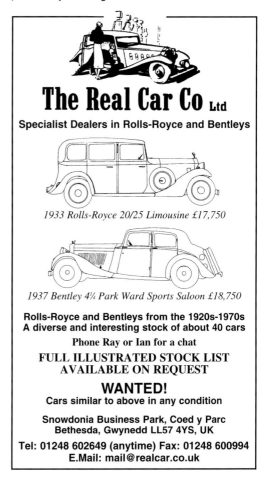

c1930 Rolls-Royce Phantom II Continental Sports Saloon, 7668cc, 6 cylinder engine, excellent condition.
£67,000–70,000 BLE

1933 Rolls-Royce Phantom II Continental Sports Saloon, coachwork by Barker, restored, finished in black, polished aluminium wheel discs, good condition throughout
£67,000–70,000 COHN

1934 Rolls-Royce Phantom II Limousine, six-light coachwork by Windovers, sliding division and occasional seats to the rear, finished in burgundy and black.
£20,000–23,000 BKS

Rolls-Royce reinforced its position in the quality car market with the Phantom II in 1929. Technically, it was a radical step forward, the main innovations being an engine and gearbox in unit, and underslung rear springs. Handling and braking were improved markedly, making the Phantom II arguably the company's finest pre-war car.

▶ **c1936 Rolls-Royce 25/30hp Doctor's Coupé,** divided windscreen, rear mounted luggage trunk, twin spare wheels, Corniche steering wheel, Volkswagen door handles, little recent use, in need of recommissioning, good mechanical condition.
£8,000–10,000 BKS

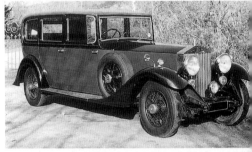

1934 Rolls-Royce Phantom II Limousine, coachwork by Hooper, chassis no. 148 PY, P100 headlamps, rear-mounted trunk, finished in black and burgundy with black leather interior, occasional seats, £5,000 engine refurbishment, good condition throughout.
£27,000–29,000 RCC

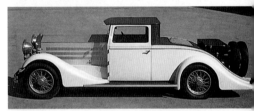

c1936 Rolls-Royce 25/30 Limousine, division, cocktail cabinets, occasional seats, restored.
£29,000–34,000 VIC

◀ **1938 Rolls-Royce 25/30hp Six-Passenger Tourer,** coachwork by Knibbs of Manchester twin side-mounted spares, twin electric horns centre spotlamp, finished in Claret with beige leather interior, steering box, front suspension and brakes overhauled, rewired, 59,000 miles from new, very good condition.
£28,000–32,000 BKS

Introduced in 1936, the new 'small' Rolls-Royce, the 25/30hp model, featured a 4257cc engine that borrowed many design features from the successful 20/25hp.

Rolls-Royce Phantom III brochure, shows four-carburettor engine that never entered production, 1935, 13½ x 9½in (34.5 x 24cm).
£180–200 PC

1935 Rolls-Royce Phantom III Top Hat Limousine, coachwork by Hooper, 7340cc V12, finished in two-tone blue, division, blue fabric to rear compartment, matching blue leather to driver's compartment, original period fittings, cockpit instruments function well, excellent condition throughout.
£25,000–28,000 H&H

▶ **1938 Rolls-Royce Phantom III Limousine,** coachwork by Hooper, chassis no. 3DL2, engine no. E78Y, 7338cc V12, 4-speed manual gearbox, finished in black with black leather driver's compartment, fawn Bedford cloth to rear, good condition.
£24,000–27,000 C

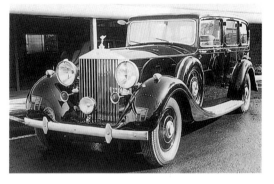

1936 Rolls-Royce Phantom III Limousine, coachwork lby Mulliner, chassis no. 3AZ28, engine no. A84A, finished in black with white leather upholstery, rear occasional tables, Philip's radio in front compartment, last used 1977,13,158 miles from new, good condition throughout.
£27,000–30,000 S

Introduced in 1936, the Phantom III featured an advanced 7.3 litre V12 engine, a light but rigid chassis and independent front suspension. For the discerning motorist, it provided impressive acceleration, exceptional roadholding and silent running. Over 700 were made.

1938 Rolls-Royce Phantom III Sedanca de Ville, coachwork by Vanvooren, 7338cc, steel body, wind-down division, occasional seats, older restoration, finished in tan and cream, driver's compartment trimmed in brown leather, rear compartment trimmed in brown fabric with floral Art Nouveau pattern, excellent condition.
£22,000–25,000 H&H

Rolls-Royce Phantom III

The Phantom III represented Rolls-Royce's determined effort to reinforce its claim to manufacture 'the best car in the world', a position challenged in the later days of the Silver Ghost and while the Phantom II was in production by very capable V12s – even a V16 – from Europe and the USA. With the PIII, Rolls-Royce went to great lengths to create an engine of unsurpassable refinement and power. In addition, the car had a one-shot chassis lubrication system that delivered oil to almost every moving part.

The PIII was never intended as an outright sporting car, and relatively few were built with open or owner/driver bodies. Rather, it was meant to provide the most modern handling and ride qualities, while carrying dignified, formal coachwork. Even so burdened – weight could be around 2.5 tons – the car's performance was praiseworthy. Testing a PIII limousine, *The Autocar* saw almost 92mph and quoted a 0–60mph time of 16.8 seconds. Coachwork varied in style, from modern-looking, razor-edged designs to more conservative shapes. With independent front suspension permitting the engine to be further forward than in previous Phantoms, leg room and space for occasional seats in the rear compartment was greater than ever.

1940 Rolls-Royce Phantom III Limousine, coachwork by Hooper, chassis no. 3DH3, rare overdrive model, finished in grey with black leather to front and beige cloth to rear, original and correct, good condition. **£25,000–28,000 RCC**

This car is one of the last Phantom IIIs to be built.

1938 Rolls-Royce Wraith Limousine, coachwork by Park Ward, 4257cc, 6 cylinders, finished in black and cream, sliding division, black leather seating to front compartment, beige cloth to rear, occasional seats, original period fittings, all brightwork and coachwork in good condition. **£15,000–17,000 H&H**

1939 Rolls-Royce Wraith Sports Saloon, coachwork by Freestone & Webb, chassis no. WHC55, engine no. S3WC, sunroof, finished in black with beige interior trim, division, unused since 1990, good original condition. **£14,500–17,000 S**

1948 Rolls-Royce Silver Wraith, finished in black and metallic grey, good condition. **£28,000–30,000 COHN**

1947 Rolls-Royce Silver Wraith Sports Saloon, coachwork by Park Ward, sunroof, picnic tables and footrests to rear, restored, bare-metal respray in black over gold, new beige hide upholstery, new veneers. **£10,000–13,000 BKS**

Rolls-Royce got back into car production post-war with the introduction of the Silver Wraith in late 1946; it was destined to be one of the longest-running models, production continuing until 1959. Similarities with the pre-war Wraith were few, the new car having a significantly shorter 10ft 7in wheelbase and an all-new F-head engine.

◄ **1954 Rolls-Royce Silver Wraith LWB Touring Limousine,** coachwork by Freestone & Webb, sunroof to rear compartment, electrically-operated division, cocktail bar, occasional seats, finished in cream over black with beige leather upholstery, 56,000 miles from new, unrestored. **£27,000–30,000 BKS**

Founded in 1923, Freestone & Webb concentrated on Rolls-Royce and Bentley chassis, their designs winning Gold Medals in the coachwork contest at nine consecutive London Motor Shows. The company was taken over by H.R. Owen in 1955 and ceased production a year later.

1947 Rolls-Royce Silver Wraith Cabriolet, coachwork by Inskip (last body produced by that company), restored, concours winner, excellent condition throughout.
£275,000+ **BLK**

1955 Rolls-Royce Silver Wraith LWB Touring Limousine, coachwork by James Young, finished in black and burgundy, blue-grey leather to front compartment, grey corded cloth to rear, picnic tables, footrests, good condition.
£23,000–25,000 **RCC**

1958 Rolls-Royce Silver Wraith Limousine, coachwork by Mulliner, 4257cc, 6 cylinder engine, 4-speed manual gearbox, power steering, independent front suspension by wishbones and coil springs, semi-elliptic leaf-spring rear suspension, ride control, servo-assisted hydraulic front brakes, mechanical rear, flagstaff mountings on wings, fitting for a shield and blue flashing light on roof, good condition throughout.
£27,000–30,000 **C**

This Silver Wraith limousine was used during Royal visits to Australia, when HM The Queen Mother rode in it. It has all the accoutrements expected of these cars, including forward-facing occasional seats.

1954 Rolls-Royce Silver Dawn, finished in two-tone grey, good condition throughout.
£20,000–22,000 **BLE**

Restored Values

The cost of a professional restoration will have an influence on, but no direct relation to, a car's market value. A restored car can have a market value lower than the cost of its restoration.

1955 Rolls-Royce Silver Dawn, 4566cc, 6 cylinders, restored, concours condition.
£33,000–35,000 COHN

1957 Rolls-Royce Silver Cloud I, 4887cc, 6 cylinders, power steering, separate front seats, finished in Sand and Sable with beige leather interior, good condition throughout.
£18,000–20,000 BLE

Rolls-Royce Silver Cloud (1955–65)

Engine: Six-cylinder, 4887cc (1955–59); V8, 6230cc.
Power output: Approximately 178bhp (4887cc); 200–220bhp (6230cc).
Transmission: Four-speed automatic; optional manual gearbox.
Brakes: Servo-assisted drums.
Maximum speed: 100–116mph
0-60mph: 10.8–14+ seconds.
Production: Approximately 7,000 (Rolls-Royce); approximately 6,500 (Bentley).

In 1955, the new Rolls-Royce Silver Cloud, and its Bentley sibling, straddled a divide between an old-world aristocracy, clinging to crumbling stately homes, and a new-world order of emerging entrepreneurs, like Berlin airlift tycoon Freddy Laker. It was the last Rolls-Royce, other than bespoke limousines, to ride on a separate chassis, on which the dwindling number of coachbuilders could still tailor bespoke bodywork. Yet it also came 'ready to wear', off the peg with so-called Standard Steel factory coachwork. Notwithstanding the car's dreadnought proportions, Rolls-Royce acknowledged that there was a new breed of owner who actually preferred to drive as well, yet initially it seemed a grudging concession, as power steering wasn't even an option for the first two years of production. In 1959, with the Silver Cloud II and S2 Bentley, Rolls gave its leviathan a V8 engine. Another sign of the times was the disappearance of the complex, pedal-operated, one-shot chassis and suspension lubrication system – a trusty chauffeur could be relied upon to keep everything oiled, but the owner/driver would probably forget. In 1962, the Silver Cloud III and S3 Bentley offered a little more power from the V8, being identified externally by quad headlamps and a lower bonnet line.

Price new: In 1965, £5,500 bought a seven-bedroomed house, 11 Austin Minis, eight Triumph Heralds – or one Rolls-Royce Silver Cloud III.

Market comment: Dark colours are always easier to sell – beware the porcelain-white, wedding hire hack, pregnant with filler and a glove box full of confetti. Bentley versions can be slightly cheaper.

ROLLS-ROYCE Model	ENGINE cc/cyl	DATES	CONDITION 1	2	3
Silver Wraith LWB	4566/6				
	4887/6	1951–59	£25,000	£17,000	£10,000
Silver Wraith SWB	4257/6				
	4566/6	1947–59	£20,000	£13,000	£10,000
Silver Wraith Drophead	4257/6				
	4566/6	1947–59	£50,000	£35,000	£25,000
Silver Dawn Std Steel	4257/6				
	4566/6	1949–52	£25,000	£15,000	£10,000
Silver Dawn Std Steel	4257/6				
	4566/6	1952–55	£30,000	£20,000	£15,000
Silver Dawn Coachbuilt	4257/6				
	4566/6	1949–55	£35,000+	£25,000	£18,000
Silver Dawn Drophead	4257/6				
	4566/6	1949–55	£60,000	£50,000	£30,000
Silver Cloud I	4887/6	1955–59	£18,000	£10,000	£8,000
SCI Coupé Coachbuilt	4887/6	1955–59	£30,000	£20,000	£15,000
SCI Conv (HJM)	4887/6	1955–59	£80,000+	£60,000+	£40,000
Silver Cloud II	6230/8	1959–62	£19,000	£10,000	£8,000
SCII Conv (HJM)	6230/8	1959–62	£80,000	£75,000	£40,000
SCII Conv (MPW)	6230/8	1959–62	£60,000	£40,000	£32,000
Silver Cloud III	6230/8	1962–65	£25,000	£12,000	£10,000
SCIII Conv (MPW)	6230/8	1962–65	£70,000	£45,000	£35,000
Silver Shadow	6230/8				
	6750/8	1965–76	£14,000	£9,000	£7,000
S Shadow I Coupé (MPW)	6230/8				
	6750/8	1965–70	£15,000	£10,000	£8,000
SSI Drophead (MPW)	6230/8				
	6750/8	1965–70	£33,000	£25,000	£18,000
Corniche FHC	6750/8	1971–77	£15,000	£11,000	£8,000
Corniche Convertible	6750/8	1971–77	£28,000	£22,000	£18,000
Camargue	6750/8	1975–85	£35,000	£25,000	£18,000

1964 Rolls-Royce Silver Cloud III Saloon, coachwork by James Young, 6230cc V8, restored, finished in Midnight blue with grey leather and navy blue carpets, smoked Sundym windows, large history file.
£20,000–23,000 COYS

The Rolls-Royce Silver Cloud and Bentley S-Type, of 1955, employed a separate chassis that could be fitted with standard or coachbuilt bodywork. Incorporating coil-spring/wishbone front suspension with semi-elliptic rear springs and a single radius arm to locate the rear axle, it also featured centralised lubrication and 4-wheel drum brakes. Power came from the 4887cc straight-6 of the Bentley R-Type Continental, producing an estimated 158bhp, which gave a top speed of 100mph. The Silver Cloud II and S2 models of 1959 used Rolls' new light-alloy V8 engine, but otherwise differed only in detail from their predecessors. For the four-headlamp Silver Cloud III/Bentley S3 models, launched in 1962, the specification remained unchanged, bar an increase of power to around 220bhp, which lifted top speed to 115mph.

A known continuous history can add value to and enhance the enjoyment of a car.

► **1961 Rolls-Royce Silver Cloud II,** 6230cc V8 engine, automatic transmission, one owner from new, well maintained, good condition throughout, history file. **£18,000–20,000 BLE**

Rolls-Royce's 6.2 litre light-alloy V8 engine, which made its debut in the Silver Cloud II and Bentley S2 models introduced in 1959, produced around 200bhp.

1964 Rolls-Royce Silver Cloud III Convertible, coachwork by Mulliner Park Ward, 6230cc V8 engine, automatic transmission, canted headlamps, finished in white with black top, well maintained, excellent condition throughout. **£38,000–42,000 BLE**

1964 Rolls-Royce Silver Cloud III, 6230cc V8, long-wheelbase version without division, finished in black over silver, good grey hide interior and upholstery, all chrome trim in good condition, automatic transmission rebuilt, well maintained, excellent condition throughout, history file. **£14,000–16,000 H&H**

1965 Rolls-Royce Silver Cloud III Flying Spur, coachwork by Mulliner Park Ward, 6230cc V8, 4-speed automatic transmission, independent coil-sprung front suspension, semi-elliptic leaf-sprung rear, hydraulic front brakes, hydro-mechanical rear, paintwork in need of attention, minor crazing to interior veneers, 83,500 miles from new.
£40,000–45,000 C

In a few instances, noteworthy coachbuilt bodies were constructed on the Silver Cloud III, which offered coachbuilders a last chance to work with a separate Rolls-Royce chassis. This example carries the very rare Flying Spur four-door, six-light saloon coachwork.

◄ **1966 Rolls-Royce Silver Cloud III Flying Spur,** coachwork by Mulliner Park Ward, 6230cc V8 engine, automatic transmission, 62,000 miles from new, one of only 21 built, excellent condition throughout.
£70,000–75,000 PALM

Did You Know?
The S1, S2 and S3 were Bentley's equivalents of the Rolls-Royce Silver Cloud I, II and III. Although virtually identical, apart from the distinctive radiator, Bentley versions can often be cheaper. This is not a factor of rarity, as with the launch of the Silver Cloud II in 1959, Rolls-Royce versions outnumbered Bentley offerings for the first time.

1962 Rolls-Royce Phantom V Two-Door Coupé, coachwork by James Young, 6.2 litre V8, automatic transmission, left-hand drive, finished in fawn with red interior, air conditioning, 45,000 miles from new, excellent condition throughout.
£200,000+ BLK

Only two four-seater, two-door coupés were built in this style by James Young.

1965 Rolls-Royce Phantom V Limousine, 6230cc V8, automatic transmission, good condition throughout.
£60,000–65,000 COHN

1974 Rolls-Royce Phantom VI, 6230cc V8, finished in dark blue, very good condition throughout.
£48,000–52,000 BLE

► **1968 Rolls-Royce Silver Shadow Two-Door Coupé,**
coachwork by Mulliner Park Ward, 6230cc, rechromed,
resprayed in metallic blue, grey leather interior trim and
upholstery, well maintained, history file.
£9,500–11,000 H&H

Restored Values

The cost of a professional restoration will have an
influence on, but no direct relation to, a car's
market value. A restored car can have a market
value lower than the cost of its restoration.

◄ **1970 Rolls-Royce
Silver Shadow,** 6750cc
V8, finished in Oxford blue
over silver-grey, dark blue
leather interior trim and
door cappings in good
condition, in need of
recommissioning.
£4,500–6,000 BRIT

1972 Rolls-Royce Silver Shadow Four-Door Saloon, 6750cc V8, finished in brown with black vinyl roof and cream leather upholstery, interior in need of some refurbishment, one-owner car, fewer than 94,000 miles recorded, good condition throughout.
£7,000–9,000 **BKS**

Introduced in 1965, the Rolls-Royce Silver Shadow (and Bentley T1) represented a complete break with tradition, being the first of the Crewe factory's models to employ unitary construction. All-round independent suspension was another feature.

1972 Rolls-Royce Silver Shadow LWB Saloon, 6750cc V8, restored in 1994, brakes overhauled, bare-metal respray in Brewster green, new door and windscreen seals, beige Connolly hide interior, air conditioning, 70,000km from new, well maintained, very good condition throughout.
£13,000–15,000 **BKS**

1975 Rolls-Royce Silver Shadow, brakes, suspension, exhaust and air conditioning overhauled, finished in Pewter with green leather interior, service history, 73,000 miles from new, excellent condition.
£10,000–12,000 **Mot**

◀ **1975 Rolls-Royce Silver Shadow,** 6750cc V8 engine, automatic transmission, suspension and brakes overhauled, coachwork in good condition, finished in Silver Sand, 31,000 miles from new, engine, gearbox and steering in excellent condition, beige hide interior in good condition. **£11,000–13,000 BRIT**

▶ **1977 Rolls-Royce Silver Shadow II,** 6750cc V8 engine, automatic transmission, full service history, very good condition throughout. **£8,500–10,000 BRIT**

The Silver Shadow II was built between 1977 and 1980. Its discreet facelift included revised bumper styling and a front air dam, while the interior received a modified fascia.

A known continuous history can add value to and enhance the enjoyment of a car.

◀ **1978 Rolls-Royce Silver Shadow II,** 6750cc V8 engine, finished in silver over maroon with red hide interior, service history, good original condition throughout. **£5,500–7,000 BRIT**

▶ **1980 Rolls-Royce Silver Shadow II,** 6750cc V8, Bentley-type alloy wheels, finished in Claret with beige Everflex roof, beige leather interior piped in Claret, 53,000 miles from new, Rolls-Royce service history, mechanically sound, excellent condition throughout. **£16,000–18,000 BRIT**

◄ **1980 Rolls-Royce
Silver Shadow II,**
6750cc V8 engine, finished
in Walnut with tan hide
upholstery, new carpets
with lambswool overrugs,
service history, good
condition throughout.
£8,500–10,000 BRIT

**The final models of the
Silver Cloud II benefited
from being fitted with an
electric headlamp
wash/wipe system.**

► **1980 Rolls-Royce Silver
Shadow II Four-Door Saloon,**
6750cc V8, automatic transmission,
power-assisted rack-and-pinion
steering, finished in Willow gold
with magnolia hide interior, split-
level air conditioning, rear picnic
tables, 48,000 miles from new,
full service history, excellent
condition throughout.
£12,000–14,000 BKS

1980 Rolls-Royce Silver Shadow II, 6750cc V8, good condition throughout.
£12,000–14,000 BLE

◄ **1977 Rolls-Royce Silver Wraith
LWB Saloon,** 6750cc V8, power
steering, left-hand drive, finished in
Chestnut with Sand Everflex roof
and matching Connolly hide interior,
62,000km from new, very good
condition throughout.
£15,000–18,000 BKS

**To satisfy the market for
chauffeur-driven cars, a long-
wheelbase version of the Silver
Shadow – with optional division –
was introduced in 1969, being
christened Silver Wraith II on the
introduction of the 'II' range. This
car once belonged to the thriller
writer Alastair Maclean.**

1979 Rolls-Royce Silver Wraith II, 6750cc V8, finished in Golden Sand with brown Everflex roof and matching interior, service history, 68,000 miles from new, good condition throughout.
£12,000–14,000 BLE

1986 Rolls-Royce Silver Spirit, 6750cc V8, well maintained, good condition throughout.
£14,000–16,000 BLE

◄ **1983 Rolls-Royce Silver Spirit,** 6750cc, new steering rack, front suspension compliance bushes and exhaust, finished in Ocean blue with matching blue leather interior, bodywork and interior in very good condition.
£10,500–13,000 H&H

◄ **1976 Rolls-Royce Camargue,** 6750cc V8, extensive body renovation in 1994, finished in cream, service history, 66,700 miles from new.
£16,000–18,000 BRIT

With its two-door, Pininfarina-styled coach-work, the Camargue was a new direction for Rolls-Royce when it arrived in the spring of 1975. This imposing coupé was also one of the most expensive cars in the world at that time, costing in excess of £29,000 – almost £10,000 more than the Corniche Convertible. Mechanically, it was similar to the Silver Shadow, although the engine produced slightly more power. Production of the Camargue ran until 1985, 531 examples being built.

1980 Rolls-Royce Camargue, left-hand drive, resprayed 1994 in pale yellow, tan interior, good condition throughout.
£14,000–16,000 BKS

Rover

Although Rover had produced cars in Coventry from 1904, it wasn't until the late 1920s that the recognisable brand qualities of solid, middle-class motoring became established. Rover's earlier riposte to the cheap and cheerful Austin 7 had failed, and with mounting losses, Spencer Wilks, formerly of Hillman, was appointed general manager in 1929. He soon established the Rover quality-first credo that positioned the company firmly in the upper middle market, above the likes of Ford, Austin and Morris. By the outbreak of WWII, Rover was building 11,000 cars a year and making a

profit of over £200,000. After the war, Spencer's brother, Maurice, who also worked at Rover, was a prime-mover behind the Land Rover. Meanwhile, the successive P4, P5 and P6 Rovers earned a loyal following as production climbed steadily. Spencer Wilks retired in 1962; in 1965, Rover took over Alvis, and in 1967 was merged into BMC. Although not top dog among the myriad marques under the BMC banner, it was the Rover name that survived and emerged when the combine was renamed the Rover Group in 1986. These days, of course, the Rover Group is owned by BMW.

1929 Rover 10/25hp Riviera Saloon, Weyman fabric-covered coachwork, rear trunk, older restoration, folding roof and bodywork in good condition, fitted with electric cooling fan, well maintained, good condition.
£5,750–6,500 CGC

1934 Rover 14 Sports Saloon, 1577cc, 6 cylinder, Speed-Fourteen triple-carburettor engine, pre-selector gearbox, dashboard-controlled chassis lubrication system, Ace wheel discs, braking system in need of attention, aluminium coachwork showing signs of age and some cracking, finished in deep purple, blue leather interior in good condition, stored since 1973, in need of recommissioning.
£4,000–5,000 BRIT

Cross Reference
See Colour Review

1936 Rover 14hp Four-Door Saloon, restored, finished in black and burgundy with brown leather interior, new headlining, paintwork and interior in need of attention, othewise good condition throughout.
£2,750–3,500 BKS

Rover's 14/6 model was launched in 1934 on an underslung chassis that retained its predecessor's 1577cc, overhead-valve, 6 cylinder engine. The frame enabled the adoption of low-line bodies, among them attractive streamlined versions of both saloon and coupé. The specification included a 4-speed freewheel gearbox, hydraulic brakes, Luvax-Bijur automatic lubrication and electric windscreen wipers.

ROVER Model	ENGINE cc/cyl	DATES	CONDITION 1	CONDITION 2	CONDITION 3
10hp	998/2	1920–25	£5,000	£3,000	£1,500
9/20	1074/4	1925–27	£6,000	£4,000	£2,000
10/25	1185/4	1928–33	£7,000	£4,000	£2,500
14hp	1577/6	1933–39	£6,000	£4,250	£2,000
12	1496/4	1934–37	£7,000	£4,000	£1,500
20 Sports	2512/6	1937–39	£7,000	£4,500	£2,500

◄ **1951 Rover 75,** 2103cc, 6 cylinder engine, complete body restoration, resprayed, mechanically sound, underside and chassis in good condition, original leather interior faded. **£2,750–3,500 BRIT**

With its transatlantic-inspired styling, the P4 model of 1949 met with criticism from a number of traditional Rover customers, yet it went on to achieve great success, spawning a line of motor cars that remained in production until 1964. Early models were recognisable by their central 'Cyclops' foglamp, which was dropped in 1952. Other improvements included full hydraulic braking for 1951 and a floor-mounted gearchange a couple of years later.

1954 Rover 60, 1997cc, 4 cylinders, 60bhp, finished in black, stored since 1970, engine partially dismantled, but complete, bodywork and interior in good condition, 32,000 miles from new. **£500–800 LF**

Rover P4 (1950–64)

Engine: Four-cylinder, 1997 or 2286cc; six-cylinder, 2103–2638cc.
Power output: 60–77bhp (four-cylinder); 75–123bhp (six-cylinder).
Maximum speed: 78–100+mph.
0–60mph: 15–23 seconds.
Production: 130,342.
Rover traditionalists choked in their cravats when the normally conventional car maker introduced the P4 in 1950. Gone were the traditional separate wings and running boards; instead, the car had a daring and up-to-the-minute, American-inspired, slab-sided, full-width body. If the exterior caused the odd sharp intake of breath, on the inside everything was reassuringly Rover: a leather, wood and Wilton

combination of comfort and sober good taste. There were other Rover virtues, too: a massive separate chassis, high build quality and long-lasting four- and six-cylinder engines. The whole package added up to steady, reliable transport for steady professional types. By the mid-1950s, everyone had become used to the once-controversial contours, and since then, the cars have earned the affectionate appellation of 'Auntie' Rovers because of the amiable qualities that made many a P4 a much loved member of the family.
P4 fact: The design was closely based on the American Studebaker Commander, and it was rumoured that a Studebaker body had been dropped on to a Rover chassis to create a prototype. Later destroyed, it was referred to as the 'Roverbaker'.

1963 Rover 95, 2625cc, 6 cylinder engine, finished in white, good condition throughout.
£1,200–1,400 **GAZE**

1956 Rover 60, 1997cc, 4 cylinders, finished in grey with original red leather upholstery, good condition throughout.
£1,750–2,250 **BRIT**

1962 Rover 100, 2625cc, 6 cylinder, inlet-over-exhaust engine, 100bhp, manual gearbox, body completely restored, bare-metal respray in maroon, blue leather upholstery, excellent mechanical condition, interior fair.
£2,750–3,500 **LF**

1963 Rover 110, 2625cc, 6 cylinder engine, excellent original condition.
£3,500–4,000 **WILM**

1965 Rover P5 Coupé, 3 litre, 6 cylinder engine, restored 1993, new wings all-round, new carpets, refurbished wood cappings, service history.
£1,750–2,500 **BARO**

◄ **1966 Rover P5 Mk III Saloon,** 3 litres, automatic transmission, finished in grey with red leather interior, stored for five years, well maintained.
£1,200–1,500 **BKS**

Introduced in 1965, the Mk III P5 was outwardly different from its predecessors by having a new radiator badge and continuous chrome side-strip. The interior boasted reclining front seats, while power steering came as standard. The 2995cc, straight-6 engine produced 108bhp at 4,500rpm.

1967 Rover 3.5 Litre Saloon, 3528cc V8, finished in Admiralty blue with buckskin leather interior, one of first P5B series to be built, good mechanical condition, structurally and bodily sound, 63,600 miles from new, original.
£2,250–2,750 BRIT

Cross Reference
See Colour Review

1969 Rover 3.5 Litre Saloon, 3528cc V8, finished in Zircon blue, service history, very good original condition.
£2,000–2,500 BRIT

The replacement for the Rover 3 Litre appeared during 1967, powered by the Buick-derived, all-alloy, 3.5 litre V8. This new engine not only gave a considerable increase in power, but also proved very durable, covering a vast mileage before major work became necessary.

1971 Rover 3.5 Litre Coupé, 3528cc V8, 3-speed automatic transmission, finished in blue and grey with grey leather interior trim and upholstery, 69,233 miles from new, museum stored for some time, good condition.
£2,500–3,000 H&H

1972 Rover 3.5 Litre Coupé, 3528cc V8, 160bhp, automatic transmission, power-assisted steering, 110mph top speed, finished in burgundy with off-white leather interior, stored 1988–97, original condition.
£3,250–3,750 BKS

▶ **1973 Rover 3.5 Litre Coupé,** 3528cc V8, automatic transmission, restored, very good condition throughout.
£7,000–8,000 BC

Auction Prices

Miller's only includes cars declared sold. Our guide prices take into account the buyer's premium, VAT on the premium, and the extent of any published catalogue information relating to condition and provenance. To identify cars sold at auction, cross-refer the source codes at the ends of photo captions with the Key to Illustrations on page 330.

ROVER Model	ENGINE cc/cyl	DATES	CONDITION 1	2	3
P2 10	1389/4	1946–47	£3,200	£2,500	£1,000
P2 12	1496/4	1946–47	£3,500	£2,800	£1,200
P2 12 Tour	1496/4	1947	£7,500	£3,500	£1,500
P2 14/16	1901/6	1946–47	£4,200	£3,000	£1,000
P2 14/16 Sal	1901/6	1946–47	£3,700	£2,500	£700
P3 60	1595/4	1948–49	£5,000	£2,500	£1,000
P3 75	2103/6	1948–49	£4,000	£3,000	£800
P4 75	2103/6	1950–51	£4,000	£2,000	£1,200
P4 75	2103/6	1952–64	£3,500	£1,800	£1,200
P4 60	1997/4	1954–59	£3,200	£1,200	£1,200
P4 90	2638/6	1954–59	£4,000	£1,800	£1,200
P4 75	2230/6	1955–59	£3,800	£1,200	£1,000
P4 105R	2638/6	1957–58	£4,000	£2,000	£1,000
P4 105S	2638/6	1957–59	£4,000	£2,000	£1,000
P4 80	2286/4	1960–62	£3,000	£1,200	£800
P4 95	2625/6	1963–64	£3,000	£1,600	£500
P4 100	2625/6	1960–62	£3,800	£2,000	£1,000
P4 110	2625/6	1963–64	£3,800	£2,000	£1,000
P5 3 Litre	2995/6	1959–67	£4,000	£2,500	£1,000
P5 3 Litre Coupé	2995/6	1959–67	£5,500	£3,800	£1,000
P5B (V8)	3528/8	1967–74	£6,250	£4,500	£1,500
P5B (V8) Coupé	3528/8	1967–73	£6,250	£4,500	£1,500
P6 2000 SC Series 1	1980/4	1963–65	£2,200	£800	-
P6 2000 SC Series 1	1980/4	1966–70	£2,000	£800	-
P6 2000 SC Auto Series 1	1980/4	1966–70	£1,500	£600	-
P6 2000 TC Series 1	1980/4	1966–70	£2,000	£900	-
P6 2000 SC Series 2	1980/4	1970–73	£2,000	£900	-
P6 2000 SC Auto Series 2	1980/4	1970–73	£1,500	£800	-
P6 2000 TC Series 2	1980/4	1970–73	£2,000	£900	-
P6 3500 Series 1	3500/8	1968–70	£2,500	£1,400	-
P6 2200 SC	2200/4	1974–77	£1,750	£850	-
P6 2200 SC Auto	2200/4	1974–77	£2,500	£1,000	-
P6 2200 TC	2200/4	1974–77	£2,000	£1,000	-
P6 3500 Series 2	3500/8	1971–77	£3,000	£1,700	-
P6 3500 S Series 2	3500/8	1971–77	£2,000	£1,500	-

◄ **1972 Rover 2000 Saloon,** 1978cc, 4 cylinder engine, 4-speed manual gearbox, finished in Sand with beige interior trim and upholstery, 45,000 miles from new, very good condition.
£1,000–1,300 H&H

1974 Rover 3500S, V8, 4-speed manual gearbox, power steering, electric cooling fan, Sundym glass, finished in Monza red, full hide interior, 4,000 miles recorded since 1994, excellent condition throughout.
£900–1,100 BARO

1975 Rover 3500 V8 Estate, body refurbished, resprayed in white, stored for some time, good condition throughout.
£1,700–2,000 CGC

Restored Values

The cost of a professional restoration will have an influence on, but no direct relation to, a car's market value. A restored car can have a market value lower than the cost of its restoration.

▶ **1976 Rover 3500S,** 3528cc V8, one of the last to be built, finished in Almond with brown Everflex roof, sunroof, underside rustproofed from new, full service history, 43,912 miles recorded, coachwork in good condition.
£5,250–6,000 BRIT

Rugby

◀ **1929 Rugby Tourer,** 2474cc, 4 cylinder engine, artillery wheels, restored, finished in Oxford blue over black, blue leather interior, black duck hood, excellent condition.
£6,500–8,000 BRIT

Between 1922 and 1929, Durant Motors manufactured the Star in New Jersey. Initially, the car competed successfully with the Ford Model T, being notable for its rugged strength. The 30hp car was favoured by those seeking rather more style than Ford had to offer. By the mid-1920s, it was being built for export under the name 'Rugby' and, as such, became highly regarded, especially in South Africa, New Zealand and Australia.

Salmson

◀ **1929 Salmson S4–61 Coupé,** 1730cc, servo-assisted brakes, independent front suspension, restored, resprayed, retrimmed, running order.
£3,500–5,000 BKS

In France, Salmson vied with Amilcar for a major slice of the light sports car market, and in the 1920s had a reputation for developing high output from efficient 4 and 6 cylinder engines. The 1930s saw a parallel operation carried on in the UK by British Salmson Aero Engines Ltd. By then, both French and British versions had become more sophisticated, the twin-cam S4 being the mainstay of production.

Singer

For 50 years, from 1905 to 1955, the Coventry firm of Singer managed to remain independent. During the 1920s, it offered appealing and truly competitive alternatives to Austin and Morris products. There was the occasional outstanding model, too, such as the Singer Nine of 1933.

However, by 1937, and thanks in part to a bewildering model range, the company had to be reorganised to remain afloat. In 1955, it was acquired by the Rootes Group and was slowly sapped of identity and distinction, until it expired in 1970.

SINGER Model	ENGINE cc/cyl	DATES	CONDITION 1	2	3
10	1097/4	1918–24	£5,000	£2,000	£1,000
15	1991/6	1922–25	£6,000	£3,000	£1,500
14/34	1776/6	1926–27	£7,000	£4,000	£2,000
Junior	848/4	1927–32	£6,000	£3,000	£1,500
Senior	1571/4	1928–29	£7,000	£4,000	£2,000
Super 6	1776/6	1928–31	£7,000	£4,000	£2,000
9 Le Mans	972/4	1932–37	£13,000+	£8,000	£5,000
Twelve	1476/6	1932–34	£10,000	£7,000	£6,000
1.5 Litre	1493/6	1934–36	£3,000	£2,000	£1,000
2 Litre	1991/6	1934–37	£4,000	£2,750	£1,000
11	1459/4	1935–36	£3,000	£2,000	£1,000
12	1525/4	1937–39	£3,000	£2,000	£1,000

1934 Singer 9 Le Mans Sport, 972cc, overhead-camshaft, 4 cylinder engine, 38bhp, centre-lock wire wheels, 75mph top speed, finished in white with black leather upholstery and black carpets, excellent condition throughout.
£6,000–7,000 LF

The overhead-camshaft Singers were renowned for their advanced engine design and enjoyed many competition successes during the 1930s. Long before its take-over by the Rootes Group in the 1950s, Singer was an independent company that enjoyed a large customer base. Its slogan in 1934, for the Olympia Motor Show, was 'Singer for Certainty, Safety and Comfort'.

1967 Singer Chamois Deluxe Saloon, 875cc, rear-mounted, 4 cylinder Coventry-Climax engine, 4-speed manual gearbox, finished in dark green with black interior trim, 50,000 miles from new, bodywork and interior in good condition.
£600–800 H&H

This car once belonged to the newspaper proprietor Eddie Shah.

Singer Gazelle (1956–67)

Engine: Four-cylinder; 1494, 1497, 1592 or 1725cc.
Power output: 49–65bhp.
Transmission: Four-speed manual with optional overdrive; optional automatic.
Maximum speed: 78–85mph.
0–60mph: 15–26.6 seconds.

In 1955, the Rootes Group acquired the Singer company to add yet another layer to the fine social distinctions of the suburban driveway. At the top of the Rootes hierarchy was Humber, but lower down, the new unit-construction Hillman, Singer and Sunbeam shared a common bodyshell with nuances of styling, comfort and performance to separate them in the pecking order of middle-class motoring. The plain-Jane, mass-market Hillman Minx was definitely lower-middle, while the two-door Sunbeam Rapier was 'sporty-middle'. The Singer Gazelle was middle-middle, a cut above the Minx with fillets of wood, carpet and leather to flatter vanity and aspiration. The result was an overlapping, three-tier platform to pitch against the likes of Austin, Morris, Ford and Vauxhall. Initially, as a sop to Singer fans, the Gazelle retained the old Singer 1497cc, overhead-camshaft engine, while the Hillman and Sunbeam had 1390cc units, but from 1958, the trio shared a common range of engines in different states of tune that eventually grew to 1725cc. Today, any real distinction between these badges of suburban rank may seem slight, but to drivers in the 1950s and 1960s, they still had real value. While the Minx sold around 700,000, the plush Gazelle filled a much smaller niche further up the social scale, scoring just over 83,000 sales. In today's classic-car pecking order, the little touch of class that marked the Gazelle when new still makes it more pricey than a Minx.

Standard

Formed in 1903, Standard was specialising in medium-range cars by the 1920s, but struggling to compete. In 1929, John Black joined the company and engineered its resurgence, building a reputation for keenly-priced, well-built, reliable and comfortable cars. In 1945, Standard acquired the defunct Triumph marque as an upmarket badge. Standard-Triumph was merged into Leyland in 1961 and, ironically, the Standard name was the first to be dropped, in 1963.

Of the late-era Standards, the Phase I beetle-backed Vanguard is a favourite accessory among swing-era nostalgics, while the Standard 8 and 10 make interesting, less common alternatives to the Morris Minor and Austin A30/35.

1949 Standard Vanguard, 2088cc, 4 cylinders, bare-metal respray, new chromework, original radio in working order, excellent condition.
£2,500–3,000 PC

1953 Standard Vanguard Series II, 2088cc, 4 cylinder engine, 3-speed manual gearbox with overdrive, column change, engine, gearbox and bodywork refurbished.
£4,500–5,000 STAN

STANDARD Model	ENGINE cc/cyl	DATES	CONDITION 1	2	3
12	1609/4	1945–48	£2,000	£950	£250
12 DHC	1509/4	1945–48	£3,200	£2,000	£500
14	1776/4	1945–48	£3,000	£950	£250
Vanguard I/II	2088/4	1948–55	£2,200	£1,000	£250
Vanguard III	2088/4	1955–61	£1,800	£900	£200
Vanguard III Est	2088/4	1955–61	£2,000	£1,000	£250
Vanguard III Sportsman	2088/4	1955–58	£2,500	£1,200	£400
Vanguard Six	1998/6	1961–63	£2,000	£1,000	£500
Eight	803/4	1952–59	£1,250	£500	-
Ten	948/4	1955–59	£1,400	£800	-
Ensign I/II	1670/4	1957–63	£1,000	£800	-
Ensign I/II Est	1670/4	1962–63	£1,000	£850	-
Pennant Companion	948/4	1955–61	£1,800	£850	£300
Pennant	948/4	1955–59	£1,650	£825	£250

Stirling

◀ **1901 Stirling 5hp Four-Seater Rally Cart,** Ackerman steering, varnished wooden wheels, candle lamp, finished in red and black with black leather upholstery, original condition.
£18,000–21,000 BKS

Bicycle manufacturer Adolphe Clément moved into the infant motor industry in 1899 by acquiring from Panhard-Levassor the licence to build a light voiturette with a rear-mounted, single-cylinder engine. Marketed in France as the Clément Panhard, it proved relatively reliable and commercially successful. In 1900, Scottish coachbuilders J & C Stirling acquired the rights to the 5hp Clément Panhard, which was marketed variously as the Stirling, Panhard-Stirling and Clément Stirling.

Sunbeam

Sunbeam's light was finally snuffed out for good in 1976, but in the long, and often rocky, ride from its birth at the dawn of the century, there were several periods of achievement and distinction. Before WWI, the company notched up considerable competition success, and later went on to become the first British make to win a Grand Prix. In the 1920s, Sunbeam also produced some fine touring and sports cars, rivalling Alvis and Bentley offerings into the 1930s. As part of the unwieldy Sunbeam-Talbot-Darracq combine, the company collapsed in 1935 and was acquired by Rootes.

Sunbeams were known as Sunbeam-Talbots from 1935 to 1953, then simply as Sunbeams. Initially, the cars continued in a sporting vein: the 1959 Alpine was a pretty sports car, and the Ford V8-engined Tiger an enjoyable handful. However, in 1964, Chrysler took over, and the last Sunbeams were little more than plain-Jane Hillmans and Humbers in slightly sporting garb.

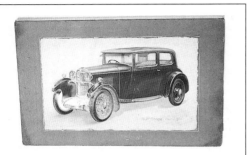

Sunbeam 16hp four-light coupé advertising picture, c1930, 6x10in (15x25cm).
£13–17 DHA

1954 Sunbeam Alpine II, non-standard front bumper, excellent condition, concours winner.
£11,000–11,500 PC

1953 Sunbeam Alpine Sports, 2267cc, gearbox converted from column change to floor change, finished in Coronation red with black hood, metal-framed sidescreens, in need of cosmetic attention and recommissioning.
£5,500–7,000 BKS

Sunbeam-Talbot

The two British car makers Sunbeam and Talbot first had links in 1920, when they became involved in the Sunbeam-Talbot-Darracq Group. Later, in 1938, the two names were combined on a car under the aegis of the Rootes Brothers. In 1948, traditional styling gave way to the handsome 80 and 90 sports saloons and tourers. Initially, the 90 had a 2 litre engine, but in Mk II form, this was replaced by a 2.3 litre overhead-valve derivative of the Humber Hawk engine. The new engine layout, which gave greater performance, resulted in the now famous Monte Carlo Rally win of 1955. The Mk II also had the benefit of independent front suspension.

The last model to bear the Sunbeam-Talbot name was the slightly restyled Mk IIA of 1952, 'Talbot' being deleted in 1953. All subsequent models were simply named 'Sunbeam', including the 2.25 litre models announced as the Mk III in 1954.

1954 Sunbeam Talbot Cut-away Display Car, 2267cc, overhead-valve, 4 cylinder engine, 4-speed manual gearbox, independent front suspension, semi-elliptic leaf springs to rear, 4-wheel drum brakes, finished in green with brown interior, good condition throughout.
£9,000–11,000 C

This vehicle was originally built as a motor show exhibit in the early 1950s. The engine, transmission, etc have been cut-away to display internal features and are connected to an electric motor to demonstrate their operation. For many years, it was owned by the Staffordshire Police Motor Training Centre, where it was used for practical workshop training.

▶ **1956 Sunbeam 90 Mk III Four-Door Saloon,** 2267cc, overhead-valve, 4 cylinder engine, 70bhp, independent front suspension, 4-wheel drum brakes, ventilated disc wheels, finished in two-tone green with matching interior, one owner from new, fewer than 46,000 miles recorded, well maintained, good condition throughout.
£3,750–4,500 BKS

SUNBEAM-TALBOT/ SUNBEAM Model	ENGINE cc/cyl	DATES	CONDITION 1	2	3
Talbot 80	1185/4	1948–50	£3,500	£2,250	£1,000
Talbot 80 DHC	1185/4	1948–50	£6,000	£4,500	£2,000
Talbot 90 Mk I	1944/4	1949–50	£4,000	£2,100	£750
Talbot 90 Mk I DHC	1944/4	1949–50	£7,000	£4,750	£2,000
Talbot 90 II/IIa/III	2267/4	1950–56	£5,000	£3,000	£1,500
Talbot 90 II/IIa/III DHC	2267/4	1950–56	£7,000	£5,000	£2,250
Talbot Alpine I/III	2267/4	1953–55	£11,000	£7,500	£3,750
Talbot Ten	1197/4	1946–48	£3,500	£2,000	£750
Talbot Ten Tourer	1197/4	1946–48	£7,000	£4,000	£2,000
Talbot Ten DHC	1197/4	1946–48	£6,500	£4,000	£2,000
Talbot 2 Litre	1997/4	1946–48	£4,000	£2,500	£1,000
Talbot 2 Litre Tourer	1997/4	1946–48	£7,500	£4,000	£2,250
Rapier I	1392/4	1955–57	£1,200	£700	£300
Rapier II	1494/4	1957–59	£1,800	£900	£300
Rapier II Conv	1494/4	1957–59	£3,000	£1,500	£450
Rapier III	1494/4	1959–61	£2,000	£1,200	£400
Rapier III Conv	1494/4	1959–61	£3,500	£1,600	£600
Rapier IIIA	1592/4	1961–63	£2,000	£1,200	£400
Rapier IIIA Conv	1592/4	1961–63	£3,600	£1,700	£650
Rapier IV/V	1592/4 1725/4	1963–67	£2,000	£700	£250
Alpine I-II	1494/4	1959–62	£6,000	£3,500	£1,800
Alpine III	1592/4	1963	£6,500	£4,000	£1,250
Alpine IV	1592/4	1964	£6,500	£4,000	£1,250
Alpine V	1725/4	1965–68	£7,000	£4,000	£1,250
Harrington Alpine	1592/4	1961	£8,000	£4,750	£1,250
Harrington Le Mans	1592/4	1962–63	£10,000	£6,500	£3,000
Tiger Mk 1	4261/8	1964–67	£15,000	£10,000	£6,000
Tiger Mk 2	4700/8	1967	£13,000	£8,000	£6,000
Rapier Fastback	1725/4	1967–76	£1,100	£700	£250
Rapier H120	1725/4	1968–76	£1,500	£800	£300

1964 Sunbeam Venezia Coupé, coachwork by Touring, 88bhp, overdrive, front disc brakes, chrome wire wheels, finished in Midnight blue with original red leather upholstery, good condition throughout.
£3,500–5,000 **BKS**

In the 1950s and early 1960s, the Rootes Group flirted with more than one Italian styling studio, but probably the most successful partnership was with Touring of Milan. An outcome of this was the Sunbeam Venezia, which was built in small numbers on the Rapier floorpan during 1963–4. Unfortunately, it came at the wrong time and did not survive Chrysler's take-over of Rootes in 1964.

> **Miller's is a price GUIDE not a price LIST**

1963 Sunbeam Alpine Series III, factory hardtop, resprayed in blue, black interior, good condition throughout.
£2,500–3,000 **BKS**

Aimed at the US market, the Sunbeam Alpine was produced between 1959 and 1968. Built on the Hillman Husky II floorpan, it employed Sunbeam Rapier running gear and a 1.5 litre, overhead-valve, 4 cylinder engine that was common to many other Rootes products. In Alpine form, the engine boasted an aluminium cylinder head and twin carburettors. It produced 78bhp, sufficient to propel the sleekly-styled two-seater to within a whisker of 100mph. The Alpine was progressively improved through Series II–V, gaining a 1.6 litre engine in 1960, and losing its distinctive tailfins with the advent of the Series IV in 1964.

◀ **1966 Sunbeam Alpine Series V,** 1725cc, 4 cylinder engine, aluminium cylinder head, 4-speed manual gearbox, factory hardtop, full tonneau cover, completely restored, finished in black, excellent condition throughout.
£6,000–7,000 **BRIT**

Talbot

1925 Talbot 10/23 Two-Seater with Dickey, finished in Royal blue over black, red leather interior, original, running well, good condition.
£11,000–13,000 **SVV**

1930 Talbot 14/45 Four-Door Cabriolet, coachwork by Tickford, 6 cylinder engine, around £6,000 spent on refurbishment, resprayed in blue, matching leather interior, in need of small amount of work to complete restoration.
£7,500–9,000 **BKS**

TALBOT Model	ENGINE cc/cyl	DATES	CONDITION 1	2	3
25hp and 25/50	4155/4	1907–16	£35,000	£25,000	£15,000
12hp	2409/4	1909–15	£22,000	£15,000	£9,000
8/18	960/4	1922–25	£8,000	£5,000	£2,000
14/45	1666/6	1926–35	£16,000	£10,000	£5,000
75	2276/6	1930–37	£22,000	£12,000	£7,000
105	2969/6	1935–37	£30,000	£20,000+	£15,000
Tourers and coachbuilt cars command a higher value.					

Toyota

1967 Toyota Corona RT 40 Saloon, 1490cc,
4 cylinder engine, finished in red, good condition.
£750–1,500 TEC

1968 Toyota 2000 GT Coupé, 4,800 miles from new,
unrestored, excellent condition.
£40,000–45,000 RM

Announced at the Tokyo Motor Show in 1965, the 2000 GT
seemed almost too good to be true: a 2 litre, twin-cam six
and all-independent suspension wrapped in a strikingly
handsome, closed two-seater body. The design was
both beautiful and functional. This combination, together
with low production numbers, has created one of the
rarest and most desirable of all Japanese cars.

1970 Toyota 2000 GT, 1988cc, 6 cylinders, alloy wheels, finished in red, good condition throughout.
£35,000–40,000 TEC

1972 Toyota Crown Saloon MS65, 2563cc, 6 cylinders,
finished in metallic blue, good condition.
£750–1,500 TEC

▶ 1976 Toyota Celica TA22 ST, 1600cc, 4 cylinder
engine, very good condition throughout.
£2,500–3,000 TEC

TOYOTA Model	ENGINE cc/cyl	DATES	CONDITION 1	2	3
Celica TA22 & TA23 Coupé	1588/4	1971–78	£3,400	£1,800	£500
RA28 Liftback	1968/4	1971–78	£3,500	£1,500	£400
Crown MS65, MS63, MS75, Saloon, Estate, Coupé	2563/6	1972–75	£2,500	£1,000	£500

Plus a premium of £200 to £400 for the Coupé and £200 to £500 for the Twin-Cam GT.

1977 Toyota Celica RA28 GT Lift Back, 2000cc, 4 cylinders, finished in red, good condition throughout.
£1,900–2,300 TEC

1977 Toyota Celica ST RA28 Lift Back, 2000cc,
4 cylinders, finished in dark green, very good condition.
£1,900–2,300 TEC

1982 Toyota Crown MS112 Saloon, 2794cc, 6 cylinder
engine, good condition throughout.
£2,000–3,000 TEC

Triumph

From the immediate post-war era to the end of the line in 1980, no other single British marque amassed such a comprehensive portfolio of mainstream sports cars and saloons. On the sporting side, the variety and range of the Triumph TR series far outstripped MG's offerings, while the marque even nudged into the lower end of the luxury Grand Tourer market with the Triumph Stag. Where saloons were concerned, the 1960s were particularly rich, with the cheap, capable and pretty Herald, the sporting Vitesse, the later Dolomite and Toledo, and the larger saloons that offered appealing alternatives to Rovers. Today, all Triumphs of the post-war era remain affordable, and most rate highly as durable and stylish starter classics.

1947 Triumph 1800 Roadster with Dickey, 1776cc, body-off restoration during 1980s, unused since, engine rebuilt, timber sill members and other sections of framework replaced as necessary, bare-metal respray in black, new red interior trim and vinyl hood, very good condition.
£13,000–15,000 BRIT

Introduced in 1946, the distinctive Roadster was one of Triumph's new designs following the company's take-over by the Standard Motor Company. Initially, the car was powered by a 1776cc engine, in effect an overhead-valve version of the pre-war Standard 14 unit. The coachwork was of aluminium on an ash framework with steel front wings, and the design drew heavily on the pre-war Dolomite Roadster. During a four-year production run, some 4,500 examples were built. Mid-way through 1948, the 2088cc engine from the Standard Vanguard was fitted, the model becoming known as the 2000.

1949 Triumph 2000 Roadster, 2088cc, 4 cylinders, engine rebuilt 1997, new kingpins and bushes, rear springs retempered, aluminium coachwork in good general condition, but in need of some refurbishment, good mechanical condition.
£7,000–9,000 BRIT

1949 Triumph 2000 Roadster, 2088cc, all-synchromesh gearbox, hypoid rear axle, finished in black, black leather interior trim and upholstery in good condition, hood sound and serviceable.
£11,000–13,000 BRIT

1949 Triumph 2000 Roadster, 2088cc, 4 cylinders, restored, very good condition throughout.
£12,000–14,000 BC

1952 Triumph Mayflower, 1247cc, 4 cylinder engine, extensively refurbished, engine and steering rebuilt, new clutch, new shock absorbers and bushes, braking system overhauled, new front wings and sills, bare-metal respray in grey, interior retrimmed in blue, very good condition.
£2,400–2,800 BRIT

In the immediate post-war years, Triumph achieved considerable success with its Renown and Roadster, and in 1949 made a bid for the quality small-car market with the 10hp Mayflower. With its razor-edged styling, the Mayflower echoed the lines of the larger Renown and was one of the most distinctive small cars of the period.

> **Miller's is a price GUIDE not a price LIST**

1955 Triumph TR2, 1991cc, 4 cylinder engine, overdrive, original right-hand drive model, restored, reconditioned engine, overdrive unit and ancillary components, new exhaust system, steering, suspension braking and cooling systems overhauled, new body panels, bare-metal respray, new Everflex hood, interior retrimmed to original specification in brown vynide, instruments fully functional.
£5,750–6,500 BRIT

Introduced in 1953, the TR2 achieved almost instant success, the North American market eagerly devouring a large proportion of its production. The TR2 utilised a rugged chassis and was powered by a twin-carburettor, 90bhp version of the sturdy Standard Vanguard engine. Fitted with optional overdrive, the car could attain over 105mph, while 35mpg could be obtained.

1956 Triumph TR3, fitted with later 2.1 litre engine, finished in red with black interior, engine and chassis in good condition, bodywork and interior very good.
£5,500–7,000 BKS

Launched in 1955, the TR3 was an improved version of the acclaimed TR2, from which it differed visually by the addition of an 'egg-crate' grille. Mechanical improvements included larger-bore SU carburettors and better porting to increase the power output of the rugged 1991cc, 4 cylinder engine. In late 1956, the TR3 became the first series-production British car to be fitted as standard with disc front brakes.

1959 Triumph TR3A, 1990cc, left-hand drive, restored, engine overhauled, gearbox and overdrive reconditioned, new starter, radiator and alloy petrol tank, rewired, finished in red with red interior trim, fitted with retrotrip, competition seats and roll-over bar.
£8,000–9,000 H&H

Triang TR4/4A pedal car in moulded plastic over a steel frame, authentic one-piece grille, working headlamps, bumpers, windscreen frame, wire wheels, non-original steering wheel, fair condition.
£150–200 CARS

1957 Triumph TR3, 1991cc, 4 cylinder engine, original right-hand-drive model, finished in pale blue with black leather trim, Heritage Trust certificate, good condition throughout.
£7,500–9,000 BRIT

1959 Triumph TR3A, 2 litre engine, 100bhp, Girling front disc brakes, Phase III Vanguard rear axle, left-hand drive, body-off restoration 1998, all mechanical components overhauled or replaced as necessary, body rebuilt using all original panels, new floorpans, bare-metal respray in red, black interior, new glass, chrome trim, electrics and carpets, excellent condition throughout.
£11,500–13,000 BKS

Cosmetically revised, but mechanically indistinguishable from the TR3, the TR3A was phased in during 1957. It featured a full-width grille incorporating combined sidelights and indicators, and for the first time, there were locking door and boot handles. The interior was also improved.

1965 Triumph TR4A, 2138cc, 4 cylinders, overdrive, Surrey top, finished in British Racing green, good mechanical condition, history file.
£6,500–7,500 BRIT

TRIUMPH Model	ENGINE cc/cyl	DATES	CONDITION 1	2	3
TLC	1393/4	1923–25	£6,000	£4,000	£1,500
TPC	2169/4	1926–30	£6,000	£4,000	£2,000
K	832/4	1928–34	£4,000	£2,000	£1,000
S	1203/6	1931–33	£5,000	£3,000	£1,500
G12 Gloria	1232/4	1935–37	£6,000	£4,000	£2,000
G16 Gloria 6	1991/6	1935–39	£7,000	£4,500	£2,000
Vitesse/Dolomite	1767/4	1937–39	£14,000	£10,000	£6,000
Dolomite	1496/4	1938–39	£7,000	£4,000	£2,000

Triumph TR4/4A (1961–67)

Engine: Overhead-valve, four-cylinder, 2138cc.
Power output: 100-104bhp.
Brakes: Front discs, rear drums.
Maximum speed: 110mph.
0–60mph: 11.4 seconds.
Production: 68,718.
Price new: £1,095.

'TR' stands for Triumph Roadster, but those two letters also stand for TRadition in a big way. Forget the Michelotti styling; the TR4 evolved directly from the earlier, true-Brit TR2 and TR3 roadsters. Sure, the new Italian suit may have sported such technical innovations as real wind-up windows, but this last of the four-cylinder TRs still has that 'vintage' sports car feel – especially in earlier TR4 form – and a contented burble that transfixes anyone with a pair of string-back gloves and a gap-toothed Terry Thomas smile.

Pick of the bunch: There are two choices: the TR4, which ran until 1965, and the TR4A that was so proud of its independent rear suspension that it bore the letters 'IRS' on its rump. The TR4A is softer and more refined in road manners and appointments. The earlier live-axle TR4 is more true-Brit. Overdrive is desirable and, in effect, gives you a 7-speed gearbox.

What to watch: The Michelotti-styled body is a real rotter, from an era when little was known of automotive rustproofing. Ironically, the revised chassis layout of the later TR4A is more prone to rust, having a number of complex closing panels to trap water.

TR4 facts: The Porsche 911 popularised the Targa top, but the TR4 was years ahead; Triumph's version was called a Surrey top. A 2+2 coupé version of the TR4 was offered by Wimbledon Triumph dealer L.F. Dove, approximately 55 examples being built.

1967 Triumph TR4A, 2138cc, 4 cylinder engine, independent rear suspension, Surrey hardtop and serviceable vinyl hood, restored 1991/92, fewer than 500 miles covered since, finished in red, dry stored, all major mechanical components in good condition,.
£6,000–7,000 BRIT

1969 Triumph TR6, 2498cc, 6 cylinders, 150bhp, stainless steel exhaust system, finished in red, engine, fuel system and steering overhauled, new brake master cylinder, reconditioned wheels.
£5,500–6,500 BRIT

1969 Triumph TR6, 2498cc, completely restored, very good condition.
£11,000–12,500 BC

▶ **1971 Triumph TR6,** 2498cc, finished in red, very good condition.
£5,500–6,500 H&H

Triumph's first 6 cylinder TR, the TR5 was restyled for 1969 by Karmann, having a full-width front end and Kamm tail.

1972 Triumph TR6, 2498cc, 6 cylinders, 150bhp, 4-speed manual gearbox with overdrive, genuine right-hand drive model, finished in green with black interior, 93,000 miles from new, good condition throughout, history file.
£4,500–5,000 H&H

1973 Triumph TR6, 2498cc, 6 cylinders, 150bhp engine, finished in red, good condition throughout.
£8,000–9,000 BLE

1975 Triumph TR6, 2498cc, converted to right-hand drive, reconditioned engine, new clutch, front suspension overhauled, finished in Mimosa yellow, serviceable black double-duck hood, structure in excellent condition.
£5,000–6,000 BRIT

▶ **1973 Triumph TR6,** 2498cc, 6 cylinders, 150bhp, restored, excellent condition throughout.
£9,000–10,000 WILM

All At Sea

A Triumph that really handled like a barge was the German Amphicar, built from 1961 to 1967. It was powered by Triumph's 1147cc Herald engine. Apparently, the ride was a little choppy, too.

1973 Triumph TR6, 2498cc, 6 cylinders, 150bhp, finished in maroon with beige hood, good condition throughout.
£8,500–9,000 BLE

TRIUMPH Model	ENGINE cc/cyl	DATES	CONDITION 1	2	3
1800/2000 Roadster	1776/				
	2088/4	1946–49	£14,000	£8,000	£5,000
1800	1776/4	1946–49	£4,000	£2,000	£1,000
2000 Renown	2088/4	1949–54	£4,000	£2,000	£1,000
Mayflower	1247/4	1949–53	£2,000	£1,000	£500
TR2 long-door	1247/4	1953	£10,000	£8,000	£5,000
TR2	1247/4	1953–55	£9,000	£6,000	£5,000
TR3	1991/4	1955–57	£9,000	£8,500	£3,500
TR3A	1991/4	1958–62	£11,000	£8,500	£3,500
TR4	2138/4	1961–65	£9,000	£6,000	£3,000
TR4A	2138/4	1965–67	£9,000	£6,500	£3,000
TR5	2498/6	1967–68	£9,000	£7,500	£4,000
TR6 (PI)	2498/6	1969–74	£8,000	£7,500	£3,500
Herald	948/4	1959–61	£1,000	£400	£150
Herald FHC	948/4	1959–61	£1,500	£550	£300
Herald DHC	948/4	1960–61	£2,500	£1,000	£350
Herald 'S'	948/4	1961–64	£800	£400	£150
Herald 1200	1147/4	1961–70	£1,100	£500	£200
Herald 1200 FHC	1147/4	1961–64	£1,400	£800	£300
Herald 1200 DHC	1147/4	1961–67	£2,500	£1,000	£350
Herald 1200 Est	1147/4	1961–67	£1,300	£700	£300
Herald 12/50	1147/4	1963–67	£1,800	£1,000	£250
Herald 13/60	1296/4	1967–71	£1,300	£600	£200
Herald 13/60 DHC	1296/4	1967–71	£3,500	£1,500	£500
Herald 13/60 Est	1296/4	1967–71	£1,500	£650	£300
Vitesse 1600	1596/6	1962–66	£2,000	£1,250	£550
Vitesse 1600 Conv	1596/6	1962–66	£3,500	£1,800	£600
Vitesse 2 Litre Mk I	1998/6	1966–68	£1,800	£800	£300
Vitesse 2 Litre Mk I Conv	1998/6	1966–68	£4,500	£2,200	£1,000
Vitesse 2 Litre Mk II	1998/6	1968–71	£2,000	£1,500	£300
Vitesse 2 Litre Mk II Conv	1998/6	1968–71	£5,000	£2,500	£600
Spitfire Mk I	1147/4	1962–64	£2,000	£1,750	£300
Spitfire Mk II	1147/4	1965–67	£2,500	£2,000	£350
Spitfire Mk III	1296/4	1967–70	£3,500	£2,500	£450
Spitfire Mk IV	1296/4	1970–74	£5,000	£2,500	£350
Spitfire 1500	1493/4	1975–78	£3,500	£2,500	£750
Spitfire 1500	1493/4	1979–81	£5,000	£3,500	£1,200
GT6 Mk I	1998/6	1966–68	£5,000	£4,000	£1,200
GT6 Mk II	1998/6	1968–70	£6,000	£4,500	£1,400
GT6 Mk III	1998/6	1970–73	£7,000	£5,000	£1,500
2000 Mk I	1998/6	1963–69	£2,000	£1,200	£400
2000 Mk III	1998/6	1969–77	£2,000	£1,200	£500
2.5 PI	2498/6	1968–75	£2,000	£1,500	£900
2500 TC/S	2498/6	1974–77	£1,750	£700	£150
2500S	2498/6	1975–77	£2,500	£1,000	£150
1300 (FWD)	1296/4	1965–70	£800	£400	£150
1300TC (FWD)	1296/4	1967–70	£900	£450	£150
1500 (FWD)	1493/4	1970–73	£700	£450	£125
1500TC (RWD)	1296/4	1973–76	£850	£500	£100
Toledo	1296/4	1970–76	£850	£450	£100
Dolomite 1500	1493/4	1976–80	£1,350	£750	£125
Dolomite 1850	1854/4	1972–80	£1,450	£850	£150
Dolomite Sprint	1998/4	1976–81	£5,000	£4,000	£1,000
Stag	2997/8	1970–77	£9,000	£5,000	£2,000
TR7	1998/4	1975–82	£4,000	£1,200	£500
TR7 DHC	1998/4	1980–82	£5,000	£3,500	£1,500

1975 Triumph TR6, 2498cc, restored, engine rebuilt, stainless steel exhaust system, tinted windscreen, finished in British Racing green, 73,000 miles from new, original specification, good condition.
£7,000–8,000 BRIT

1981 Triumph TR7 Convertible, 1998cc, refurbished 1994, finished in red, with good black vinyl hood, good condition throughout.
£1,500–2,000 BRIT

1963 Triumph Italia, coachwork by Vignale, completely restored, unused since, mechanical components overhauled, finished in silver, new red leather upholstery, excellent condition throughout.
£6,500–8,000 BKS

By the end of the 1950s, the TR3/3A was overdue for replacement, and Michelotti put in a bid to style its successor. His Italia 2000 had a handsome GT body built by Vignale on a TR3A chassis. It was recognisably related to the later TR4 and was made in small numbers between 1960 and early 1963.

1965 Triumph Special, 850cc, twin-cylinder Motor Guzzi engine, 5-speed gearbox, Triumph Herald chassis and running gear, aluminium two-seater Morgan-style coachwork, very low mileage, very good condition.
£3,250–3,750 BKS

This unusual special was constructed by a retired motor engineer in 1990, using a combination of new and secondhand parts.

Auction Prices

Miller's only includes cars declared sold. Our guide prices take into account the buyer's premium, VAT on the premium, and the extent of any published catalogue information relating to condition and provenance. To identify cars sold at auction, cross-refer the source codes at the ends of photo captions with the Key to Illustrations on page 330.

Triumph Herald (1967–73)

Body styles: Saloon, coupé, convertible, estate and van.
Construction: Separate backbone chassis with bolt-on steel body panels.
Engine: Four-cylinder, 948-1296cc.
Power output: 38-61bhp.
Maximum speed: 70-85mph.
0-60mph: 18-28 seconds.
Production: 486,000.

1964 Triumph Herald 1200 Convertible, finished in white with red interior, dry stored since 1987, good condition.
£1,500–2,000 BKS

The Triumph Herald was one of the most successful small cars of the 1960s. Powered by a 1147cc, overhead-valve engine that developed 48bhp, it was capable of returning 40mpg. It also had an extraordinarily tight, 25ft turning circle. Its chassis-type construction with bolt-on body panels simplifies restoration work.

Starter Triumphs: *Herald and Vitesse saloons and convertibles; Spitfire; Dolomite, Toledo and variants.*

- The Herald's a top-down winner when it comes to budget, wind-in-the-hair motoring – an Italian-styled four-seater convertible with a 25ft turning circle that's tighter than a London taxi, and an engine that's so accessible, it's like having your own inspection pit. They are very modestly priced, too.
- Of course, it's not all good news. The Herald's performance is hardly shattering, particularly with the early, rather asthmatic, 948cc Standard 10 engine. It's also prone to rust, and the handling was legendary – for being so darned awful, in the earlier models at least. In the wet and in sudden throttle-off conditions, the car's high-pivot, swing-axle rear suspension would pitch it suddenly into unpredictable oversteer.
- But who'd be daft enough to try to race a Herald on public roads? What's more relevant is the smiles per mile as you and your family potter along over hill and dale, burning fossil fuel at a miserly 35–40mpg.
- Heralds do fray quite ferociously, and you'll want to inspect the separate chassis, which provides structural strength. The front-hinged bonnet is both a strength and weakness. It gives unrivalled access to the front running gear and engine, but once the rot sets in, it can flap around like a soggy cardboard box.
- Because of its separate chassis, the Herald saloon is one car that can be safely turned into a convertible. The roof literally unbolts, and a number of rag-top conversion kits are available.

Pick of the bunch: The Herald's no winged-messenger, so avoid early cars with the puny 948cc engine, and go for at least the 1147cc or, preferably, one of the last 1296cc cars.

- The Herald's chassis formed the basis of a number of sporting Triumphs, including the twin-headlamp Vitesse. Similar in looks to the Herald, but with a 1600 or 2000cc engine, the Vitesse will heave you along with plenty more urge – almost to 100mph in 2 litre form. The Herald chassis also formed the basis of the pretty little two-seater Spitfire, again with wonderful engine access provided by a front-hinged, one-piece bonnet. The Spitfire ran from 1961 to 1980, which means there are plenty to choose from.

1967 Triumph Vitesse Saloon, 1998cc, 6 cylinder engine, 4-speed manual gearbox, finished in two-tone blue with blue interior trim and upholstery, 49,000 miles from new, excellent condition throughout, history file. **£2,000–2,500 H&H**

Triumph Trivia

A Triumph Herald was the first car owned by Scottish saloon car ace John Cleland, who reminisced fondly, 'It handled abominably, but it taught me a lot about driving because it was such a handful.'

1972 Triumph Spitfire Mk IV, restored late 1980s, finished in Pimento with black interior, concours winner. **£5,000–5,500 BKS**

Launched in 1962, the Spitfire was so successful that its basic design remained virtually unchanged until 1970. A restyled Spitfire, the Mk IV, with revised bonnet and rear-end was announced for 1971. It retained the 1296cc, overhead-valve four, introduced on the Mk III, but had a new 'swing-spring' rear suspension to tame the previous handling quirks, and an all-synchromesh gearbox. When production ceased in 1980, over 300,000 Spitfires had been built.

Triumph GT6 (1966–73)

Engine: Overhead-valve, six-cylinder, twin SU carburettors, 1998cc.
Power output: 95-104bhp.
Transmission: Four-speed manual; optional overdrive.
Maximum speed: 107-112mph.
0–60mph: 10-11 seconds.
Price new: £985.
Production: 40,926.

The Triumph GT6 has forever been plagued by unfair comparison, both by devotees and detractors of this dinky GT. To be fair, some of the fault must lie with Triumph for claiming GT credentials for its Spitfire-based coupé, when the term 'Grand Tourer' still had some meaning as short-hand for luxury, close-coupled, continent-gobbling tin-tops in the mould of Jaguar, Aston, Jensen and Ferrari.

The Triumph's trouble, even now, is the same as when it was new: the MGB GT was a direct tin-top counterpart of the MGB roadster; the Triumph GT6 also looked like a direct fixed-head counterpart of the Triumph Spitfire, but it wasn't. In place of the Spitfire's modest four-cylinder engine, the GT6 had beefy 2 litre, six-cylinder power that gave it a marginal edge over the MGB's straight-line performance. On bendy bits, though, the GT6 was no match, and the Press rounded on its poor handling. Although later improved, the GT6 was never a mountain goat. Today, none of this should matter, but the collective consciousness of the classic car crowd makes elephants look forgetful. That's why you can buy a very nice Triumph GT6 for less than a comparable MGB GT – and, come to think of it, that's not such a bad idea.

Triumph Stag (1970–77)

Engine: Double-overhead-camshaft V8, cast-iron block, alloy cylinder heads, twin carburettors, 2997cc.
Power output: 146bhp.
Transmission: Four-speed manual with optional overdrive; three-speed automatic.
Brakes: Front discs, rear drums.
Maximum speed: 115+mph.
0–60mph: 10.5 seconds.
Production: 25,877.

With crisp, convertible four-seater styling and a burbling V8, British Leyland's blueprint for the Triumph Stag must surely have come straight out of Dearborn, Michigan, where Ford's Mustang had created the 'pony car' idiom and galloped off with record-breaking sales. Where the Mustang had a wild stallion on its grille, British Leyland substituted a leaping Stag and a litany of blunders. Instead of the redoubtable 3.5 litre Rover V8, available in-house and off the shelf, Triumph insisted on developing its own 3 litre V8, which earned a rotten reputation as soon as it hit the road, and from which the Stag never recovered. Over the next seven years, fewer than 26,000 Stags were made, and with all the money having been swallowed up by developing an engine for a single, low-selling model, there was nothing left to develop the Stag into the car it could have become.

What to watch: Specialists and enthusiasts have long since found the solution to the Stag's main bugbears of overheating, warped cylinder heads and blown head gaskets, yet there are still rogue Stags out there. Evidence of regular and careful maintenance to engine and radiator is essential; be very wary of a car that overheats on a test run – the damage has probably already been done. Many have done what Triumph should have done originally and installed Rover's lusty and robust 3.5 litre V8 – this is an acceptable, and even desirable, practice.

Stag-gering facts: In May 1996, an enthusiast who had stumped up £53,067 to restore his 1974 Triumph Stag sold it at auction for £16,100; the design of the Stag was executed by Italian styling house Michelotti, which also penned the TR4, Herald and 2000 saloon.

1974 Triumph GT6 Mk III, 1998cc, 6 cylinders, manual gearbox with overdrive, Webasto-type sunroof, finished in magenta, 39,000 miles from new, original, unrestored.
£4,750–5,500 BRIT

Introduced in 1966, the Triumph GT6 was an attractive fastback coupé based on the contemporary Spitfire, but fitted with the 6 cylinder engine from the Vitesse. Its Michelotti styling was particularly pleasing, and it remained in production until 1974.

1973 Triumph Stag, manual gearbox with overdrive, mechanical components overhauled, bodywork restored, new upholstery, carpets, hood and chrome, excellent condition.
£8,000–9,000 Mot

1971 Triumph Stag, 2997cc V8, automatic transmission, refurbished, finished in yellow, interior wood trim replaced with walnut veneer, new carpets and black canvas hood, good mechanical condition.
£3,500–4,000 BRIT

1974 Triumph Stag, 2997cc V8, automatic transmission, factory replacement engine, gearbox rebuilt, all other mechanical components overhauled or replaced as necessary, coachwork refurbished.
£6,500–7,500 BRIT

Triumph Trivia

Israeli psychic and spoon bender Uri Geller credits his Triumph Spitfire with his vegetarianism. He was just about to take a pot-shot at a bird with a rifle when an almighty crash startled him. His Spitfire had rolled down the road and impaled itself on a tree. Some folk might blame a faulty handbrake, but Uri suspects supernatural intervention.

◄ **1978 Triumph Stag,** 2997cc V8, automatic transmission, new exhaust system, Kenlowe fan, factory hardtop, restored, finished in white, with tan interior trim and upholstery, 57,000 miles from new, very good condition.
£5,250–5,750 H&H

1980 Triumph Dolomite Sprint, 1998cc, 4 cylinder engine, 4-speed manual gearbox with overdrive, Webasto sunroof, fully Waxoyled, finished in Russet brown with beige interior trim and upholstery, 59,000 miles from new, excellent condition throughout.
£2,300–2,700 H&H

◀ **1980 Triumph Dolomite Sprint,** 1998cc, 4 cylinder engine, 4-speed manual gearbox with overdrive, finished in red with black interior trim and upholstery, one owner from new, well maintained, 55,518 miles recorded, award winner, concours condition throughout, history file.
£3,500–4,000 H&H

TVR

◀ **1978 TVR Taimar,** 2994cc Ford V6, restored, engine rebuilt, reconditioned gearbox and steering rack, finished in maroon with cream side flashes, good mechanical condition.
£5,500–6,000 BRIT

The Taimar continued the theme of the 3000M, which had been in production from 1972. However, there were slight differences in the styling, among them a large lift-up hatchback. The Taimar continued in production until late 1979, when it was replaced by the Tasmin.

TVR Model	ENGINE cc/cyl	DATES	CONDITION 1	2	3
Grantura I	1172/4	1957–62	£4,000	£3,000	£2,000
Grantura II	1558/4	1957–62	£4,500	£3,000	£2,000
Grantura III/1800S	1798/4	1963–67	£5,000	£3,000	£2,200
Tuscan V8	4727/8	1967–70	£12,000	£7,000	£6,000
Vixen S2/3	1599/4	1968–72	£5,000	£3,000	£1,500
3000M	2994/6	1972–79	£7,000	£4,000	£3,000
Taimar	2994/6	1977–79	£7,500	£5,000	£3,500

c1918 Ford Model T Ambulance, older restoration, original, good condition throughout.
£8,000–10,000 TUC

1924 Ford Model T Dropside Truck, restored, finished in black with gold lettering and red coachlines, undersealed, interior retrimmed in black vinyl, good condition throughout.
£9,000–10,000 S

Commercial derivatives of the Model T were simple, cheap, and easy to drive and maintain. They considerably outnumbered the cars and, being capable of speeds in excess of 35mph, gave an impression of considerable power in the days when London buses were limited to 12mph, and no traffic moved faster than 20mph.

◄ **1924 Ford Model T Charabanc,** 2892cc, 4 cylinders, 11-seater open coachwork, artillery wheels, finished in green, good condition.
£13,000–15,000 TUC

1925 Ford Model T 1 Ton Truck, Manchester-built example, artillery wheels, fabric-covered rear bed, cab roof rack, right-hand drive, restored, very good condition throughout.
£9,000–10,000 TUC

► **1933 Ford Model B Fire Engine,** 2000cc, 4 cylinder, side-valve engine, three-speed manual gearbox, transverse-leaf-spring suspension, mechanical drum brakes all-round, cycle-type front wings, brass bell, fire extinguisher and ladder, finished in red, museum stored for some years, original condition throughout, in need of tidying.
£2,250–3,000 H&H

1934 Dodge 3 Ton Truck, 3497cc, 6 cylinder, side-valve engine, restored, finished in maroon and black, new timber flatbed platform.
£6,500–7,500 BRIT

1935 Clement-Talbot AY-35 Ambulance, wood and metal coachwork, restored.
£11,000–12,000 BAm

◀ **1949 Jowett Bradford Utility,** 1005cc, twin-cylinder engine, finished in brown with black wings, red interior trim, original, good condition throughout.
£2,500–3,000 BRIT

Available in Light Van and Utility variants, the Jowett Bradford of the immediate post-war period was favoured by small businesses due to its ruggedness, reliability and economy. The twin-cylinder engine dated from the vintage era, but proved virtually indestructible. Many examples of the Bradford were still in regular commercial use as late as the 1970s.

1962 Thames Flatbed Transporter, 2700cc, 6 cylinder Zodiac engine, 4-speed column-change gearbox, 85mph top speed, aluminium checker-plate floor, aluminium ramps, hand winch, finished in Lotus green with yellow signwriting.
£7,750–9,000 COYS

This vehicle was built in 1994 as a replica of the original Team Lotus transporter. It was based on a Ford Thames van, which was stripped of its body and had its chassis extended.

▶ **1977 Checker Aerobus,** 5735cc V8, good mechanical condition.
£5,500–7,000 BRIT

The Checker Yellow Cab is as synonymous with New York as the Austin FX4 is with London. Approximately 250 examples of the 12-seater, eight-door Aerobus were produced, and this one was originally owned by an old-people's home in the USA. It is believed to be the only example resident in the UK.

c1904 Edwardian Pedal Car, wooden construction with wrought-iron axles, metal wheels, tyres missing, rope-and-bobbin steering, candle-type front lamp.
£800–900 C

1928 Triang Pedal Car, finished in blue with yellow coachlines, bulb horn, all original.
£450–500 PC

Bugatti T35 Grand Prix Replica, 50cc, air-cooled Honda petrol engine, self-starter, automatic gearing, leaf-spring suspension, alloy wheels, aero screen, dashboard instrumentation, capable of 10–12mph.
£3,500–4,000 C

Alfa Romeo P3 Monoposto Replica, 50cc air-cooled Honda petrol engine, self starter, automatic gearing, leaf-spring suspension with friction dampers, wire wheels, outside exhaust, aero screen, dashboard instrumentation, woodrim steering wheel.
£4,000–5,000 C

1950s Austin J40 Pedal Car, pressed-steel construction, dummy engine, electric lighting and horn, opening boot, chrome-plated brightwork, original paintwork showing signs of wear, otherwise good condition.
£700–900 C

1950s Triang Ford Zodiac Pedal Car, pressed-steel construction, chrome grille, battery-operated headlamps, non-original badges and windscreen surround, restored.
£250–300 CARS

1985 Porsche 936 Replica, 5hp petrol engine, 2-speed transmission, fibreglass body, rear spoiler, battery-operated headlights, excellent condition throughout.
£4,000–5,000 S(NY)

1960s Blue Streak Willys Knight Pedal Car, restored, finished in bronze with black wings, good condition.
£200–250 GAZE

c1939 Humber Super Snipe Estate, 4.2 litres,
6 cylinders, restored, RAF markings.
£4,500–5,000 EAFG

c1940 Volkswagen VW82/KDF Kubelwagen, 1131cc,
air-cooled, 4 cylinder engine, 25bhp, 4-speed gearbox,
rear-wheel drive.
£6,000–7,000 MVT

c1940 Bedford MW 15cwt GS, 3519cc, 6 cylinders,
72bhp, 4-speed gearbox, rear-wheel drive, good condition.
£2,500–3,500 MVT

**Vauxhall supplied almost 66,000 15cwt 4x2 trucks
during WWII, the most common being this GS type.**

1941 Dodge WC10 Carryall, 3572cc, 6 cylinder engine,
85bhp, 4-wheel drive, 4-speed gearbox, single-speed
transfer box, restored, engine rebuilt.
£9,000–10,000 PC

c1940 Leyland Retriever GS, 5895cc, 4 cylinders,
73bhp, 4-speed gearbox with 2-speed transfer box.
£3,500–5,000 MVT

1940 Bedford MWR FFW Wireless Truck, 3519cc,
overhead-valve petrol engine, restored, very good condition.
£3,500–4,000 EAFG

1941 White M3 Half-Track, completely restored,
British markings.
£7,000–8,000 EAFG

c1942 GMC CCKW-353 2½ Ton Truck, 4416cc,
overhead-valve, 6 cylinder petrol engine, winch,
machine-gun mount, restored.
£5,000–5,500 PC

1942 Willys Jeep, 2199cc, 4 cylinder side-valve engine, soft top and sidescreens, restored, good condition.
£4,500–5,000 EAFG

1942 Bedford QLT Troop Carrier, completely restored, very good condition.
£3,500–4,000 NTMV

1943 Morris C4 Mk II 15cwt, 3519cc, side-valve petrol engine, 70bhp, 4-speed gearbox rear-wheel drive, RAF markings.
£3,000–4,000 MVT

1943 GMC CCK W352 SWB Truck, 4424cc, 6 cylinders, 5-speed gearbox with overdrive, open-cab, restored, good condition.
£2,000–2,500 EAFG

◀ **1943 Ford F15 Anti-Aircraft Truck,** 3917cc, side-valve V8 engine, British-built on Canadian chassis, No.13 cab, fitted with deactivated 20mm Polston gun on towable gun carriage, only known surviving example, restored, very good condition.
£13,000–15,000 PC

▶ **1943 Ford WOT2 15cwt GS,** 3621cc side-valve V8 engine, rear-wheel drive, restored, very good condition throughout.
£3,500–4,000 EAFG

Ford built almost 60,000 15cwt WOT2 chassis throughout WWII. Most had the GS type of body, as fitted to this example, but some carried special-purpose bodies, such as enclosed vans and fire-service vehicles. At first, the WOT2 was provided with an open cab and folding windscreen, but later examples were equipped with a semi-enclosed cab.

c1944 Humber 8 cwt FWD GS Truck,
4086cc, 6 cylinder, side-valve engine, 85bhp at
3,400rpm, 4-wheel drive, 4-speed gearbox
with 2-speed transfer box, hydraulic brakes,
transverse-leaf-spring independent front
suspension, restored, RAF markings.
£3,500–4,500 MVT

**Humber also built a heavy utility car, field
ambulance, truck and armoured vehicles on
the FWD chassis.**

1944 Bedford OY Truck, 3519cc, overhead-valve,
6 cylinder engine, rear-wheel drive, restored,
good condition throughout.
£3,000–3,500 NTMV

1944 GMC DUKW, 4424cc, 6 cylinder petrol
engine, 94bhp, 5-speed gearbox with
overdrive, 2-speed transfer box, amphibious,
restored, excellent condition.
£24,000–28,000 MVT

1944 Ford T16 Bren Gun Carrier, 3621cc, side-valve
V8, restored, good condition throughout.
£6,000–7,000 EAFG

1945 Ford WOA2A Heavy Utility, 3621cc, side-valve V8,
30hp, 4-speed gearbox, rear-wheel drive, mechanical
drum brakes, leaf-spring suspension, completely
restored, Army film and photographic unit markings, only
known restored example in the UK, very good condition.
£11,000–12,000 NMV

**The WOA2A was built by Ford in Britain between 1941
and 1947 It was available in two body styles: saloon
and estate.**

◄ **1951 Dodge M43 Ambulance,** 4-wheel drive,
all original equipment, very good condition.
£4,500–5,000 BAm

This ambulance was used in the film *The Dirty Dozen*.

◀ **1952 GAZ 67 Utility,** 2430cc, Ford side-valve engine, 4-wheel drive, restored, good mechanical condition, serviceable weather equipment, Soviet markings.
£2,000–2,500 BRIT

The Gorky Automobile Works, in the former Soviet Union, produced its first vehicle in 1932, with assistance from Ford. The organisation supplied vehicles for both civilian and military use. Gaz 67 utility vehicles, such as this example, remained in production until the 1960s.

1954 Austin Champ, 2838cc, 4 cylinders, 5-speed gearbox, 4-wheel drive, mostly original.
£3,000–3,500 NMV

c1955 Ferret Mk I Scout Car, Rolls-Royce B60 engine, restored, good condition.
£5,000–5,750 WITH

1955 Austin K9 Cargo FFW, 3995cc, 6 cylinders, 4-speed gearbox, 2-speed transfer box, completely restored.
£1,500–2,000 EAFG

1956 Volvo TP21 SUGGA, 3.6 litre, 6 cylinder side-valve engine, good condition.
£7,000–8,000 MVT

This command car was built exclusively for the Swedish Army, between 1952 and 1957, by Volvo's truck division.

1965 Austin Gipsy, 2199cc, 4 cylinders, 2,400 miles from new, good original condition.
£3,300–3,700 BRIT

Clearly prompted by the success of the Land Rover, BMC introduced the Austin Gipsy in 1958. A choice of petrol or diesel power units was offered, the former being the redoubtable 2.2 litre, 4 cylinder unit from the Austin Sixteen of 1945–49. Both short- and long-wheelbase versions were available with a variety of bodies. Production ceased in 1968 following the amalgamation of Austin and Rover.

1959 Auto Union DKW F91/4 Munga, 3 cylinder, 2-stroke engine, 4-wheel drive, restored, British markings.
£1,300–1,500 EAFG

Bob Murray, Classic Encounter, depicting a Mk VB Spitfire making a low pass over an Aston Martin DB6, water colour and gouache, framed, mounted and glazed, 19¾x25½in (50x65cm).
£750–800 BKS

▶ Michael Wright, Ghost in the Dolomites, depicting a Rolls-Royce 40/50hp in the Fiorentini Valley with Monte Pelmo in the distance, mixed media, framed, mounted and glazed, 24¾x19¾in (63x50cm).
£2,500–3,000 BKS

Charles Shaw, Smokers Prefer Shell, original lithographed Shell advertising poster, 1936, 30¼x44¾in (76.5x114cm).
£1,000–1,200 S

Edward McKnight Kauffer, Dinton Castle Near Aylesbury, original lithographed Shell advertising poster, 1936, some tears to margin, 30¼x44¾in (76.5x114cm).
£650–700 S

Brooklands Totalisator amusement machine, working, original key, original metal decoration and plating, worm-free wooden body, 1930s, excellent condition.
£1,800–2,000 BKS

Mr Bibendum, Michelin promotional suit, featuring corrugated head, limbs, legs and torso, original white boots, yellow and blue sash, 1960s.
£2,500–3,000 BKS

Lodge Plugs garage advertising totem in the form of a spark-plug, aluminium and wood construction, c1930, 29in (75cm) high.
£300–350 C

A pair of driving goggles with original tinted visor, 1930s.
£40–50 BRIT

An Art Deco silver and glass post holder, 6in (15cm) long.
£150–170 BRIT

◄ A set of three Shell BP service buttons, 1950s.
£200–250 BRIT

A set of six enamelled silver cocktail sticks, depicting road signs, 1935.
£200–220 BRIT

A Champion Spark Plugs silver ashtray, hallmarked London, 1938, 4in (10cm) square.
£250–300 BRIT

► A silver St Christopher dashboard plaque by P. Vincenze, 1930s, 2in (5cm) diam.
£150–200 BRIT

A Black Cat Cigarettes advertising vesta box, 1912, 2x2¼in (5x5.5cm).
£300–400 BRIT

◄ An Oldfield oil rear lamp, nickel finish 10in (25.5cm) high.
£120–140 CGC

A Lucas inspection lamp, correct 2-pin connection plug, as supplied with Rolls-Royce, Bentley, Sunbeam, Lagonda and other pre-war quality cars, 12in (30.5cm) long.
£100–120 CGC

A brass bulb horn, inscribed 'Lucas – King of the Road', 11in (28cm) long.
£25–30 CGC

▶ A Latil elephant's head car mascot, by F. Bazin, French, signed, 1920s, wooden base.
£900–1,000 S

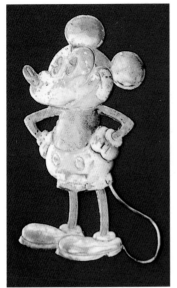

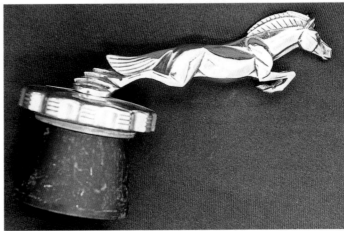

An Art Deco horse car mascot, by Brau, 8in (20cm) long.
£600–700 DRJ

A nickel-on-brass Mickey Mouse radiator grille badge, slight wear, 5¾in (14.5cm) high.
£150–180 BKS

A cockerel radiator cap mascot, French, 1920s, 5½in ((14cm) high.
£250–275 ChA

A monkey car mascot, French, c1920, 7¾in (19.5cm) high, turned wooden base.
£450–500 ChA

A squirrel car mascot, by M. Leverrier, French, 1920s, 6½in (16.5cm) high, turned and polished wooden base, good condition.
£380–420 ChA

▶ An opalescent glass *Perche* mascot, by Lalique, wheelcut and moulded, French, 1929–39, 6¼in (16cm) long.
£1,500–2,000 S

A glass eagle's head mascot, by
Lalique, excellent original condition
with correct moulded 'R. Lalique'
and 'France' on base,
French, 1920s.
£800–900 BKS

A silver bull's head mascot, by
Garrards, hallmarked London 1936,
3¾in (9.5cm) high, mounted on a
radiator cap.
£3,300–3,700 S

A bronze and ivory elephant mascot,
unsigned, French, 1920, 6in (15cm)
high, mounted on radiator cap.
£400–450 ChA

A silver setter mascot, unsigned,
British, c1940, 7in (18cm) high.
£230–250 ChA

A leaping greyhound mascot, French, c1939,
6in (15cm) high, mounted on a marble base.
£900–1,100 ChA

◄ A Riley woman skier mascot, c1935,
6½in (16.5cm) high.
£550–600 ChA

A nickel-plated bronze
mascot, by L'As, French,
signed, 1920s, 3½in
(8.5cm) high, mounted on
a radiator cap above a
turned wooden base.
£2,000–2,500 S

A Chrysis glass mascot, by Lalique, French,
c1930, etched 'R. Lalique' under base,
5¾in (14.5cm) high.
£1,200–1,500 S

◄ A Pathfinder mascot, by G. Poivin, French,
c1920, 5in (12.5cm) high.
£400–500 ChA

A chrome-plated Schneider
Supermarine S6B mascot,
painted tail, spinning
propeller, original pivoting
stand, c1930, 6¼in (15.5cm)
wingspan, mounted on a
turned wooden base.
£600–700 S

**Desmo made several
racing seaplane
mascots. This particular
version features a
pivoting action that
allows it to bank when
the car turns.**

A ballet dancer mascot,
French, c1930,
9¾in (25cm) high.
£230–250 ChA

A Pierce-Arrow mascot, American, c1932,
6in (15cm) high.
£450–500 ChA

A lighthouse mascot, with illuminator,
by P. Ross, c1910, 8in (20cm) high.
£170–200 ChA

A Magnificent mascot, by P. de Soete, Belgian,
c1930, 4½in (11.5cm) high.
£900–1,000 ChA

◄ A Spirit of Triumph mascot, 1930s,
8¼in (21cm) high, on turned wooden base.
£350–400 ChA

A nickel Duval Unique mascot,
French, 1930s, 7½in (19cm) high.
£380–420 ChA

A stylised head mascot, by
L. Auscher, French, c1920,
4¾in (12cm) high.
£700–750 ChA

A 1936 Olympics commemorative
mascot, German, 7in (18cm) high.
£100–120 ChA

◄ A bronze elephant mascot, by A.
Zeitlin, signed, the base fitted with
integral radiator cap screw fitting,
c1905, 10¼in (26cm) high.
£1,700–1,900 S

A Buick mascot, by Teinstedt,
c1915, 3½in (9cm) high, damaged.
£230–250 ChA

A Lalique ram's head glass mascot,
greenish tint to glass (usually clear).
£2,000–2,500 BKS

A French Gueron fish mascot, mint
condition, c1930, 5½in (14cm) high.
£275–325 ChA

A limited-edition 1:8 scale model of a supercharged Le Mans Bentley 4½ Litre, by Sapor Model Technik, electrically-operated engine and transmission, working brakes, electric lights, working gearshift and dashboard controls, leather seats and interior, folding hood, one of only 25 made, 24in (61cm) long.
£8,000–9,000 C

A stainless steel and aluminium scale model of a 1962 Ferrari 250 GTO engine and gearbox, black crackle-finished cam covers with polished Ferrari logo, 6 twin-choke Weber-style carburettors, gear-selector quadrant with chromed gate, supported on turned aluminium stands, 22½in (57cm) long.
£1,750–2,500 BKS

A detailed 1:5 scale model of a Mercedes-Benz 300SL chassis, by M. Jelesjevie, many movable parts, 30in (76cm) long.
£10,000–11,000 C

A 1960s Mamod Roadster Steam Car, good condition, 16in (41cm) long.
£50–55 GAZE

A scratch-built 1:12 model of a 1962 Ferrari 250 GTO, body with opening doors, bonnet and boot, Perspex windscreen, side and rear windows, engine vents and headlight covers, wire Borrani-style wheels, detailed engine bay and cockpit.
£18,000–22,000 BKS

A 1:8 scale model of a Bugatti Atlantique T57 coupé, by Herr Strauss, leather interior, seats and panels, polished wooden dashboard and door trims, full instrumentation, detailed engine compartment, chromed brightwork, wire wheels, 22in (56cm) long.
£6,000–7,000 C

A detailed 1:14 scale model of an Alfa Romeo 8C 2300 Spyder Tourer, by P. and Gerald Wingrove, Perspex windscreen, nickel-effect radiator surround, Boyce MotoMeter-style radiator cap/water temperature gauge, opening bonnet with six nickel-effect, spring-in-tube-style bonnet clips, semi-elliptic road springs, hinged and bolted tie-bars and lever-arm shock absorbers, wire wheels, detailed engine, interior trimmed in maroon faux leather.
£4,600–5,200 BKS

A one-off 1:8 scale model of a 1934 Rolls-Royce Phantom II Shooting Brake, by Nick Bock, detailed engine bay, nickel-plated brightwork, polished aluminium bonnet with opening louvres, wire wheels, opening doors, leather upholstery, 27in (68.5cm) long.
£7,500–8,500 C

A Shell Economy Model 4 petrol pump, by Gilbert & Barker, hand-cranked, 1930s, 102in (260cm) high.
£700–1,000 CRC

A Milwaukee freestanding petrol pump, hand-cranked, with rubber hose, 10 gallon delivery dial and bronze gun, 60in (152.5cm) high.
£130–140 BKS

A Pratts petrol pump, by Gilbert & Barker, hand-cranked, restored, original apart from globe, 1920, 96in (244cm) high.
£750–850 TPS

A Wakefield 5 gallon forecourt oil-delivery cistern, hand-cranked.
£45–50 BKS

A BP glass petrol pump globe, late 1920s, 14in (35.5cm) high.
£300–350 MSMP

► A Carless Coalene Mixture petrol pump globe, moulded glass by Hailwood & Ackroyd, hand-painted, some fading to paint and minor chipping to base, 1936.
£13,000–16,000 S

Ace glass petrol pump globes, 1950s, each 17in (43cm) high.
£250–300 each MSMP

A Barratt fold-front, petit wicker, two-person picnic set, lid converts into tray, kettle, burner, teaspoons, 2 Minton cups and saucers food boxes, milk bottle, c1902.
£230–270 BKS

◄ A Drew & Sons tea basket, complete and original, 1905–10, good condition.
£700–800 PPH

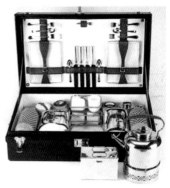

A Coracle four-person picnic set, black leathercloth case with wedge-shaped lid, fitted interior with 2 wicker-covered bottles, copper kettle, burner stand and burner glasses, china cups and saucers, ceramic butter jar, milk bottle, oil container, 2 sandwich boxes with ceramic bases, cutlery in lid, 1920s.
£1,400–1,700 BKS

◄ A Coracle four-person wicker picnic set, sandwich box, stacking cups and saucers, milk bottle, drinks bottle in woven cover, cutlery in lid, brass hinges and padlock, c1905.
£1,150–1,400 BKS

A Coracle four-person wicker picnic set, 1930s, good condition.
£175–200 PPH

A Keller leather-cased four-person picnic set, kettle, burner, china cups and saucers, stacking tumblers, wicker-covered bottles, silver cutlery in lid, ceramic-based sandwich box, food boxes, various ceramic jars, mid-1920s, excellent condition.
£700–800 BKS

A French leather trunk with wooden slats, brass fittings and corners, original internal tray, c1903.
£1,400–1,700 BKS

A Louis Vuitton wardrobe trunk, fitted hangers, drawers, combination duo hatbox drawer with original divider, velvet lining, brass fittings, c1920, excellent condition.
£11,500–13,000 BKS

▶ A Louis Vuitton shoe trunk, 36 compartments with drawers, fold-up lid, brass fittings, unmarked interior, original Vuitton key, c1925.
£14,000–15,000 BKS

A Louis Vuitton leather cabin trunk, correct in every detail, all original clothes cases intact, original lining, padded inside lid, c1900.
£11,500–13,000 BKS

A Shell double-sided, illuminated hanging garage sign, printed glass each side, undamaged, 1920s.
£1,000–1,100 BKS

An Automobile Association single-sided enamel village sign, last series, 29in (73.5cm) diam, good condition.
£170–190 MSMP

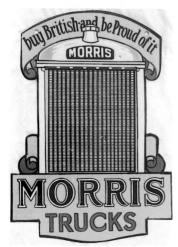

◄ A Morris Trucks enamel sign, good condition, c1920, 22in (56cm) high.
£1,000–1,100 BRUM

An Edwardian Electra angled brass, 30-hour dashboard clock, 2¾in (7cm) diam.
£75–85 CGC

A Clevecol enamel sign, 30in (76cm) wide.
£75–80 CGC

A Smith's Quick-Test Brake-Dynamometer enamel sign, c1930.
£80–90 GAZE

A Motoral French tinplate sign, c1910, 20in (51cm) wide.
£350–395 JUN

A Heuer helmet alarm clock, Niki Lauda colours, c1976, 5in (13cm) high.
£50–60 LE

A Dragonfly Motor Oils and Greases flanged, double-sided enamel sign, very good condition, 18in (45.5cm) wide.
£375–400 MSMP

An Ospedol Motor Oils double-sided, enamel forecourt sign, 22in (56cm) wide, damaged.
£150–180 CGC

◄ An Amilcar enamel sign, c1925, 36in (91.5cm) high, good condition.
£500–600 GIRA

A Stepney Tyres enamel sign, 1918–20, 29in (73.5cm) high.
£600–650 BRUM

A Smiths London clock, 4½in (11.5cm) diam.
£30–35 DRJ

Vauxhall

Although owned by General Motors since 1925, Vauxhall has managed to maintain a distinct British identity throughout much of its long life, which began when the first Vauxhall motor car rolled out of the Vauxhall Iron Works, alongside the River Thames, in 1903. In the Edwardian and vintage eras, the expensive, sporting Prince Henry models and the later 30/98 were very highly regarded, but in 1925, poor financial control led to the company's take-over by General Motors.

After that, Vauxhall moved into the mainstream middle market, which has remained its domain ever since. Throughout the 1950s and into the 1960s, British Vauxhalls absorbed American styling influences, but still retained an essentially British character, more Uncle Stan than Uncle Sam. From the mid-1970s, model lines converged with those of Opel in Germany, also owned since the 1920s by General Motors.

1924 Vauxhall OE 30-98 Velox Four-Seater Tourer, 4224cc, overhead-valve engine, twin SU carburettors, 4-branch exhaust, heavy-duty brake drums, in need of cosmetic attention.
£48,000–53,000 BKS

Introduced initially as a 4.5 litre side-valve model, borrowing many features from the landmark pre-WWI Prince Henry model, the E-Type 30-98 was described as a gentleman's fast touring car, but it quickly made its mark in competition on the circuits and in speed hillclimbs.

1933 Vauxhall Cadet Grosvenor 17hp Saloon, restored, finished in dark blue and black, very good condition.
£9,000–11,000 BKS

VAUXHALL Model	ENGINE cc/cyl	DATES	CONDITION		
			1	2	3
D/OD	3969/4	1914–26	£35,000	£24,000	£18,000
E/OE	4224/4	1919–28	£90,000+	£60,000+	£35,000
Eighty	3317/6	1931–33	£10,000	£8,000	£5,000
Cadet	2048/6	1931–33	£7,000	£5,000	£3,000
Lt Six	1531/6	1934–38	£5,000	£4,000	£1,500
14	1781/6	1934–39	£4,000	£3,000	£1,500
25	3215/6	1937–39	£5,000	£4,000	£1,500
10	1203/4	1938–39	£4,000	£3,000	£1,500
Wyvern LIX	1500/4	1948–51	£2,000	£1,000	£500
Velox LIP	2200/6	1948–51	£2,000	£1,000	£500
Wyvern EIX	1500/4	1951–57	£2,000	£1,320	£400
Velox EIPV	2200/6	1951–57	£3,000	£1,650	£400
Cresta EIPC	2200/6	1954–57	£3,000	£1,650	£400
Velox/Cresta PAS/PAD	2262/6	1957–59	£2,850	£1,300	£300
Velox/Cresta PASY/PADY	2262/6	1959–60	£2,700	£1,500	£300
Velox/Cresta PASX/PADX	2651/6	1960–62	£2,700	£1,300	£300
Velox/Cresta PASX/PADX Est	2651/6	1960–62	£2,700	£1,300	£300
Velox/Cresta PB	2651/6	1962–65	£1,600	£800	£100
Velox/Cresta PB Est	2651/6	1962–65	£1,600	£800	£100
Cresta/Deluxe PC	3294/6	1964–72	£1,500	£800	£100
Cresta PC Est	3294/6	1964–72	£1,500	£800	£100
Viscount	3294/6	1964–72	£1,700	£900	£100
Victor I/II	1507/4	1957–61	£2,000	£1,000	£250
Victor I/II Est	1507/4	1957–61	£2,100	£1,100	£300
Victor FB	1507/4	1961–64	£1,500	£900	£200
Victor FB Est	1507/4	1961–64	£1,600	£1,000	£300
VX4/90	1507/4	1961–64	£2,000	£900	£150
Victor FC101	1594/4	1964–67	£1,600	£900	£150
Victor FC101 Est	1594/4	1964–67	£1,800	£1,000	£200
101 VX4/90	1594/4	1964–67	£2,000	£1,500	£250
VX4/90	1975/4	1969–71	£1,000	£600	£100
Ventora I/II	3294/6	1968–71	£1,000	£375	£100
Viva HA	1057/4	1963–66	£1,000	£350	£100
Viva SL90	1159/6	1966–70	£1,000	£350	£100
Viva Brabham	1159/4	1967–70	£2,000	£1,000	£800
Viva	1600/4	1968–70	£500	£350	£100
Viva Est	1159/4	1967–70	£500	£400	£100

Starter Vauxhalls: PA Cresta/Velox, 1957-62; F-Type Victor, 1957-61.

- As our price table shows, all Vauxhalls of the 1950s and 1960s are affordable, but two models that really stand out for their glamorous styling are the Detroit-inspired PA Cresta/Velox and F-Type Victor, which today are very appealing to anyone nostalgic for the 1950s.

- They look for all the world like classic Yank tanks, yet their flanks clothe ordinary British mechanicals and running gear that are generally readily available and easy to maintain. The earlier E-Type Cresta, Velox and Wyvern also offer a touch of star-spangled razzmatazz, but their numbers have thinned to a level where they are not quite as practical as the later PA. Later cars, like the PB Cresta and FB Victors are also practical buys; compared to the extravagant PA they are almost muted.

- The glorious PA Cresta is a monster by British standards, a genuine six-seater with enough body rock 'n' roll to please any Elvis fan. Mechanically, they offer little to worry about with their strong 2.2 and 2.6 litre engines, and ancillaries like front discs, starter motors and dynamos are straight out of the MGB.

- **Pick of the PAs:** Some prefer the looks of the pre-1960 models, with their three-piece rear window, but later versions have a slightly more eager 2.6 litre lump in place of the earlier 2.2. Bodies are a different matter. Legend has it that PA Crestas rusted so rapidly that by the time they reached the end of the Luton production line, they would have failed today's MoT test. Actually, their resistance to rust was pretty much in line with other cars of the era. The big difference is that there's just more metal to rust. When you go to look at one, take a metal detector, because a festering rust box will be a labour of love rather than a sound purchase.

- Compared to contemporary saloon rivals, the F-Type Victor was a fine car to drive, with a tough and flexible engine. The mechanicals are all pretty sturdy, but the early cars really did have a deserved reputation for rusting, as their bodyshells offered more mud traps than a Florida swamp. In fact, by the end of 1959, Vauxhall was already receiving corrosion complaints, and in response, added underseal and splash panels.

1962 Vauxhall Cresta, 2.6 litre, 6 cylinder engine, windscreen visor, finished in two-tone blue, in need of restoration.
£800–1,100 GAZE

1962 Vauxhall Victor Saloon, 1507cc, 4 cylinders, front end damaged, complete, in need of restoration.
£200–250 SWO

1980 Vauxhall Silver Aero, 2279cc, 4 cylinder turbocharged engine, body side-skirts, electrically-adjusted Recaro front seats.
£3,200–3,700 BRIT

The Silver Aero was a factory concept car, based on the Cavalier Sports Hatch. It was first exhibited at the 1980 Motor Show, and although public response was encouraging, this example remains the only one built. It remained the property of Vauxhall for its first eight years.

Volkswagen

1969 Volkswagen Beetle, 1493cc, reconditioned engine, finished in red, original interior, good condition.
£1,400–1,600 RBB

1970 Volkswagen Beetle, 1300cc, all-synchromesh gearbox, 12 volt electrics, body refurbished, resprayed in Plum, grey interior trim, bodywork in excellent condition, mechanics and interior in good condition.
£1,700–2,000 LF

VOLKSWAGEN Model	ENGINE cc/cyl	DATES	CONDITION 1	2	3
Beetle (split rear screen)	1131/4	1945–53	£5,000	£3,500	£2,000
Beetle (oval rear screen)	1192/4	1953–57	£4,000	£2,000	£1,000
Beetle (slope headlamps)	1192/4	1957–68	£2,500	£1,000	£600
Beetle DHC	1192/4	1954–60	£6,000	£4,500	£2,000
Beetle 1500	1493/4	1966–70	£3,000	£2,000	£1,000
Beetle 1302 LS	1600/4	1970–72	£2,500	£1,850	£850
Beetle 1303 S	1600/4	1972–79	£3,000	£2,000	£1,500
1500 Variant/1600	1493/4 1584/4	1961–73	£2,000	£1,500	£650
1500/1600	1493/4 1584/4	1961–73	£3,000	£2,000	£800
Karmann Ghia/I	1192/4	1955–59	£5,000	£3,000	£1,000
Karmann Ghia/I DHC	1192/4	1957–59	£8,000	£5,000	£2,500
Karmann Ghia/I	1192/4	1960–74	£5,500	£3,000	£1,800
Karmann Ghia/I DHC	1192/4	1960–74	£7,000	£4,500	£2,000
Karmann Ghia/3	1493/4	1962–69	£4,000	£2,500	£1,250

Volvo

In Latin, Volvo means 'I roll', and that's what Volvos are famous for – rolling on and on and on. Although the company was founded in Sweden in 1927, it wasn't until the 1947 launch of the PV444 that the company's products came to wider international notice. With its quasi-American styling, scaled down to European proportions, the PV444 brought Volvo into the mainstream. Its unitary construction, high levels of comfort, fine driving dynamics and rugged dependability made a winning combination. The PV544 refined the theme further. In the late 1950s, the 121 continued in the same mould and endured through various model designations (122, 131, 132 and 123GT) up to 1970. Today, they are still enjoyed as robust, stylish classic workhorses. A little more exotic is the P1800 sports car which, despite its more delicate looks, has Volvo's characteristic sturdiness, even if body parts aren't as readily available or as cheap. The complex curves can also make repair and renovation quite costly.

1969 **Volvo 131 Amazon,** completely restored, excellent mechanical condition, history file.
£3,000–3,500 Mot

1972 **Volvo P1800E,** completely restored, finished in yellow, concours condition.
£7,000–8,500 WILM

◀ 1972 **Volvo P1800ES,** 2 litre, fuel-injected, 4 cylinder engine, finished in bronze metallic with black hide upholstery, 30,000 miles from new, concours condition.
£6,000–7,500 PORT

VOLVO Model	ENGINE cc/cyl	DATES	CONDITION 1	2	3
PV444	1800/4	1958–67	£4,000	£1,750	£800
PV544	1800/4	1962–64	£4,000	£1,750	£800
120 (B16)	1583/4	1956–59	£3,000	£1,000	£300
121	1708/4	1960–67	£3,500	£1,500	£350
122S	1780/4	1960–67	£4,500	£1,500	£250
131	1780/4	1962–69	£4,000	£1,500	£350
221/222	1780/4	1962–69	£2,500	£1,500	£300
123GT	1986/4	1967–69	£3,000	£2,500	£750
P1800	1986/4	1960–70	£4,500	£2,500	£1,000
P1800E	1986/4	1970–71	£4,200	£2,500	£1,000
P1800ES	1986/4	1971–73	£4,800	£3,000	£1,000

White

◀ **1911 White Tourer,** completely restored, finished in white with black hood, running well, good condition throughout.
£22,000–25,000 RM

White cars were built in Cleveland, Ohio, between 1900 and 1918, during which time, a total of 9,122 steam cars and 8,927 petrol-engined cars were produced. Considered to be in the upper echelon of early cars, Whites were quite expensive and had some famous owners, including John D. Rockefeller and Buffalo Bill Cody. After ceasing passenger car production, the White Motor Company concentrated on commercial vehicles.

Willys

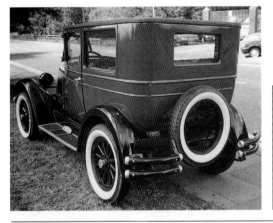

◀ **1927 Willys Overland Whippet Two-Door Saloon,** 2199cc, 4 cylinders, 3-speed manual gearbox, left-hand drive, wooden artillery wheels, external petrol gauge, finished in maroon and black with grey interior trim and upholstery, good condition throughout.
£7,500–9,000 H&H

Auction Prices

Miller's only includes cars declared sold. Our guide prices take into account the buyer's premium, VAT on the premium, and the extent of any published catalogue information relating to condition and provenance. To identify cars sold at auction, cross-refer the source codes at the ends of photo captions with the Key to Illustrations on page 330.

Winton

1915 Winton Model 21/Six Five-Passenger 3/4 Limousine, 6 cylinder in-line engine, 48.6hp, 3-speed gearbox, McKee headlights, restored, excellent condition throughout.
£60,000–70,000 BLK

Wolseley

Although one of the early pioneers in British car manufacturing, Wolseley hardly had an independent existence at all. The first four-wheeled vehicle was built in 1899 or 1900, and in 1901, the marque was taken over by Vickers. Early products were a mixed bag, usually with well engineered engines that didn't always have the chassis and running gear to match. Financial difficulties led to the company's acquisition in 1927 by William Morris, and after 1935, Wolseleys served as upmarket Morrises with overhead-valve engines. After the 1952 merger of Austin and Morris to form BMC, Wolseley survived as a group brand until 1975.

1934 Wolseley 21/60 County Four-Door Saloon, 2677cc, overhead-camshaft, 6 cylinder engine, 4-speed gearbox with central control, P100 headlamps, wire wheels, older restoration, finished in white and black with tan leather interior, good condition throughout. **£8,500–10,000 BKS**

1936 Wolseley Cabriolet, Lucas P100 headlamps, chrome electric horns, new hood, leather seating and trim, very good condition. **£11,000–12,000 PC**

SERVICE
WOLSELEY
AND SALES

1950s Wolseley Sales and Service printed tin sign, fair condition, 36in (91.5cm) diam. **£180–220 MSMP**

1957 Wolseley 15/50 Four-Door Saloon, finished in black with red leather interior, 42,722 miles from new, original, well maintained, excellent condition throughout. **£4,000–4,750 BKS**

Descended from the Wolseley 4/44 of 1956, the 15/50 combined its predecessor's running gear and unitary-construction with a larger, 1489cc B-series engine offering 75mph performance. It incorporated a welcome improvement in the form of a floor-mounted gear-change, rather than its predecessor's column change.

WOLSELEY Model	ENGINE cc/cyl	DATES	CONDITION 1	2	3
8	918/4	1939–48	£3,000	£2,000	£1,000
10	1140/4	1939–48	£3,500	£2,000	£1,000
12/48	1548/4	1939–48	£4,000	£2,000	£1,250
14/60	1818/6	1946–48	£4,500	£2,500	£1,500
18/85	2321/6	1946–48	£6,000	£3,000	£2,000
25	3485/6	1946–48	£7,000	£4,000	£2,500
4/50	1476/4	1948–53	£2,500	£1,000	£450
6/80	2215/6	1948–54	£3,000	£1,500	£750
4/44	1250/4	1952–56	£2,500	£1,250	£750
15/50	1489/4	1956–58	£1,850	£850	£500
1500	1489/4	1958–65	£2,500	£1,000	£500
15/60	1489/4	1958–61	£2,000	£700	£400
16/60	1622/4	1961–71	£1,800	£800	£400
6/90	2639/6	1954–57	£2,500	£1,000	£500
6/99	2912/6	1959–61	£3,000	£1,500	£750
6/110 Mk I/II	2912/6	1961–68	£2,000	£1,000	£500
Hornet (Mini)	848/4	1961–70	£1,500	£750	£400
1300	1275/4	1967–74	£1,250	£750	£400
18/85	1798/4	1967–72	£950	£500	£250

Commercial Vehicles

1939 Austin Heavy 12/4 Landaulette Taxicab, coachwork by Jones Brothers, 4 cylinder petrol engine, 4-speed manual gearbox, finished in black, blue interior trim and upholstery, black hood, one of only three known to survive, original, good condition throughout.
£7,000–8,000 H&H

This vehicle was one of the last of the pre-war taxicabs to be built. It was operated throughout the war in London, finally retiring from service in 1955, and has been used in many films.

1951 Austin Commercial Recovery Vehicle, A90 4 cylinder engine, fully-operational Harvey Frost crane, originally built as a Three-Way van, converted to recovery vehicle with 2+1 seating to the cab, finished in blue and black, engine overhauled, good condition.
£2,000–2,500 S

1959 Austin Princess DA2 Herbert Lomas Ambulance, accommodation for 4 stretcher patients, restored to original condition, bell replaced by later siren.
£4,000–5,000 BAm

◀ **1966 Austin Minivan,** 848cc, stored for 10 years, fair condition, in need of recommissioning.
£600–700 BKS

Following the Mini saloon's introduction in August 1959, the van arrived in 1960. Built on a longer wheelbase, its front-wheel drive and compact independent rear suspension enabled it to match many more expensive, medium-sized vans for interior space. Austin and Morris versions were built for the first nine years, after which it became known simply as the Mini Van. A 998cc engine was offered in 1967, but most buyers opted for the more economical 848cc.

1977 Leyland Mini Van, 848cc, brakes overhauled, new sills, resprayed in Old English white, mechanically sound.
£1,200–1,500 BRIT

1969 BMC LD Ambulance, coachwork by Wadham Stringer, restored, finished in St John Ambulance livery.
£2,000–3,000 BAm

1920 Ford Model T Truck, 3310cc, 4 cylinder engine, 2-speed manual gearbox, recently overhauled, finished in green with black wings and bonnet, black spoked wheels, very good condition throughout.
£4,250–5,500 H&H

1951 Bedford KZ Ambulance, restored to original condition, period first aid equipment, finished in St John Ambulance livery.
£5,000–6,000 BAm

1913 Ford Model T Bus, right-hand drive, finished in green with black wings, green spoked wheels, original, unrestored.
£9,000–11,000 TUC

1925 Ford Model T Depot Hack, varnished wooden body, black wings and bonnet, artillery wheels, older restoration, good condition.
£6,500–7,500 TUC

◄ **1953 Ford E494C 5cwt Van,** 933cc, side-valve engine, 3-speed gearbox, mechanical brakes, transverse-leaf springs front and rear, restored, finished in green and black with matching interior, good condition throughout.
£5,000–6,000 BKS

Introduced in 1948, Ford's E494A Anglia and its E494C commercial vehicle derivatives offered 60mph performance while returning 35–40mpg. The 5cwt van version proved deservedly popular as a delivery vehicle with large companies and individual traders alike.

1975 Ford Escort Van, 1098cc, 4 cylinder petrol engine, 4-speed manual gearbox, finished in light blue with black interior, unused, never registered, 477 miles recorded.
£2,500–3,000 H&H

1937 Morris 8 Series I Commercial Van, 918cc, restored, good condition throughout.
£5,500–6,500 MOR

◄ **1958 Morris 5 Ton Series III Dropside Truck,** one owner from new, dry stored from 1977, partially restored, good mechanical condition, body and cab fair.
£2,000–2,500 LF

From its earliest days, the van and lorry division of Morris had been a separate marque, Morris-Commercial. Following the merger of Morris' parent, the Nuffield Group, with Austin in 1952 to form BMC, things began to change. The Series III truck was introduced in 1955 and was available as an Austin or a Morris with only minor cosmetic changes, and by 1958, a third option, the BMC, was also on the market.

Children's Cars

Strega Rocking Car, over 150 handmade components, finished in red and yellow, slight wear.
£500–600 S

1960s Triang Thunderbolt Pedal Car, original finish in red with white logo and sidestrip, good condition.
£150–200 CARS

◄ **Triang Sharna Rolls-Royce Corniche,** moulded plastic body on steel frame, working lights, indicators and horn, 12 volt rechargeable battery, good condition.
£350–400 CARS

AMF Fire Chief Patrol Pedal Car, working bell, windscreen surround missing, in need of complete restoration.
£75–100 CARS

Auction Prices

Miller's only includes items declared sold. Our guide prices take into account the buyer's premium, VAT on the premium, and the extent of any published catalogue information relating to condition and provenance. To identify items sold at auction, cross-refer the source codes at the ends of photo captions with the Key to Illustrations on page 330.

1980s Toys Toys Turbo Racer FI Pedal Car, moulded plastic body with sponsors' logos, very good condition.
£50–75 CARS

Jaguar D-Type Motorised Racing Car, Villiers engine, centrifugal clutch, disc brake, pneumatic tyres, fibreglass body, full-width screen, finished in silver, little use.
£1,500–1,750 BKS

1990 Jaguar D-Type 2/3 Scale Motorised Car, 180cc, air-cooled, single-cylinder engine, starter, 2-speed gearbox with reverse, independent front suspension, hydraulic disc brakes, rack-and-pinion steering, electric lights, horn and instruments, leather upholstery.
£11,000–12,000 RM

1972 Ferrari 312 PB Motorised Sports Racer, 50cc, water-cooled Derbi engine, aluminium coachwork, independent suspension, 80km/h top speed.
£4,000–5,000 Pou

RaySon ERA Motorised Racing Car, 5hp, Briggs and Stratton 4-stroke engine, centrifugal expanding clutch, rear disc brake, pneumatic tyres, tubular-steel chassis, GRP bodywork, finished in British Racing green, black interior, little use, very good condition.
£1,750–2,000 BKS

Harrington Junior Coach, built by Johnson's Midget Motors for Harringtons of Brighton, 125cc, Villiers 2-stroke, single-cylinder engine, aluminium coachwork on ash frame, central driving position, accommodation for 2 or 3 small passengers, finished in original Costin's Coaches of Bedfordshire livery in maroon and blue, one family ownership from new, stored since 1970s.
£3,500–4,000 C

Replica, Kit & Reproduction Cars

1986 Bugatti Type 59 Replica, 1998cc, 6 cylinder Triumph Vitesse engine, Vitesse running gear, aluminium bodywork, dual aero screens, finished in Bugatti blue, cockpit upholstered in black vinyl, period-style instrumentation, 13,000 miles from new, good condition throughout
£7,500–9,000 RCC

Only 25 of these Bugatti Type 59 replicas were built by Mike King Racing.

Dax Cobra Replica, 4200cc, 6 cylinder Jaguar engine, 4-speed manual gearbox, Jaguar running gear, finished in blue, completed 1994, excellent condition.
£11,500–13,000 H&H

1986 Gravetti Cobra Replica, 3528cc Rover V8, Jaguar-based suspension, Halibrand alloy wheels, GRP bodywork, serviceable black hood and tonneau cover, sidescreens, finished in Midnight blue.
£9,000–10,500 BRIT

1986 AC Cobra Replica, 5 litre Ford V8, 4-speed gearbox, round-tube chassis, E-Type Jaguar running gear, side exhausts, Halibrand knock-off alloy wheels, fibreglass body, finished in Flame red, interior retrimmed in magnolia leather, good condition throughout.
£12,000–14,000 BKS

◀ **1978 Ferrari 250 GTO Replica,** based on Datsun 260Z, 2656cc, 6 cylinder engine, Borrani-style wire wheels, new exhaust system, reupholstered in 1996, major mechanical components in good condition.
£6,000–7,500 BRIT

1990 KVA Ford GT 40 Replica, 3500cc V8 engine, 4-speed manual gearbox, many parts individually fabricated, correct-style sill-mounted fuel tanks, finished in white with black interior trim and upholstery, 5,293 miles from new, excellent condition throughout.
£10,000–13,000 H&H

1966 Jaguar C-Type Replica, 3781cc, 6 cylinder engine, one of only 10 built, good condition throughout.
£40,000–45,000 BC

1984 Househam Dutton Phaeton, 3500cc Rover V8, fully balanced engine with half-race camshaft, electronic ignition, 4-barrel Weber carburettor, tubular exhaust manifolds, uprated oil pump and clutch, 250bhp, 5-speed manual gearbox, spare wheel with carrier, finished in British Racing green, hood and sidescreens in mohair, heater, history file.
£5,000–6,000 H&H

This is one of two Duttons built by L.W. Househam & Son, its sibling having the distinction of winning the first Formula K race for kit cars in 1984.

1986 Lynx D-Type, blueprinted 4.2 litre E-Type engine, rebuilt Jaguar 4-speed, all-synchromesh, close-ratio gearbox, XJ6-specification front disc brakes, standard 4.2 E-Type rear brakes, Koni shock absorbers and uprated rear coil springs, 16in Dunlop alloy wheels, all-alloy monocoque long-nose style body, full-width windscreen, metal tonneau cover over passenger seat, one of only 42 built, one owner from new, good condition.
£55,000–60,000 RM

1981 Kougar V12 Two-Seater Sports, tuned 6.9 litre engine, 6 Weber 401DF carburettors, 430bhp at 3,000rpm, close-ratio E-Type gearbox, Powr-Lok limited-slip differential, Compomotive alloy wheels, 0–60mph in 5.4 seconds, full-width windscreen and aero screens, finished in red with blue/grey interior, detachable roll-over bar, 4-point competition harnesses, good condition.
£14,500–16,000 BKS

Introduced in 1977, the Kougar was a traditionally styled sports car based on Jaguar components, Rover's V8 becoming a powerplant option in the 1980s. In both forms, the lightweight Kougar possessed formidable acceleration. This car is the only Jaguar V12-engined Kougar to be built by the factory.

Lotus Eleven Le Mans S2 Replica, 1500cc, 4 cylinder Coventry-Climax engine, gearbox, suspension, brakes and wheels to correct specification, chassis as original, aluminium bodywork with metal tonneau and wrap-around windscreen, finished in Lotus green with red seats, eligible for VSCC and AMOC events. road legal.
£12,000–14,000 COYS

c1986 Maserati 450S Replica, built by Wymondham Engineering, race-prepared, 4.9 litre, Maserati double-overhead-camshaft V8, twin-plug heads, 4 twin-choke Weber 38DCN carburettors, 375bhp, Getrag 5-speed gearbox, tubular chassis frame, coil-and-wishbone front suspension, Jaguar independent rear suspension, Borrani alloy wheels, unused since 1995, excellent mechanical condition.
£35,000–38,000 BKS

This car is a faithful reconstruction of one of the all-time greats of sports car racing, built at an estimated cost of £100,000 for the Cannonball Run in the USA.

Restoration Projects

c1904 Albion 16hp Chain-Driven Rolling Chassis, engine and gearbox fitted, artillery wheels, no documentation or history.
£1,700–2,000 S

1928 Austin 7 Tourer, originally a Gordon England Cup model, fitted with current military tourer body c1935, one owner since 1933, last used 1956, dry stored since, no documentation.
£1,800–2,200 BKS

1929 Austin 12hp Burnham Saloon, 4 cylinder side-valve engine, nickel radiator, opening rooflight, scuttle-mounted sidelamps, leather upholstery, complete in all major respects, unused in recent years, in need of restoration and recommissioning.
£5,500–7,000 BKS

Bugatti Type 57 Atalante Body Frame, one of four exact replica body frames made from seasoned ash by marque experts A.B. Price Ltd in 1995.
£3,500–4,000 BKS

Of all the factory body styles specially designed by the talented Jean Bugatti for the T57 chassis, the Atalante is one of the most appealing.

Cross Reference
See Colour Review

1909 Ford Model T Tourer, 2892cc, restored 1950s, in need of recommissioning.
£16,000–18,500 TUC

1933 Invicta 12/45 Four-Door Saloon, coachwork by Carbodies, basically sound, spare engine, in need of a few minor mechanical components.
£4,000–5,000 BKS

Introduced in 1932 and built to the same high standards as Invicta's larger models, the 12hp had a 1.5 litre, overhead-camshaft Blackburne six and was available with tourer or saloon coachwork. There was also a high-performance version – the supercharged 12/90 – but the smaller Invicta had arrived too late to influence the company's fortunes, and production ceased in 1933 after about 50 cars had been built.

1913 Ford Model T, original lamps and brass radiator, two-piece windscreen, no bodywork.
£4,000–5,000 TUC

1936 Lagonda Rapier Tourer, 1104cc, 4 cylinder in-line engine, twin SU carburettors, 4-speed pre-selector gearbox, cable-operated drum brakes, left-hand drive, four-seater aluminium coachwork, wire wheels.
£8,500–11,000 Pou

1923 Morris Cowley 11.9hp Bullnose Two-Door Tourer, coachwork by Wheller & Bristow of Yeovil, later SU carburettors, front wheel brakes, mechanically complete, windscreen, hood, dashboard and instruments missing, only example known to exist.
£3,000–4,000 BKS

1925 Morris Cowley 11.9hp Bullnose Two-Seater with
Dickey, Hotchkiss engine, generally sound and original.
£5,750–6,750 BKS

1959 Morris Minor 1000 Traveller, complete, running order.
£500–750 CGC

◄ 1931 Riley 14/6 Deauville Four-Door Saloon,
1633cc, 6 cylinder engine, 50bhp, complete, engine and
transmission reconditioned, body stripped for rebuild,
one of only three Deauvilles known to exist.
£4,000–5,000 BKS

The Deauville saloon was the creation of
coachbuilders Hancock & Warman. It was an elegant,
metal-panelled car with comfortable seating for five,
priced in 1929 at £525.

Microcars

1962 BMW Isetta 250, 247cc, left-hand drive, older
restoration, finished in pale blue with brown/grey interior,
roof in need of recovering, otherwise good condition in
most respects.
£5,000–6,500 BKS

BMW acquired the rights to the Isetta from the Italian
Iso company in the early 1950s. Fitted with the 247cc,
single-cylinder engine from the BMW R25 motorcycle,
it was good for around 55mph and returned 55mpg.
Three- and four-wheel versions were built, both with
a side-hinged single front door, which carried the
jointed steering column, and a roll-top sunroof. Later
models were of 297cc and capable of 65mph. Over
161,000 Isettas were built between 1955 and 1962.

1965 Peel Trident, restored, museum stored for some
years, in need of recommissioning.
£5,500–7,000 BKS

Peel Engineering, built microcars in the 1950s and
1960s, one of which was almost certainly the world's
smallest car – the P50. Launched in 1962, it could be
fitted inside a box measuring 5ft x 3ft 6in x 4ft. The
single-cylinder power unit was a 49cc, DKW fan-
cooled two-stroke, which produced enough power to
propel the single-seater to 30mph. The same engine
was used in the two-seat Trident, although some had
100cc Vespa motors. The Trident had a hinged
canopy topped by a Perspex bubble, and consumed
fuel at almost 100mpg. In all, about 50 were built.

◄ 1964 Trojan 200, left-hand drive, restored, finished in
maroon with plaid and grey interior, good condition in
most respects.
£1,750–2,250 BKS

Trojan had manufactured unconventional light cars in
the 1920s and 1930s, and the acquisition of the rights
to the Heinkel bubblecar in 1961 marked the
company's return to motor manufacture after a break
of 25 years. While closely resembling the Isetta, the
Trojan 200 was both lighter and roomier, even having
children's seats in the rear. Around 7,000 were built
before the firm quit car production again in 1965.

Racing & Rallying

For the owners of classic and historic motor cars, there is a growing number of events to keep their vehicles exercised. These cater for all types of motor car and owner, from the highly competitive race meeting to the gentle wine run. In particular, the opportunities for historic racing are varied, ranging from piloting an Austin 7 up Prescott Hill during a VSCC event to campaigning a Ferrari 512M in Jonathan Baker's Group 4 Championship, or from meandering from London to Brighton in a De Dion to storming the hillclimbs and racing circuits of France in a GT40 during the Tour de France. Virtually every field of motorsport is catered for, and a multi-million-pound bank account is not a prerequisite; all you really need is enthusiasm.

Today, competition-themed auctions occur on a regular basis, the most well-known being the Coys International Historic Festival at Silverstone,

Brooks' sale at the Goodwood Festival of Speed and Christie's at Pebble Beach. Historic racing is big business, and not only with the drivers, dealers, collectors, restorers and tuners – the public's imagination is captured by these wonderful old machines, which hark back to an age when cars had their own distinctive appearance and their drivers were the great heroes of their day. Prestigious events include the Mille Miglia Retrospective, Coys International Historic Festival, Goodwood Revival, Tour de France, Carrera Panamericana and Monterey Historics. As a result of these events, interest is growing. Recent sales have seen some very important cars come under the hammer. All are eligible for a large number of events, and they will prove very competitive in the right hands.

Tim Schofield

1930 MG M-Type Midget, 847cc, overhead-camshaft, 4 cylinder engine, metal body, converted for racing in the 1930s, long-distance fuel tank, spare wheel, cutaway door, finished in red with tan interior, FIA papers.
£6,000–7,500 BKS

◄ **1936/1997 Riley 2½ Litre Competition Special,** assembled in 1997 from pre-war Riley components, 2443cc, mildly-tuned Big Four engine, twin SU carburettors, 4-branch exhaust manifold, accurate replica Riley Sprite chassis, rebuilt Merlin axle, raked steering column, finished in dark blue.
£20,000–22,000 COYS

In 1934, 1½ Litre Rileys were second and third at Le Mans, and among countless other successes were three wins in the Tourist Trophy. Ever since their heyday, Rileys have remained popular as the basis for one-off sports and racing cars.

1958 Vanwall VW10 Formula 1 Single-Seater, ex-Stirling Moss, 2.5 litre, fuel-injected, 4 cylinder Vanwall racing engine, up to 285bhp at 7,300rpm, disc brakes, lightweight space-frame, NACA-style flush air intakes, sunken exhaust, well maintained.
£800,000+ BKS

Of the nine 'teardrop'-bodied Vanwall F1 cars built and raced by the Vandervell Products team in 1956–58, this car is the only example to have been preserved by its original manufacturer as an unmodified, assembled, running entity throughout most of the intervening years. It is also the actual chassis with which Stirling Moss won the 1958 Dutch and Portuguese Grands Prix, finished 2nd in the French Grand Prix, and set fastest lap at the Nürburgring during that season's tumultuous German Grand Prix.

▶ **1939 Lancia/British Salmson Competition Special,** British Salmson S4C engine, Lancia Augusta chassis, unused for years, partly dismantled, including a 2.3 litre British Salmson 6 cylinder engine and Cotal gearbox.
£1,000–1,500 BKS

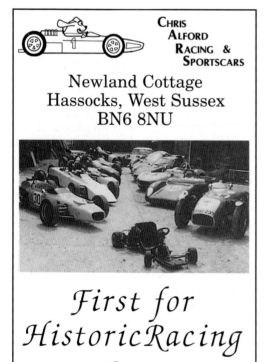

1951 Cooper-Jap 500 F3 Mk IV, restored, finished in British Racing green, excellent condition throughout.
£9,000–11,000 Car

1968 Russell Alexis Ford Mk XIV Formula Ford, 1600cc, later Alexis Mk XV body, very original example of an early Formula Ford.
£14,000–16,000 Car

1970 Tyrrell-Cosworth 001 Formula 1 Single-Seater, ex-Jackie Stewart/Peter Revson, fitted with dummy Cosworth DFV V8 engine, restored, very good condition.
£150,000–180,000 BKS

This 3 litre F1 car is the prototype machine that launched the new Tyrrell marque in 1970. It was designed by Derek Gardner for reigning World Champion Jackie Stewart, and was produced in such secrecy that when Stewart visited Gardner's home for an initial cockpit fitting, even the designer's young daughter – who was a great Stewart fan – was unaware of his visit. Manufacture of the monocoque was subcontracted to Gomm Metal Developments, whose proprietor, Mo Gomm, swore each of his employees to secrecy on the family Bible!

◀ **1988 Lotus 100T Formula 1 Single-Seater,** ex-Nelson Piquet, turbocharged, Honda 1.5 litre V6 engine, 6-speed gearbox, double-wishbone suspension, carbon-composites monocoque and separate body, triple-deck rear aerofoil, fitted with internally-complete exhibition engine, excellent condition throughout.
£40,000–45,000 COYS

1944 Alfa Romeo 2500S 'Bucci' Two-Seater Sports, bodywork constructed in Argentina by Nestor Salerno, restored, engine rebuilt at a cost of £25,000, brakes, steering and front suspension rebuilt, finished in red with matching interior, excellent condition throughout, FIA papers.
£90,000–110,000 BKS

1978 Lola T492 Sports 2000, 2000cc, twin carburettors, 5-speed gearbox, suitable for historic endurance races.
£16,500–18,500 Car

1960 Austin-Healey Sebring Sprite, 1000cc engine, close-ratio gearbox, limited-slip differential, adjustable rear shock absorbers, full mechanical restoration, new body to original specification, roll cage, very good condition, FIA papers, ready to race.
£20,000–24,000 BKS

At the start of the 1961 season, Cyril Simson made this car available to the Castrol-backed works team for the Sebring four-hour, small-capacity GT race, in which it was driven by Pat Moss and Paul Hawkins in support of Stirling Moss in John Sprinzel's similar car. Then it was taken over by Simson and Hawkins for the major Sebring 12-hour race that followed.

Dealer Prices

Miller's guide prices for dealer cars take into account the value of any guarantees or warranties that may be included in the purchase. Dealers must also observe additional statutory consumer regulations, which do not apply to private sellers. This is factored into our dealer guide prices. To identify dealer cars cross-refer the source codes at the ends of photo captions with the Key to Illustrations on page 330.

1956 Lotus Eleven Le Mans, ex-Team Lotus, Coventry-Climax 1500cc engine, de Dion rear axle, 4-wheel disc brakes, lightweight aluminium bodywork, completely restored using all original parts.
£45,000–55,000 HLR

1968 Chevron B8 BMW, rebuilt, race-ready.
£57,500–65,000 Car

1961 Alfa Romeo Giulietta Sprint Zagato Coupé, 1.3 litre, double-overhead-camshaft, 4 cylinder engine, 116bhp, lightweight aluminium coachwork, 125mph top speed, engine rebuilt, bare-metal respray in white and red.
£22,000–25,000 BKS

Alfa Romeo's successful Giulietta range debuted in 1954 with the arrival of the Bertone-styled Sprint coupé, the Berlina saloon appearing in the following year. Veloce models with improved performance followed, and the agile Giulietta SV quickly established an enviable record in production car racing. Nevertheless, to fully exploit the car's potential, lighter, more aerodynamic bodywork was deemed necessary. This resulted in the ultimate Giuliettas: Bertone's Sprint Speciale and the Sprint Zagato, both on the short-wheelbase Spider platform.

1991 Ferrari F40 LM, coachwork by Pininfarina, 3 litre, double-overhead-camshaft V8, 4 valves per cylinder, twin IHI turbochargers, converted to unleaded fuel, tubular-steel chassis, one-piece composite body, carbon fibre doors, bonnet and bootlid, Plexiglass windows, 600km from new, never raced, 'as-new' condition throughout.
£275,000+ BKS

Developed for competition by Michelotto of Padova, on behalf of Ferrari, the LM had a reinforced chassis, deep front air dam, stiffer suspension, and uprated brakes. Only 17 F40 LMs were built.

Military Vehicles

c1940 Austin K2 Ambulance, 3462cc, 6 cylinders, 63bhp, 4-speed gearbox, 2-wheel drive, accommodation for 4 stretchers or 10 sitting wounded, restored.
£4,000–6,200 MVT

c1940 GMC AFKX 352 1½–3 Ton 4x4, 4064cc, 6 cylinders, 88bhp, 4-speed gearbox, 2-speed transfer box, hydraulic brakes, leaf-spring suspension.
£4,000–5,000 MVT

c1940 Morris Quad 4x4 Artillery Tractor, 3519cc, 4 cylinder, side-valve petrol engine, 5-speed gearbox, single-speed transfer box, rigid axles, leaf-spring suspension, winch, good unrestored condition.
£3,000–3,500 WITH

1941 Dodge WC6 ½ Ton Command Car, 3572cc, 6 cylinders, 85bhp, 4-wheel drive, 4-speed gearbox, single-speed transfer box.
£8,000–10,000 MVT

c1941 White Half-Track M16, 6325cc, 6 cylinders, originally multiple gun carrier, in need of complete restoration.
£3,000–3,500 RRM

▶ **1942 Ford GPW Jeep,** 4 cylinder, side-valve engine, 3-speed synchromesh gearbox, 2- or 4-wheel drive, left-hand drive, hand-operated windscreen wipers, machine-gun swivel post, good condition throughout.
£5,000–6,000 S

A known continuous history can add value to and enhance the enjoyment of a car.

1942 Ford GPW Jeep with Trailer, completely restored, very good condition throughout.
£6,000–7,000 NTMV

1942 GM Otter Light Reconnaissance Armoured Car, 2- or 4-wheel drive, 4-speed gearbox, single-speed transfer box, fitted with deactivated Boys anti-tank rifle and Bren gun.
£8,000–10,000 EAFG

c1943 Bedford OXC Truck 30cwt 4x2 Tractor, 3519cc, 6 cylinders, 72bhp, 4-speed gearbox, hydraulic brakes with vacuum servo for mechanical trailer brake, modified by Scammel with couplings for 6 ton semi-trailer, good condition throughout.
£3,000–3,750 MVT

c1943 GMC CCKW 353 LWB Truck, 4416cc, 6 cylinders, 5-speed gearbox, 2-speed transfer box, restored, good condition throughout.
£3,500–4,000 RRM

c1943 Canadian Chevrolet 15cwt 4x4, 3540cc, 6 cylinder, petrol engine, 85bhp, 2- or 4-wheel drive, 4-speed gearbox, single-speed transfer box, good condition throughout.
£3,500–4,500 MVT

The 15cwt GMP chassis was made by both Chevrolet and Ford, the latter fitting a 3917cc, side-valve V8 developing 95bhp. Various bodies were fitted, including Van, Office, Wireless, Cable Layer, Personnel and Water Tanker.

c1944 Ford Carrier Windsor, 3917cc, side-valve V8, 95bhp, centre-mounted 4-speed gearbox, Helicab spring suspension.
£6,000–7,500 MVT

c1944 MIA/Ward La France 10 Ton Wrecker, 8.2 litre engine, 130bhp, 5-speed gearbox, 2-speed transfer box, ladder chassis, Garwood wrecking gear, good condition.
£6,000–7,000 MVT

c1945 Bedford QLW Air Portable Tipper, 3519cc, 6 cylinder petrol engine, 72bhp, all-wheel drive, 4-speed gearbox, 2-speed transfer box, 5-ton winch,.
£3,000–4,000 MVT

Some 52,250 QL trucks were built, being fitted with a variety of bodies, including QLR Radio, QLB Bofors Gun Tractor, QLT Troop Carrier (longer body) and QLD GS Cargo. They were used by all branches of the armed services.

c1955 Scammel Constructor 20 ton 6x6 GS FV12101, 10.4 litre, 6 cylinder Meadows engine, 175bhp, 6-speed gearbox, 2-speed transfer box, 15 ton winch, very good condition.
£2,500–3,250 MVT

1958 Ferret Mk I, 4258cc, 6 cylinders, 5-speed pre-selector gearbox, forward/reverse transfer box, in need of restoration.
£3,500–4,500 RRM

Cross Reference
See Colour Review

◄ c1958 Skoda/Tatra 810 Half-Track, 11.8 litre, air-cooled V8 engine, 120bhp, 4-speed gearbox, 2-speed transfer box, leaf-spring suspension, bogies on torsion bars, German markings, good condition throughout.
£4,000–5,000 MVT

This armoured personnel carrier is a Czechoslovakian version of the WWII German Sd.Kfz 251

Tractors & Traction Engines

Many may think that the vintage and classic tractor movement is the preserve of farmers and those from the agricultural industry, but that is not the case, for tractor enthusiasts come from all walks of life. Unlike collectors' cars, tractors have not been subject to a 'boom and bust' period; prices having remained steady and appreciated gradually. Some makes, however – such as the Ferguson-Brown, Field Marshall and Turner – have seen a rapid increase in demand, principally because they are British and also because, in some way, they represent stages in the development of the tractor.

For those interested in starting a collection, a 1950s Ferguson TE20 (known as the 'Little Grey Fergie') can be bought at auction for between £400 and £1,000. An Allis Chalmers Model B can also be purchased for between £350 and £700, depending on condition. For the more serious collector, Field Marshall Series I, II and III tractors will make between £3,000 and £8,000. The importance of condition, however, should not be overestimated; many collectors are as happy to have an ex-farm tractor as a Class 1 restoration. In contrast to cars, tractors are low-maintenance vehicles and often are easier to restore.

The provenance of a tractor can increase its value; special editions also achieve a premium.

In recent years, some very rare tractors have come on to the market, among them a 1913 Saunderson & Mills Model G, which made £31,500, and a 1925 Nichols Shepard Red River Line Special, which made £36,000.

Overall, interest in vintage and classic tractors is growing rapidly, especially the latter, which increasingly are being purchased not only for collection and restoration, but also for ploughing matches and rallies. Of course, buying a tractor for these purposes will lead to the acquisition of all the implements and machinery of that particular make. Most makes are supported by clubs, and now specialist magazines, further opening up the market place.

On a much grander scale, traction engines are humbling to stand by and were impressive feats of engineering for their time. In April 1999, the Russell collection of traction engines was offered and confirmed the continued demand for these incredible machines. Top price was for the famous 1925 Wm Allchin 7nhp General-Purpose engine, which made £37,250. Few traction engines survive, and they must be considered an investment, but they can be expensive to maintain without help or advice.

William King

1939 Allis-Chalmers Model C, completely restored, excellent condition throughout.
£1,300–1,700 CGC

Farmall Model F12, petrol/paraffin engine, in need of complete restoration.
£550–650 CGC

1948 Case Model DC4, 4 cylinder, petrol/tvo engine, Case magneto, Eagle hitch, older restoration, running, good condition throughout.
£1,250–1,400 CGC

1953 Ferguson Model TED20, petrol/tvo engine, new vertical exhaust and manifold elbow, water pump, clutch and first gear selector, good condition.
£600–700 CGC

1952 Field Marshall Series III Contractor's Tractor,
Brougham winch, on same farm from new, in good
ex-farm condition.
£6,800–7,500 CGC

1964 Fordson Super Dexta, 3 cylinder diesel engine,
restored, very good condition.
£1,000–1,200 CGC

1959 Hatz Model TL16, single-cylinder, air-cooled diesel
engine, restored, good condition throughout.
£1,300–1,700 CGC

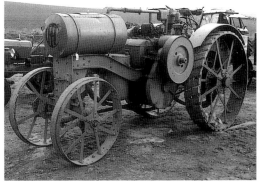

International Titan Model 10–20, KW Model T magneto,
2 belt pulleys, steel treads.
£5,500–7,000 CGC

1941 John Deere Model BW, twin-cylinder engine, electric
start, pto and pulley wheel, in need of restoration.
£2,000–2,500 CGC

1920 Nichols & Shepard Model 20–35, gas/petrol
engine, in need of complete restoration.
£3,000–3,500 CGC

1914 Aveling & Porter Class BS 10 Ton Road Roller, single-cylinder motion rated at 5nhp, no boiler certificate, new welded firebox, original canopy, in need of restoration. **£5,750–7,000 CGC**

1914 Foden 5 Ton Steam Wagon, 2-speed, 14ft platform body with sides and hinged tail boards, cab rebuilt, boiler and firebox in good condition, insured for original full working pressure of 200psi, good condition throughout. **£28,000–32,000 S**

Dealer Prices

Miller's guide prices for dealer vehicles take into account the value of any guarantees or warranties that may be included in the purchase. Dealers must also observe additional statutory consumer regulations, which do not apply to private sellers. This is factored into our dealer guide prices. To identify dealer vehicles cross-refer the source codes at the ends of photo captions with the Key to Illustrations on page 330.

◄ **1886 Marshall Convertible Traction Engine,** single-cylinder motion rated at 6nhp, hydraulic tested at 200psi, second oldest Marshall traction engine in preservation. **£29,000–34,000 CGC**

Horse-Drawn Vehicles

c1900 Governess Cart, in need of restoration. **£400–600 A&H**

Ralli Car, by W. Warham of Middlesborough, to fit 11–12hh pony, 40in English-pattern wheels and triple spring, tightly-curled splash boards, finished in red and green with contrasting linings, brown leather upholstery, adjustable seating, in need of refurbishment. **£750–900 TSh**

It is thought that this Ralli Car once belonged to the late Dr Sparrow, the well-known hunting artist.

19thC Double Brougham, to fit 15hh upwards, single or pair, shafts and pole, iron-bound wheels, full elliptic springs, handbrake, finished in black with red lining, interior lined in varnished wood, original buttoned leather seating, doors decorated with coats of arms and mounted with ivory inside. **£2,750–3,500 TSh**

1880 Hearse, pole, plume and horse covers, restored. **£11,000–12,000 CALD**

Cyclecars

c1920 **Briggs & Stratton Model D Buckboard,** restored, museum stored for some time, in need of recommissioning.
£3,000–4,000 BKS

In 1919, the Briggs & Stratton Company, of Milwaukee, acquired the rights to the Smith Flyer buckboard and Smith Motor Wheel. The latter was a self-contained power unit for motorising bicycles. The American Motor Vehicle Company was first to attach one of Smith's powered wheels to a buckboard, calling the resulting five-wheeler the Red Bug. The rights to this were soon acquired by Smith, and production of the renamed Smith Flyer began in 1916. Briggs & Stratton doubled the power output to 2hp and fitted improved flywheel-magneto ignition to their Model D buckboard, production of which continued until the rights were sold, again, in 1924.

c1920 **Way Cyclecar,** front-mounted, single-cylinder, 2-stroke Beardmore-Precision engine, Moss motorcycle-type gearbox without reverse, countershaft and belt drive to rear wheels, solid tyres, wire-spoked wheels, in need of restoration.
£1,500–2,000 BKS

This cyclecar is thought to be the only example of its type in existence, and possibly the prototype for a model that never entered production. It was intended to take a two-seat, tandem-type body, but this appears never to have been fitted. The Beardmore-Precision engine is the only one of its type made by the Birmingham-based company in the immediate post-WWI period.

> **Miller's is a price GUIDE not a price LIST**

Invalid Cars

◄ 1920 **Stanley Invalid Carriage,** 125cc Villiers engine, hand and power-operated, in need of complete restoration.
£1,200–1,400 CGC

> ## Auction Prices
>
> Miller's only includes cars declared sold. Our guide prices take into account the buyer's premium, VAT on the premium, and the extent of any published catalogue information relating to condition and provenance. To identify cars sold at auction, cross-refer the source codes at the ends of photo captions with the Key to Illustrations on page 330.

Tricycles

1905 **Rekette Tricycle,** 8hp, restored, finished in dark green with black leather upholstery, tandem seating arrangement, one of two known to exist, very good condition throughout.
£16,000–18,000 AT

1910 **AC Sociable Tricycle,** air-cooled, single-cylinder engine, 2-speed epicyclic gear, chain drive, sloping dash, tiller steering, front wheel brakes, original seasoned ash and birch frame, repanelled 1994, finished in green with matching seats, new vinyl hood, not running.
£6,000–7,000 S

Automobile Art

Nicholas Watts, Spirit of Le Mans, depicting Luigi Chinetti in an Alfa 8C 2300, limited-edition print, signed by Chinetti.
£120–130 BKS

Jose Maria Jorge, 1957 Mille Miglia, the Ferrari 335S of Alfonso de Portago and Ed Nelson, oil on canvas, signed by artist, mounted and framed, 34½ x 31in (87.5 x 79cm).
£1,700–2,000 BKS

◀ Tony Upson, mural depicting a 1939 Mercedes-Benz W154 with factory logo, acrylic on board, framed 48 x 96in (122 x 244cm).
£400–500 BKS

Tony Upson, mural of an Auto Union, acrylic on board, framed 48 x 96 (122 x 244cm).
£400–500 BKS

Bob Murray, Old Number 1 wins the 1930 Le Mans, depicting Wolf Banarto driving a Speed Six Bentley and leading Caracciola in his Mercedes at the Mulsanne corner, mixed media painting, framed and glazed, 24¾ x 28¾in (63 x 73cm).
£400–500 BKS

After Roy Nockolds, a limited-edition black and white lithograph depicting Richard Seaman in a Mercedes at the 1938 German Grand Prix, 26 x 36in (66 x 91.5cm).
£100–120 BKS

Michael Wright, 1932 Targa Florio, depicting Amedeo Ruggeri in his Maserati 8C 2800 passing the grandstands ahead of a Bugatti, mixed media, signed, mounted, framed and glazed, 8 x 11½in (20.5 x 29cm).
£350–400 S

◀ Tony Upson, mural of a 1926 Bugatti Type 35B, acrylic on board, 48 x 96in (122 x 244cm).
£800–850 BKS

Nicholas Watts, Ferrari – The First Grand Prix Victory, depicting José Gonzalez in the Ferrari 375/F1 leading Juan Fangio in the Alfa Romeo and followed by Gigi Villoresi in another Ferrari at the 1951 British Grand Prix, Silverstone, limited-edition print, signed by José Gonzalez and Gigi Villoresi.
£120–130 MPG

Tony Upson, a large mural depicting the side view of a driver at the wheel of a Ferrari during the 1948 Monza Gran Premio dell' Autodromo, acrylic on board, 48 x 96in (122 x 244cm).
£575–650 BKS

After Roy Nockolds, depicting Hawthorn and Collins in Ferraris and Fangio in a Maserati at the 1957 German Grand Prix, colour lithograph, 26 x 36in (66 x 91.5cm).
£100–120 BKS

Michael Wright, 1991 Grand Premio d'Italia, depicting Ayrton Senna in the Marlboro McLaren MP4/6 making the fastest lap, watercolour and gouache, signed and titled, mounted, framed and glazed, 23¼ x 20in (59 x 51cm).
£750–800 S

Nicholas Watts, Monaco Grand Prix Europe, May 22 1955, depicting the eventual-winner Trintignant in the Ferrari 625 climbing the hill by Beau Rivage and being hotly pursued by Villoresi in the Lancia D50, mixed media painting, signed by the artist and boldly autographed by Maurice Trintignant, framed and glazed, 29½ x 42¾ in (75 x 109cm).
£3,000–3,500 BKS

> **Cross Reference**
> See Colour Review

Automobilia

A bronze sculpture depicting a Ferrari 250 GTO, by Italian artist Lorenzo Vandi, well detailed, 15¾in (40cm) long.
£1,500–1,800 BKS

◀ A ceramic Les Leston ashtray, in the form of a racing steering wheel, produced by Beswick Co, 1960s.
£35–45 CARS

A bronze sculpture depicting Phil Hill driving a Ferrari 250 TR at Sebring in 1958, 24in (61cm) long.
£900–1,100 BKS

A cold-cast bronze sculpture, depicting Stirling Moss driving a Jaguar XK120, limited edition of 200, 1998, 28in (71cm) long.
£200–250 LF

A hollow-cast bronze sculpture, depicting a racing car with driver and mechanic, mounted on a serpentine-style marble base, 13in (33cm) long.
£1,700–1,900 BKS

A Dunhill chauffeur's uniform, comprising a khaki double-breasted cloth jacket with light blue collar, removable buttons, adjustable sleeves and 2 external pockets, button-at-knee breeches, cotton-lined double-breasted top coat with light blue collar, peaked cap with light blue band, RAC chauffeur's badge with Dunhill motif, c1914.
£2,000–2,300 BKS

A Harrods fur muffler, in original box, 1930/40s.
£45–55 LF

▶ An Austin Seven and Big Seven sales brochure, late 1930s, 10x8in (25.5x20cm).
£45–50 LF

A French plate, inscribed 'Voyages Comique', one of a series depicting motoring scenes, 8in (20cm) diam.
£40–45 PC

A set of six Champion Spark Plugs tin plates, depicting famous racing drivers and cars, with facsimile autographs, each plate 8in (20cm) diam., good condition.
£300–350 LE

Two Energol BP lampshades, in original crate, unused.
£450–500 GAZE

◄ A Rolls-Royce cigarette case, with integral lighter.
£65–75 CGC

A Mobiloil oil can, 1930s, 21in (53.5cm) high.
£40–50 JUN

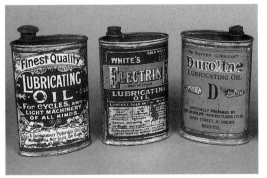

Four illustrated oil tins, Duroline, Electrine Lubricating Oil, Bosphorus Burning Oil, early 1900s, 4½in (11.5cm) high.
£45–55 CGC

◄ A Shell 1pt oil can, 1930s, good condition.
£50–60 GAZE

BADGES

Two badges and a medallion, presented by the Automobile Club of Great Britain and Ireland, 1903, comprising a Gordon Bennett Steward's lapel badge in green and white enamel with matching cord, a green enamel lapel badge for Mecredy-Percy Camp Ardscull tied with blue ribbon, and an AC medal, engraved 'A.C. Wright, 2nd Prize, Class A, Clough-Castlewellan July 7th 1903' in original presentation case.
£500–600 S

A cast bronze prototype Automobile Club of Great Britain & Ireland 'Royal' badge, by Sydney March, signed and dated 1907, with St. Christopher on obverse and profile of HM King Edward on reverse, 4¼in (11cm) wide.
£1,700–1,900 S

> **Miller's is a price GUIDE not a price LIST**

An RAC Life Member's badge, hollow-cast motor wheel supported by a double-wing style Mercury, rectangular Union flag and profile of the King, slight wear, some dents to wheel, numbered A30, c1908, 8in (20cm) high.
£600–650 BKS

COMPONENTS

A Marelli magneto, 1920s, 7in (18cm) high.
£250–300 BRIT

A pair of Lucas G51 electric projectors, correct rear bayonet fittings, side-mounted stirrup fittings and correct concave front glasses in front of silvered reflectors, c1922, unused, front rims 8in (20cm) diam.
£760–820 BKS

Two Bosch electric horns, 1930s, largest 8in (20cm) long.
£120–140 each BRIT

A pair of Scintilla rear lights, 1930s, unused, 5in (12.5cm) wide.
£750–850 BRIT

MASCOTS

A Voisin nickel crouching Icarus, signed 'Ch. Paillet AEL', with Courieult book *Automobiles Voisin*, which traces the history of the mascot.
£875–950 BKS

A nickel L'Oeuf d'Elephant mascot, gilded finish, mounted on a turned wooden base, originally fitted to a Bugatti, 5in (12.5cm) high.
£1,700–1,900 S

A Lalique Coq Nain glass mascot, acid etched 'R Lalique France' on base, 8¼in (20.5cm) high.
£900–1,000 S

A Lalique Tête de Coq clear glass mascot, moulded 'Lalique France', 7¼in (18cm) high.
£1,000–1,200 S

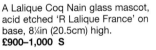

A chrome-plated Dolphin Girl mascot, mounted on a turned wooden base, 1930s.
£560–630 BKS

◄ An Art Deco Cartier fox mascot, worn finish, 9in (23cm) long.
£250–375 DRJ

Auction Prices

Miller's only includes items declared sold. Our guide prices take into account the buyer's premium, VAT on the premium, and the extent of any published catalogue information relating to condition and provenance. To identify items sold at auction, cross-refer the source codes at the ends of photo captions with the Key to Illustrations on page 330.

◄ A British silver-plated eagle, on a turned wooden base, 8in (20cm) high.
£650–700 ChA

A French nickel-plated bronze The Kid mascot, by Jean Verschneider, 6¼in (15.5cm) high.
£1,150–1,400 S

A French Pathfinder mascot, by G. Poitvin, c1920, 7in (18cm) high.
£500–600 ChA

A Pinocchio glass mascot, by Walt Disney Productions, with original painted highlights, 1940/50s.
£425–475 S

This mascot was based on the character played by Jackie Coogan in the film *The Kid*.

MODELS

Models of two cars driven by Juan-Manuel Fangio, the Mercedes W196 that won the 1954 French Grand Prix, and the Maserati 250F that won in Argentina in 1957, plus miniature figure of Fangio, exact representations of the real cars, detailed painted finish.
£350–400 BKS

1957 Dinky Toys catalogue, excellent condition, 5x6in (12.5x15cm).
£30–40 GAZE

A Matchbox No. 29 milk float, 1956, 2in (5cm) long.
£15–20 GAZE

A Schuco clockwork Grand Prix Racer, yellow, 7in (18cm) long.
£90–110 CGC

> A known continuous history can add value to and enhance the enjoyment of a car.

◄ 1996 Anson metal die-cast model of a Porsche 911 Carrera 4 Cabriolet, movable parts, 1:14 scale, mounted on a wooden base, 12in (30.5cm) long, with original box.
£50–60 PC

An Alfa Romeo P2 tinplate clockwork toy, by Compagnie Industrielle de Jouets, finished in red with brown seats, some wear to paintwork, c1929, 21in (53cm) long.
£1,800–2,000 S

A 1:4 scale model of Nigel Mansell's 1992 Williams FW14B, finely detailed, mounted on a base board fitted with Perspex cover, one of three commissioned by Williams Grand Prix Engineering, certificate of authenticity signed by Adrian Newey, 43¼in (110cm) long.
£7,000–8,000 S

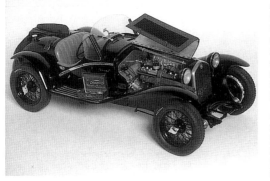

A scratch-built 1:12 scale model of the 1970 Ferrari 312PB, by Michel Conti, full front and rear light fittings, windscreen and headlight covers, cast alloy-style wheels, solid slick racing tyres, detailed engine bay, highly detailed cockpit with full instrumentation, pedal assembly, handbrake, gear lever, faux leather Ferrari steering wheel, racing seat and full race harness, mounted on a polished wooden stand.
£9,000–10,000 BKS

◄ A 1:8 scale model of an Alfa Romeo 8C 2300 Spider Corsa, by M. Jelesvic, leather upholstery and trim, instrumentation, engine detailing, wire spoke wheels, shock absorbers, detachable spare wheel, finished in black with nickel-plated brightwork, 19in (48.5cm) long.
£6,000–7,000 C

PETROL PUMPS

An Anglo American Oil Co (Angloco) hand-cranked combination petrol delivery pump, mounted on original support board, in need of restoration, 48in (122cm) high.
£180–220 BKS

A Hammond hand-cranked, double-glass-cylinder, wall-mounted petrol delivery pump, two 1 gallon glass delivery tubes, body painted green with Hammond delivery clock, complete with rubber hose.
£125–150 BKS

A Bowser hand-cranked, freestanding, skeleton petrol pump, complete with rubber hose, bronze gun, upper sight feed and delivery chamber, painted orange, numbered H6907, 1920s, 68in (173cm) high.
£120–150 BKS

A Bowser T45 hand-cranked petrol pump, 1930s, 84⅛in (215cm) high.
£400–500 CRC

An Avery Hardoll petrol pump, restored in Shell livery, complete with hose, nozzle and glass Shellmax globe, wired for illumination, 1930s, 94½in (240cm) high.
£1,000–1,150 S

A Shell petrol pump, 1930s, 85in (216cm) high.
£400–450 PC

A Shell upper-cylinder lubricant dispenser, 1930s, 19in (48cm) high.
£145–185 JUN

An Avery Hardoll AH 288 petrol pump, electric clock face, restored, painted in green, good condition, 84in (213.5cm) high.
£700–800 TPS

A Power petrol pump, 1960s, 86in (218.5cm) high.
£325–375 PC

A Gulf 2-stroke service petrol pump, c1970s, 73in (185.5cm) high.
£250–300 PC

GLOBES

A shield-shaped BP petrol pump globe, good yellow and green colour, no chips or cracks.
£140–160 BKS

> **Cross Reference**
> See Colour Review

A Cleveland No.1 glass petrol pump globe, 1930s.
£350–400 MSMP

A Cleveland Discol petrol pump globe, 1960s, 26in (66cm) wide.
£30–35 MSMP

An Esso Autodiesel pump globe.
£110–130 GAZE

PICNIC SETS, VANITY CASES & TRAVEL GOODS

A W. Thornhill two-person sterling silver tea set, kettle, burner and case, tea infuser, sugar container housed in teapot, 3 silver-topped cut-glass bottles, 2 teaspoons, original bone china cups with gilt edges, matching saucers, housed in a compact black leather case with original pigskin leather dividers and cover, hallmarked, excellent condition.
£10,000–11,000 BKS

A Drew & Sons two-person footrest picnic set, contained within a padded, woven decorated cloth step board, wooden compartments containing fine china gilt-rimmed cups and saucers, sandwich box, leather-covered Thermos flask, drinks bottle, two Drew metal beakers, teaspoons and knife held inside lid, 1902.
£600–900 BKS

A Derry & Toms four-person picnic set, saucepan and burner, cups, saucers, milk bottles, plates, wicker-covered drinks flask, leather-covered Thermos flask, ceramic preserves jar with leather strap, 2 condiment bottles, contained within a black leather case, leather carrying handle, c1910.
£400–600 BKS

Miller's is a price GUIDE not a price LIST

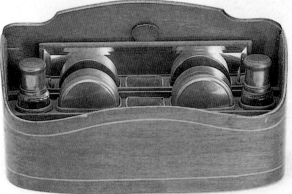

A large interior vanity set, comprising glass bottles, powder box and vanity mirror in a wooden box, 1920s.
£250–300 BKS

A Louis Vuitton wardrobe trunk, internally fitted hangers, drawers, cases, original support struts, good condition, c1920, 44in (112cm) high.
£8,000–9,000 BKS

A Louis Vuitton Malle Courier cabin trunk, leather edges, brass corners, brass handle and catches, wooden struts, original lining and drawers intact, original lid lining intact, excellent condition, c1925.
£4,000–5,000 BKS

A Brexton Willow four-person picnic hamper, 1950s, 21 x 14 x 9in (53.5 x 35 x 22.5cm).
£100–120 PPH

ENAMEL SIGNS

A Goodyear enamel sign, 1920s, 45 x 30in (114.5x76cm).
£150–200 JUN

A Maserati Automobili Servizio enamel sign, in red, white and blue on yellow ground, some minor chips and rusting, 37¾ x24¾ in (96 x 63cm).
£2,500–3,000 S

An Austin Mobiloil tin sign, poor condition, early 1920s, 27 x 19in (68.5 x 48cm).
£175–195 JUN

A Mobiloil shaped tin sign, 24 x 21in (61 x 53cm).
£25–35 BKS

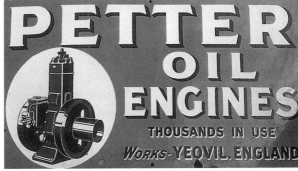

A Petter Oil Engines single-sided enamel sign, good condition, c1940, 20 x 40in (51 x 102cm).
£220–250 MSMP

A Shell Lubricating Oils double-sided enamel sign, 1915–20, 20x22in (51x56cm).
£800–900 BRUM

A Shell Ascent of Peak Hill enamel sign, 1920s, 30in (76cm) square.
£350–400 JUN

A Shell enamel sign, 1925–30, 33x20in (84x51cm).
£1,300–1,450 BRUM

CLOCKS & WATCHES

A Rolls-Royce Cushion Clock, polished case, quartz movement, Spirit of Ecstacy motif beneath dial, original box, 3¼in (8cm) high.
£35–40 LF

▶ An Esso Extra Oil combination advertising sign and mechanical clock, with front glass and hanging chains.
£200–250 BKS

A Jaeger 8-day clock, 4in (10cm) diam.
£70–80 DRJ

BOOKS

Fangio, edited by Denis Jenkinson and based on the film *Fangio* by Hugh Hudson and Giovanni Volpe, signed by Fangio, 1973.
£70–90 GPCC

◄ David Hayhoe, *Grand Prix Data Book – Formula 1 Racing Facts and Figures 1950 to Date*, signed by over 100 F1 personalities, including 11 world champions, 1989.
£500–600 GPCC

Hispano-Suiza 12 cylinder, limited edition of 500, numbered, with original box, 1934.
£350–400 GIRA

Geo Ham, *Oy et Voitures du Grand Prix*, dedicated to Michael Dore, 1924.
£550–600 GIRA

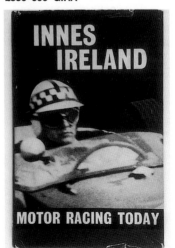

◄ Innes Ireland, *Motor Racing Today*, signed by Innes Ireland, Lofty England and Sir Jack Brabham, first edition, 1961.
£90–95 GPCC

Motor Racing Memorabilia

RACE SUITS & HELMETS

A Les Leston helmet worn by Jack Brabham, silver with leather peak, framed photograph of Brabham wearing same helmet.
£2,500–3,000 BKS

A Linea Sport Nomex race suit worn by Emerson Fittipaldi during his 1973.
£8,750–9,750 BKS

► A pair of racing overalls worn by Jimmy Clark at Indianapolis in 1963 when driving for Lotus-Ford, embroidered 'Jim Clark' on left breast and 'Lotus-powered by Ford' on back.
£12,000–13,000 BKS

A 1978 Bell Helmets Racewear hold-all belonging to Ronnie Peterson, containing worn Bell helmet with hinged visor, spare helmet peak, 5 pairs of unused Bell earplugs, original bottle of Bell anti-fog solution and spare visor fixing circlip.
£14,000–16,000 BKS

A Herbert Johnson helmet, believed to have been used by Mike Hawthorn in the 1950s, painted dark blue, cork and leather lined interior, webbed canvas, leather band inside helmet with handwritten inscription 'Jo-Jo, you win the bet, I take my hat off to you, all the best, Mike'.
£1,200–1,400 BKS

COMPONENTS

A Benetton B-191 front wing end-plate, used during 1991 Italian Grand Prix, made of Kevlar, wing degree angle notations written on inside, signed and inscribed 'Monza '91' by Michael Schumacher, 48in (122cm) long.
£600–700 BKS

A Ferrari World Championship shield-shaped, bevelled-edge glass panel, etched 'Campione de Mondo, M. Hawthorn Ferrari', with Scuderia Ferrari central shield, slight chipping to edges, dated '1958', complete with hanging chains, 27in (68.5cm) wide.
£330–400 S

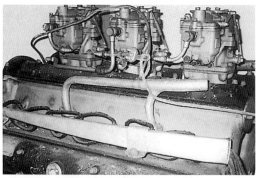

1936 Alfa Romeo 4.5 litre, 12C-36/37 and Tipo 412 V12 racing engine, ex-Scuderia Ferrari/Alfa Corse/Enrico Nardi, triple Weber 36DCRA carburettors, AC 45XL spark plugs, Magneti Marelli Tipo MVE-SL25DAS distributor mounted on each cylinder head, sports car-style starter motor, superficial corrosion to cylinder heads, stored for many years, internal state unknown.
£115,000–130,000 BKS

This important racing engine is believed to have been one of the supercharged, 4.5 litre, quad-cam V12 power units created by Alfa Romeo's experimental department for use in the Scuderia Ferrari-operated Grand Prix cars of 1936–37. Such V12s powered the Alfa Romeo 12C-36 and low-chassis 12C-37 cars, with which the quasi-works Scuderia Ferrari confronted the German Mercedes-Benz and Auto Union racing teams. It was acquired direct from Scuderia Ferrari by the late Enrico Nardi, who told his family that it was the engine that powered Nuvolari to victory in the 1936 Vanderbilt Cup race.

PHOTOGRAPHS

A photograph of double World Champion Alberto Ascari's Maserati 250F in the paddock during the 1954 British Grand Prix at Silverstone, standing immediately behind the car in racing overalls is Ascari's Argentine team-mate, Onofre Marimon.
£230–260 BKS

Restored Values

The cost of a professional restoration will have an influence on, but no direct relation to, a car's market value. A restored car can have a market value lower than the cost of its restoration.

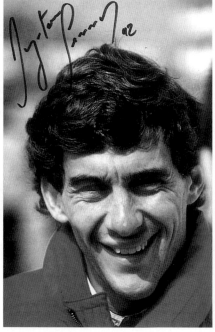

A signed photograph of Ayrton Senna, taken in 1990 during testing at Imola, mounted, framed and glazed, 15¾ x 12in (40 x 30cm).
£600–700 BKS

TROPHIES

The Sir Charles Wakefield Trophy, presented to Sir Henry Segrave for attaining the speed of 231.362mph on Daytona Beach driving *The Golden Arrow* on 11 March 1929, silver, designed by Phoebe Stablet, mounted on a marble base, 1929 London assay marks, 24in (60cm) high, original oak carrying case.
£27,000–32,000 BKS

An Aix-le-Bains Fastest Lap Trophy, presented to Stirling Moss, 3 June 1951, 12½in (32cm) high.
£1,700–2,000 BKS

A Grand Prix de Bruxelles trophy, presented to Innes Ireland, tulip-shaped bowl supported by three figures of victory, mounted on a polished slate base with presentation engraving, 1961.
£1,000–1,100 BKS

A silver-plated, two-handled Monaco Grand Prix Trophy, presented to Jochen Rindt, inscribed '1970 Coupe de SAS Le Prince Souverain, 28th Grand Prix of Monaco', Principality Crown and Arms armorial to front, original condition, mounted on a marble base, 9¾in (25cm) high.
£23,000–26,000 BKS

▶ An ERA Club car badge, c1938, very good condition, 4in (10cm) high.
£300–350 LE

A British Monte Carlo Rally Drivers Club car badge, 1950s, 4in (10cm) high.
£220–250 LE

Key to Illustrations

Each illustration and descriptive caption is accompanied by a letter code. By referring to the following list of auctioneers (denoted by *), dealers (•), clubs, museums and trusts (§), the source of any item may be immediately determined. Inclusion in this edition no way constitutes or implies a contract or binding offer on the part of any of our contributors to supply or sell the goods illustrated, or similar articles, at the prices stated. Advertisers in this year's directory are denoted by †.

If you require a valuation, it is advisable to check whether the dealer or specialist will carry out this service and if there is a charge. Please mention Miller's when making an enquiry. A valuation by telephone is not possible. Most dealers are willing to help you with your enquiry; however, they are very busy people and consideration of the above points would be welcomed.

AS • Ashted Service Station of Kenilworth, The Willows Meer End Road, Kenilworth, Warwicks CV8 1P Tel: 01676 532289

AT • Andrew Tiernan Vintage & Classic Motorcycles, Old Railway Station, Station Road, Framlingham, Nr Woodbridge, Suffolk IP13 9EE Tel: 01728 724321

AUS §† Austin A30-35 Owners Club, Barbara Scott, Membership secretary, Ardbeg Farm Cottage, Ardmory Road, Ardbeg, Bute, Scotland PA20 0PG Tel: 01872 273938

BAm § British Ambulance Society, Paul M. Tona, 5 Cormorant Drive, Hythe, Hampshire SO45 3GG. Tel: 01703 841 999

BARO *† Barons, Brooklands House, 33 New Road, Hythe, Southampton, Hampshire SO45 6BN Tel: 01703 840081

BC •† Beaulieu Garage Ltd, Beaulieu, Hampshire SO42 7YE Tel: 01590 612999

BHM • Brands Hatch Morgans Ltd, Borough Green Garage, Maidstone Road, Borough Green, Kent TN15 8HA Tel: 01732 882017

BKS *† Robert Brooks (Auctioneers), 81 Westside, London SW4 9AY Tel: 0171 228 8000

BLE •† Ivor Bleaney, PO Box 60, Salisbury, Wiltshire SP5 2DH Tel: 01794 390895

BLK • Blackhawk Collection, 1092 Eagles Nest Place, Danville, California 94506-5872, USA Tel: 925 736 3444

BRIT * British Car Auctions Ltd, Classic & Historic Automobile Division, Auction Centre, Blackbushe Airport, Blackwater, Camberley, Surrey GU17 9LG Tel: 01252 878555

BRUM • Fred Brumby Tel: 01487 842999

C * Christie, Manson & Woods Ltd, 8 King Street, St James's, London SW1Y 6QT Tel: 0171 839 9060

CALD * Phillip Caldwell, New South Wales, Australia Tel: 0411 529 414

Car • Chris Alford Racing and Sportscars, Newland Cottage, Hassocks, Sussex BN6 8NU Tel: 01273 845966

CARS •† C.A.R.S. (Classic Automobilia & Regalia Specialists), 4-4a Chapel Terrace Mews, Kemp Town, Brighton, Sussex BN2 1HU Tel: 01273 60 1960

CGC *† Cheffins Grain & Comins, 2 Clifton Road, Cambridge, Cambs CB2 4BW Tel: 01223 358731

ChA • The Chapel Antiques, The Chapel, Chapel Place, Tunbridge wells, Kent, TN1 1YR. Tel: 01892 619921

COHN • Terry Cohn, Rotherwood Lodge, Jumps Road, Churt, Surrey GU10 2JZ Tel: 01252 795000

COR •† Claremont Corvette, Snodland, Kent ME6 5NA Tel: 01634 244444

COUG § Cougar Club of America, Barrie S Dixon, 11 Dean Close, Partington, Gt. Manchester M31 4BQ

COYS * Coys of Kensington, 2/4 Queens Gate Mews, London SW7 5QJ Tel: 0171 584 7444

CPUK § Club Peugeot UK (General Secretary), Pole Position, 2 Steeple Heights Drive, Biggin Hill, Westerham, Kent TN16 3UN

CRAY § Crayford Convertible Car Club, 58 Geriant Road, Downham, Bromley, Kent BR1 5DX Tel: 0181 461 1805

CRC § Craven Collection of Classic Motorcycles, Brockfield Villa, Stockton-on-the-Forest, Yorkshire YO3 9UE Tel: 01904 488461/400493

CVPG/ CVPS § Chiltern Vehicle Preservation Group

DB • David Baldock

DHA • Durham House Antiques Centre, Sheep Street, Stow-on-the-Wold, Glos GL54 1AA Tel: 01451 870404

DHAM • Duncan Hamilton & Co Ltd, PO Box 222, Hook, Basingstoke, Hampshire RG27 9YZ Tel: 01256 765000

DRAK • John Drake, 5 Fox Field, Everton, Lymington, Hampshire SO41 0LR Tel: 01590 645623

DRJ • The Motorhouse, D.S. & R.G. Johnson, Thorton Hall, Thorton, Bucks MK17 0HB Tel: 01280 812280

EAFG § East Anglia Fighting Group, 206 Colchester Road, Lawford, Nr Manningtree, Essex Tel: Colchester 395177

EPP • Epping Motor Company, 558 High Road, Ilford, Essex IG3 8EQ Tel: 0181 590 3103

ESM • East Sussex Minors, The Workshop, Bearhurst Farm, Stonegate, Sussex TN5 7DU Tel: 01580 200203

FHD •† F.H. Douglass, 1a South Ealing Road, Ealing, London W5 4OT Tel: 0181 567 0570

FHF • Foulkes-Halbard of Filching, Filching Manor, Filching, Wannock, Polegate, Sussex BN26 5QA Tel: 01323 487838

FORD • Affordable Classics, The Old Garage, 22 Ridgewell Road, Great Yeldham, Halstead, Essex CO9 4RG Tel: 01787 237887

GAZE * Thomas Wm Gaze & Son, 10 Market Hill, Diss, Norfolk IP22 3JZ Tel: 01379 651931

GILB § Gilbern Owners' Club, Alan Smith, Hunters Hill, Church Lane, Peppard Common, Oxon RG9 5JL Tel: 01491 628379

GIRA • Girauto, Porte d'Orange, 84860 Caderousse, FRANCE Tel: 04 90 51 93 72

GPCC § Grand Prix Contact Club, David Hayhoe, 43 New Barn Lane, Ridgewood, Uckfield, East Sussex TN22 5EL Tel: 01825 764918

GPT •† Grand Prix Top Gear, The Old Mill, Mill End, Standon, Hertfordshire SG11 1LR Tel: 01279 843999

GW •† Graham Walker Ltd, 28 Bumpers Lane, Chester, Cheshire CH1 4LN Tel: 01244 381777

H&H *† H & H Classic Auctions Ltd, Whitegate Farm, Hatton Lane, Hatton, Warrington, Cheshire WA4 4BZ Tel: 01925 730630

HEND • Hendon Way Motors, 393-395 Hendon Way, London NW4 3LP Tel: 0181 202 8011

HLR § Historic Lotus Register, Victor Thomas (President), Badgers Farm, Short Green, Winfarthing, Norfolk IP22 2EE Tel: 01953 860508

JUN •† Junktion, The Old Railway Station, New Bolingbroke, Boston, Lincolnshire PE22 7LB Tel: 01205 480068

KHP • Kent High Performance Cars, Unit 1-2 Target Business Centre, Bircholt Road, Parkwood Industrial Estate, Maidstone, Kent ME15 9YY Tel: 01622 663308

LE •† Laurence Edscer, Flat B Semple Mews, Semple House, Gardeners Lane, Romsey, Hants SO51 6AD Tel: 01703 814665

LF * Lambert & Foster, 77 Commercial Road, Paddock Wood, Kent TN12 6DR Tel: 01892 832325

LOM • Lombarda Sport Ltd, 2 Railway Mews, Notting Hill, London W10 6HN Tel: 0171 792 9773

MEE • Nicholas Mee & Company Ltd, 36-38 Queensgate Place Mews, London SW7 5BQ Tel: 0171 581 0088

MIN § Mini Cooper Register, Philip Splett, Public Relations Officer, Burtons Farm, Barling Road, Barling Magna, Southend, Essex SS3 0LZ

MOR § Morris Register, Mr & Mrs A.V. Peeling, Enrolment Secretariat, 171 Levita House, Chalton Street, London NW1 1HR

Mot • Motospot, North Kilworth, Nr Lutterworth, Leicestershire LE17 6EP Tel: 01455 552548/0850 450269

MPG • MotorPost Gallery, 5 Shadwell Park Court, Leeds, Yorkshire LS17 8TS Tel: 0113 225 3525

MSMP • Mike Smith Motoring Past, Chiltern House, Ashendon, Aylesbury, Bucks HP18 0HB Tel: 01296 651283

MUN •† Munich Legends Ltd, The Ashdown Garage, Chelwood Gate, East Sussex RH17 7DE Tel: 01825 740456

MVT § Military Vehicle Trust, 7 Carter Fold, Mellor, Lancashire BB2 7ER Tel: 01254 812894

NMV § Norfolk Military Vehicle Group, Fakenham Road, Stanhoe, King's Lynn, Norfolk PE31 8PX Tel: 01485 518052

NTMV § North Thames Military Vehicle Preservation Society, 22 Victoria Avenue, Grays, Essex RM16 2RP

PALM *† Palm Springs Exotic Car Auctions, 602 East Sunny Dunes Road, Palm Springs, California 92264, USA Tel: 760 320 3290

PARA •† Paragon Porsche, Five Ashes, East Sussex TN20 6HY Tel: 01825 830424

PC Private Collection

PeL § Panhard et Lavassor Club GB, Martin McLarence, 18 Dovedale Road, Offerton, Stockport, Cheshire SK2 5DY

PORT • Portfield Sports & Classics Ltd, Quarry Lane, Chichester, West Sussex PO19 2NX Tel: 01243 528500

Pou * Poulain Le Fur Commissaires Priseurs Associes, 20 rue de Provence, 75009 Paris, France Tel 01 42 46 81 81

PPH • Period Picnic Hampers Tel: 0115 937 2934

RBB * Russell, Baldwin & Bright, Fine Art Salerooms, Ryelands Road, Leominster, Herefordshire HR6 8NZ Tel: 01568 611122

RCC •† Real Car Co Ltd, Snowdonia Business Park, Coed y Parc, Bethesda, Gwynedd LL57 4YS Tel: 01248 602649

RM * RM Classic Cars, 825 Park Avenue West, Chatham, Ontario Tel: 00 519 352 4575

RRM • RR Motor Services Ltd, Bethersden, Ashford, Kent TN26 3DN Tel: 01233 820219

S *† Sotheby's, 34-35 New Bond Street, London W1A 2AA Tel: 0171 293 5000

S(NY) * Sotheby's, 1334 York Avenue, New York, NY 10021, USA Tel: 00 1 212 606 7000

SCS • Sports & Classic Specialists, Seacott, 56 Cleveleys Avenue, Cleveleys, Lancashire Tel: 01253 858584

SJR • Simon J Robinson (1982) Ltd, Ketton Garage, Durham Road, Coatham, Munderville, Darlington, Co. Durham DL1 3LZ Tel: 01325 311232

STAN § Standard Motor Club, Tony Pingriff (Membership secretary), 57 Main Road, Meriden, Coventry, West Midlands CV7 0LP

SVV • Smallbone Vintage Vehicles, 116/118 Raddlebarn Road Selly Oak, Birmingham, West Midlands B29 6HQ Tel: 0121 472 7139

SWO * G.E. Sworder & Sons, 14 Cambridge Road, Stansted Mountfitchet, Essex CM24 8BZ Tel: 01279 817778

TALA • Talacrest, 74 Station Road, Egham, Surrey TW20 9LF Tel: 01784 439797

TEC § Toyota Enthusiasts' Club, c/o Secretary/Treasurer Billy Wells, 28 Park Road, Feltham, Middlesex TW13 6PW Tel/fax: 0181 898 0740

THOR • Thoroughbred Cars Tel: 0181 501 2727

TPS • Trevor's Pump Shop, 2 Cement Cottages, Station Road, Rainham, Kent ME8 7UF Tel: 01634 361231

TSh * Thimbleby & Shorland, 31 Great Knollys Street, Reading, Berkshire RG1 7HU Tel: 01734 508611

TUC •† Tuckett Bros., Marstonfields, North Marston, Bucks MK18 3PG Tel: 01296 670500

TWY • Twyford Moors Classic Cars, Unit C Burnes Shipyard, Old Bosham, Nr Chicester, West Sussex PO18 8LJ Tel: 01243 576586

UMC •† Unicorn Motor Company, Brian R. Chant M.I.M.I., Station Road, Stalbridge, Dorset DT10 2RH Tel: 01963 363353

VIC •† Vicarys of Battle Ltd, 32 High St, Battle, Sussex TN33 0EH Tel: 01424 772425

WCL • Waterside Classics Ltd, 3 Alleysbank Road, Farmeloan Estate, Rutherglen, Glasgow, Scotland G73 1AE Tel: 0141 647 0333

WILM •† Wilmington Classic Cars, Lewes Road Wilmington, Polegate, East Sussex BN26 5JE Tel: 01323 486136

WITH • Witham Specialist Vehicles, Honey Pot Lane, Colsterworth, Grantham, Lincolnshire NG33 5LY Tel: 01476 861361

Glossary

We have attempted to define some of the terms that you will come across in this book. If there are any terms or technical expressions that you would like explained or you feel should be included in future, please let us know.

Aero-screen A small, curved windscreen fitted to the scuttle of a sports car in place of the standard full-width screen. Used in competition to reduce wind resistance. Normally fitted in pairs, one each in front of the driver and passenger.

All-weather A term used to describe a vehicle with a more sophisticated folding hood than the normal Cape hood fitted to a touring vehicle. The sides were fitted with metal frames and transparent material, in some cases glass.

Barchetta Italian for 'little boat', an all-enveloping open sports bodywork.

Berline *See* **Sedanca de Ville**.

Boost The amount of pressure applied by a supercharger or turbocharger.

Boxer Engine configuration with horizontally-opposed cylinders.

Brake A term dating from the days of horse-drawn vehicles. Originally the seating was fore and aft, the passengers facing inwards.

Brake horsepower (bhp) This is the amount of power produced by an engine, measured at the flywheel (*See* **Horsepower**).

Cabriolet The term Cabriolet applies to a vehicle with a hood that can be closed, folded half-way or folded right back. A Cabriolet can be distinguished from a Landaulette because the front of the hood reaches the top of the windscreen, whereas on a Landaulette, it only covers the rear half of the car.

Chain drive A transmission system in which the wheels are attached to a sprocket, driven by a chain from an engine-powered sprocket, usually on the output side of a gearbox.

Chassis A framework to which the car body, engine, gearbox, and axles are attached.

Chummy An open-top, two-door body style, usually with a single door on each side, two seats in the front and one at the rear.

Cloverleaf A three-seater, open body style, usually with a single door on each side, two seats in the front and one at the rear.

Concours Concours d'Elegance is a competition in which cars are judged by their condition. Concours has become a byword for a vehicle in excellent condition.

Cone clutch A clutch in which both driving and driven faces form a cone.

Connollising Leather treatment produced by British firm Connolly to rejuvenate and restore suppleness to old and dry leather.

Convertible A general term (post-war) for any car with a folding soft top.

Continental A car specifically designed for high-speed touring, usually on the Continent. Rolls-Royce and Bentley almost exclusively used this term during the 1930s and post-WWII.

Coupé In the early Vintage and Edwardian period, Coupé was only applied to what is now termed a Half Limousine or Doctor's Coupé, which was a two-door two-seater. The term is now usually prefixed by Drophead or Fixed-Head.

Cubic capacity The volume of an engine obtained by multiplying the area of the bore by the stroke. Engine capacity is given in cubic centimetres (cc) in Europe and cubic inches (cu in) in the USA. 1 cubic inch equals 16.38cc (1 litre = 61.02cu in).

De Ville A style of coachwork in which the driver/chauffeur occupies an open driving position, and the passengers a closed compartment – thus, Coupé de Ville or Sedanca de Ville. In America, these vehicles are known as Town Cars.

Dickey Seat A passenger seat, usually for two people, contained in the boot of the car and without a folding hood (the boot lid forms the backrest). See also Rumble Seat.

Doctor's Coupé A fixed or drophead coupé without a dickey seat, the passenger seat being slightly staggered back from the driver's to accommodate the famous doctor's bag.

Dog Cart A form of horse-drawn vehicle originally designed for transporting beaters and their dogs to a shoot (the dogs were contained in louvred boxes under the seats; the louvres were kept for decoration long after the practice of carrying dogs in this way had ceased).

Dos-à-dos Literally back-to-back, i e the passenger seating arrangement.

Double-duck Double-layered fabric used in construction of folding convertible tops.

Drophead coupé Originally a two-door two-seater with a folding roof.

Dry sump A method of lubricating engines in which the oil is contained in a separate reservoir rather than in a sump at the bottom of the cylinder block. Usually, two oil pumps are used, one to remove oil from the engine to the reservoir, the other to pump it back to the engine.

Fender American term used to describe the wing of a car.

F-head An engine design in which the inlet valve is in the cylinder head, while the exhaust valve is in the cylinder block. Also referred to as inlet-over-exhaust.

Fixed-head coupé (FHC) A coupé with a solid fixed roof.

Golfer's coupé Usually an open two-seater with a square-doored locker behind the driver's seat to accommodate golf clubs.

Hansom As with the famous horse-drawn cab, an enclosed two-seater with the driver out in the elements, either behind or in front of the passenger compartment.

Homologation To qualify for entry into some race series, the rules can require that a minimum number of road-going production versions of the race car are built. These are generally known as 'homologation specials'.

Hood American term used to describe the bonnet of a car.

Horsepower (hp) The unit of measurement of engine power – one horsepower represents the energy expended in raising 33,000lb by one foot in 60 seconds.

Landau An open town carriage for four people with a folding hood at each end, which would meet in the middle when erected.

Landaulette A horse-drawn Landaulette carried two people and was built much like a coupé. The roof line of a Landaulette is always angular, in contrast to a Cabriolet, and the folding hood is very often made of patent leather. A true Landaulette only opens over the rear compartment and not over the front seat at all. (Also Landaulet.)

L-head An engine design in which the inlet and exhaust valves are contained within the cylinder block. (*See* **Side-valve**.)

Limousine French in origin and used to describe a closed car equipped with occasional seats and a division between the rear and driver's compartments.

Monobloc engine An engine with all its cylinders cast in a single block.

Monocoque A method of constructing a car without a separate chassis, structural strength being provided by the arrangement of the stressed panels. Most modern, mass-produced cars are built in this way.

Monoposto Single-seater (Italian).

Nitrided Used to describe engine components, particularly crankshafts, that have been specially hardened to withstand the stresses of racing or other high-performance applications.

OHC Overhead camshaft, either single (SOHC) or double (DOHC).

OHV Overhead valves.

Phæton A term dating back to the days of horse-drawn vehicles and used to describe an open body, sometimes with a Dickey or Rumble Seat for the groom at the rear. It was an owner/driver carriage and designed to be pulled by four horses. A term often misused during the Veteran period, but still in common use, particularly in the USA.

Post Vintage Thoroughbred (PVT) A British term created by the Vintage Sports Car Club (VSCC) to describe selected models made in the vintage tradition between 1931 and 1942.

Roadster A two-seater, open sporting vehicle, the hood of which is removed completely rather than being folded down, as on a drophead coupé. Early versions without side windows.

Roi des Belges A luxurious open touring car with elaborately contoured seat backs, named after King Leopold II of Belgium. The term is sometimes incorrectly used to describe general touring cars.

Rotary engine A unique form of car engine in which the cylinders, pistons and crankshaft of the normal reciprocating engine are replaced by a triangular rotor that rotates about an eccentric shaft within a special waisted chamber. One or more rotor/chamber assemblies may be used. On the whole, the engine having a third of the number of parts of a comparable reciprocating engine. The engine was designed by Dr Felix Wankel and has been used in a range of sports cars by Mazda.

Rpm Engine revolutions per minute.

Rumble Seat An American term for a folding seat for two passengers, used to increase the carrying capacity of a standard two-passenger car. (*See* **Dickey seat**.)

Runabout A low-powered, lightweight, open two-seater from the 1900s.

Saloon A two- or four-door car with four or more seats and a fixed roof.

Sedan *See* **Saloon**.

Sedanca de Ville A limousine body with an open driving compartment that can be covered with a folding or sliding roof section, known in America as a Town Car.

Side-valve Used to describe an engine in which the valves are located in the cylinder block rather than the head.

Sociable A cyclecar term used to describe the side-by-side seating of the driver and passenger.

Spider/Spyder An open two-seater sports car, sometimes a 2+2 (with two small occasional seats behind the two front seats).

Station wagon American term for an estate car.

Supercharger An engine-driven pump for forcing the fuel/air mixture into the cylinders to gain extra power.

Surrey An early 20thC open four-seater with a fringed canopy. A term from the days of horse-drawn vehicles.

Stanhope A single-seat, two-wheeled horse-drawn carriage with a hood. Later, a four-wheeled, two-seater, sometimes with an underfloor engine.

Stroke The distance an engine's piston moves up-and-down within its cylinder. The stroke is invariably measured in millimetres, although in the USA, inches may be used.

Superleggera Italian for 'super lightweight' and used to describe a method of construction devised by Touring of Milan, whereby an aluminium skin was attached to a framework of steel tubes to produce a light, yet strong, structure. One of the best-known proponents of this method was Aston Martin, which employed Superleggera construction in some of its DB series cars.

Tandem A cyclecar term used to describe the fore-and-aft seating of the driver and passenger.

Targa A coupé fitted with a removable central roof section.

Tonneau A rear-entrance tonneau is a four-seater to which access is provided through a centrally-placed rear door. A detachable tonneau meant that the rear seats could be removed to make a two-seater. Today, 'tonneau' usually refers to a waterproof cover that can be fitted over the cockpit of an open car when the roof is detached.

Torpedo An open tourer that has coachwork with an unbroken line from the bonnet to the rear of the body.

Tourer An open four- or five-seater with three or four doors, a folding hood (with or without sidescreens) and seats flush with the body sides. This body style began to appear in about 1910 and, initially, was known as a torpedo (*see above*), but by 1920, the word 'tourer' was being used instead – except in France, where 'torpedo' continued in use until the 1930s.

Turbocharger An exhaust-gas-driven pump for forcing the air/fuel mixture into the engine's cylinders to produce extra power.

Unitary construction Used to describe a vehicle without a separate chassis, structural strength being provided by the arrangement of the stressed panels. (*See* **Monocoque**.)

Veteran All vehicles manufactured before 31 December 1918; only cars built before 31 March 1904 are eligible for the London to Brighton Commemorative Run.

Victoria Generally an American term for a two- or four-seater with a very large folding hood. If a four-seater, the hood would only cover the rear seats. In some cases, applied to a saloon with a 'bustle' back.

Vintage Any vehicle manufactured between the end of the veteran period and 31 December 1930. (*See* **Post Vintage Thoroughbred**.)

Vis-à-vis Face-to-face; an open car in which the passengers sit opposite each other.

Voiturette A French term used to describe a very light car, originally coined by Léon Bollée.

Wagonette A large car for six or more passengers, in which the rear seats face each other. Entrance is at the rear, and the vehicle is usually open.

Waxoyled Used to describe a vehicle in which the underside has been treated with Waxoyl, a proprietary oil and wax spray that protects against moisture.

Weyman A system of body construction employing Rexine fabric panels over a Kapok filling to prevent noise and provide insulation.

Wheelbase The distance between the centres of the front and rear wheels of a vehicle.

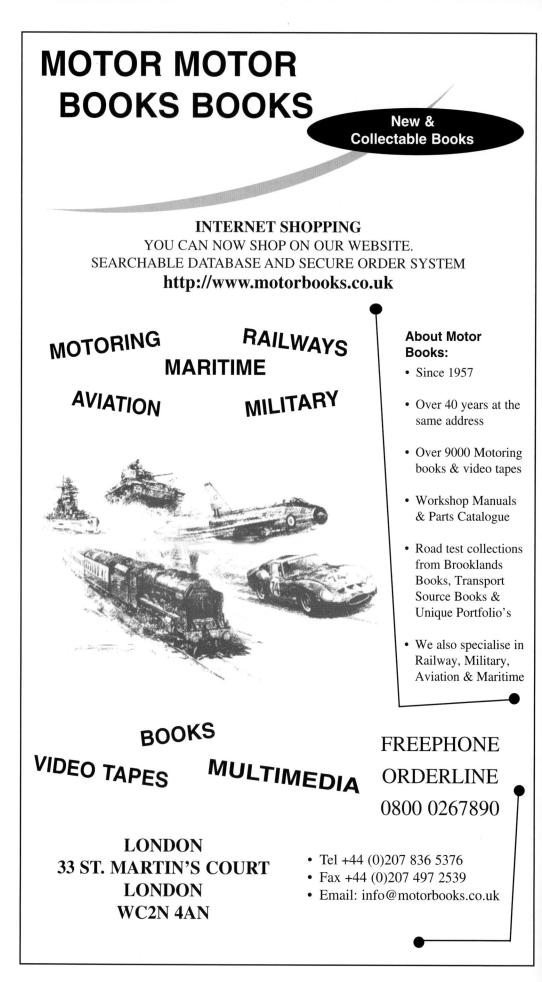

MOTOR MOTOR
BOOKS BOOKS

New & Collectable Books

INTERNET SHOPPING
YOU CAN NOW SHOP ON OUR WEBSITE.
SEARCHABLE DATABASE AND SECURE ORDER SYSTEM
http://www.motorbooks.co.uk

FERRARI   FIAT & ABARTH   ROVER

MINI   ALVIS   PORSCHE   TRIUMPH

RELIANT   MERCEDES

MORGAN

MORRIS   VOLKSWAGEN

RENAULT   BUGATTI

CITROEN   LANCIA   CORVETTE

ALFA ROMEO   FORD   MUSTANG

JAGUAR   DAIMLER   MASERATI

ROLLS-ROYCE & BENTLEY   B.M.W.   M.G.

RILEY   ROOTES   PONTIAC

AUSTIN-HEALEY   TVR   CADILLAC

About Motor Books:

- Since 1957

- Over 40 years at the same address

- Over 9000 Motoring books & video tapes

- Workshop Manuals & Parts Catalogue

- Road test collections from Brooklands Books, Transport Source Books & Unique Portfolio's

- We also specialise in Railway, Military, Aviation & Maritime

FREEPHONE
ORDERLINE
0800 0267890

**OXFORD
8 THE ROUNDWAY
HEADINGTON
OXFORD OX3 8DH**

- Tel +44 (0)1865 766215
- Fax +44 (0)1865 763555
- Email: info@motorbooks.co.uk

Directory of Car Clubs

If you would like your Club to be included in next year's directory, or have a change of address or telephone number, please inform us by 31 May 2000.

750 Motor Club Ltd, Worth Farm, Little Horsted, Sussex TN22 5TT Tel: 01825 750760
AC Owners' Club, R A Morpeth, The Clovers, Mursley, Buckinghamshire MK17 0RT
ABC Owners' Club, D A Hales, The Hedgerows, Sutton St Nicholas, Hereford HR1 3BU
Tel: 01432 880726
Alexis Racing and Trials Car Register, Duncan Rabagliati, 4 Wool Road, Wimbledon, London SW20 0HW
Alfa Romeo 1900 Register, Peter Marshall, Mariners, Courtlands Avenue, Esher, Surrey KT10 9HZ
Alfa Romeo Owners' Club, Michael Lindsay, 97 High Street, Linton, Cambridgeshire CB1 6JT
Allard Owners' Club, Michelle Wilson, 10 Brooklyn Court, Woking, Surrey GU22 7TQ
Tel: 01483 773428
Alvis Owners' Club, Charles Mackonochie, 2 Sunny Bank Cotts, Colts Hill, Capel, Tonbridge, Kent TN12 6SW Tel: 01892 832118
Alvis Register, Mr J. Willis, The Vinery, Wanborough Manor, Nr Guildford, Surrey GU3 2JR
Tel: 01483 810308
Armstrong Siddeley Owners' Club Ltd, Peter Sheppard, 57 Berberry Close, Bournville, Birmingham, West Midlands B30 1TB
Assoc of British Volkswagen Clubs, Dept PC, 76 Eastfield Road, Burnham, Bucks SL1 7PF
Association of Healey Owners, Tony Heyworth, 10 Blagrove Lane, Wokingham, Berkshire RG11 4BA
Association of Old Vehicle Clubs in Northern Ireland Ltd,
Secretary Trevor Mitchell, 38 Ballymaconnell Road, Bangor, Co Down, N Ireland BT20 5PS
Tel: 01247 467886
Association of Singer Car Owners, Anne Page, 39 Oakfield, Rickmansworth, Hertfordshire WD3 2LR
Tel: 01923 778575
Aston Martin Owners' Club Ltd, Jim Whyman, AMOC Ltd, 1A High Street, Sutton Nr Ely, Cambridgeshire CB6 2RB
Tel: 01353 777353
Austin A30-35 Owners' Club, Barbara Scott, Membership Secretary, Ardbeg Farm Cottage, Ardmory Road, Ardbeg, Bute, Scotland PA20 0PG
Tel: 01872 273938
Austin Atlantic Owners' Club, Lee Marshall, Membership Secretary, Wildwood, 21 Cornflower Cl, Stamford, Lincolnshire PE9 2WL
Austin Big 7 Register, R E Taylor, 101 Derby Road, Chellaston, Derbyshire DE73 1SB
Austin Cambridge/Westminster Car Club, Mr J Curtis, 4 Russell Close, East Budleigh, Budleigh Salterton, Devon EX9 7EH
Tel: 01395 446210
Austin Eight Register, Ian Pinniger, 3 La Grange Martin, St Martin, Jersey, Channel Islands JE3 6JB
Austin Gipsy Register 1958-1968, Mike Gilbert, 24 Green Close, Rixon, Sturminster Newton, Dorset DT10 1BJ
Austin Healey Club, Colleen Holmes, 4 Saxby St, Leicester LE2 0ND
Austin J40 Car Club, Mary Rowlands, 21 Forest Close, Lickey End, Bromsgrove, Worcestershire B60 1JU
Austin Maxi Club, Mrs C J Jackson, 27 Queen Street, Bardney, Lincolnshire LN3 5XF

Austin Sheerline & Princess Club, Ian Coombes, 44 Vermeer Cresc, Shoeburyness, Essex S53 9TJ
Austin Swallow Register, G L Walker, School House, Rectory Road, Great Haseley, Oxon OX44 7JP
Austin Ten Drivers' Club Ltd, Ian M Dean, P.O. Box 12, Chichester, Sussex PO20 7PH
Tel: 01243 641284
Bean Car Club, Gerry Langham, Terries, Holyport Road, Maidenhead, Berkshire SL6 2HA
Tel: 01628 25387
Bentley Drivers' Club, 16 Chearsley Road, Long Crendon, Aylesbury, Buckinghamshire HP18 9AW
Berkeley Enthusiasts' Club, Paul Fitness, 9 Hellards Road, Stevenage, Hertfordshire SG1 3PN
Tel: 01438 724164
BMW Car Club, PO Box 328, Andover, Hampshire SP10 1YN Tel & Fax: 01264 337883
BMW Drivers' Club, Samantha Easton, 41 Norwich St, Dereham, Norfolk NR19 1AD
Tel: 01362 691144
Borgward Drivers' Club, Mr D C Farr, 19 Highfield Road, Kettering, Northants NN15 6HR
Tel: 01536 510771
Brabham Register, Ed Walker, The Old Bull, 5 Woodmancote, Dursley, Gloucestershire GL11 4AF
Tel: 01453 543243
Bristol Owners' Club, John Emery, Vesutor, Marringdean Road, Billingshurst, Sussex RH14 9HD
British Ambulance Society, Roger Leonard (General Secretary), 21 Victoria Road, Horley, Surrey RH6 9BN
Tel/Fax: 01293 776636
British Salmson Owners' Club, D Cannings, 61 Holyrood Gardens, Edgware, Middlesex HA8 5LS
Brough Superior Club, Justin Wand (Secretary), Flint Cottage, St Paul's Walden, Hitchin, Hertfordshire SG4 8ON
BSA Front Wheel Drive Club, Barry Baker, 164 Cottimore La, Walton-on-Thames, Surrey KT12 2BL
Bugatti Owners' Club Ltd, Sue Ward, Prescott Hill, Gotherington, Cheltenham, Gloucs GL52 4RD
Bullnose Morris Club, Richard Harris, PO Box 383, Hove, Sussex BN3 4FX
Cambridge-Oxford Owners' Club, 32 Reservoir Rd, Southgate, London N14 4BG
Capri Club International, 18 Arden Business Centre, Arden Road, Alcester, Warwickshire B49 6HW
Capri Drivers' Association, Mrs Moira Farrelly (Secretary), 9 Lyndhurst Rd, Coulsdon, Sy CR5 3HT
Citroën Car Club, PO Box 348, Bromley, Kent BR2 2QT Tel: Membership 01689 853999
General fax/answerphone 07000 248 258
email: members@citroencarclub.org.uk
website: http://www.citroencarclub.org.uk
Citroën Traction Owners' Club, Peter Riggs, 2 Appleby Gardens, Dunstable, Beds LU6 3DB
Classic and Historic Motor Club Ltd,
Tricia Burridge, Stream Cottage, Yarley Cross, Wells, Somerset BA5 1LS Tel: 01749 675404
Classic Corvette Club (UK), Andy Greenfield, 17 Sudeley Gardens, Hockley, Essex SS5 4XQ
Tel: 01702 200881
Classic Hearse Register, Paul Harris.
Tel: 01268 472313
Club Alfa Romeo 2600/2000 International,
Roger Monk, Knighton, Church Close, West Runton, Cromer, Norfolk NR27 9QY

Club Alpine Renault UK Ltd, 1 Bloomfield Close, Wombourne, Wolverhampton, W. Midlands WV5 8HQ

Club Lotus, Lotus Lodge, PO Box 8, Dereham, Norfolk NR19 1TF Tel: 01362 694459

Club Marcos International, Mrs I Chivers, Membership Sec, The Spinney, Littleworth Lane, Whitley, Melksham, Wilts SN12 8RE
Tel: 01225 707815

Club Peugeot UK, Peter Beale, 49 Upper Green, Tewin, Welwyn, Herts AL6 0LX Tel: 01438 717323

Club Triumph, Derek Pollock, 86 Waggon Road, Hadley Wood, Hertfordshire EN14 0PP

Clyno Club, Swallow Cottage, Langton Farm, Elmesthorpe, Leicestershire LE9 7SE

Connaught Register, Duncan Rabagliati, 4 Wool Road, Wimbledon, London SW20 0HW

Cougar Club of America, Barrie S Dixon, 11 Dean Close, Partington, Greater Manchester M31 4BQ

Crayford Convertible Car Club, 58 Geriant Road, Downham, Bromley, Kent BR1 5DX
Tel: 0181 461 1805

Crossley Register, 7 Manor Rd, Sherborne St John, Nr Basingstoke, Hampshire RG24 9JJ

DAF Owners' Club, S K Bidwell, Club Sec, 56 Ridgedale Road, Bolsover, Chesterfield, Derbyshire S44 6TX

Daimler and Lanchester Owners' Club, PO Box 276, Sittingbourne, Kent ME9 7GA
Tel: 07000 356285 email: daimleruk@aol.com

De Tomaso Drivers' Club, Phil Stebbings, Founder & Club Sec, Flint Barn, Malthouse Lane, Ashington, Sx RH20 3BU Tel/fax: 01903 893870

Delage Section of the VSCC Ltd, Peter Jacobs, Secretary, Clouds' Reach, The Scop, Almondsbury, Bristol BS32 4DU

Delorean Owners' Club, Linehill House, Sapey Common, Clifton-upon-Teme, Worcs WR6 6EP Tel: 01886 853294

Diva Register, Steve Pethybridge, 8 Wait End Road, Waterlooville, Hants PO7 7DD Tel: 01705 251485

DKW Owners' Club, David Simon, Aurelia, Garlogie, Skene, Westhill, Aberdeenshire, Scotland AB32 6RX

Droop Snoot Group, John Smerdon, 17 Priors Rd, Tadley, Hampshire RG26 4QJ

Dutton Owners' Club, Mark Young, 6 Binyon Close, Badsey, Evesham, Worcestershire WR11 5EY

Early Ford V8 Club, S Wade, Forge Stones, Heath Road, Boughton Monchelsea, Maidstone, Kent ME17 4HS

East Anglia Fighting Group, 206 Colchester Road, Lawford, Nr Manningtree, Essex
Tel: Colchester 395177

Elva Owners' Club, Roger Dunbar, 8 Liverpool Terr, Worthing, Sussex BN11 1TA Tel/fax: 01903 823710
email: roger.dunbar@elva.com
web: www.elva.com

Enfield & District Veteran Vehicle Trust, Whitewebbs Museum, Whitewebbs Road, Enfield, Middlesex EN2 9HW Tel: 0181 367 1898

Facel Vega Car Club, Mr M Green, Secretary, 17 Stanley Road, Lymington, Hampshire SO41 3SJ

Fairthorpe Sports Car Club, Tony Hill, 9 Lynhurst Crescent, Uxbridge, Middx UB10 9EF

Ferrari Club of GB, Daytona House, 47 Hill Top Rd, Newmillerdam, Wakefield, West Yorkshire WF2 6PZ
Tel: 01924 257735

Fiat 500 Club, Janet Westcott, Membership Sec, 33 Lionel Ave, Wendover, Aylesbury, Bucks HP22 6LP

Fiat Dino Register, Mr Morris, 59 Sandown Park, Tunbridge Wells, Kent TN2 4RT

Fiat Motor Club (GB), Mrs S Robins, Hon Membership Sec, 118 Brookland Road, Langport, Somerset TA10 9TH

Fiat Osca Register, Mr M Elliott, 36 Maypole Drive, Chigwell, Essex IG7 6DE Tel: 0181 500 7127

Fire Service Preservation Group, Andrew Scott, 50 Old Slade Lane, Iver, Buckinghamshire SL0 9DR

Ford Avo Owners' Club, W Arnold, 21 Carey, Hockley, Tamworth, Staffordshire B77 5QB
Tel: 01827 250622

Ford Capri Enthusiasts' Register, Glyn Watson, 7 Louis Avenue, Bury, Lancashire BL9 5EQ
Tel: 0161 762 9952

Ford Classic and Capri Owners' Club, 1 Verney Close, Covingham, Swindon, Wiltshire SN3 5EF Tel: 01793 523574

Ford Corsair Owners' Club, Mrs E Checkley, 7 Barnfield, New Malden, Surrey KT3 5RH

Ford Cortina 1600E Owners' Club, D Johnson, 16 Woodlands Close, Sarisbury Green, Southampton, Hants SO31 7AQ Tel: 01489 602576

Ford Escort 1300E Owners' Club, Steve Ramek, 93 Thorkhill Road, Thames Ditton, Surrey KT7 0UQ
Tel: 0181 339 0572

Ford Executive Owners' Register, G Young, 31 Brian Road, Chadwell Heath, Essex RM6 5DA

Ford Granada Mk 1 Owners' Club, Jonathan Lillystone, 65 Perry Street, Darwen, Lancashire BB3 3DG Tel: 01254 761814

Ford Mk II Independent O.C. International, B & J Enticknap, 173 Sparrow Farm Drive, Feltham, Middx TW14 0DG Tel: 0181 384 3559

Ford Mk III Zephyr and Zodiac Owners' Club, Dave Barnes, 27 Shirley Grove, Edmonton, London N9 8ES Tel: 0181 443 2648

Ford Mk IV Zephyr & Zodiac Owners' Club, Richard Cordle, 29 Ruskin Drive, Worcester Park, Surrey KT4 8LG Tel: 0181 649 0685

Ford Model T Ford Register of GB, Mrs Julia Armer, 3 Strong Close, Keighley, Yorkshire BD21 4JT Tel: 01535 607978

Ford RS Owners' Club, PO Box 4044, Pangbourne, Reading, Berkshire RG8 7XL Tel: 01189 841583

Ford Y&C Model Register, Bob Wilkinson, 9 Brambleside, Thrapston, Northants NN14 4PY

The Gentry Register, Barbara Reynolds, General Secretary, Barn Close Cottage, Cromford Road, Woodlinkin, Nottinghamshire NG16 4HD

Gilbern Owners' Club, Alan Smith, Hunters Hill, Church Lane, Peppard Common, Oxon RG9 5JL
Tel: 01491 628379

Ginetta Owners' Club, Dave Baker, 24 Wallace Mill Gardens, Mid Calder, Livingstone, West Lothian, Scotland EH53 0BD Tel: 01506 8883129

Gordon Keeble Owners' Club, Ann Knott, Westminster Rd, Helmdon, Brackley, Northants NN13 5QB Tel: 01280 702311

Grand Prix Contact Club, David Hayhoe, 43 New Barn Lane, Ridgewood, Uckfield, E Sussex TN22 5EL Tel: 01825 764918

Heinkel Trojan Owners' and Enthusiasts' Club, Peter Jones, 37 Brinklow Cl, Matchborough West, Redditch, Worcestershire B98 0HB
Tel: 01527 501318

Heinz 57 Register, Barry Priestman, Secretary, 58 Geriant Rd, Downham, Bromley, Kent BR1 5DX

Historic Commercial Vehicle Society (HCVS), Iden Grange, Cranbrook Road, Staplehurst, Kent TN12 0ET

Historic Lotus Register, Victor Thomas, President, Badgers Farm, Short Green, Winfarthing, Norfolk IP22 2EE Tel: 01953 860508

Historic Sports Car Club, J Keech, HSCC, Silverstone Circuit, Silverstone, Towcester, Northamptonshire NN12 8TN
Tel: 01327 858400

Historic Volkswagen Club, Rod Sleigh, 28 Longnor Road, Brooklands, Telford, Shropshire TF1 3NY Tel: 01952 242167

Holden UK Register, G R C Hardy, Clun Felin, Woll's Castle, Haverfordwest, Pembrokshire, Dyfed, Wales SA62 5LR

Humber Register, R N Arman, Northbrook Cottage, 175 York Road, Broadstone, Dorset BH18 8ES

Imp Club, Michelle Ross, 71 Evesham Road, Stratford upon Avon, Warwickshire CV37 9BA Tel: 01789 204778

Invicta Military Vehicle Preservation Society, 58 Ladds Way, Swanley, Kent BR8 8HW Tel: 01322 408738

Isetta Owners' Club, Mick & Kay West, 137 Prebendal Avenue, Aylesbury, Bucks HP21 8LD

Jaguar Car Club, Jeff Holman, Barbary, Chobham Road, Horsell, Woking, Surrey GU21 4AS Tel: 01483 763811

Jaguar Drivers' Club, JDC Jaguar Hse, Stuart St, Luton, Bedfordshire LU1 2SL Tel: 01582 419332

Jaguar Enthusiasts' Club, Graham Searle, Sherborne, Mead Road, Stoke Gifford, Bristol BS12 6PS Tel: 0117 969 8186

Jaguar/Daimler Owners' Club, 130–132 Bordesley Green, Birmingham, West Mids B9 4SU

Jensen Owners' Club, Keith Andrews, 2 Westgate, Fulshaw Park, Wilmslow, Cheshire SK9 1QQ Tel: 01625 525699

Jowett Car Club, Pauline Winteringham, 33 Woodlands Road, Gomersal, Cleckeaton, Yorks BD19 4SF Tel: 01274 873959

Jupiter Owners' Auto Club, Geoff Butterwick, Cowlishaw Cottage, Yarmouth Road, Melton, Woodbridge, Suffolk IP12 1QF Tel: 01394 385709

Karmann Ghia Owners' Club, Astrid Kelly (Membership Secretary), 7 Keble Road, Maidenhead, Berkshire SL6 6BB Tel: 01628 39185

Kieft Racing and Sports Car Club, Duncan Rabagliati, 4 Wool Road, Wimbledon, London SW20 0HW

Lagonda Club, Colin Bugler (Hon Secretary), Wintney House, London Road, Hartley Wintney, Hook, Hants RG27 8RN Tel & Fax: 01252 845451

Lancia Motor Club, Dave Baker (Membership Secretary), Mount Pleasant, Penrhos, Brymbo, Wrexham, Clwyd, Wales LL11 5LY

Land Rover Register (1947–1951), Richard Lines, Ricoli, Conisholme Road, North Somercotes, Louth, Lincolnshire LN11 7PS Tel: 01507 358314

Land Rover Series One Club, David Bowyer, East Foldhay, Zeal Monachorum, Crediton, Devon EX17 6DH

Land Rover Series Two Club Ltd, Laurence Mitchell Esq, PO Box 251, Barnsley S70 5YN

Landcrab Owners' Club International, Bill Frazer, PO Box 218, Cardiff, Wales CF3 9HZ

Lea Francis Owners' Club, R Sawers, French's, High Street, Long Wittenham, Abingdon, Oxfordshire OX14 4QQ

Lincoln-Zephyr Owners' Club, Colin Spong, 22 New North Road, Hainault, Ilford, Essex IG6 2XG

London Bus Preservation Trust, Mike Nash, 43 Stroudwater Park, Weybridge, Surrey KT13 0DT Tel: 01932 856810

London Vintage Taxi Association, Steve Dimmock, 51 Ferndale Crescent, Cowley, Uxbridge, Berkshire UB8 2AY

Lotus Cortina Register, Andy Morrell, 64 The Queens Drive, Chorleywood, Rickmansworth, Hertfordshire WD3 2LT

Lotus Drivers' Club, PO Box 387, St Albans, Hertfordshire AL4 9BJ

Lotus Seven Club, Julie Richens, PO Box 7, Cranleigh, Surrey GU6 8YP

Marcos Owners' Club, 51 London Road, Bromley, Kent BR1 4HB Tel: 0181 460 3511

Marendaz Special Car Register, John Shaw, 107 Old Bath Road, Cheltenham, Gloucs GL53 7DA Tel: 01242 526310

Marina/Ital Drivers' Club, Mr J G Lawson, 12 Nithsdale Road, Liverpool, Lancashire L15 5AX

Maserati Club, Dave Smith, 39 Ventnor Avenue, Middlesex HA7 2HX Tel: 0181 907 1972

Matra Enthusiasts' Club (MEC), Greig Dalgleish, The Hollies, Crowborough Hill, Crowborough, Sussex TN6 2HH Tel: 01892 652964

Mercedes-Benz Club Ltd, Brightstone, Over Old Road, Harbury, Gloucestershire GL19 3BJ

Mercedes-Benz Owners' Club, N Ireland Area Organiser, Trevor Mitchell, 38 Ballymaconell Road, Bangor, Co Down, N Ireland BT20 5PS

Messerschmitt Enthusiasts' Club, C Archer, Kitterick, Shaftesbury Avenue, Woking, Surrey GU22 7DU Tel: 01483 769270

Messerschmitt Owners' Club, Mrs Eileen Hallam, Birches, Ashmores Lane, Rusper, Sussex RH12 4PS Tel: 01293 871417

Metropolitan Owners' Club, Nick Savage, The Old Pump House, Nutbourne Common, Pulborough, Sussex RH20 2HB Tel: 01798 813713

MG Car Club, Kimber House, PO Box 251, Abingdon, Oxon OX14 1FF Tel: 01235 555552

MG Octagon Car Club, Unit 19 Hollins Business Centre, Rowley Street, Stafford ST16 2RH Tel: 01785 251014

MG Owners' Club, Octagon House, Swavesey, Cambridgeshire CB4 5QZ Tel: 01954 231125

MG 'Y' Type Register, Mr J G Lawson, 12 Nithsdale Road, Liverpool, Lancashire L15 5AX

Midget & Sprite Club, Nigel Williams, 15 Foxcote, Kingswood, Bristol, Gloucestershire BS15 2TX

Military Vehicle Trust, Simon Johnson, 7 Carter Fold, Mellor, Lancashire BB2 7ER Tel: 01254 812894

Mini Cooper Club, Mary Fowler, 59 Giraud Street, Poplar, London E14 6EE Tel: 0171 515 7173

Mini Cooper Register, Philip Splett, Public Relations Officer, Burtons Farm, Barling Road, Barling Magna, Southend, Essex SS3 0LZ

Mini Marcos Owners' Club, R Porter, 23 Switchback Road North, Maidenhead, Berkshire SL6 7UF Tel: 01628 621614

Mini Moke Club, Paul Beard, 13 Ashdene Close, Hartlebury, Herefordshire DY11 7TN

Mini Owners' Club, 15 Birchwood Road, Lichfield, Staffordshire WS14 9UN

MK I Consul, Zephyr and Zodiac Club, 180 Gypsy Road, Welling, Kent DA16 1JQ Tel: 0181 301 3709

Mk I Cortina Owners' Club, Karen Clarke, 6 Hobson's Acre, Gunthorpe, Nottingham NG14 7FF Tel: 0115 966 3995

Mk II Consul, Zephyr and Zodiac Club, Liam Cotton, 8 Chestnut Close, Moira, Swadlincote, Derbyshire DE12 6EP Tel: 01283 219508

Mk II Granada Owners' Club, Paul Farrer, 58 Jevington Way, Lee, London SE12 9NQ Tel: 0181 857 4356

Model A Ford Club of Great Britain, Mike Cobell, 10–14 Newland Street, Coleford, Forest of Dean, Gloucestershire GL16 8AN Tel: 01594 834321

Morgan Sports Car Club, Carol Kennett, Old Ford Lodge, Ogston, Higham, Derbys DE55 6EL

Morgan Three-Wheeler Club Ltd, E Eyes, 280 Commonwealth Way, Abbey Wood, London SE2 0LD Tel: 0181 311 7282

Morris Cowley and Oxford Club, Derek Andrews, 202 Chantry Gardens, Southwick, Trowbridge, Wiltshire BA14 9QX

Morris Marina Owners' Club, 39 Portley Road, Dawley, Telford, Shropshire TF4 3JW Tel: 01952 504900

Morris Minor Owners' Club, PO Box 1098, Derby DE23 8ZX Tel: 01332 291675

Morris Minor Owners' Club, N Ireland Branch,
Mrs Joanne Jeffery, Secretary, 116 Oakdale,
Ballygowan, Newtownards, Co Down, N Ireland
BT23 5TT

Morris Register, Mr & Mrs A V Peeling,
Enrolment Secretariat, 171 Levita House,
Chalton Street, London NW1 1HR

Moss Owners' Club, S Jarbutt, 89 London Rd Sth,
Merstham, Surrey RH1 3AX Tel: 01737 645165

Naylor Car Club, John W Taylor (Secretary),
c/o Naylor Brothers Restoration, Airedale Garage,
Hollins Hill, Shipley, Yorkshire BD17 7QN

Norfolk Military Vehicle Group, Fakenham Road,
Stanhoe, King's Lynn, Norfolk PE31 8PX
Tel: 01485 518052

**North Thames Military Vehicle Preservation
Society,** 22 Victoria Ave, Grays, Essex RM16 2RP

NSU Owners' Club, Rosemarie Crowley,
58 Tadorne Road, Tadworth, Surrey KT20 5TF
Tel: 01737 812412

Ogle Register, Chris Gow, 108 Potters Lane,
Burgess Hill, Sussex RH15 9JN Tel: 01444 248439

Opel GT UK Owners' Club, Dean Hayes,
11 Thrale Way, Parkwood, Rainham, Kent ME8 9LX
Tel: 01634 379065

Opel Manta Owners' Club, Richard Miller,
186 Norman Place Rd, Coundon, Coventry CV6 2BU

Opel-Vauxhall Drivers' Club, E Morphew,
41 Norwich Street, Dereham, Norfolk NR19 1AD
Tel: 01362 691144

Panhard et Levassor Club GB, Martin McLarence,
18 Dovedale Road, Offerton, Stockport, Cheshire
SK2 5DY

Panther Enthusiasts' Club UK, George Newell
(Secretary), 91 Fleet Road, Farnborough, Hampshire
GU14 9RE Tel: 01252 540217

Pedal Car Collectors' Club (PCCC),
c/o A P Gayler, 4/4a Chapel Terrace Mews,
Kemp Town, Brighton, Sussex BN2 1HU
Tel/Fax: 01273 601960

Piper (Sports and Racing Car) Club, Clive Davies,
Pipers Oak, Lopham Rd, East Harling, Norfolk
NR16 2PE Tel: 01953 717813

Porsche Club Great Britain, Robin Walker,
c/o Cornbury House, Cotswold Business Village,
London Road, Moreton-in-Marsh, Gloucestershire
GL56 0JQ Tel: 01608 652911/01296 688760

Post Office Vehicle Club, 7 Bignal Rand Close,
Wells, Somerset BA5 2EE

Post War Thoroughbred Car Club, 87 London St,
Chertsey, Surrey KT16 8AN

Post-Vintage Humber Car Club, Neil Gibbins,
32 Walsh Crescent, New Addington, Croydon, Surrey
CR0 0BX Tel: 01689 849851

Pre 1940 Triumph Owners' Club, Jon Quiney,
2 Duncroft Close, Reigate, Surrey RH2 9DE

Pre 67 Ford Owners' Club, Alistair Cuninghame,
13 Drum Brae Gardens, Edinburgh, Scotland
EH12 8SY Tel: 0131 339 1179

Pre-War Austin Seven Club Ltd, Stephen Jones,
1 The Fold, Doncaster Road, Whitley, Nr Goole,
Yorkshire DN14 0HZ

Radford Register, Chris Gow, 108 Potters Lane,
Burgess Hill, Sussex RH15 9JN
Tel: 01444 248439

Railton Owners' Club, Barrie McKenzie, Fairmiles,
Barnes Hall Road, Burncross, Sheffield, Yorkshire
S35 1RF Tel: 01742 468357

Rapier Register, D C H Williams, Smithy, Tregynon,
Newtown, Powys, Wales SY16 3EH
Tel: 01686 650396

Rear Engine Renault Club, Kevin Gould,
2 Barleyfield Close, Heighington, Lincoln LN4 1TX
Tel: 01522 874990

Register of Unusual Micro-Cars, Jean Hammond,
School House Farm, Hawkenbury, Staplehurst, Kent
TN12 0EB

Reliant Owners' Club, Graham Chappell,
19 Smithey Close, High Green, Sheffield, Yorkshire
S30 4FQ

Reliant Sabre and Scimitar Owners' Club,
PO Box 67, Teddington, Middlesex TW11 8QR
Tel: 0181 977 6625

Renault Owners' Club, J Henderson,
24 Long Meadow, Mansfield Woodhouse, Mansfield,
Nottinghamshire NG19 9QW

Riley MC Ltd, J Hall, Treelands, 127 Penn Road,
Wolverhampton WV3 0DU

Riley Register, J A Clarke, 56 Cheltenham Road,
Bishops Cleeve, Cheltenham, Glos GL52 4LY

Riley RM Club, Mrs Jacque Manders, Y Fachell,
Ruthin Road, Gwernymynydd, Mold, Clwyd, Wales
CH7 5LQ

Rochdale Owners' Club, Alaric Spendlove,
7 Whiteleigh Avenue, Crownhill, Plymouth, Devon
PL5 3BQ Tel: 01752 791409

Rolls-Royce Enthusiasts' Club, Peter Baines,
The Hunt House, Paulerspury, Northamptonshire
NN12 7NA

Ronart Drivers' Club, Simon Sutton (Membership
Secretary), Orchard Cottage, Allan Lane, Fritchley,
Belper, Derbyshire DE56 2FX
Tel: 01773 856901

Rover P4 Drivers' Guild, Colin Blowers,
32 Arundel Road, Luton, Bedfordshire LU4 8DY
Tel: 01582 572499

Rover P5 Owners' Club, G Moorshead,
13 Glen Avenue, Ashford, Middx TW15 2JE
Tel: 01784 258166

Rover P6 Owners' Club, M Jones,
48 Upper Aughton Road, Birkdale, Southport
PR8 5NH Tel: 01704 560929

Rover SD1 Club, PO Box 255, Woking, Surrey
GU21 1GJ Tel: 01483 888432

Saab Enthusiasts' Club, PO Box 96, Harrow,
Middlesex HA3 7DW Tel: 01249 815792

Saab Owners' Club of GB Ltd, John Wood,
Membership Secretary, PO Box 900, Durham
DH1 2GF Tel: 01923 229945

Scimitar Drivers' Club International, Steve Lloyd,
45 Kingshill Park, Dursley, Gloucestershire
GL11 4DG Tel: 01245 320734

Scootacar Register, Stephen Boyd, Pamanste,
18 Holman Close, Aylsham, Norwich, Norfolk
NR11 6DD Tel: 01263 733861

Simca Owners' Register, David Chapman,
18 Cavendish Gardens, Redhill, Surrey RH1 4AQ

Singer Owners' Club, Secretary, Martyn Wray,
11 Ermine Rise, Great Casterton, Stamford,
Lincolnshire PE9 4AJ
Tel: 01780 62740

South Wales Austin Seven Club, Mr H Morgan,
Glynteg, 90 Ammanford Road, Llandybie,
Ammanford, Wales SA18 2JY

Spartan Owners' Club, Steve Andrews,
28 Ashford Drive, Ravenhead, Nottinghamshire
NG15 9DE Tel: 01623 793742

Sporting Fiats Club, Graham Morrish,
19 Oakley Wood Road, Bishops Tachbrook,
Leamington Spa, Warwickshire CV33 9RW
Tel: 01926 335097

Stag Owners' Club, The Old Rectory, Aslacton,
Norfolk NR15 2JN

Standard Motor Club, Tony Pingriff (Membership
Secretary), 57 Main Road, Meriden, Coventry,
West Midlands CV7 0LP

Star, Starling, Stuart and Briton Register,
D E A Evans, New Wood Lodge, 2A Hyperion Rd,
Stourton, Stourbridge, West Midlands DY7 6SB

Sunbeam Alpine Owners' Club, PO Box 226,
Grimsby, Lincolnshire DN37 0GG

Sunbeam Rapier Owners' Club, Peter Meech,
12 Greenacres, Downtown, Salisbury, Wilts SP5 3NG
Tel: 01725 21140

Sunbeam Talbot Alpine Register, Derek Cook, Memebership Secretary, 47 Crescent Wood Road, Sydenham, London SE26 6SA

Sunbeam Talbot Darracq Register, J Donovan, Blackwell House, 21 Stubbs Wood, Chesham Bois, Amersham, Bucks HP6 6EY Tel: 01494 721972

Sunbeam Tiger Owners' Club, Brian Postle, Beechwood, 8 Villa Real Est, Consett, Co Durham DH8 6BJ Tel: 01207 508296

Swift Club and Swift Register, John Harrison, 70 Eastwick Drive, Bookham, Leatherhead, Surrey KT23 3NX Tel: 01372 452120

Tornado Register, Dave Malins, 48 St Monica's Ave, Luton, Bedfordshire LU3 1PN Tel: 01582 37641

Toyota Enthusiasts' Club, c/o Secretary/Treasurer Billy Wells, 28 Park Rd, Feltham, Middx TW13 6PW Tel/Fax: 0181 898 0740

TR Drivers' Club, Jeff Black, 3 Blackberry Close, Abbeymead, Gloucs GL4 7BS Tel: 01452 614234

TR Register, 1B Hawksworth, Southmead Ind Park, Didcot, Oxfordshire OX10 7HR Tel: 01235 818866

Trident Car Club, David Rowlinson, 23 Matlock Cres, Cheam, Sutton, Surrey SM3 9SS Tel: 0181 644 9029

Triumph 2000/2500/2.5 Register, Alan Crussell, 10 Gables Close, Chalfont St Peter, Bucks SL9 0PR Tel: 01494 873264 email: t2000register@compuserve.com website: http://www.kvaleberg.com/t2000.html

Triumph Dolomite Club, 39 Mill Lane, Upper Arncott, Bicester, Oxfordshire OX6 0PB Tel: 01869 242847(am only)

Triumph Mayflower Club, John Oaker, 19 Broadway North, Walsall, West Midlands WS1 2QG Tel: 01922 33042

Triumph Razoredge Owners' Club, Stewart Langton, 62 Seaward Ave, Barton-on-Sea, Hampshire BH25 7HP Tel: 01425 618074

Triumph Roadster Club, J Cattaway, 59 Cowdray Park Rd, Little Common, Bexhill-on-Sea, Sussex TN39 4EZ Tel: 01424 844608

Triumph Spitfire Club, Corwin van Heteren, Waltersingel 34A, 7314 Apeldoorn, The Netherlands.

Triumph Sports Six Club Ltd, Main Street, Lubenham, Market Harborough, Leics LE16 9TF Tel: 01858 434424

Trojan Owners' Club, Derrick Graham, President, Troylands, St Johns, Earlswood Common, Redhill, Surrey RH1 6QF Tel: 01737 763643

Turner Register, Dave Scott, 21 Ellsworth Road, High Wycombe, Buckinghamshire HP11 2TU

TVR Car Club, c/o David Gerald, TVR Sports Cars Tel: 01386 793239

United States Army Vehicle Club, Simon Johnson, 7 Carter Fold, Mellor, Lancashire BB2 7ER Tel: 01254 812894

Vanden Plas Owners' Club, Nigel Stephens, The Briars, Lawson Leas, Barrowby, Grantham, Lincolnshire NG32 1EH

Vauxhall Owners' Club, Roy Childers (Membership Secretary), 31 Greenbanks, Melbourn, Nr Royston, Cambridgeshire SG8 6AS

Vauxhall PA/PB/PC/E Owners' Club, Steve Chapman, 333 Eastcote Lane, South Harrow, Middlesex HA2 8RY Tel: 0181 423 2440

Vauxhall VX4/90 Drivers' Club, Jason Callear, 1 Milverton Drive, Uttoxeter ST14 7RE

Vectis Historic Vehicle Club, Nigel Offer, 10 Paddock Dr, Bembridge, Isle of Wight PO35 5TL

Veteran Car Club Of Great Britain, Jessamine Court, High Street, Ashwell, Baldock, Hertfordshire SG7 5NL Tel: 01462 742818

Victor 101 Club, Joan Caldwell, 43 Princess Street, Widnes, Cheshire WA8 6NT Tel: 0151 510 0251

Vintage Austin Register, Frank Smith, Hon Sec, The Briars, Four Lane Ends, Oakerthorpe, Alfreton, Derbyshire DE55 7LH Tel: 0773 831646

Vintage Sports Car Club Ltd, The Secretary, The Old Post Office, West Street, Chipping Norton, Oxon OX7 5EL Tel: 01608 644777 email: wiggle@globalnet.co.uk

Viva Owners' Club, Adrian Miller, The Thatches, Snetterton North End, Snetterton, Norwich, Norfolk NR16 2LD

Volkswagen Owners' Club (GB), PO Box 7, Burntwood, Walsall, West Midlands WS7 8SB

Volkswagen Split Screen Van Club, Mike & Sue Mundy, The Homestead, Valebridge Rd, Burgess Hill, Sussex RH15 0RT Tel: 01444 241407

Volvo Enthusiasts' Club, Kevin Price, 4 Goonbell, St Agnes, Cornwall TR5 0PH

Volvo Owners' Club, John Smith, 18 Macaulay Ave, Portsmouth, Hants PO6 4NY Tel: 01705 381494

Vulcan Register, D Hales, The Hedgerows, Sutton St Nicholas, Herefordshire HR1 3BU Tel: 01432 880726

VW Type 3 and 4 Club, J Bourne, Brookside, Hamsey Road, Barcombe, Lewes, Sussex BN8 5TG Tel: 01273 400463

Wolseley 6/80 and Morris Oxford MO Club, Don Gould, 2 Barleyfield Close, Heighington, Lincoln LN4 1TX Tel: 01652 635138

Wolseley Hornet Special Club, Kylemor, Crown Gardens, Fleet, Hampshire GU13 9PD Tel: 01252 622411

Wolseley Register, Mike Schilling, 46 Mansewood Road, Glasgow G43 1TN

XR Owners' Club, PO Box 47, Loughborough, Leicestershire LE11 1XS Tel: 01509 882300

FOUNDED IN 1930

THE VETERAN CAR CLUB OF GREAT BRITAIN · FOR PRE-1919 CARS

For details of membership, telephone or write to:
The Secretary, The Veteran Car Club of Great Britain,
Jessamine Court, High Street, Ashwell, Hertfordshire SG7 5NL
Tel: 01462 742818   Fax: 01462 742997

BE PROUD TO BE A MEMBER

Directory of Auctioneers

Academy Auctioneers & Valuers, Northcote House, Northcote Avenue, Ealing, London W5 3UR
Tel: 0181 579 7466

Aylesbury Motor Auctions, Pembroke Road, Stocklake, Aylesbury, Bucks HP20 1DB Tel: 01296 339150

Barons, Brooklands House, 33 New Road, Hythe, Southampton, Hampshire SO45 6BN Tel: 01703 840081

Bernaerts, Verlatstraat 18-22, 2000 Antwerp, Belgium Tel: +32 (0)3 248 19 21

C Boisgirard, 2 Rue de Provence, Paris, France 75009 Tel: 00 33 147708136

Bonhams, 65–69 Lots Road, Chelsea, London SW10 0RN Tel: 0171 393 3900

British Car Auctions Ltd, Classic & Historic Automobile Division, Auction Centre, Blackbushe Airport, Blackwater, Camberley, Surrey GU17 9LG Tel: 01252 878555

Brooks (Auctioneers), 81 Westside, London SW4 9AY Tel: 0171 228 8000

Phillip Caldwell, New South Wales, Australia Tel: 0411 529 414

Mervyn Carey, Twysden Cottage, Benenden, Cranbrook, Kent TN17 4LD Tel: 01580 240283

Chapman, Moore & Mugford, 9 High Street, Shaftesbury, Dorset SP7 8JB Tel: 01747 852400

H C Chapman & Son, The Auction Mart, North Street, Scarborough, Yorkshire YO11 1DL Tel: 01723 372424

Cheffins, Grain & Comins, 2 Clifton Road, Cambridge CB2 4BW Tel: 01223 358721/213343

Christie Manson & Wood International Inc, 502 Park Avenue, (including Christie's East), New York, NY 10022, USA Tel: (212) 546 1000

Christie Manson & Wood Ltd, 8 King Street, St James's, London SW1Y 6QT Tel: 0171 839 9060

Christie's (Monaco), SAM, Park Palace, Monte Carlo 98000 Tel: 00 337 9325 1933

Christie's Pty Ltd, 1 Darling Street, South Yarra, Melbourne, Victoria 3141, Australia Tel: 010 613 820 4311

Christie's South Kensington Ltd, 85 Old Brompton Rd, London SW7 3LD Tel: 0171 581 7611

Classic Automobile Auctions BV, Goethestrasse 10, 6000 Frankfurt 1, Germany Tel: 010 49 69 28666/8

Coys of Kensington, 2–4 Queen's Gate Mews, London SW7 5QJ Tel: 0171 584 7444

Dickinson, Davy and Markham, Wrawby Street, Brigg, Humberside DN20 8JJ Tel: 01652 653666

David Dockree, Cheadle Hulme Business Centre, Clemence House, Mellor Road, Cheadle Hulme, Cheshire SK7 1BD Tel: 0161 485 1258

Evans & Partridge, Agriculture House, High Street, Stockbridge, Hampshire SO20 6HF Tel: 01264 810702

Thomas Wm Gaze & Son, 10 Market Hill, Diss, Norfolk IP22 3JZ Tel: 01379 651931

Greens (UK) Ltd, Worcestershire WR14 2AY Tel: 01684 575902

H & H Classic Auctions Ltd, Whitegate Farm, Hatton Lane, Hatton, Warrington, Cheshire WA4 4BZ Tel: 01925 730630

Halls Fine Art Auctions, Welsh Bridge, Shrewsbury, Shropshire SY3 8LA Tel: 01743 231212

Hamptons Antique & Fine Art Auctioneers, 93 High St, Godalming, Surrey GU7 1AL Tel: 01483 423567

Andrew Hartley, Victoria Hall Salerooms, Little Lane, Ilkley, Yorkshire LS29 8EA Tel: 01943 816363

Kidson Trigg, Estate Office, Friars Farm, Sevenhampton, Highworth, Swindon, Wilts SN6 7PZ Tel: 01793 861000

Kruse International, PO Box 190, 5400 County Road 11A, Auburn, Indiana 46706, USA Tel: (219) 925 5600

Lambert & Foster, 77 Commercial Rd, Paddock Wood, Kent TN12 6DR Tel: 01892 832325

Lawrences Auctioneers, Norfolk House, 80 High Street, Bletchingley, Surrey RH1 4PA Tel: 01883 743323

Thomas Mawer & Son, The Lincoln Saleroom, 63 Monks Road, Lincoln, Lincolnshire LN2 5HP Tel: 01522 524984

Mealy's, Chatsworth Street, Castle Comer, Co Kilkenny, Southern Ireland Tel: 00 353 56 41229

Morphets of Harrogate, 6 Albert Street, Harrogate, Yorkshire HG1 1JL Tel: 01423 530030

Neales, 192–194 Mansfield Road, Nottingham, Nottinghamshire NG1 3HU Tel: 0115 962 4141

John Nicholson, The Auction Rooms, Longfield, Midhurst Road, Fernhurst, Surrey GU27 3HA Tel: 01428 653727

Onslow's, The Depot, 2 Michael Road, London SW6 2AD Tel: 0171 371 0505

Palm Springs Exotic Car Auctions, 602 East Sunny Dunes Road, Palm Springs, California 92264, USA Tel: 760 320 3290

Palmer Snell, 65 Cheap Street, Sherborne, Dorset DT9 3BA Tel: 01935 812218

J R Parkinson Son & Hamer Auctions, The Auction Rooms, Rochdale Road (Kershaw Street), Bury, Lancashire BL9 7HH Tel: 0161 761 1612/7372

Phillips, Blenstock House, 101 New Bond Street, London W1Y 0AS Tel: 0171 629 6602

Phillips, 20 The Square, Retford, Notts DN22 6BX Tel: 01777 708633

Phillips, Alphin Brook Road, Alphington, Exeter, Devon EX2 8TH Tel: 01392 439025

Phillips Scotland, 207 Bath Street, Glasgow, Scotland G2 4HD Tel: 0141 221 8377

Poulain Le Fur, 20 rue de Provence, 75009 Paris, France Tel: 01 42 46 81 81

RM Classic Cars, 825 Park Avenue West, Chatham, Ontario, Canada Tel: 00 519 352 4575

Rogers, Jones & Co, The Saleroom, 33 Abergele Road, Colwyn Bay, Wales LL29 7RU Tel: 01492 532176

Martyn Rowe, The Truro Auction Centre, Calenick Street, Truro, Cornwall TR1 2SG Tel: 01892 260020

RTS Auctions Ltd, 35 Primula Drive, Eaton, Norwich, Norfolk NR4 7LZ Tel: 01603 505718

Sotheby's, 34–35 New Bond St, London W1A 2AA Tel: 0171 293 5000

Sotheby's, 1334 York Avenue, New York, NY 10021, USA Tel: (212) 606 7000

Sotheby's, BP 45, Le Sporting d'Hiver, Place du Casino, Monaco/Cedex MC 98001 Tel: 0101 3393 30 88 80

Sotheby's Sussex, Summers Place, Billingshurst, Sussex RH14 9AD Tel: 01403 833500

Sotheby's Zurich, Bleicherweg 20, Zurich, Switzerland CH-8022 Tel: 41 (1) 202 0011

Specialised Postcard Auctions, 25 Gloucester Street, Cirencester, Glos GL7 2DJ Tel: 01285 659057

G E Sworder & Sons, 14 Cambridge Road, Stansted Mountfitchet, Essex CM24 8BZ Tel: 01279 817778

Taylors, Honiton Galleries, 205 High Street, Honiton, Devon EX14 8LF Tel: 01404 42404

Thimbleby & Shorland, 31 Great Knollys St, Reading, Berkshire RG1 7HU Tel: 01734 508611

Walker, Barnett & Hill, 3–5 Waterloo Road Salerooms, Clarence Street, Wolverhampton, West Midlands WV1 4JE Tel: 01902 773531

Wellers Auctioneers, The Saleroom, Moorfield Road, Slyfield Grn, Guildford, Surrey GU1 1SG Tel: 01483 447447

Welsh Bridge Salerooms, Welsh Bridge, Shrewsbury, Shropshire SY3 8LH Tel: 01743 231212

Wintertons Ltd, Lichfield Auction Centre, Wood End Lane, Fradley, Lichfield, Staffordshire WS13 8NF Tel: 01543 263256

World Classic Auction & Exposition Co, 1092 Eagles Nest Place, Danville, California 94506-5872, USA Tel: 925 736 3444

Directory of Museums

Bedfordshire
Shuttleworth Collection,
Old Warden Aerodrome, Nr Biggleswade
SG18 9EP Tel: 01767 627288

Buckinghamshire
West Wycombe Motor Museum,
Cockshoot Farm, Chorley Road, High
Wycombe, West Wycombe HP14 3AR

Cheshire
Mouldsworth Motor Museum,
Smithy Lane, Mouldsworth, Chester
CH3 8AR Tel: 01928 731781

Co. Durham
North of England Open Air Museum,
Beamish, Stanley DH9 0RG

Cornwall
Automobilia Motor Museum,
The Old Mill, Terras Road, St Stephen,
St Austell PL26 7RX Tel: 01726 823092

Cumbria
Cars of the Stars Motor Museum,
Standish Street, Keswick CA12 5LS
Tel: 01768 73757
Lakeland Motor Museum,
Holker Hall, Cark-in-Cartmel,
Nr Grange-over-Sands LA11 7SS
Tel: 01539 558509

Derbyshire
The Donnington Collection,
Donnington Park, Castle Donnington
DE74 2RP Tel: 01332 810048

Devon
Totnes Motor Museum,
Steamer Quay, Totnes, TT9 5AL
Tel: 01803 862777

Essex
Ford Historic Car Collection,
Ford Motor Co, Eagle Way, Brentwood
CM13 3BW

Gloucestershire
Bristol Industrial Museum,
Princes Wharf, City Docks, Bristol
BS1 4RN Tel: 0117 925 1470
The Bugatti Trust,
Prescott Hill, Gotherington, Cheltenham
GL52 4RD Tel: 01242 677201

Cotswold Motor Museum, Sherbourne St,
Bourton-on-the-Water, Nr Cheltenham
GL54 2BY Tel: 01451 821255

Greater Manchester
Manchester Museum of Transport,
Boyle Street, M8 8UW

Hampshire
Gangbridge Collection,
Gangbridge House, St Mary Bourne,
Andover SP11 6EP
National Motor Museum,
Brockenhurst, Beaulieu SO42 7ZN
Tel: 01590 612123/612345

Humberside
Bradford Industrial Museum,
Moorside Mills, Moorside Road, Bradford
BD2 3HP Tel: 01274 631756
Hull Transport Museum,
36 High Street, Hull, HU1 1NQ
Peter Black Collection,
Lawkholme Lane, Keighley BD21 3BB
Sandtoft Transport Centre,
Sandtoft, Nr Doncaster DN8 5SX

Southern Ireland
Kilgarven Motor Museum,
Kilgarven, Co. Kerry Tel: 00 353 64 85346
National Museum of Irish Transport,
Scotts Garden, Killarney, Co. Kerry

Northern Ireland
Ulster Folk and Transport Museum,
Cultra Manor, Holywood, Co. Down
Tel: 01232 428428

Isle of Man
Manx Motor Museum,
Crosby Tel: 01624 851236
Port Erin Motor Museum,
High Street, Port Erin Tel: 01624 832964

Jersey
Jersey Motor Museum,
St Peter's Village Tel: 01534 482966

Kent
Dover Transport Museum,
Old Park, Whitfield, Dover CT16 2HL
**Historic Vehicles Collection of C.M.
Booth,** Falstaff Antiques, 63–67 High
Street, Rolvenden, TN17 4LP
Tel: 01580 241234

The Motor Museum,
Dargate, Nr Faversham, ME13 9EP
Ramsgate Motor Museum,
West Cliff Hall, Ramsgate CT11 9JX
Tel: 01843 581948

Lancashire
British Commercial Vehicles Museum,
King Street, Leyland, Preston PR5 1LE
Tel: 01772 451011
Bury Transport Museum,
Castlecroft Road, off Bolton Street, Bury
Tameside Transport Collection,
Warlow Brook, Friezland Lane, Greenfield,
Oldham OL3 7EU

London
British Motor Industry Heritage Trust,
Syon Park, Brentford
Science Museum,
Exhibition Road, South Kensington
SW7 2DD Tel: 0171 589 3456

Norfolk
Caister Castle Car Collection,
Caister-on-Sea, Nr Great Yarmouth
Tel: 01572 787251

Nottinghamshire
Nottingham Industrial Museum,
Courtyard Buildings, Wallaton Park

Scotland
Grampian Transport Museum,
Main Street, Alford, Aberdeenshire
AB33 8AD Tel: 01975 562292
Highland Motor Heritage,
Bankford, Perthshire
Melrose Motor Museum,
Annay Road, Melrose TD6 9LW
Tel: 01896 822 2624
Moray Motor Museum, Bridge Street,
Elgin IV30 2DE Tel: 01343 544933
Museum of Transport,
Kelvin Hall, 1 Bunhouse Road, Glasgow
G3 8DP Tel: 0141 357 3929
Myreton Motor Museum,
Aberlady, Longniddry, East Lothian
EH32 0PZ Tel: 01875 870288
Royal Museum of Scotland,
Chambers Street, Edinburgh EH1 1JF
Tel: 0131 225 7534

Shropshire
Midland Motor Museum,
Stanmore Hall, Stourbridge Road,
Bridgnorth WV15 6DT
Tel: 01746 762992

Somerset
Haynes Sparkford Motor Museum,
Sparkford, BA22 7LH Tel: 01963 440804

Surrey
Brooklands Museum,
The Clubhouse, Brooklands Road,
Weybridge KT13 0QN Tel: 01932 857381
Dunsfold Land Rover Museum, Dunsfold
GU8 4NP Tel: 01483 200567

Sussex
Bentley Motor Museum,
Bentley Wild Fowl Trust, Harvey's Lane,
Ringmer, Lewes BN8 5AF
Foulkes-Halbard of Filching,
Filching Manor, Filching, Wannock,
Polegate BN26 5QA Tel: 01323 487838

Tyne & Wear
Newburn Hall Motor Museum,
35 Townfield Garden, Newburn NE15 8PY
Tel: 0191 264 2977

USA
Behring Automotive Museum,
3700 Blackhawk Plaza Circle, Danville,
California, CA 94506. Tel: (510) 736 2280

Wales
Conway Valley Railway Museum,
Ffordd Hen Eglwys, Betws-y-Coed,
Gwynedd LL24 0AL Tel: 01690 710568

Warwickshire
Heritage Motor Centre,
Banbury Road, Gaydon CV35 0YT
Tel: 01926 645040
Museum of British Road Transport,
St Agnes Lane, Hales Street, Coventry
CV1 1PN Tel: 01203 832425

West Midlands
**Birmingham Museum of Science &
Industry,** 136 Newhall Street, Birmingham
B3 1RZ Tel: 0121 235 1651
Black Country Museum,
Tipton Road, Dudley DY1 4SQ

Wiltshire
Science Museum,
Red Barn Gate, Wroughton, Nr Swindon
SN4 9NS Tel: 01793 814466

Yorkshire
The Automobilia Transport Museum,
Heritage Centre, Leeds Road,
Huddersfield Tel: 01484 450446

Index to Advertisers

Bibliography

Baldwin, Nick; Georgano, G. N.; Sedgwick, Michael; and Laban, Brian; *The World Guide to Automobiles*, Guild Publishing, London, 1987

Colin Chapman *Lotus Engineering*, Osprey, 1993.

Flammang, James M; *Standard Catalog of Imported Cars*, Krause Publications Inc, 1992.

Georgano, G. N.; ed: *Encyclopedia of Sports Cars*, Bison Books, 1985.

Georgano, Nick; *Military Vehicles of World War II*, Osprey 1994.

Harding, Anthony; Allport, Warren; Hodges, David; Davenport, John; *The Guinness Book of the Ca*r, Guinness Superlatives Ltd, 1987

Hay, Michael; *Bentley Factory Cars*, Osprey, 1993.

Hough, Richard; *A History of the World's Sports Cars*, Allen & Unwin, 1961.

Isaac, Rowan; *Morgan*, Osprey, 1994.

McComb, F. Wilson; *MG by McComb*, Osprey, 1978.

Nye, Doug; *Autocourse History of the Grand Prix Car 1966–1991*, Hazleton Publishing, 1992.

Posthumus, Cyril, and Hodges, David; *Classic Sportscars*, Ivy Leaf, 1991.

Robson, Graham; *Classic and Sportscar A–Z of Cars of the 1970s*, Bay View Books, 1990.

Sedgwick, Michael; Gillies, Mark; *Classic and Sportscar A–Z of Cars of the 1930s*, Bay View Books, 1989.

Sedgwick, Michael, Gillies, Mark; *Classic and Sportscar A–Z of Cars 1945–70*, Bay View Books, 1990.

Sieff, Theo; *Mercedes Benz*, Gallery Books, 1989.

Vanderveen, Bart; *Historic Military Vehicles Directory*, After the Battle Publications, 1989.

Willson, Quentin; Selby David, *The Ultimate Classic Car Book*, Dorling Kindersley, 1995.

Classic Car Connections

the home of the classic car
enthusiast on the world wide web.
Featuring, cars for sale, die-cast models,
books, magazines, car clubs, news,
features, workshop tips and much more.

http://www.cccns.co.uk/

don't surf the web . . . drive it!

UNICORN MOTOR COMPANY

Brian R. Chant, M.I.M.I.
Station Road, Stalbridge,
Dorset DT10 2RH
Telephone: (01963) 363353
Fax: (01963) 363626

CLASSIC CAR SALES, REPAIRS & LOW BAKE OVEN REFINISHING

*Inspections and valuations
undertaken. Interesting cars
sold on commission*

Viewing by
appointment only

TRADE MEMBER

BEAULIEU GARAGE LIMITED

Beaulieu, Hampshire, England SO42 7YE
Telephone: 01590 612999
Fax: 01590 612900   Mobile: 0836 642279
Email: philipscott@beaulieugarage.demon.co.uk
Website: www.beaulieugarage.demon.co.uk

We have for sale one of the largest selections of
classic and vintage cars in the South of England.
Located within yards of the famous National
Motor Museum and within easy commuting
distance of London and Heathrow. Round off
your trip to the Museum and pop in to see us.

Index

Italic page numbers denote colour pages; **bold** numbers refer to information and pointer boxes

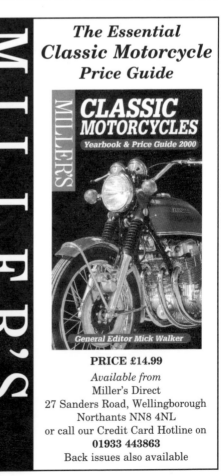